Inequalities and the Progressive Era

Inequalities and the Progressive Era

Progressive Era

Breakthroughs and Legacies

Edited by

Guillaume Vallet

*Associate Professor in Economics, University of Grenoble
Alpes, and Research Fellow at Centre de Recherche en
Économie de Grenoble (CREG), and Institut de Recherche
pour l'Economie Politique de l'Entreprise (IREPE), France
and Associate Researcher, Institute of Sociological Research of
Geneva, Switzerland*

 **Edward Elgar**
PUBLISHING

Cheltenham, UK • Northampton, MA, USA

Published by
Edward Elgar Publishing Limited
The Lypiatts
15 Lansdown Road
Cheltenham
Glos GL50 2JA
UK

Edward Elgar Publishing, Inc.
William Pratt House
9 Dewey Court
Northampton
Massachusetts 01060
USA

A catalogue record for this book
is available from the British Library

Library of Congress Control Number: 2020932120

This book is available electronically in the **Elgar**online
Economics subject collection
DOI 10.4337/9781788972659

ISBN 978 1 78897 264 2 (cased)
ISBN 978 1 78897 265 9 (eBook)

Printed and bound by CPI Group (UK) Ltd, Croydon CR0 4YY

Contents

Contributors

Vladimir Babashkin is Full Professor of History and Sociology at the Russian Presidential Academy of National Economy and Public Administration (RANEPA) in Moscow, Russia. In Russia, he is one of the leading academics on the history of Russia. More specifically, as a specialist of the history of Russian peasantry, he has published several articles and books on the topic. He is also a member of the advisory board of Russian Peasant Studies.

Thomas Briggs is a PhD student of economics at Colorado State University, United States. His fields of interest are political economy, health economics and regional economics, with a focus on stratification. Thomas' work has been primarily the quantitative analysis of interdisciplinary studies.

Bernardo Buarque de Hollanda is Associate Professor at the School of Social Sciences, and researcher at the Center for Research and Documentation on Brazilian Contemporary History, at FGV Foundation (CPDOC/FGV). His main topics of research are literary history and modernism; social thought and intellectuals in Brazil; and the social history of football and organized soccer supporting groups. He has published extensively on these topics, such as *O descobrimento do futebol: modernismo, regionalismo e paixão esportiva* (2004).

Christine Castelain-Meunier is a researcher in Sociology at the Centre National de la Recherche scientifique (CNRS) at the Ecole des Hautes Etudes en Sciences Sociales (EHESS), France. She works on gender issues and is an expert on masculinity. She has published many books and papers on the issue of gender, especially on men (see, for instance, her best-seller in France: *Les métamorphoses du masculin* (2005)), on fatherhood (see, for instance, her recent book *L'instinct paternel. Plaidoyer en faveur des nouveaux pères* (2019)). She campaigned successfully for paternity leave, introduced in 2001. She has edited a number of books or special issues on those topics, in the international review *Enfances, Familles, Générations* in particular.

Virgile Chassagnon is Full Professor of Economics at the University of Grenoble Alpes, France (research fellow at CREG Research Center). He is the director of the Doctoral School of Economics. He is also the director of the Research Institute for the Political Economy of the Firm (IREPE) and associated research fellow at

TRIANGLE Research Center in Lyon. His research includes the study of the nature, the boundaries and the governance of complex economic organizations from a progressive and evolutionary institutional approach, where he develops a theory of the firm as a power-based entity (also called TFEP). As a leading expert in this field, he has published several books and over 50 research articles, notably in established academic journals (*Journal of Institutional Economics, Journal of Economic Issues, Journal of Business Ethics, Journal of the History of Economic Thought, Technological Forecasting and Social Change*, and *History of Economic Ideas*).

Robert W. Dimand is Full Professor of Economics at Brock University, Canada. He has published more than one hundred articles in leading journals such as the *Journal of Economic Perspectives, History of Political Economy*, the *Journal of the History of Economic Thought*, the *European Journal of the History of Economic Thought* and the *Journal of Money, Credit and Banking*. He has published many books on the history of economic thought such as *James Tobin* (2014), *Irving Fisher* (2019), *The Elgar Companion to John Maynard Keynes* (edited with Harald Hagemann, 2019) and *The Routledge Handbook of the History of Women's Economic Thought* (edited with Kirsten Madden, 2018).

Benjamin Dubrion is Associate Professor of Economics at Sciences Po Lyon, France, and a member of the research laboratory Triangle (UMR CNRS 5206). He works in the fields of organizational economics and human resource management. His latest topics of research are on "old institutionalism." He has published in several French academic journals on economics and human resource management.

Odile Goerg is Full Professor Emerita of Modern African History at the University of Paris-Paris Diderot, France. She is one of the leading French experts in the studies of urban history in Africa. Her research deals with social and cultural history in an urban context, especially through leisure (cinema). In particular, she works on Sierra Leone and Guinea. She has published more than 50 papers, chapters in books, or books on several issues dealing with Africa. Her latest book is *Tropical Dream Palaces: Cinema in Colonial West Africa*, published in 2019.

Stephany Griffith-Jones is Emeritus Professorial Fellow, Institute of Development Studies, Sussex University, England. Stephany Griffith-Jones has authored or edited 25 books, including *Time for a Visible Hand: Lessons from the 2008 World Financial Crisis* (2010, co-edited with José Antonio Ocampo and Joseph Stiglitz), and *The Future of National Development Banks* (2018, co-edited with José Antonio Ocampo).

Francisca Granda is Professor of Political Economy and Research in the College Program in the Department of Economics at Pontifical Catholic University (PUCE) in Quito, Ecuador. She obtained a master's degree in Political Science from New York University, a master's degree in Latin American Studies from Universidad Andina Simón Bolívar and a degree in Economics from PUCE. Her research focuses on the political economy of institutional change in Ecuador, with an emphasis on inequality and political participation. Her most recent works deal with the influence of economic crises on inequality of opportunity in education in the Andean countries, state intervention in popular and solidarity economies, and trust measures in different public policies in Ecuador.

Odile Lakomski-Laguerre is Associate Professor in Economics at the University of Picardie, France. She works on money as an institution, and she is also the French specialist on Schumpeter's thought. She has published the book *Les Institutions Monétaires du Capitalisme. La Pensée Economique de J.A. Schumpeter* (2002), and articles in leading journals such as *History of Political Economy* and the *Journal of Evolutionary Economics*. She has also written several chapters of books, translated from German and edited in a French version of Schumpeter's book on money, *Das Wesen des Geldes* (2005).

Catherine Maumi is Full Professor of History of Architecture and Urban Planning at the Ecole nationale supérieure d'architecture de Paris La Villette (ENSAPLV), HESAM University, France. She was previously Professor at the ENSAG, University of Grenoble Alpes. Her research focuses mainly on American architectural and urban cultures, and questions more specifically the relations between architecture, city and nature, and the idea of environmental planning. She is the leading French specialist on Frank Lloyd Wright. She has published several articles in academic journals, chapters of books and books on those topics, in particular her distinguished book published in French, *Broadacre City: la nouvelle frontière* (2015).

Stephen Meardon is Associate Professor of Economics at Bowdoin College in Brunswick, Maine. His scholarship in the fields of the history and politics of international trade and Latin American studies has been published in *History of Political Economy*, the *Journal of the History of Economic Thought*, and the *European Journal of the History of Economic Thought*, among other journals. From 2013 to 2018 he was the editor of the *Journal of the History of Economic Thought*, and from 2017 to 2020 Director of Texas A&M International University's Center for the Study of Western Hemispheric Trade.

Alex Millmow is an Associate Professor in Economics at the School of Business at Federation University Australia. Alex's research interests include the economics of Joan Robinson, the making of the Australian economic profession and the role of economic ideas in steering public policy. In 2004 he completed his doctorate at the Australian National University on "The Power of Economic Ideas: The Rise of Macroeconomic Management in Australia" which was subsequently published. Alex has also published over 50 journal articles including the *Economic Record, Economic Papers, Economic Analysis and Policy* and the *History of Economics Review*. He is the current President of the History of Economic Thought Society of Australia (HETSA). In 2017 he published *A History of Australasian Economic Thought*.

Christian Morrisson is Emeritus Professor at the University Paris 1 Panthéon-Sorbonne, France. A former Chief of Division at the OECD, he also worked for major international institutions such as the World Bank, the International Bureau of Labor and the European Commission. He has published 25 books and more than 60 articles in leading economic journals, especially the highly selective *American Economic Review, Economic Journal, Journal of Development Economics,* and *World Development*. In 2019 he published with Bechir Talbi, *Politiques économiques et développement au Maghreb depuis l'Indépendance*.

Tidiane N'Diaye is an anthropologist, economist and writer. He worked as an economic analyst at the French institute of statistics ("INSEE"), and as a Professor of Economics at "Sup-de-co Caraïbes," France. He is one of the leading French and Senegalese intellectuals on both the economy and history of Caribbean and African countries. He has published a French best-seller on slavery, *Le génocide voilé* (2017, 2nd edn), for which he was awarded the "Prix Renaudot Essai" in 2008.

Alexander Nikulin is Full Professor at the Russian Presidential Academy of National Economy and Public Administration (RANEPA) in Moscow, Russia. He is also Head of the Chayanov Research Center and Head of the Centre of Agrarian Studies of the RANEPA. He works and publishes on Russian peasantry. He is the editor-in-chief of *Russian Peasant Studies*.

Jeffrey Nathaniel Parker is an Assistant Professor of Sociology at the University of New Orleans, United States. He earned his PhD in Sociology at the University of Chicago in 2019. In his research, he studies the intersection of gentrification, business interests, and reputation in cities, having focused especially on merchants as pivotal stakeholders in changing neighborhoods. Motivated to better understand how people balance financial- and identity-based interests in their communities, his research has examined the circumstances in which merchants come to either embrace or repudiate gentrification in their own neighborhoods and the ways they attempt to manage those neighborhoods' reputations. He is starting a project about the intersection of race, class, and capitalism in the production of regional reputation in the American South during and after the Civil Rights Movement.

Steven Pressman is an Emeritus Professor of Economics and Finance at Monmouth University in West Long Branch, United States. He also serves as co-editor of the *Review of Political Economy*, as Associate Editor and Book Review Editor of the *Eastern Economic Journal*, and is a member of the Editorial Advisory Board of the journal *Basic Income Studies*. He is presently at Colorado State University. He has published around 120 articles in refereed journals and as book chapters, and has authored, or edited 13 books, including *50 Major Economists* (2nd edn (2006)), and *Leading Contemporary Economists* (2008). His main areas of research are poverty and income distribution, and government tax and spending policies.

Michel Rocca is Full Professor of Economics at the University of Grenoble Alpes, France (research fellow at CREG). He is the former Dean of the Department of Economics at the University of Grenoble Alpes (2008–12), and Vice-President of the University Pierre Mendès-France of Grenoble (2012–16). A specialist on labor issues, he also works on institutionalism, especially "Old Institutionalism." For many years, he has been examining the works of R. T. Ely. He has published several papers on institutionalist issues in French academic journals.

Cherry Schrecker is Full Professor of Sociology at the University Grenoble Alpes, France and member of the research laboratory PACTE. She has worked on the history of sociology and on the founding and development of the New School for Social Research, a progressive university in New York. A major focus during the research was on the role played by Alvin Johnson in ensuring the School's continuity. Other research interests lie in the domain of the sociology of health, and she is also involved in research into issues related to death and dying. She has published in international reviews, such as *The American Sociologist, Sociologies Pratiques* and *Anthropologie & Santé*.

Florencia Sember is a researcher at the National Council of Scientific and Technical Research, in Argentina (CONICET). She received her PhD in Economics from the University of Paris 1 Panthéon-Sorbonne, France and the Università di Macerata, Italy. Her research focuses on the history of economic thought. She has written on eminent scholars such as Taussig, Prebisch and Ricardo in books or leading academic journals (*European Journal of the History of Economic Thought, Journal of the History of Economic Thought*).

Robert Skidelsky is a British economic historian, best known for his award-winning biographies of John Maynard Keynes. Indeed, Robert is one of the greatest specialists on Keynes. He has also written many relevant papers and books on the British economy. For instance, the second volume of Skidelsky's three-volume biography of John Maynard Keynes, *The Economist as Saviour, 1920–1937*, won the Wolfson History Prize in 1992. The third volume, *Fighting for Britain, 1937–1946*, won the Duff Cooper Prize in 2000, the James Tait Black Memorial Prize for biography in 2001, the Arthur Ross Book Award for international relations in 2002 and the Lionel Gelber Prize for International Relations, and was short-listed for the Samuel Johnson Prize for non-fiction writing in 2001.

Hidetomi Tanaka is Full Professor of Economics at the University of Jobu, Japan. He is an expert in the history of Japanese economic thought and has written numerous papers on economists from the seventeenth century to the present day. He has contributed to a book published in Germany about Miura Baien, an Edo scholar, and has published more than 20 books on the Japanese economy in Japan. He is also a prominent critic in Japan, and books on pop-star economics have been translated into various languages.

Patricia Thane is Visiting Professor in History, Birkbeck College, London; Emeritus Professor, University of London; and formerly Professor of Contemporary History, University of Sussex. She has written widely on the history of the British welfare state, on women's history and labor history. Her most recent book is *Divided Kingdom: A History of Britain since 1900* (2018). She has been a Visiting Professor at Nanjing University, China, and in Australia, Japan, Taiwan, Chile and New York.

Guillaume Vallet is Associate Professor of Economics at the University of Grenoble Alpes, France (research fellow at CREG), and associate researcher at the Institute of Sociological Research in Geneva, Switzerland. He holds two PhDs, one in economics (obtained at the University Pierre Mendès-France of Grenoble (France) in 2009) and the other in sociology (earned from the University of Geneva (Switzerland) and the Ecole des Hautes Etudes en Sciences Sociales (EHESS) of Paris (France) in 2014). In his research, he studies monetary economics, the political economy of gender and the history of economy thought during the Progressive Era. He has published in several distinguished academic journals (*Revue d'Economie Politique, Economy and Society*), especially on Albion W. Small (*Business History, Journal of the History of Economic Thought*).

Foreword

Stephany Griffith-Jones

Inequalities and the Progressive Era is a unique and very important book. It is an original contribution on two levels. First, it focuses on the "Progressive Era" (1890s–1930s), and the treatment of social and economic inequalities in that period. Each chapter, written by distinguished scholars, highlights the extent to which inequalities during the "Progressive Era" offer an angle to both better understand and deal with inequalities today, through the implementation of particular economic and social policies. The book makes it possible to deal with important issues or authors of the "Progressive Era," who have at times been insufficiently discussed, such as R. T. Ely, A. W. Small, and J. Dewey. Second, the authors come from all parts of the world, thereby giving the book a valuable international flavor.

This dual lens implies the book makes valuable contributions to the in-depth understanding of contemporary debates regarding the treatment of inequalities, and the necessary policy response to this major challenge of our times.

Relying both on a multidisciplinary and multicountry approach, this book characterizes a very broad concept of inequalities, including: inequalities of rights, inequalities of opportunity, geographical inequalities, income and wealth inequalities, inequalities of race, and gendered inequalities. Such a broad approach is very valuable.

Given that the authors of the "Progressive Era" had established a clear link between the economic and the democratic system, in particular through the role of the state, the current lessons to draw from their contributions to economic and social policies reveal valuable insights into the treatment that the state could give to inequalities.

More than just theoretical, historical and empirical reflections (important as these are), this book aims to rethink the nature of economic and social policies related to the treatment of inequalities. It is therefore highly relevant to current policy debates, giving a valuable historical depth to these debates.

Acknowledgements

This is a book I have always wanted to do. As such, I have many people to thank. First, I would like to thank my wife, Stephanie, for her support and love, as well as my three children who understood that at times daddy had to work. I would also like to thank all the authors for agreeing to participate, thereby transforming this project into reality; Louis-Philippe Rochon and Sergio Rossi for their continued support and for agreeing to publish this book in their series. I also want to acknowledge the financial support of the University of Grenoble Alpes. Finally, I would like to thank everyone at Edward Elgar Publishing for their support, encouragement and professionalism. It has been a real pleasure to work with them every step of the way.

Introduction

Whoever looks at the major socio-economic advances of the twentieth century will find that the literature dealing with the period following the Great Depression of 1929 abounds with ideas of reform and progress of various kinds in Western countries. In that sense, the New Deal era in the United States, and most importantly the postwar boom tend to be regarded as the most significant phases in this process. Whether on the economic level (i.e. sustained growth), on the social level (i.e. the establishment of a welfare state), or on the political level (i.e. decolonization, the extension of the franchise to women), this historical period is usually associated with major breakthroughs around the globe.

Yet it was at an earlier point that the seeds of political, social and economic reform were sown. That period, known as the "Progressive Era," is primarily associated with American history and society, and social scientists agree that it begins in the 1890s and ends in the 1920s. As its name suggests, the Progressive Era calls to mind a large raft of policy advances which dramatically transformed American society beyond recognition.

Although that vision truthfully reflects a tangible historical reality, it would be erroneous to view the Progressive Era as unfolding smoothly over time and as an exclusively American phenomenon, for two major reasons.

Firstly, within this thirty-year span lie several distinct sub-periods instead of a single macro-phase. The first stage, that is the end of the nineteenth century in the United States, marks the onset of what Mark Twain and Charles Dudley Warner would term "the Gilded Age."[1] This period includes the start of the American Civil War (1861–65) in a context of rising urbanization and industrialization (the American version of Walt Rostow's takeoff stage).[2] At the same time as the country enjoyed an economic boom, American moral values were also remodeled, revealing a society in the throes of a deep identity crisis.

Many historians have observed the gradual erosion of – or perhaps a shift away from – traditional moral values in the rural postbellum world, as they were gradually supplanted by individualism and personal success as seen in the constant pursuit of wealth. Seen in this light, life during the Gilded Age was even harsher than what major thinkers like Alexis de Tocqueville had observed when he went on his seminal American tour in the 1830s.[3]

In all, the Gilded Age was a double-edged sword for Americans: a time of momentous economic prowess giving rise to greater individualist pursuits, but also of widening inequalities in different areas, such as employment, race, gender and territory, among others.

Although class warfare did not bring about a proletarian revolution in the United States, rising inequality crystallized into a new intellectual consciousness keen on the notion of "progress," which in turn enabled reforms to take place around the start of the twentieth century. From the 1900s to the Roaring Twenties, American society experienced momentous breakthroughs. Workers,[4] among other social groups, benefited from improved working conditions. In the same spirit, on August 18, 1920, the United States ratified the 19th Amendment, thereby granting women the vote.

These advances, however, did not soften the blows of the Great Depression or of the First World War. Despite their belated involvement in the conflict in 1917, the USA was not insulated from the collateral damage of the war, which was historically significant. The Progressive Era challenged the idea of American exceptionalism, which had been a point of serious contention among American intellectuals as early as the 1870s. Is the USA an isolated case in Western history? A historical one-off requiring special treatment? Or, rather, should America be regarded as a major offshoot of European society?

For various reasons, America's Progressive Era cannot be easily divorced from its global context. It is during this era that many nation states were formed – sometimes through abrupt convulsions such as the First World War – and that colonialism solidified its hold elsewhere. Besides the USA and Europe, similar trends of thought emerged in other parts of the world, which shared the goal of human progress. One key feature of the Progressive Era was the increased mobility of some social groups such as intellectuals. As a result, the intelligentsia could draw parallels between differing contexts and gradually began to believe in the possibility of spreading reform from one society to the next. By way of illustration, many American social scientists were educated on the European continent, particularly in Germany. Their initial motive was to learn how to remold America along the lines of European and, above all, German progressive ideas.

In addition, it should be remembered that the Progressive Era coincided with progress and discoveries of different kinds. For instance, cinematography was invented in the 1890s thanks to the endeavors of Léon Bouly and Auguste and Louis Lumière, following the pioneering work of Thomas Edison who invented the Kinetograph in 1891. In France, such technological breakthroughs gave incentives to Charles Pathé to develop the industry of cinema during the *Belle Époque* period (1871–1914). Likewise, Gustave Eiffel's radical innovations are evidence of this age of progress.[5] Such a period was also characterized by the creation of new competitions in several fields, such as the *Tour de France* in 1903. Indeed, sport exemplifies the global atmosphere and environment of the Progressive Era: progress, technology, competition, opportunities, but also inequalities.[6]

Likewise, the Progressive Era coincided with a string of historical phenomena of great significance, related to the growth of imperialism, the expansion of trade and industry, and the intensification of worldwide economic competition. In a sense, in the First World War, we find the culmination of tensions between different factions and the embodiment of changes within the capitalist order, which was symbolically reflected by the handover of global leadership from the British Empire to the United States.

In short, the Progressive Era was a time of profound upheaval, whose intellectual landscape bore the marks of pioneering thinkers from all corners of the globe – most notably in the fields of social sciences.

The present work purports to explore this period, which was both eventful for the United States as well as for a number of other countries. It seeks to do so from two overarching perspectives.

First of all, our chosen period, which starts in the 1890s and ends in the 1930s, encompasses more than the usual timespan. Besides vindicating some historical research, this allows for greater coherence: the 1930s were characterized by inequalities caused by the Great Depression as well as by the innovative public policies devised as a response to them. It therefore appears necessary to connect this period to the pioneering ideas beforehand which gave rise to the upheavals of the 1930s.

As far as I am concerned, I do not share the view that the New Deal owed its existence solely to the crisis of 1929. Rather, its rationale should be analyzed against the historical backdrop of both America and that of capitalism more largely. The remodeling of capitalism which occurred in the 1930s was the ultimate outcome of forty or so years of profound thinking, intense debating, and the burgeoning social movements of various persuasions.

It is my view that these reflections, debates and social movements are all united by the same theme, namely, that of inequalities. Whichever form it took, it then ceased to be branded as natural, unavoidable or normal. In this regard, the Progressive Era was a turning point, in the sense that it saw a shift in the perception of inequalities among all the key sections of society – in academia as well as in the media and in the political class.

A second feature of this work is the wealth of its contributions from international authors, each of whom sketches out a unique facet of the Progressive Era. Each contributor has dealt with a particular type of inequality, focusing on a specific geographical area, or on the responses of progressive thinkers – some of them being underestimated, in spite of their paramount intellectual contributions – to their particular contexts. Our decision to broaden the geographical scope to Europe, Asia, Africa and Oceania reflects a willingness to illustrate the global impact of the Progressive Era, which was key to the formation of a number of nation states. This is also helpful in identifying the particulars of each economic, social and political context presented in the chapters of this book. The raft of interventionist measures adopted in the aftermath of the Great Depression varied in scope and nature from country to country. In that sense, a provocative view would stress that there is nothing exceptional about American exceptionalism, just as there are exceptionalisms to be found elsewhere. Therefore, contingency of the context and exceptionalism should be distinguished.

Likewise, the Progressive Era also marked a scientific milestone, in terms of the proposals for radical reforms which emerged in this period. Although progressive authors' thoughts were plural, all share an important intellectual trait which transcends their own fields of interest and backgrounds. As they pushed for new policy measures, they asserted the importance of questioning the nature of the overarching socio-economic framework which governed individual interactions instead of blaming the victims. This methodological stance in turn enabled them to question the orthodoxy of conventional wisdom and, most crucially, to challenge the naturalization of social behavior. In concrete terms, this amounted to a huge step forward in the fight against the prejudices of their time, be they racism, sexism or eugenics.

In the United States in particular, intellectual leaders of the Progressive Era saw in science the best means to improve global welfare and to promote the public good. This explains why Edward A. Ross, a prominent sociologist of the Progressive Era, defined progressivism as "intelligent social engineering" (Ross 1907: 41).[7] Indeed, intellectual leaders of the Progressive Era had faith in their expertise to guide the state – in their eyes, the unique institution capable to play this economic, social and moral role – in devising and implementing new types economic and social policies. As Leonard summarizes, "the progressives venerated science not only because it was their necessary instrument of social improvement. For the social gospel progressives at the forefront of American economic reform, science was a place of moral authority where the public-spirited could find religious meaning in scientific inquiry's values of dispassionate analysis, self-sacrifice, pursuit of truth, and service to a cause greater than oneself" (Leonard 2016: 16).[8]

Against this backdrop, the present work provides an account of the duality of the Progressive Era, as a transition was underway: that of the end of nineteenth-century *laissez-faire* capitalism toward the regulated capitalism of the Glorious Thirty, of the formation of nation states – including its imperialist and colonialist corollaries, as mentioned above – toward nascent postmodernity and the democratic renewal which followed the Second World War; of the emergence of social sciences to their institutionalization and professionalization. Hence, focusing on inequalities, as well the political and academic responses they inspired, is essential to understand the extent to which the

Progressive Era fully deserved its name. "Progress" did not materialize immediately at the time, but the thoughts bequeathed by the great figures of that
time, often visionaries, all carried faith in betterment.

These intellectuals believed in the possibility of reconciling liberty with
equality, as they sought to achieve both individual and collective emancipation. What they aspired to was the ability of individuals to recognize who they
truly are, both for their own sake as well as for the sake of global well-being (of
the societies of which they were a part). Indeed, both individual and collective
progresses were related in their eyes. In the United States, for instance, progressives rejected individualism in the context of American industrialization
of the Progressive Era, emphasizing the primacy of moral challenges, namely
the need to improve the public good. In other words, each individual should
have the equal ability to realize oneself but without jeopardizing the "cohesive
wholeness" of society. American progressives clearly gave society primacy
over individuals, with the belief that "what is good for the organism is good for
its constituent parts" (Leonard 2016: 106).

Likewise, it should be noted that American progressives focused mainly on
the issue of the equality of opportunity. On the one hand, they were dealing
with individuals capable of self-government: in the name of the primacy of
society over individuals, such a stance led paradoxically some American
progressives to exclude individuals or social groups from this capability of
self-government, such as blacks and women for instance.[9] On the other hand,
American progressives coped with the equality of opportunity because they
believed in a sort of "elitism of experts," whose unique scientific expertise was
supposed to demonstrate the social need for superior intellectual leadership.

More generally, at stake was the emergence, preservation and expansion
of democracy itself. Indeed, many such thinkers strove to reconcile economic
efficiency with democracy against the backdrop of a rival model, that of the
USSR, which had risen from the ashes of the First World War. They were
dedicated to achieving a more equitable distribution of wealth and to the
self-determination of all peoples, hence their common rejection of *laissez-faire*
capitalism. The latter was seen as economically inefficient, unfair and then
harmful for society.

Another factor contributing to this ideological stance was the precedence
they gave to reality and life over abstract theoretical – economic in particular
– models. They unanimously criticized the figure of the ivory tower thinker,
while insisting that reflection should go hand in hand with action. This gave
a noble dimension to intellectual pursuits – in effect politicizing their research.
Through scientific study and intellectual work, they aimed to reduce the gap
between the existing status quo and the potential for radical social change –
which resulted in a "cultural lag" (William Ogburn) or a "social lag" (Charles
Merriam).

More than merely conducting research on inequalities, and devising alternative systems for slicing up the cake of wealth, the ultimate goal of progressive thinkers was to "offer a different kind of cake." This implied the need for a buoyant and meritocratic social ecosystem, where each individual would occupy a position reflecting their ability to realize their potential. Likewise, this was consistent with the view of evolving societies. The latter were viewed as living organisms, whose whole is greater than the sum of its parts. Consequently, the intellectual courage of those thinkers cannot be overemphasized, as their views and stances made them vulnerable to attack: their "fighting spirit" was sometimes the target of vehement criticism from radicals and they risked being ostracized or even prosecuted. They did not hold back from challenging conventional wisdom and confronting the proponents of the status quo – the latter did so either out of fear or because they had vested interests.

Symmetrically, focusing in this book on some progressives is not intended to embellish their portrait, and to hide some of their weaknesses and their contradictions. As we mentioned, some progressives of that time were "ambiguous," and maybe conservative, with respect to some topics. Therefore, it is important not to underestimate the existence, and spread of, a significant current consisting of tendencies (in every way) antithetical to progressivism at the time (i.e. eugenics, nationalism, racism and sexism, among others).

However, in spite of this, we qualify the authors of this book as progressives because they have contributed significantly to the global improvement of society through their original and innovative thoughts, and their commitment to struggle. Ensuring that progressive ideas would take root in academia and in society at large was an uphill battle (whose final outcome was far from predetermined). Therefore, our decision to focus on other progressive thinkers than mere American ones reflects a willingness to address the issue of inequalities in its different forms and meanings, and thus to rethink what inequalities mean and refer to.

It is within this contextual framework that the theme of inequalities during the Progressive Era should be placed, which is precisely what the present work seeks to do. But this volume lays no claim to comprehensiveness. Other influential authors and geographical spheres of interest will be conspicuous by their absence. The choices made regarding the corpus of the volume reflect our goal to convey a sense of the most salient aspects of progressive ideas. Besides, all the contributions neatly share an overall thematic unity. In particular, this meant the need for contextual background – met in several chapters when necessary – was an essential part of our work. The multidisciplinary approach adopted in this volume is most appropriate in view of the pedagogical tasks at hand.

The present work is divided into three distinct sections, for a total of twenty-two chapters. The first section, "Foundations of inequalities," includes contributions addressing the question of the nature and origin of various forms of inequality. The second section, "Fighting income, capital and land inequalities," provides an overview of inequalities caused by "physical capital" (dependent on machines, industry and land), and subsequently examines the distribution of these inequalities within that period on a global level. Such an appraisal in turn leads to establishing proposals for progressive reforms, with a view to reducing inequalities. The third section, "Fighting social inequalities," follows a similar pattern to the second section. It is centered on other (alternative) forms of social inequalities in a broad sense (related to gender, architecture, community and ethnicity), and examines the reformist agenda laid out by certain progressive thinkers.

It is our hope that this collective work will attract the interest of not only academics, but also students, politicians and that of all readers with a mind of civic engagement. The progressive figures and economic, social and political contexts discussed throughout these twenty-two chapters all strive to reconcile conducting theoretical research with concrete policy proposals for reform. However risky the tendency to draw historical parallels might be, the present work does help make sense of the dynamics of inequalities inherent in capitalism. It opens up new perspectives in the contemporary desire to usher in a new phase of capitalism, at a time when inequalities are aggravated.[10]

In the same vein, each contributor has aimed for optimal clarity in addressing the subject of inequality, so as to make this knowledge accessible to all – the primary condition for intellectual emancipation which progressive thinkers held so dear. In the words of Albion W. Small: "Science would be like music in a population of deaf if there were no provision for its publicity" (Small and Vincent 1894: 156).[11]

Guillaume Vallet

University of Grenoble Alpes, Centre de Recherche en Économie de Grenoble (CREG); Institut de Recherche pour l'Economie Politique de l'Entreprise (IREPE) (France)
Institute of Sociological Research, Geneva (Switzerland)

NOTES

1. See Mark Twain and Charles Dudley Warner (1973), *The Gilded Age: A Tale of Today*. Chicago, IL: American Publishing Company.
2. See Walt W. Rostow (1961), *The Stages of Economic Growth*. Cambridge: Cambridge University Press.
3. See Alexis de Tocqueville (2012 [1835 and 1840]), *Democracy in America* (2 vols). London: Penguin Classics.
4. But mainly male and white workers.
5. These innovations refer to the composition of the structure of the Eiffel Tower, the latter being erected for the *Exposition Universelle* held in Paris in 1889.

These innovations were also critical to build the supporting frame of the Statue of Liberty.

6. In relation to the creation of the Tour de France in 1903, mention should be made of the invention of the modern bicycle (the "Rover Safety Bicycle") by John Kemp Starley in 1884.

7. Edward A. Ross (1907), *Sin and Society: An Analysis of Latter-Day Iniquity.* New York: Macmillan.

8. Thomas C. Leonard (2016), *Illiberal Reformers: Race, Eugenics, and American Economics in the Progressive Era.* Princeton, NJ: Princeton University Press.

9. It should be mentioned that some American intellectuals of the Progressive Era were sometimes ambiguous on the subjects of racism, sexism and eugenism (see Leonard, *Illiberal Reformers*). With respect to footnote 7, Ross was a eugenicist for instance. Likewise, Jim Crow laws enforcing racial segregation in the Southern United States enacted in the late nineteenth and early twentieth centuries should not be forgotten.

10. See, for instance, Thomas Piketty (2014 [2013]), *Capital in the Twenty-First Century.* Cambridge, MA: Harvard University Press; Thomas Piketty (2019), *Capital et Ideologie.* Paris: Seuil.

11. Albion W. Small and George E. Vincent (1894), *An Introduction to the Study of Society.* New York, Cincinnati, Chicago: American Book Company.

PART I

Foundations of inequalities

1. The question of inequalities during the Progressive Era in the United States: the "Golden Mean" program of the economist Richard T. Ely

Michel Rocca

1. INTRODUCTION

"Markets can also concentrate wealth, pass environmental costs on to society and abuse workers and consumers. For all these reasons, it is plain that markets must be tamed and tempered to make sure they work to the benefit of most citizens. And that has to be done repeatedly, to ensure that they continue to do so. That happened in the United States in the "Progressive Era", when competition laws were passed for the first time. [. . .] Markets, by themselves, even when they are stable, often lead to high levels of inequality, outcomes that are widely viewed as unfair" (Stiglitz 2012: xlii). In 2012 Joseph Stiglitz carried out a diagnostic of the state of society already assessed in the same terms by the economist Richard T. Ely as far back as 1884 during "the age of the robber barons" (Ely 1884). This diagnostic was to be Ely's first step toward formulating a "Golden Mean" program with a view to reforming an American Society of the Gilded (1865–1901), deemed to be intrinsically unequal.

A leading "light" of the Progressive Era in the United States (1880s–1930s), Richard T. Ely (1854–1943) was an eminent American late nineteenth-century academic (Coats 1993).[1] Ely is viewed as a major organizer and forerunner of the profession of economist, especially by institutional economists. Furthermore, Ely advocated social reform and intellectual alternatives borrowed from the German Historical School (GHS) teachings (Gough 1991; Rutherford 2009).

Richard T. Ely promoted a project inspired by his education (from 1877 to 1880, Ely studied in Halle, Heidelberg and Berlin before obtaining academic positions in the United States), and more particularly by his life as a young intellectual seduced by the Europe of the 1870s. While this project displayed an ambition to build a progressive, stable and harmonious society, it also

explicitly aimed to avoid confrontation between the classes leading to revolutions affecting the order of society (Ely 1918: 124). This fear of revolution
would be the driving force behind the project of a very religious, philosophically conservative man of aristocratic stock.

Ely marked the Progressive Era by the political and intellectual magnitude
of the project he proposed in four main works,[2] as well as a vast canon of
publications, monographs and articles.[3]

The "Golden Mean" project comprised three main components developed
progressively over a lifetime dedicated to economic research and militant
action in favor of societal reform. The first component was a radical criticism
of the unequal order resulting from the industrial society of the late nineteenth
century (Section 2). Using the methods of the GHS, as well as empirical
approaches, Ely's criticism, addressing the unequal society of the United
States, was actually an analysis of poverty related to the conditions of workers.
The analysis of the end of the Pullman strike in 1894 was the culmination
of Ely's criticism. The second component formulated a theoretical proposal
designed to enable American capitalism to avoid conflict between the classes
by envisaging the introduction of a new "bundle of rights," particularly in relation to private property (Section 3). The principles of a new socio-economic
order promoting the general interest rather than the privileges of just a few
were explained in his work of 1914, which allocated to the state a normative
role in economic life, thereby redefining the rights of access to wealth. The
third component put forward a relatively precise template for action in order to
implement the institutional reforms necessary for this new conception of rights
(Section 4).

In conclusion, we will demonstrate that, while Ely's project did indeed have
an impact on American society, it was only much later that the second New
Deal took effect (Section 5).

2. ELY AND THE CRITICISM OF CAPITALISM: A HOTBED OF INEQUALITIES . . . JUSTIFIED BY THE "OLD POLITICAL ECONOMY"

Ely's works were developed during singular, ambivalent periods in the United
States: the Gilded Age and the Progressive Era. These periods experienced
both a rapid growth of the main economic activities (railroads, factories,
banks, mines, etc.) and the first major crises in the American capitalist
system. Rapidly increasing wealth among major entrepreneurs benefiting from
industrial concentration was contrasted by growing inequalities and the
rise of severe poverty. Over the period 1883–85, Ely's academic works
were unprecedentedly guided by this characterization of an unequal society,
explaining it through the application of an unfounded economic doctrine that

was self-satisfying, even justifying the status quo. The work "The Past and the Present of Political Economy" (1884) took up the essence of these writings to serve up Ely's first overall reflection, published as a book.

During his most productive period (1884–1914), Ely's works presented a methodical criticism of capitalism. From the outset, he leveled criticism at both the order of society and the economic thought underpinning it. These somewhat abrasive articles were nevertheless acknowledged for their qualities and their considerable originality (Dorfman 1949).[4]

A first criticism therefore analyzed the unequal mechanisms of the capitalism of the Gilded Age. Ely believed that this capitalism displayed the particularity of amplifying "more natural human inequalities" (greater intelligence, gifts, ability, talents) (Bradizza 2013: 30–31). As an intellectual and Christian militant, Ely examined these inequalities constructed by the American Society of the Gilded Age through the prism of increasing poverty. Faithful to the methods of the GHS, Ely studied this poverty in great detail in several monographic and highly empirical texts. A summary text entitled "Pauperism in The United-States" was published in 1891.

Through an approach not previously adopted by other economists, this explanation of the unequal mechanisms of capitalism targeted the exercise of capital ownership rights in the USA, which prevented the fair distribution of wealth created by production.

The second criticism demonstrated that this increase in inequalities resulted from the adoption of an economic policy that was inappropriate, as the latter was based on the ideas of the "Old Political Economy" or, in other words, classical English economics (Kloppenberg 1986: 208). According to Ely, "[the old political economy] doctrines purporting to disclose natural laws harmonizing private and public interests and to support a laissez-faire policy allow the greedy and avaricious to use them as a tool for keeping down and oppressing the labor class" (Ely 1884: 64).

Ely believed that classical economic theory posed a whole host of problems, which were presented in his 1889 book, *An Introduction to Political Economy*. He identified three levels of problems. Philosophically speaking, the conception of the classical theory prevented both ethical concerns and the very idea of change from being considered (Frey 2008). Emblematic of the status quo, of a "theological determinism" and ultimately of a form of "absolutism" (Rader 1966), this theory was impermeable to the problems of society, and in particular of the most deprived, whom Ely felt should be the prime concern. Finally, through a strictly deductive axiom aimed at identifying the laws of economics, this theory produced solutions incorrectly deemed valid at all times and in all circumstances. The criticism of a belief that the market is the optimum form of resource allocation was already present.

This explains Ely's decision to examine the social sciences from a moral standpoint in order to demonstrate how society works and to endeavor to improve it (Ely 1886b). There is a direct link to the ideas of Gustav von Schmoller, a pioneer of the "historical method" of the second GHS during the 1870s.[5] Furthermore, by studying the social experimentation observed in Pullman in 1885, Ely showed that other solutions, while difficult, were possible in order to develop more harmonious social rules in American capitalist society (Ely 1885).

3.   ELY AND THE "SOCIAL THEORY OF RIGHTS": BUILDING A FAIRER SOCIETY

Ely's criticism called directly for the transformation of capitalism, rejecting the *laissez-faire* approach. This rejection led to a new means to promote the development of economic discipline (Rocca and Vallet 2019). In particular, Ely believed that it was essential to make space for the effective analysis of human choices in economic life and to develop the precise methods of investigation to facilitate this (Ely 1889). In our view, E. W. Morehouse's work (1969) provides the most faithful summary of this desire for renewal, the aim of which was to understand economic and social phenomena rather than hunting for improbable laws that governed them.

Incidentally, these new theoretical perspectives were accompanied by a number of somewhat ironic utterings that the history of thought has retained as being revealing of institutional intuition,[6] as well as by the formulation of theoretical outlines for economic research: a more inductive form of research (not just counter-factual), more concerned with collecting facts (not just identifying the supposed laws of economics) and with proposing solutions for reform (rather than simply serving a liberal approach to economic phenomena). However, this criticism of classical economics was not the culmination of Ely's approach, even if the history of thought sees it as a founding element of the institutional school: such a criticism was rather the means of transformation capitalism.

Calling on his analysis of institutions (and not merely the price-setting on the market), Ely clearly laid out his project in his major work published in 1914. In *Property and Contracts in Their Relations to the Distribution of Wealth* (995 pages in two volumes), Ely extended his criticism of *laissez-faire* policy and classical theory to an analysis of property rights as a factor preventing change. He believed that these property rights should be altered through robust state action (Ely 1914).

In *Socialism and Social Reform* (1894), Ely's choice already appeared clear: he rejected the idea – hotly debated at the time – of taxing the income (of the rich) to finance the redistribution of wealth, favoring institutional change instead. The latter was supposed to establish a fairer and globally more effi-cient wage-profit-sharing than the simple distribution of incomes (Bradizza 2013: 87). As a progressive conservative, and despite the marked inequalities observed in the USA at the end of the nineteenth century, Ely made a clear choice: to prioritize the path of resources obtained through work over income (of the poorest) obtained through redistribution made possible by taxing incomes (of the wealthiest).

In *Property and Contracts in Their Relations to the Distribution of Wealth*, Ely confirmed this path toward reform, becoming the pre-institutional the-oretician who very directly inspired his student, John R. Commons. Indeed, this work marked a fundamental milestone in the development of institutional thought, explicitly connecting an investigative methodology, a theory of prop-erty rights and an application to the theoretical problem of the distribution of wealth (Obeng-Odoom 2015: 889). According to Rutherford (2001: 176–7), Ely earned a specific place in the laying of the foundations of institutional tradition with his 1914 work: "Except for material on intangible property, little of this emphasis on law and economics came directly from Veblen. The major sources were the legal-economic work of Richard Ely (who taught Commons) and H. C. Sumner (who taught Hamilton). They, in turn, had been very much impacted by their exposure to the German Historical School."

Property and Contracts in Their Relations to the Distribution of Wealth also sparked the most virulent criticism of Ely from liberal economists: taking up the accusations voiced by Simon Newcomb of Johns Hopkins University in 1884, this attack returned to his supposed socialist leanings[7] and the need to remove him from the university.

This major work developed three ideas in particular:

1. The long-term accumulation of capital was fundamentally unstable as a result of the existence of the distribution of hereditary property rights. As Kummerow notes (2004: 2), "rather than 'trickling down', property rights 'pump up' wealth and income, tending to increase [the] concentration of wealth and political power over time." This could foster investment in the short or medium term but could tend to weaken demand in the long run because the average propensity to consume falls with income. Therefore, if hereditary property rights give a larger percentage of national income to the wealthy, less consumption and more saving would be the outcome. Ely believed that this economic system generated poverty that could not be reduced, assuming forms similar to the conditions of slavery (Ely 1914: 806).
2. This situation of poverty and growing economic inequalities could only improve if the fundamental rights were to change in society. In Ely's opinion, an institutional reform of property rights was the only means of achieving a fair and efficient economy. In tangible terms, it was impossible

to continue believing that capitalism was synonymous with total freedom of action of the owner – a total freedom that the Constitution was supposed to guarantee and the judges were to supervise.

Based on numerous appendices to the chapters of *Property and Contracts in Their Relations to the Distribution of Wealth*, Ely analyzed judgments and characterized the influence of a property right (over capital) that the courts of justice deemed absolute and inalienable. Globally speaking, Ely had a different theoretical conception of the role of law in economic functioning, seeing law as promoting social well-being.

Ely defended a change in the principle of constitutionally inalienable property rights, as the following quotation summarizes:

> Property has its social side, as represented by the right of taxation, the right of eminent domain, the right to exercise the police power, the right to control transfers, especially by way of inheritance, the right to exempt certain property from execution and distress in order that a man may not be deprived of the means of doing his part in the work of the world by working at his trade or calling. An absolute right of property, free from these restrictions for the benefit of organized society, would [. . .] result in the dissolution of society. It is these considerations that sustain one of the main theses of the book, that private property is established and maintained for social purposes. (Swayze 1915: 825)

The trend favored by Ely was an increased incorporation of what he termed "public interest" (now referred to as general interest) in exercising private property rights (and not its abolition).

3. The necessary change in property rights was possible without contracting the Constitution (this was incidentally the case for the abolition of slavery). According to Ely, the rights specifically linked to the distribution of wealth should be progressively reformed. In practice, reforms were not intended to abolish property rights but rather to impose an allocation of wealth created in a more socially fair manner. Different institutions would have to be modified:

> In the existing socio-economic order, there are five fundamental institutions of first rank: (1) property, public and private; (2) inheritance; (3) contract and its conditions; (4) vested rights; and (5) personal conditions. In addition, there are five fundamental forces of second rank: (1) custom; (2) competition; (3) monopoly; (4) authority; and (5) benevolence. It is these fundamental institutions and forces that radical socio-economic reformers desire to change. It must be admitted. (Swayze 1915: 822)

A change in the "bundle of rights" should thus be designed to achieve new balances between the individual freedoms to be protected at all costs (capital ownership right) and social institutions that restrict owners while also guaranteeing the individual freedom of worker-citizens. From 1914 Ely advocated not only the introduction of new tools to steer the economy, but more particularly a set of constraints designed to achieve these new equilibria. The constraints were either new institutions (the creation of unions, for example) or new rules (legal provisions with regard to wages, sharing the wealth created and child labor).

This project of Ely's was not isolated.[8] It was even relayed and amplified by many of the students who became professors or leading politicians during the Progressive Era. Summarizing the literature on this point, Kummerow (2004: 7) lists the variety and strength of the relays from which Ely's ideas benefited:

- Wesley Mitchell contributed to improving information by helping to create institutions to produce national accounts data.
- John R. Commons lobbied effectively for the legalization of labor unions.
- Thorstein Veblen attacked the assumption of rationality, developing the idea that people act through "habits" to achieve status in social contexts, rather than as individually autonomous decision-makers.
- Woodrow Wilson (Ely 1900), who minored in Economics under Ely at Johns Hopkins, became a reformist president whose administration passed child labor laws and pure food and drug laws.
- Frederick Jackson Turner wrote a key essay on the closing of the American frontier and hence the need to conserve natural resources.
- Theodore Roosevelt did not study under Ely, but read his works, commenting that "Professor Ely taught me to be radical in my economics and then sane in my radicalism" (Ely 1938: 248). Roosevelt especially paid attention to Ely's 1900 work on monopoly and was known as a "trust buster." Roosevelt also set aside public land for conservation purposes.
- Many other Ely students developed institutions for land-use regulation, property taxation and real-estate valuation.

While the "Golden Mean" was theoretically sound and very clear in its aims, it also displayed the originality of containing the definition of its means of implementation.

4.   ELY, A PALADIN[9] COMMITTED TO THE REFORM OF SOCIETY'S INSTITUTIONS

On a personal note, Ely had a conception of the role of the state that was influenced by his faith. In contrast to the Darwinian approach to society dominant in the USA at the time, he relied on a redemptive conception of the role of the state: "In Ely's eyes, government was the God-given instrument through which we had to work. Its preeminence as a divine instrument was based on the post-Reformation abolition of the division between the sacred and the secular and on the State's power to implement ethical solutions to public problems" (Quandt 1973: 402–3). The state was thus the key driving force in reducing inequalities.

Likewise, Cranfill specified the vision that Ely had of reducing inequalities, seen as "inequalities of opportunity." Imbued with his militant actions, "Ely believes in social progress toward a condition under which each member of society secured equal opportunity to develop to the full extent of his capacity. [. . .] The State with all of its institutions coordinated and cooperating should be ready to step in on the side of the weak and to check the strong when the latter showed any tendencies to exploit or harass the weak" (Cranfill 1941: VII).

Henceforth, the meaning of the reform of institutions was clearly established. While the change in property law was to be designed with a view to reducing the effects of "unequal opportunities," it was not simply a case of empty words, or naivety in the "Golden Mean" program. This program corresponded to a state of mind: the reform had to be undertaken by an elite, trained to manage social change (Herzberg 2001: 137). In Ely's mind, this elite was the group of intellectuals and politicians who identified with the Wisconsin Idea (Cavalieri 2016).

This elite had its means of action and the methods necessary to implement this change. In defining the means, Ely adopted a rather singular approach for the time. In *Property and Contracts in Their Relations to the Distribution of Wealth*, he meticulously established that it was essentially the decisions of judges, those stringent defenders of the Constitution, that prevented the fair distribution of wealth from occurring. The numerous appendices to the chapters listed a plethora of scenarios in which the judge's decision was over-protective of property rights, presenting the latter as an intangible right and, more often than not, rejecting the salaried worker's requests for reparations or better pay. Ely felt that action on means needed to be twofold: first, creating commissions bringing together intellectuals, employers and representatives of the civil society tasked with studying possible reforms – Ely would be the initiator and a member of the first commissions; and second, increasing the awareness of judges who would be trained in a "social theory of property" (Ely's own expression throughout his works) developed on the basis of ethical considerations to guide institutional change (Morehouse 1969: 15). On this, Ely was directly influenced by Knies (Heidelberg) and Wagner (Berlin).

With regard to methods, the "Golden Mean" program was clearly not a public policy mechanism that was sufficiently detailed to be immediately operational (Frey 2008: 310). As a reformist intellectual, Ely put forward new principles capable of providing a reasoned framework for institutional change. In addition to a general call for greater democracy, Ely discussed an "incentive mechanism," which can be pieced together by reading his autobiography published in 1938 (Ely 1938). This mechanism, conducive to "social change" – which scholars of his life and works believe remained the aim underpinning Ely's approach – comprised three complementary ideas.

First, Ely spent several decades developing his global influence on how economic policy should be implemented. He maintained ongoing relations with numerous politicians of the Progressive Era (in particular, Robert – "Bob Fighting" – La Folette), as well as with President Wilson, who freely acknowledged the influence of his former professor on his actions (Wilson 1913). This influence was not solely intellectual, as Wilson's first term in office saw the adoption of a proportional income tax, the Federal Reserve Act and "new regulations on the economy" (Pequet and Thies 2010: 74), as called for by Ely and his students.

Second, building on this general influence on policy matters, Ely and his friends (in particular Commons) participated widely in the work of a wide range of policy reform commissions, most particularly that of the commissions of the "experimental" state of Wisconsin, now recognized as the laboratory of the New Deal (Gonce 1996). At the same time, Ely initiated a number of professional associations boasting a major reformist impact. In particular, Da Costa (2010) points to the decisive role of the American Association for Labor Legislation (created by Ely) in the fight to adopt social legislation in the United States.

Ely believed deeply in the supervision of private enterprise by the institutions, which defined the limits of freedom vis-à-vis the collective interest (Groves 1969: 8). More precisely, Ely developed an original means of acting on economic policy: "The men and women of the progressive movement should be seen as pioneers of the welfare state. Their aim was not to strengthen government authority as such, but they were determined to remedy the most urgent and dangerous ills of industrial society and in doing so, they quickly learned that they could not achieve their goals without using the power of the administrative state" (Hofstadter 1963: 15).

Finally, Ely gambled on comprehensive change in the means of teaching the elite in universities, prioritizing a more analytical mindset and innovative scientific approaches (in particular, the analysis of facts by "sifting and winnowing"). These ambitions were put into practice by means of teaching in interactive seminars, the involvement of professionals and company visits – an avalanche of new practices in the world of American academia in the early twentieth century. In this respect, Ely had a major impact on the social sciences in the USA, as he taught the most economists during this period (Tilman 1987: 142), while developing both the most prominent research and advisory institutions and the most original methods. In particular, he was the first person to create a department of agricultural economics in the United States, in 1909.

5.   CONCLUSION

Ely gradually disappeared from American social sciences after the early twentieth century, though he had an acknowledged scientific excellence and connections to the recognized between-the-wars institutional stream (Rutherford 2012). The history of thought nevertheless acknowledges his role as a pioneer in the ascension of Old Institutionalism, be it through the theoretical insights contained in his major works or through the training of the main professors forming this movement over several decades (Fine 1951). While this pioneering role is recognized even by his most virulent critics (in particular, S. Newcomb), neoclassical thought nevertheless made every effort to limit his place in the history of thought, granting him only a few mundane lines in the *New Palgrave*.

During his lifetime, Ely frequently faced quite strenuous opposition: a famous "trial" (Rolnick 1955; Schlabach 1963), as well as public attacks on his methods and the quality of the work conducted by the institutions that he founded. One of the most virulent attacks was that of Jorgensen in 1925, relating to the *Institute for Research in Land Economics and Public Utilities* (Jorgensen 1925). Despite this, the influence of the work of the research "institutions" that he created is now commonly acknowledged (Rocca and Vallet 2019).

Assisted by Commons, Ely remains the pioneering author of major institutional developments that marked the twentieth century in the United States. The provisions of the second New Deal with regard to social legislation and public intervention, for example, are the direct result of Wilson's experience and the work of commissions influenced by Ely's philosophy (Higgs 1987).

In his final work in 1938, Ely nevertheless felt that the reformist provisions of the second New Deal were ultimately of an overly socializing nature. This is evidence of a man torn between the firm conviction of a desire to reform capitalism and the profound influence of a conservative education.

NOTES

1.   *Outlines of Economics* (1893), initially published in 1889 under the title *An Introduction to Political Economy*, was the most influential economics textbook in late nineteenth-century United States. *The Times* (October 7, 1937) stated that "probably not since the publication of Adam Smith's *Wealth of Nations* has a book of its kind had wider circulation." Ely founded the American Economic Association (AEA). His book *The Labor Movement in America* (1886a) – for many years the reference manual for United States labor economists – founded United States institutional labor economics (Kaufmann 2003). To labor relations specialists, Ely's work echoed the 1897 work of the Webbs.

2. Four of Ely's works are generally recognized as being truly significant, with respect to their originality, their political scope or the analytical and theoretical synthesis provided: (1) "The Past and the Present of the Political Economy" (1884) provides a synthesis of the criticisms of classical political economics; (2) *The Labor Movement in America* (1886a) is the founding act of the tradition of institutional labor economics in the United States (Kaufmann 2003; McNulty 1980: ch. 6); (3) *Outlines of Economics* (1893), updated several times with co-authors, is a seminal book that remains the most influential economics textbook in late nineteenth-century United States, as mentioned in footnote 1. This textbook was immediately translated into several languages, and more than 500,000 copies were sold in the USA; (4) *Property and Contracts in Their Relations to the Distribution of Wealth* (1914) forms the very heart of his theoretical proposal, justifying the reform of property rights with a view to establishing a more equitable economy. The specific contributions of each of these four works to the "Golden Mean" project are explained in greater detail in the following pages.

3. In more than one hundred academic publications and extensive correspondence, Ely's most telling publications were written between 1884 and 1914. His autobiography (*Ground Under Our Feet*) naturally appeared much later (1938). Archived in the Library of the State Historical Society of Wisconsin, Ely's correspondence (the "Ely papers") has been examined and analyzed on several occasions. Two such analyses are reference works. The first is that of H. C. Taylor (1966), devoted to one of Ely's co-authors (E. W. Morehouse). The second work, by B. G. Rader (1966), is more familiar. Furthermore, E. W. Morehouse (1969) provides a periodized and thematic review of Ely's works.

4. In the introduction to his work, Bradizza (2013: 7) offers an extensive review of the opinions concerning the influence of Ely's publications. Bradizza provides a list of authors who consider that Ely's works over the period 1880–90 were highly influential.

5. The development of the GHS comprised two "schools" of thought, the first forming around Hildebrand, Roscher and Knies, and the second around authors such as Gustav von Schmoller or Adolph Wagner, for instance.

6. See, for instance, the following quotation: "At bottom, it [supply-and-demand analysis] is only a truism proved by the experience of cooks. When fish is scarce it is dear. In sooth, a beautiful discovery! Nevertheless, there is nothing necessary in this. Suppose a religious law which forbids one to eat fish; it might be very scarce and at the same time cheap" (Ely 1884: 39).

7. In 1917 Ely wrote, "In our work in this state, we have three watch words, namely patriotic, sanely progressive, and anti-Bolshevik" (quoted by Tilman 1992: 102). In 1938 Ely (1938: 224) once again explained his aversion for socialism, something quite clearly confirmed by the literature (Wilkins 1958).

8. This project was not dissimilar to the work of Henry George, and in particular his denunciation of a market economy characterized by owners acquiring wealth (see this volume, Chapter 14).

9. In reference to the title of the article written by M. N. Rothbard (2002).

REFERENCES

Bradizza, Luigi. 2013. *Richard T. Ely's Critique of Capitalism*. New York: Palgrave Macmillan.

Cavalieri, Marco. 2016. "Inside Institutions of Progressive-Era Social Sciences: The Interdisciplinarity of Economics and Sociology." *Journal of Economic Issues* 50, no. 2: 345–61.

Coats, Alfred W. 1993. *The Sociology and Professionalization of Economics*. London and New York: Routledge.

Cranfill, Samuel Elliott. 1941. "The Contributions of Richard T. Ely to Economic Thought." *LSU Historical Dissertations and Theses* 7843. Available at https://digitalcommons.lsu.edu/gradschool_disstheses/7843.

Da Costa, Isabelle. 2010. "John Commons' Institutionalism and the Origins of the Welfare State in the United States." *Papers in Political Economy* 42 [journal available online].

Dorfman, Joseph. 1949. *The Economic Mind in American Civilization*. New York: Viking Press.

Ely, Richard T. 1884. "The Past and the Present of Political Economy." *Studies in Historical and Political Science of Johns Hopkins University* Second Series: 5–64.

Ely, Richard T. 1885. "Pullman: A Social Study." *Harper's Magazine* 70 (February): 452–66.

Ely, Richard T. 1886a. *The Labor Movement in America*. New York: T. Y. Crowell.

Ely, Richard T. 1886b. "Ethics and Economics." *Science* 7, no. 175: 529–33.

Ely, Richard T. 1889. *An Introduction to Political Economy*. New York: Chautauqua Press.

Ely, Richard T. 1891. "Pauperism in the United States." History of Economic Thought Articles 152, no. 413: 395–410.

Ely, Richard T. 1894. *Socialism and Social Reform*. New York: Thomas Y. Crowell & Co.

Ely, Richard T. 1900. "Letter to Woodrow Wilson." *The Papers of Woodrow Wilson*, April 20. Geneva: Archives of the League of Nations, 11 (1898–1900): 535.

Ely, Richard T. 1914. *Property and Contracts in Their Relations to the Distribution of Wealth*. New York: Macmillan.

Ely, Richard T. 1918. "Private Colonization of the Land." *American Economic Review* 8, no. 3: 522–48.

Ely, Richard T. 1938. *Ground Under Our Feet: An Autobiography*. New York: Macmillan.

Fine, Sydney. 1951. "Richard T. Ely, Forerunner of Progressivism, 1880–1901." *The Mississippi Valley Historical Review* 37, no. 4: 599–624.

Frey, Donald E. 2008. "The Impact of Liberal Religion on Richard Ely's Economic Methodology." *History of Political Economy* 40, no. 5: 299–314.

Gonce, Richard A. 1996. "The Social Gospel, Ely, and Commons' Initial Stage of Thought." *Journal of Economic Issues* 30, no. 3: 641–65.

Gough, Robert J. 1991. "Richard T. Ely and the Development of the Wisconsin Cutover." *Wisconsin Magazine of History* 75, no. 1: 2–38.

Groves, Harold M. 1969. "R. T. Ely: An Appreciation." *Land Economics* 45, no. 1: 1–9.

Herzberg, David L. 2001. "Thinking through War: The Social Thought of Richard T. Ely, John R. Commons, and Edward A. Ross during the First World War." *Journal of the History of the Behavioral Science* 37, no. 2: 123–41.

Higgs, Robert J. 1987. *Crisis and Leviathan: Critical Episodes in the Growth of American Government.* New York: Oxford University Press.

Hofstadter, Richard (ed.). 1963. *The Progressive Movement, 1900–1915.* Englewood Cliffs, NJ: Prentice-Hall, Inc.

Jorgensen, Emil O. 1925. *False Education in Our Colleges and Universities: An Exposé of Prof. Richard T. Ely and His "Institute for Research in Land Economics and Public Utilities."* Chicago, IL: Manufacturers and Merchants Federal Tax League.

Kaufman, Bruce E. 2003. "John R. Commons and the Wisconsin School on Industrial Relations Strategy and Policy." *Industrial and Labor Relations Review* 57, no. 1: 3–30.

Kloppenberg, James T. 1986. *Uncertain Victory: Social Democracy and Progressivism in European and American Thought, 1870–1920.* New York: Oxford University Press.

Kummerow, Max. 2004. "Richard T. Ely's Property and Contract in Their Relation to the Distribution of Wealth (1914): Did the Historical School Institutional Economists Invent a Workable Solution to 'Recurrent Crises of Capitalism'?." Working paper, available at http://citeseerx.ist.psu.edu/viewdoc/download?doi=10.1.1.201.5389&rep=rep1&type=pdf.

McNulty, Paul J. 1980. *The Origins and Development of Labour Economics: A Chapter of the History of Social Thought.* Cambridge, MA: MIT Press.

Morehouse, Edward W. 1969. "Richard T. Ely: A Supplement." *Land Economics* 45, no. 1: 10–18.

Obeng-Odoom, Franklin. 2015. "Luigi Bradizza: Richard T. Ely's Critique of Capitalism." *Journal of Economic Issues* 49, no. 3: 887–90.

Pecquet, Gary M. and Clifford T. Thies. 2010. "The Shaping of a Future President's Economic Thought. Richard T. Ely and Woodrow Wilson at 'The Hopkins'." *The Independent Review* 15, no. 2: 257–77.

Quandt, Jean B. 1973. "Religion and Social Thought: The Secularization of Postmillennialism." *American Quarterly* 25, no. 4: 390–409.

Rader, Benjamin G. 1966. "Richard T. Ely: Lay Spokesman for the Social Gospel." *Journal of American History* 53, no. 1: 61–74.

Rocca, Michel and Guillaume Vallet. 2019. "A Noble, but Failed, Attempt by R. T. Ely, A. W. Small and The German Historical School to Influence U.S. Social Science (1890s–1930s)." *Seminar of the New School for Social Research.* March 5, New York.

Rolnick, Stanley R. 1955. "Exceptional Decision: The Trial of Professor Richard T. Ely by the Board of Regents of the University of Wisconsin, 1894." *Journal of the Arkansas Academy of Science* 8, no. 22: 198–203.

Rothbard, Murray N. 2002. "Richard T. Ely: Paladin of the Welfare–Warfare State." *The Independent Review* 6, no. 4: 585–9.

Rutherford, Malcolm. 2001. "Institutionalism Then and Now." *Journal of Economic Perspectives* 15, no. 3: 173–94.

Rutherford, Malcolm. 2009. "Towards a History of American Institutional Economics." *Journal of Economic Issues* 43, no. 2: 308–18.

Rutherford, Malcolm. 2012. "Field, Undercover, and Participant Observers in US Labor Economics: 1900–1930." History of Political Economy 44, no. 5: 185–205.

Schlabach, Theron, F. 1963. "An Aristocrat on Trial: The Case of Richard T. Ely." *Wisconsin Magazine of History* 47, no. 2: 140–59.

Stiglitz, Joseph. 2012. *Le Prix de l'Inégalité.* Paris: Les Liens qui Libèrent.

Swayze, Francis J. 1915. "Review on Property and Contract in their Relation to the Distribution of Wealth by Richard T. Ely." *The Quarterly Journal of Economics* 29, no. 4: 820–28.

Taylor, Henry C. 1966. "E. W. Morehouse: The Academic Years and the Heritage of Richard Ely." In *Innovation and Achievement in the Public Interest Essays on Government, Business and the University in Honor of the Seventieth Birthday of Edward W. Morehouse*, edited by Ward Morehouse and Nancy Morehouse Gordon. Croton-on-Hudson, NY: Wayward Press, pp. 1–17.

Tilman, Rick. 1987. "Grace Jaffe and Richard Ely on Thorstein Veblen: An Unknown Chapter in American Economic Thought." *History of Political Economy* 19, no. 1: 141–61.

Tilman, Rick. 1992. *Thorstein Veblen and His Critics, 1891–1963*. Princeton, NJ: Princeton Legacy Library.

Wilkins, Myra S. 1958. "Richard T. Ely on English Socialism." *The American Journal of Economics and Sociology* 18, no. 1: 61–8.

Wilson, Woodrow. 1913. *The New Freedom*. New York: Doubleday, Page & Company.

2. The progressive view of Old Institutionalism: business ethics, industrial democracy and reasonable capitalism

Virgile Chassagnon and Benjamin Dubrion

1. INTRODUCTION

The question of inequality has been gaining importance in economics since the publication of Piketty's (2014) book, *Capital in the Twenty-First Century*. However, few studies have focused on the historical analysis of inequality from the point of view of an unorthodox history of economic thought (see Chassagnon and Vallet 2019). This is particularly true in the case of the major developments that American authors such as Ely, Veblen, Commons and Dewey had been able to propose during the Progressive Era. Similarly, organizational economists have too often ignored the issue of inequality and the role of firms and business relationships in the fight against this phenomenon. However, when one considers the work of Old Institutionalism, one realizes that it contains many theoretical intuitions, concepts and heuristics allowing better treatment of the crucial question of social and economic inequalities in modern capitalism. Hence, this chapter aims to contribute to filling these two current theoretical gaps by showing how the principal authors of Old Institutionalism proposed a vision of the firm and of industrial democracy enabling one to think of inequality and the conditions of human development in a capitalist system seen as more just.

This chapter is organized into four sections followed by a general conclusion. Section 2 proposes the definition of institutional business ethics. Section 3, starting from labor problems, questions the place that Old Institutional thought gives to work in an economic democracy. Section 4 defines the business enterprise in institutionalism with reference to the concepts of going concern and organized institution. Section 5 shows that modern capitalism creates significant inequality because of the industrial sabotage committed by the paradigm of shareholder value and the new captains of industries. It indicates the institutional changes needed to transition to good capitalism based on reasonable values.

2.   TOWARDS INSTITUTIONAL BUSINESS ETHICS

The ethical question was central for several economists who, from the end of the nineteenth century in the United States, were considered to be at the origin of the institutional economic analysis. In Old Institutional thought, the economy is seen as fundamentally composed of ethical values, a point of view in opposition to that of classical English economists whose ideas dominated the entire nineteenth century. This importance given to ethics owes much to the influence of the Protestant religion on several authors of the time such as John R. Commons and especially his mentor Richard T. Ely, whose thought has been presented in Chapter 1. Both belonged to the Social Gospel, a Christian social movement in the 1880s that denounced the negative effects of industrialization and of firms, concentrating on the living conditions of workers of the time. At the end of the nineteenth century, Ely was considered one of the leaders of the Social Gospel Movement, defending the values of Christian love and fraternity that the social sciences, in particular economics, would be able to promote by mitigating the negative effects of unregulated capitalism (see Bradizza 2013).

Ely, a co-founder of the American Institute of Christian Sociology, in which he recruited Commons as secretary-treasurer, was perceived as "the most aggressive advocate of social gospel during the eighties" (Hopkins, cited in Gonce 1996: 642). Very religiously committed, Ely had never ceased to denounce the effects of, according to him, devastating *laissez-faire* resulting, in particular, in the development of social injustice, economic inequality and, more generally, poverty among workers. As an advocate of more regulation, he was one of the first authors to assert the ethical dimension of the economy and the need to found a "new political economy" or "ethical school" distinct from the classical English political economy in which the absence of ethical considerations served to justify the *laissez-faire* (Ely 1889). For Ely, the English political economy was founded on the will to analyze the economy independently of social and legal institutions. Additionally, this economic thought was based on the primacy given to the individual rather than society; on the contrary, the author defends the thesis of inseparability of ethics and the economy and that of an inversion of relations between the individual and society (Ely 1883).

Ethics and economics are inseparable insofar as the reality studied by economists, "what is", is never grasped as such but always depends on past trajectories and history and also on people's will to change things one way or another. Therefore, the economist cannot separate "what is" from "what should be" and always adopts, even implicitly, an ethical point of view on what he or she analyzes. Thus, concerning the relationship between the individual and society, the "new" political economy does not conceive of the individual as an isolated element existing by and for himself independently of others; on the contrary, his or her existence makes sense in the society that transcends it. In the words of Ely (1886: 532), "the ethical school [. . .] places society above the individual, because the whole is more than any of its parts." Highly influenced by the German Historical School, where he was trained during his studies in Germany, Ely could be regarded as the forerunner of the institutionalist economic approach in that, for him, the behavior of individuals was always explained by examining the environment.

Individuals are part of a broader social group – members of a family, a firm, a union or, at the most general level, members of society – who strongly structure their decisions and attitudes. This way of representing individual behavior as "institutionalized" is central to the characterization of what we call the institutional business ethics. In this view, De George (1987: 204) defines business ethics as a theoretical field of investigation concerning the "morality and immorality as well as the possible justification of economic systems." This field makes sense at complementary levels of analysis that implies both individuals' actions and their collective actions in firms.

For De George (1987), the microanalytical level of business ethics is that of the individual. At this level, institutional business ethics give an interesting account of the individual based on the transactions he engages in; these are viewed in the institutionalist perspective as the unit of analysis of social and economic activities. It is therefore not the individual who is central but the existing relationships between individuals. Institutional business ethics follows a relational approach in the sense that the smallest unit of analysis is the relationship that binds people to each other, and not individuals, from the outset viewed as separate, independent or "atomic human beings," to use Veblen's critical analogy (see Veblen 1904). In this respect, Commons (1934) is at the origin of a typology of transactions that exhaust economic activities according to three major modalities of relations between individuals. Bargaining transactions, which echo market coordination, are based on the assumption of equality between contractors who voluntarily negotiate transfers of property rights. These transactions involve not only two individuals in negotiation but also several who are in competition with one another for the purpose of obtaining or assigning property rights. This is one of the points of difference from the two other types of transactions that have in common qualifying situations in which the participants are in unequal positions.

Managerial transactions characterize activities in which there is a superiority or inferiority relationship of one of the participants in the transaction to the other, as is the case in the relationship between a master and a servant, or an employer and an employee. The purpose of this type of transaction is not the distribution of wealth (see Commons 1893) but its production, which raises the question of the industrial efficiency of the organization created to produce wealth. Lastly, the rationing transactions that, similarly to the above, mobilize asymmetric resources between individuals, differ in that one of them – the superior – is a collective responsible for making decisions about the distribution of wealth produced. This identification of three types of transactions makes it possible to emphasize the plural dimension of the forms of coordination of economic activities. However, in the institutional perspective, the social order cannot emerge from individual interactions alone. In other words, the micro level cannot be understood without reference to a higher level of analysis.

De George (1987) argues that in the field of business ethics, the most studied level remains that in which individuals work, invest and act collectively – namely, the firm. This idea is close to several institutional economists, such as Commons and Veblen, for whom the business enterprise constitutes a form of collective action that both constrains and provides resources for individual actions. The institution structures the behavior of its members without being conceived as *deus ex machina* because it is the product of the choices and actions of the agents. If the firm is an institution, it also has an organizational dimension in the institutional tradition because the firm is organized as a collective action. In other words, formal and informal rules regulate the behavior of its members. It finally appears as an "organized institution" (see *infra*) resulting from collective decisions that, in turn, structure individual actions (see the modern institutional view of Chassagnon 2014).

3.   LABOR PROBLEMS AND INDUSTRIAL DEMOCRACY

The way in which labor is considered is the primary research question of institutional business ethics, which could be understood from the debates that occurred, especially in the United States, from the end of the nineteenth century. It is in this intellectual context that central questions have been asked that remain relevant to the representation of workers, collective bargaining, industrial democracy and, more broadly, the emancipation of the people at work. The study of labor problems can initially be defined as the analysis of problems concerning, and solutions to, the relations between the two factors of production essential to the capitalist economic dynamic – capital and labor – more specifically at the level of the firm, the study of the often conflictual relationships between employers and employees.

In a book considered throughout the twentieth century to be the essential reference on the question of labor problems (Brissenden 1926), Adams and

Sumner (1905) suggest that with the development of big business and the difficulties experienced by workers in emancipating themselves from their work situation, labor problems are rooted in the wage system. Because this system leads to making each individual a "merchant" of his own skills, the worker is encouraged to behave as if he were an entrepreneur himself. In a liberal perspective, work is a commodity among others able to instigate or be the object of purchases and sales regulated by the price system – an idea specifically disputed by Old Institutional thought.

In progressive Old Institutional thought, the subject of the exchange in an employment relationship is not a commodity or a machine that could be fully specified in transactions, but a mutual promise, a "goodwill," to use Commons' (1919) term. In this vision, the employment relationship is based on a promise constantly renewed, based on the expectations of each of its members. From the workers point of view, the promise refers to the obedience to orders and the provision of a service considered satisfactory by the employer. From that of the latter, the promise is based on working conditions and a wage level in line with workers' expectations. The employment relationship is therefore regarded not as one of rights and duties but of freedom and exposure to the goodwill of the other. This view means that everyone owns not a tangible and objective good but an expectation that depends on the goodwill of each participant in the transaction.

For Commons (1924: 303), the will of each participant "is not an empty choosing between doing and not doing, but between different degrees of power in doing one thing instead of another." This is the fundamental asymmetry between employers and employees – asymmetry that purely liberal approaches most often refuse to recognize. From an ethical and political point of view, it is quite possible to establish a set of principles governing society and establishing the equal rights of individuals, as was constitutionally possible in the United States or France after the revolution at the end of the eighteenth century. However, from an economic point of view, the employee is coerced in his choices to a much greater degree than the employer is.

In this respect, Commons distinguishes three major forms of power and shows that the employment relationship is strongly structured by one of them for the benefit of the employer. Physical power and moral power – relying, respectively, on the use of physical violence and persuasion to guide the behavior of others – may be present in the employment relationship, but another form of power is central, namely, coercion. It depends on the wants and resources of the participants in the transaction. However, for Commons (1934: 337), "since resources are but means of satisfying the corresponding wants, and since the satisfying of wants exhausts resources in course of time, the power of each to determine the ratios of exchange depends upon their relative power to wait for the other to give in." He speaks of "waiting power." The employment relationship is marked by a lack of equality in terms of weighing the power between employers and employees (Commons 1924: 306). For instance, unlike the employee, the employer can more easily admit certain financial losses. This possibility raises the question of the means available to rebalance the employment relationship, i.e. the question of the rules to be implemented to stabilize mutual expectations that are the result of the mutual promises of employers and employees.

Thus, it is crucial to mitigate the economic inequality between the members of the employment relationship by organizing a political system of rebalancing the bargaining powers in transactions. To this end, it is necessary to institutionalize a collective mode of action allowing the employee to overcome the weakness of his individual action. Trade unionism and collective bargaining constitute collective modes of action that enhance the economic power of employees over the employer, leading to less inequality between the members of the employment relationship (Dubrion 2018). By giving more voice to employees, particularly in terms of fixing wage levels, collective bargaining became a fertile ground for the foundation of industrial democracy that was extensively questioned at the turn of the nineteenth and twentieth centuries in the United States as part of the debates on labor problems (Derber 1970). On this issue, lively debates took place at the beginning of the twentieth century between the incumbents of nascent scientific management defending the idea of non-necessity of trade unions and those of collective bargaining and institutional thought.

This is notably the case of Hoxie's (1915) work at the American Industrial Relations Commission that justified collective bargaining as a means of improving the economic power of workers in a position of individual weakness vis-à-vis those who employ them. It is through the expansion of collective bargaining that solutions to conflicts between employers and employees could be found. With regard to what has been done at the US federal level in terms of citizen representation, it appears useful to organize a system of rules, a "constitution," governing collective relations between employers and employees. In Commons' words, this is to treat the problem "in the same way that similar conflicts are met in the region of politics, namely, a constitutional form of organization representing the interests affected, with mutual veto, and therefore with progressive compromises as conflicts arise" (Commons 1911: 466–7).

Institutional business ethics assigns high importance to democratic solutions to the problems of individuals; these problems concern not only members of the employment relationship, as we have seen here, but also more broadly all members of society, as we will see later. In search of a reasonable capitalism (Commons 1934) or a "creative" democracy (Dewey 1991), institutional business ethics is driven by the recognition of the pluralism of points of view and the search for a just balance between individual and collective interests that often conflict. The democratic industrial organization does not always necessarily guarantee power sharing but aims toward what it is best able to achieve.

4.   THE BUSINESS ENTERPRISE AS A SPECIFIC GOING CONCERN

The Old Institutional economic tradition has developed a singular conception of the business enterprise perceived as the central institution of capitalism. In this approach, the firm appears as both an institution and an organization, without these two terms being understood to contradict each other. In contrast, applied to the firm, the terms of institution and organization are understood as two different but inseparable dimensions of understanding the regulatory power within the capitalist system. The firm is an institution that emerges from the rules of capitalism. This conception fully inscribes the firm in the political order that the prevailing contemporary approaches developed in economics and management tend to evade.

The firm is primarily an institution in the sense that it is a form of collective action that structures individual behavior. Commons' (1934) reflections on the nature and role of institutions make it possible to specify the institutional dimension of the firm as a going concern. Two major forms of collective action based on both informal and formal rules can be identified. For Commons, the first form of collective action, considered the most universal, is custom. It produces informal rules, habits and routines that enable individuals to secure their expectations. These rules are generally not intentionally implemented and followed, unlike the other form of collective action identified, the going concern. In contrast to custom, the going concern is an organized mode of collective action that voluntarily mobilizes participants in different transactions according to more or less precise formal rules ensuring the regulation of each person's actions. Because it involves potentially conflicting individual behaviors, it has a strong political dimension. The rules that specify it are related to each participant's expectations of the behaviors and ways of thinking of others and can then be seen as coordinating individuals' actions. Their implementation is the result of a collective will based on individual intentions and on the discretionary actions of participants.

The firm is an institution to the extent that by its collectively established rules, it assigns obligations and rights to individuals, authorizes or declines certain actions and suggests, more or less strongly, the adoption of various behaviors. In other words, "as an organization, the firm is not only an entity facing an external environment but also an (internal) institutional entity, that is to say, a cultural and normative system made of formal rules, legal devices, conventions, informal norms, and shared beliefs that structure social interactions and relationships, govern and constrain individuals' behaviors, and prevent and resolve conflicts between actors who permanently adapt to their environment" (Chassagnon 2014: 204). This institution is organized because the rules that characterize it stem from the human will. More specifically, two main types of rules structuring the behavior of the firm members are identifiable: the rules defined outside the firm by law, which give a legal existence to the firm as a corporation, and those defined internally by the private members of the going concern.

In Old Institutional thought, two subsets form the business enterprise. On the one hand, the "going plant" refers to the productive nature of the organization, where the unit of measurement is the working hour and where technological and productive efficiency issues are addressed. On the other hand, the "going business" integrates the expectations of the members of the firm measured in monetary terms and deals with conflicts of interest and stabilization of relations between individuals and groups of individuals constrained by the scarcity of resources. From an economic point of view, the question that involves the enterprise and its two interdependent subsets concerns "the whole activity of proportioning the parts so as to get the largest result or the minimum effort" (Commons 1934: 621).

However, this question makes sense in a broader context that is more political than economic. The Old Institutional thought of the firm considers the firm an institution organized above all depending on the political relations that exist not only between the members of the organization but also in society as a whole. The implementation of the rules of stabilization of relations between individuals is political because it produces relations of power and conflicts between individuals and groups of individuals in transactions. The regulation of the behavior of members of the firm is realized – in terms of both production and exchange – within a broad institutional framework specifying the nature and the functions of participants considered legitimate to cause the emergence of the rules of collective action. This framework is linked to what Commons names "rationing transactions" that actually regulate other types of transactions. These rationing transactions are thus qualified as "authoritative" (Commons 1924: 107) insofar as they legitimize the existence of individuals and their collectives, and govern the types of transactions they have between them.

If the firm as the business enterprise of Old Institutional thought differs from custom by the organized aspect of its rules, it is no less dependent on past habits and practices that ultimately contribute to limiting the scope for action of the present (see Dewey 1922). In other words, beyond legal constraints, the formal rules put in place within firms cannot be understood without reference to informal practices and past histories. As pointed out by Commons (1924: 147), "the collective will is also guided by acts of participants in the past.

Customs, practices, habits, precedents, methods of work, have been built up and handed down as working rules, which limit discretion in the present." The resulting political organization for both the firm and society determines largely the economic efficiency of the adopted rules. In this vision, while the firm is clearly seen as an economic entity, its place and function in society are primarily political. In this view, democratic values are central to the Old Institutional business ethics. We agree with Ely (1887: 975) when he argues that the firm "must in the end tend to a true democracy [. . .]. This should never be forgotten."

5.   INDUSTRIAL SABOTAGE, REASONABLE VALUE AND SOCIAL INEQUALITIES

For Old Institutional scholars, capitalism can lead to industrial inefficiency and sabotage. Originally, Veblen (1904) defined sabotage as a conscientious withdrawal of industrial efficiency, which was in fact the ability of a firm not to maximize profit but to propose a higher level of production. Sabotage implies that pecuniary transactions lead to restriction and so are a limit to the provision of public common good. For Veblen (2001: 4), sabotage was "the deliberate, although entirely legal, practice of peaceful restriction, delay, withdrawal, or obstruction to secure some special advantage or preference." In a Veblenian perspective, capital holders can increase their economic rents by controlling strategic aspects and information of an industrial system, which is a sabotage of production through interstitial disturbance. For Veblen, transactions implied a search for pecuniary rather than industrial productive gain in controlling interstices, which requires focusing on power and even controlling manipulation in industrial economics and corporate governance theory (see Knoedler 1995).

In this view, modern business practices based on the shareholder value paradigm become a form of norm in modern capitalism, and this norm is qualified as sabotage. Some works analyze the "financial sabotage" resulting from the 2008 global financial crisis (Nesvetailova and Palan 2013) or, more generally, from financial capitalism (Cornehls 2004). Financial control is seen by Veblen as involving a policy of industrial sabotage, i.e. a deliberate restriction of productivity of capital and labor to keep profits and financial rents higher. However, little work has been done on new forms of sabotage based on increasing social inequalities that are constituted by, for example, CEO compensation and the shareholder value paradigm associated with the managerial quest for high compensation.

Modern unequal business attitudes and practices contribute to the merging of industries and in doing so manage to earn high gains. Proponents of such attitudes and practices constitute a new form of "investors of capitalism" who benefit from their legal rights. Veblen (1923: 131) wrote that "any person who has the legal right to withhold any part of the necessary industrial apparatus or materials from current use will be in a position to impose terms and exact obedience, on pain of rendering the community's joint stock of technology inoperative for that extent. This is the Natural Right of Investment." The managers of multinational firms are the new Veblenian captains of industry, guilty of modern industrial sabotage by using speculative finance and short-term economic requirements as a means of both legitimation and perpetuation of their non-industrial strategies. In this perspective, they are businesses that operate by sabotaging and disorienting employees, customers, regulators or even competitors.

Through their strategic behaviors, managers are the captains of industry that manipulate the rules and norms of industrial processes to ensure higher prices including high compensation. For Veblen (1904), the goal of the captain of industry was always to make a profit, and the means was always a disturbance of the industrial system. In this Veblenian perspective, management mission and compensation are viewed as an industrial sabotage that harms public common good and contributes to the problem of misallocation of income as the main failure of current modern capitalism. Thus, it is important to link these questions to the nature of the capitalist system and to analyze in institutional thought the role that the firm's top managers would play in the advent of a more just capitalism.

In Old Institutional economics, Commons proposed a framework of analysis making the market system a reasonable capitalism, i.e. a capitalism that would constitute a form of social control of the economy. It was clearly justified in his 1934 book: a reasonable capitalism would achieve a superior ideal by improving human nature. In other words, the ambition is to put capitalism under democratic control to develop the human community and increase its capacity for emancipation. On this point, the Commons thesis placed humans and their ability to reach collective compromise at the heart of the reflections to promote social development and reform that apply very well to modern societies.

For Commons (1924), it is necessary to make capitalism good to save it. It is in this view that he proposes a theory of reasonable value, which is a behavioral or, rather, a volitional theory of value that should be an instrument of reform, including corporate reform. Even though modern considerations on firm governance do not fit the industrial realities of Commons' time, he elaborates a set of ideas on the reasonable value that supplement Veblenian views of business enterprise. The firm as a going concern is for Commons (1934) an "ongoing coordinated activity" based on working rules that govern both industrial life and human behaviors in transactions of individuals with others. For him, a going concern implies collective action in restraint, liberation and expansion of individual action. As a going concern, the firm has its own rules of conduct (see Ramstad 1991) and its top management has to have ethical beliefs as to the good to advance toward a reasonable capitalism.

Indeed, in his 1893 book on the distribution of wealth, Commons explains that class income inequalities emerge notably from the laws on property rights resulting from the sovereignty of public order. Consequently, good working rules and public policies should reduce these inequalities to make capitalism's values reasonable, which is why from a Commonsian perspective, sustainable corporate governance is not only an economic question but also a crucial legal and ethical issue of modern capitalism. This perspective implies that men are reasonable to make the CEO reasonable. As Ramstad (2001: 266) explains, Commons considers reasonable value as "nothing more than a consensus among reasonable men as to what constitutes an exchange free from duress and coercion." Capitalism must become genuinely fair. Otherwise, it is clear that market prices, including management compensation and shareholder dividends, in free economies will fail to contribute to a reasonable and good capitalism. Ethical behaviors and reasonable business practices and values are interconnected in good capitalism.

Commons' theory of reasonable value implies a new perspective on the human conditions of self-realization. For him, the "three most fundamental wishes of mankind" are security, liberty and equality (1934: 706). The rules of firm governance must make it possible to achieve conditions of self-realization for the greatest number of people and not to excessively satisfy the interests of a privileged class; this implies fair collective bargaining and an effective industrial democracy. The public order must regulate economic conflicts of interest by facilitating "agreement among equals" (Commons, 1934: 849). The public order must therefore fight against economic autocracies to increase justice in the conditions of the distribution of wealth. In Commons' (1934: 874) view, "the theory of reasonable value may be summarized, in its pragmatic application, as a theory of social progress by means of personality controlled, liberated, and expanded by collective action."

For Commons, the working rules of going concerns such as business enterprises combine efficiency and fairness in a public common-good perspective regulating social conflicts and interests, which is why the theory of reasonable value and capitalism is related to social reforms and progress of humanity (see Dugger 1979). It also explains that the view of Commons (1939) is close to that of Dewey by advocating a practicable idealism, which is a "pragmatic idealism" and not a "utopia." Commons (1934) explains that a theory of reasonable value is "a theory of the attainable" that makes reasonableness an idealism circumscribed by practicability. The practicability of reasonableness will be affirmed as a political issue that becomes a normative ideal: the ultimate objective being to build a fair compromise to reduce conflicts (or make them acceptable), a lasting compromise as a societal solution reasonable for the continuity of development of the human community. In a Deweyan perspective, Commons (1939) believed reasonableness lies in the combination of rules and compromises. Once again, reasonability is both performative (a value is reasonable only for a given period) and evolutionary (reasonableness is linked to institutional change, whereas right does not change ontologically). It is necessary to associate with reasonableness an idealism in action that aims, in Commonsian logic, at the highest possible ethical goal. This thought makes democracy a true social faith: creative democracy à la Dewey that is advocated by Commons must radically transform society and with it the modes of human association.

The production and exchange rules of the firm must be fair in a reasonable capitalism because making values truly reasonable implies questioning values that are truly just. Ramstad (2001: 254) considers that just or fair is a sister concept of reasonableness so that "Commons' theory can be understood as resolving the long-neglected issue that originally stimulated inquiry into market values – the quest for principles ensuring just prices. Indeed (. . .) at an abstract level, reasonable value itself is nothing more than a coherent and pragmatic, albeit secularized, solution to the problem of just price." The ultimate goal in the short term is to keep people together in the same ethical whole (see Dewey 1935).

6. CONCLUSION

In his recent book in French, Chassagnon (2018) explains that reasonable capitalism must allow us to overcome the financial autocracies that prevent fairness, because to be fair is to be able to catalyze the social change that tends to weaken the weakest and strengthen the strongest. Similarly, reasonable capitalism must allow us to transform economic institutions and human behavior in order to counteract social and economic inequalities. Reasonable capitalism must therefore create the conditions conducive to the most effective development of corporate finance systems and industrial democracy while making firms actors of structural change that contribute to reducing inequalities and improving social mobility rather than short-term machines that produce capital.

Three arguments must finally be specified. First, reasonable capitalism must make it possible to direct economic power toward the pursuit of the general interest, in addition to private interests, in a spirit of social responsibility. Second, a collective and ethical economic democracy based on organized aspirations must emerge and, for this, an economic representability capable of revealing reasonable values must be found. Finally, to create collective action, the power of men and women must be rebalanced through collective social bargaining to bring about shared control and a collective spirit of cooperation and trust. In this view, industrial efficiency should not deviate even from one of the three principles of reasonableness, and industrial democracy should create equitable and reasonable compromises that serve social justice in the firm.

REFERENCES

Adams, Thomas S. and Helen L. Sumner. 1905. *Labor Problems: A Text Book*. New York: The MacMillan Company.
Bradizza, Luigi. 2013. *Richard T. Ely's Critique of Capitalism*. New York: Palgrave Macmillan.
Brissenden, Paul. 1926. "Labor Economics." *American Economic Review* 16, no. 3: 443–9.
Chassagnon, Virgile. 2014. "Toward a Social Ontology of the Firm: Reconstitution, Organizing Entity, Institution, Social Emergence and Power." *Journal of Business Ethics* 124, no. 2: 197–208.
Chassagnon, Virgile. 2018. *Economie de la Firme-Monde: Pouvoir, Régime de Gouvernement et Régulation*. Louvain-la-Neuve: De Boeck.
Chassagnon, Virgile and Guillaume Vallet. 2019. "Albion W. Small's Neglected Progressive Views: Reducing Inequalities for a 'Reasonable' Capitalism." *Journal of the History of Economic Thought* 41, no. 1: 77–98.
Commons, John Rodgers. 1893. *The Distribution of Wealth*. New York: Macmillan.
Commons, John Rodgers. 1911. "Organized Labor's Attitude toward Industrial Efficiency." *American Economic Review* 1, no. 3: 463–72.
Commons, John Rodgers. 1919. *Industrial Goodwill*. New York: McGraw Hill Book Company.
Commons, John Rodgers. 1924. *Legal Foundations of Capitalism*. New York: Macmillan.
Commons, John Rodgers. 1934. *Institutional Economics: Its Place in Political Economy*. New York: Macmillan.
Commons, John Rodgers. 1939. "Twentieth-Century Economics." *Journal of Social Philosophy* 5: 29–41.
Cornehls, James V. 2004. "Veblen's Theory of Finance Capitalism and Contemporary Corporate America." *Journal of Economic Issues* 38, no. 1: 29–58.
De George, Richard T. 1987. "The Status of Business Ethics: Past and Future." *Journal of Business Ethics* 6, no. 3: 201–11.
Derber, Milton. 1970. *The American Idea of Industrial Democracy, 1865–1965*. Urbana: University of Illinois Press.
Dewey, John. 1922. *Human Nature and Conduct: An Introduction to Social Psychology*. New York: Henry Holt and Company.
Dewey, John. 1935. *Liberalism and Social Action*. New York: G. P. Putnam.
Dewey, John. 1991 [1940]. "Creative Democracy – The Task before Us." In *John Dewey: The Later Works*, edited by Jo Ann Boydston. Carbondale: Southern Illinois University Press, pp. 224–30.
Dubrion, Benjamin. 2018. "Institutionnalisme Economique versus Management Scientifique autour des Labor Problems: Quels Fondements à la Démocratie dans l'Entreprise?." *Revue de Philosophie Economique* 13, no. 2: 33–60.
Dugger, William M. 1979. "The Reform Method of John R. Commons." *Journal of Economic Issues* 13, no. 2: 369–81.

Ely, Richard T. 1883. "The Past and the Present of Political Economy." *The Overland Monthly* 2, no. 9: 225–35.

Ely, Richard T. 1886. "Ethics and Economics." *Science* 7, no. 175, June: 529–33.

Ely, Richard T. 1887. "The Nature and Significance of Corporations." *Harper's New Monthly Magazine* 74, May: 970–77.

Ely, Richard T. 1889. *An Introduction to Political Economy*. New York: Chautauqua Press.

Gonce, Richard A. 1996. "The Social Gospel, Ely, and Commons's Initial Stage of Thought." *Journal of Economic Issues* 30, no. 3: 641–65.

Hoxie, Robert. F. 1915. *Scientific Management and Labor*. New York: Appleton and Company.

Knoedler, Janet T. 1995. "Transaction Cost Theories of Business Enterprise from Williamson and Veblen: Convergence, Divergence, and Some Evidence." *Journal of Economic Issues* 29, no. 2: 385–95.

Nesvetailova, Anastasia and Ronen Palan. 2013. "Sabotage in the Financial System: Lessons from Veblen." *Business Horizons* 56, no. 6: 723–32.

Piketty, Thomas. 2014. *Capital in the Twenty-First Century*. Cambridge, MA and London: The Belknap Press of Harvard University Press.

Ramstad, Yngve. 1991. "From Desideratum to Historical Achievement: John R. Commons's Reasonable Value and the 'Negotiated Economy' of Denmark." *Journal of Economic Issues* 25, no. 3: 431–9.

Ramstad, Yngve. 2001. "John R. Commons's Reasonable Value and the Problem of Just Price." *Journal of Economic Issues* 35, no. 2 (June): 253–77.

Veblen, Thorstein. 1904. *The Theory of Business Enterprise*. New York: Charles Scribner's Sons.

Veblen, Thorstein. 1923. *Absentee Ownership and Business Enterprise in Recent Times: The Case of America*. New York: B. W. Huebsch.

Veblen, Thorstein. 2001 [1921]. *The Engineer and the Price System*. Kitchener, ON: Batouche Publishing.

3. Inequalities and the dynamics of capitalism: will democracy survive? Albion W. Small's view

Guillaume Vallet

1. INTRODUCTION

The coming of age of sociology is usually dated to the end of the nineteenth century in Europe, at the time of the alleged "method dispute" pitting proponents of a French-style sociological method against proponents of German-style interpretive sociology. Yet, against the backdrop of these debates lie the contributions of Albion W. Small (1854–1926), who founded the University of Chicago's department of sociology in 1892, thereby giving birth to American sociology. As the institutional – rather than scientific as some believed (Abbott 1999) – founder of sociology in Chicago, he actively supported a moral form of sociology, characterized by close ties to religious values and a vision of the scholar as a civil servant involved in social action.

As a parson's son, Small never departed from the influence of Christianity, invariably advocating fraternity throughout his life (Christakes 1978). He viewed his era as one of mounting challenges for the leading role of Christianity in America, hence his hope that sociology would be a "prophetic science" facilitating the analysis of social change and the definition of "sound" policies. In other words, through his criticism of Herbert Spencer and William G. Sumner, he adopted the view that the evolution of societies was not set in motion by "natural forces", but instead relied on individual actions, namely "social forces."

In addition, despite living through a period when sociology had yet to make its mark as an autonomous field of studies, he advocated a form of interdisciplinary research which would both single out sociology as a distinct field while connecting it with neighboring domains of research, unifying social sciences as a result (Small and Vincent 1894). Small had developed a keen interest in political economy ever since his student days. After hearing of Francis Lieber's work, he determined to move to Germany to read political economy (1879 to 1881), attending lectures by such renowned scholars as Adolph Wagner and Gustav von Schmoller in Berlin and Leipzig. He owed to them both his concern for preserving the unity of the social sciences as well as the need for social scientists to take up an active role as government advisers (given that they were members of the *Verein für Socialpolitik*, a scientific think tank advising the German government[1]).

On his return to the United States in 1881, he first enrolled at Colby College as a lecturer in History and Political Economy, before moving to Johns Hopkins in Baltimore in 1888–9 where he earned a PhD in history. During this time, he interacted with leading economists such as John R. Commons and Richard T. Ely, who gave lectures on political economy, Ely later sitting on his thesis committee. Ely's approach to political economy had a lasting influence on Small. Ely rejected both American "old school" economics inherited from classical economics and neoclassical economics, Ely emphasizing the importance of social, historical and political issues for economics.

As mentioned in Chapters 1 and 2 of this book, Ely favored a "social gospel" in keeping with Christian ideals (Fine 1951). According to Ely's motto of "progressive conservatism," economics should be mobilized to devise social policies that improved social welfare. His overarching goal was to reconcile an industrious work ethic with notions of solidarity and fraternity.

As the United States was in the midst of socio-economic upheaval, Small relied on his personal academic connections to militate against inequalities. He viewed his crusade against inequalities as extending beyond the problems posed by capitalism. Indeed, the scope of his reflections included a large array of ontological meditations on human nature and democracy: "What is the meaning of human life, and how may we adjust our conduct accordingly?" (Small 1907: 517). Addressing his under-discussed reflections on the treatment of inequalities during the Progressive Era is therefore the central aim of this chapter.

The present work, which relies heavily on archival documents and on Small's personal works, intends to disclose Small's multi-faceted approach to the question of inequalities. It furthermore seeks, wherever possible, to draw relevant parallels with our contemporary state of affairs. The Smallian perspective is not only concerned with tackling inequalities within society; it is also a larger concern for the survival of social order and democratic institutions.

The remainder of the chapter proceeds as follows. The second section deals with Small's views of inequalities of his time. The third section presents Small's proposals to improve the democratic functioning of industrial organizations, and the fourth section explains why Small entrusted the state to fight inequalities. The fifth section raises the issue of Small's contribution to today's capitalism. Finally, the sixth section brings concluding remarks.

2.   SMALL AND THE INEQUALITIES OF HIS TIME: WHY FIGHTING THEM MATTERS

Small wrote in a period of socio-economic upheaval characterized by increasing social inequalities. Indeed, inequalities rose significantly in the nineteenth century in the United States in the wake of industrialization (Glaeser et al., 2002). Other countries went down a similar route.[2]

What is most striking about the period of Small's writings (1890s to mid-1920s) was a spectacular rise in inequalities of all sorts, which divided society along racial, gender and geographic lines. Far from disregarding these social cleavages, Small dedicated most of his efforts to engaging with inequalities stemming from the unequal distribution of wages and capital ownership, which were particularly salient.

The first example to spring to mind regarding this issue is that of Williamson (1997) who devised an inequalities index based on the ratio of unskilled workers' wages to GDP per worker hour: w/y. This ratio indicates the income of those at the bottom of the distribution with a weighted average of the price of all the other factors of production. Each rise indicates a decline in inequalities, and vice versa. In 1914, the ratio increased from 100 in 1870 to 153/154 in a number of impoverished European countries, whilst it dropped from 100 to 58 in the USA during the same period.

Small was unequivocal in his condemnation of capital concentration:

> I am spending my life in the study of sociology because I believe – and I see more and more reasons for the belief the longer I study – that the social system in which we live and move and have our being is so bad that nobody can tell the full measure of its iniquity. In the age of so-called democracy we are getting to be the thralls of the most relentless system of economic oligarchy that history thus far records. That capital from which most of us directly or indirectly get our bread and butter is becoming the most undemocratic, in human and atheistic of all the heathen divinities. (Small 1899)

This concentration of capital manifested itself most conspicuously with the rise of trusts. The McLane report of 1832 listed only 106 manufacturing firms which held assets greater than $100,000 in the United States (Glaeser et al., 2002: 21). However, by 1917, 278 companies possessed assets in excess of $20 million. Consequently, this trend increased the number of wealthy "fat cats" at the top while leaving many more people impoverished (Lindert and Williamson 1985; Lindert 2000). Workers' conditions deteriorated both at the workplace and in their daily lives.

Even though the Roaring Twenties contributed to some degree of improvement of workers' wages and skills (Shackel and Palus 2006), as far as the concentration of capital is concerned the general trend of the period may be characterized by an overall rise of inequalities (Chassagnon and Vallet 2019).

In order to more fully understand the global changes in inequality occurring at this time, we need to account for the prior historical context. Small perfectly summarized the new challenges of his time: "The fact is that production and distribution of wealth occur now under conditions that have been changing very rapidly, not only since the so-called 'industrial revolution' of nearly a century ago, but particularly during the last twenty-five years" (Small 1905: 517).

Specifically, before the wave of progressive ideas swept across the United States of America, the 1875–1900 period was in the midst of what Mark Twain termed the "Gilded Age," during which America had been thoroughly reshaped by both post-Civil War trauma and rapid economic takeoff, which had transformed the country beyond recognition through a non-linear and peaceful path (Ross 1991).

This was a two-sided era, of great fortunes being made and of unchecked industrialization leading to deteriorating living standards for workers (Shackel and Palus 2006). The latter led to a series of major strikes (Homestead in 1892, and Pullman in 1894) and demands for labor laws which materialized with the creation of the first workers' unions (the Knights of Labor, 1869 and the American Federation of Labor, founded in 1886) and political parties sharing the same goals (the Socialist Party of America, born in 1901).

The first two decades of the twentieth century did not reverse this trend, as the "industrial question" became central (Diner 1998: 46). For instance, mention should be made of the garment workers' strike in New York (1909–10) and the Paterson silk mill strike in New Jersey (1911–13).

As the United States entered the First World War, the country had reached a climax of social disorder, in effect posing a threat to the capitalistic order and democracy at the same time. Small provided an acute summary of the situation:

> Since that time [the Civil War] a bastard individualism has run riot. The peculiar need of our stage of development is enough assimilation of the social in our philosophy of life to neutralize this unsocial factor. The law of individualization by virtue of socialization, rather than the fantasy of individualization by resisting socialization, is the peculiar lesson that our generation needs. (Small 1905: 478)

Against this backdrop, Small carried out new studies and recommended policies to counteract the excesses of American society. In his view, the first step to making progress in this respect would be to improve the conditions of workers from within the workplace.

3.   SMALL'S PROPOSALS TO IMPROVE THE DEMOCRATIC FUNCTIONING OF INDUSTRIAL ORGANIZATIONS

Small was aware of the necessity of reducing inequality by reshaping the spheres of both production and distribution. For Small, the two are interrelated, although he certainly paid more attention to the latter than to the former, since the distribution sphere is related to the highest moral standards of a society (Small 1907).

Small enumerated three factors of production: labor, capital and land. Adjudging Marx as "one of the few really great thinkers in the history of social science" (Small 1912: 804), Small was concerned with labor, which he viewed as a source of identity and meaning for all people. This is seen in Small's vindication of the Marxian labor theory of value: only labor creates a value superior to its cost, and then, capital and rent only transmit their value to price, not having the power to create surplus value. In order to create wealth, capital and rent must be in association with labor.

Unlike Marx, Small did not hold the fatalistic belief that capitalism was fated to cause class warfare, on the condition that capitalists and workers cooperate. Specifically, Small believed in a non-revolutionary path to social harmony, through what he called "moralization" and "socialization" (Christakes 1978). Moreover, Small considered that profit – and, to a lesser extent, rent – was inherent in capitalism. He thus operated a distinction between "profit" and "over profit" (Small 1912) to make his point. "Profit" is acceptable only as long as it corresponds to the remuneration of capital, as well as being oriented toward investments or subsidies, allowing labor to increase its productive capabilities. In these cases, profit serves a social goal: the profit motive is morally acceptable when it is invested to improve the efficiency of labor, and more broadly of society taken as a whole.

To that end, Small argued that the degree of control over the use of capital should be proportionate to the extent to which workers, and not merely the owner, are required to make capital productive. Accordingly, he distinguished between tool capital, management capital and finance capital, where the first is only used by the owner, the second is used by the owner subject to the influence of others, and the third is used "wholly by others than the owner, and under conditions which he does not and could not maintain by his own individual power," especially banking and financial institutions (Small 1914: 728). According to Small, over profit occurs where the use of capital is not fairly distributed between the owner and the workers, which constitutes "a rape of justice" for workers (Small 1913: 353).

However, Small did not hold capitalism per se responsible for these ills:

> Our present society is assuming the impossible, however, when it dallies with the illusion that there can be 'free competition' in a society containing, on the one hand, millions of persons with no assets but their individual powers, and on the other hand thousands of corporations with wealth and credit and legal resources. When the interests of these two types of competitors clashes, 'free competition' between them is like a boy with a pea-blower besieging the Rock of Gibraltar. (Small 1914: 723)

This quotation shows that for Small, the largest part of the problem lay in assigning too much status to capital as well as the social valuation of its concentration. As he stated, "we have given to capital the legal status of a person, by incorporating capital. Capital thus becomes a titanic superman, incomparably superior to the natural persons who find their interests challenged by this artificial being" (Small 1905: 302).

Small was particularly critical of the poor use of management capital and finance capital: both result in empowering capital owners at the expense of workers and cooperation between the actors of production. As a result, one of the consequences of capital concentration could be a drop in entrepreneurship and increasing strain on the use of capital.

For that reason, inequalities stemming from capital concentration entailed serious problems regarding the valuation of each individual, which subsequently affects social cohesion. Each individual must feel that they are efficiently involved in the production process – namely that they have a true status in the workplace. In other words, cooperation is required in industrial organizations both to improve their functioning and to prevent conflicts from arising.

Likewise, Small stressed the need for individuals to acquire wealth by reaping the fruits of their labor, especially through the use of tool capital (Dibble 1975: 134). Indeed, each individual should have the equal ability to realize oneself through labor: "Labor is dignified in proportion as it is mental mastery of materials or conditions. The wealth produced by mental mastery is the regalia of the real man" (Small 1905: 453).

Finally, the concentration of capital posed a challenge to democracy for Small, who equated capital with an economic power that could turn into political power: "The radical evil of our present wage system is not that it permits inequality of distribution, but that the inequality is so largely an index of an arbitrary personal inequality, which gives artificial weight to the will of some persons and artificially counts out the will of others" (Small 1907: 966).

In Small's mind, each individual should have the right and the ability to access equality of opportunity to realize their own selves. On his view, equality of opportunity does not mean the equality of chances or situations, but it refers to a "social and economic" climate in which each individual can realize their own human potential:

> "We want to be treated like men," means demand, not alone for higher wages, but for opportunity to be accounted as men in the councils of men. It means assertion of right to have feelings respected and opinions weighed and judgements considered on their merits, instead of having them summarily quashed at the dictation of other men's interests. (Small 1905: 459)

From that perspective, Small agrees with Alexis de Tocqueville's analysis of American democracy (Tocqueville 1961). Small said:

> The equality that we have in mind, however, is not a quotient obtained by dividing the aggregate of opportunity by the population of the State. It is not the vulgar, 'One man is as good as another'. The equality which comports with civilization, the equality which is foreshadowed in the personal endowments of people and in the workings of the social process thus far, we have called, for want of a better name, "functional equality." (Small 1905: 348)

Consequently, in combating inequalities, Small entrusted the only institution capable of acting for the collective interest, namely the state.

4.   THE PRIMACY OF THE STATE IN COMBATING INEQUALITY

In this period of great upheaval, Small entrusted the state to build coopera-tion between workers and capitalists on fairer terms, and also to protect the weak in general. Small considered the state as the fairest and most suitable institution capable of effecting a new kind of capitalism and a new model for a society promoting maximal well-being: "More and better life by more and better people, beyond any limit of time or quality that our mind can set, is the indicated content of the social process" (Small 1905: 518).

To Small, since the state was a politically organized institution embodying the general will of the people, only it can implement policies preventing capi-talists from behaving unfairly. Therefore, he bestowed moral commitments on the state. In his view, good policy-making should have an ethical drive.

Let me elaborate now on three policies that Small called on the state to enforce, as part of his general goal to promote equality of opportunities.

First, it appears necessary to reform the current legislation in order to improve workers' living conditions while preventing the wealthiest from exerting influence on the state (Small 1905: 231). Once again, at stake are improvements in cooperation and therefore in overall well-being. Creating the legal framework for reaching equality of opportunity demonstrated the extent to which the state was able to mutate, passing through many diverse stages such as the "biologic state," "economic state," and the "civic state" to reach the "ethical state" (Small 1905: 221) – that no country had yet reached in Small's period. In sum,

> the more important question is: Do the law and the social situation make it morally certain that one party can and will take an unjust advantage of the other party in deciding how the burdens and the products of industry shall be divided? (Small 1905: 518)

Second, Small emphasized the need to support cooperation within the workplace through the setting up of cooperative councils which brought together capitalists and workers. Although Small supported unions, he entrusted such cooperative councils to tackle the daily problems of their industry. He was also in favor of giving workers seats on administrative councils and on the boards of company directors, since he believed that "partnership without representation is undemocratic" (Christakes 1978: 94). Moreover, such cooperative councils would improve the economic and democratic functioning of industrial organizations through better use of "management capital" (Vallet 2017).

In this framework, the state was viewed as the moral institution capable of supervising such cooperative councils. In that sense, Small was a "corporatist." State intervention was required but did not entail the socialization of the means of production, and even "worse" for him, socialism: "All socialisms tend to gravitate towards programs which magnify societal machinery, and minimize the importance of the personal units" (Small 1905: 477).

However, Small saw the state more as a regulator of conflicts, a central institution transforming social forces from conflict into cooperation. Therefore, "a state is normal or mature in proportion as the interests operating within it find their adjustment and completion in the progress of the common interest. Each interest is normal in proportion as it lends itself to the completion of the total civic interest" (Small 1905: 281).

Lastly, Small called for state interventionism, with respect to new taxation policies. Since the state embodies the whole society, "taxation is in no strict sense simply an economic process. It is a function of the total life of the people" (Small 1907: 2017). It is worth emphasizing that Small's principles on taxation were ground-breaking at a time when few taxes were in place, most of them being tariffs on foreign goods. Specifically, it was Small's firm belief that the state would be able to overcome both individual and class egoism by imposing taxes on capital concentration.

Furthermore, Small favored several types of capital taxation: legacy taxation, "over profit" taxation and taxation on assets held by stockholders (Small 1925: 460). Interestingly, the revenue from taxation could be used to finance smaller companies and later spread to the development of the use of "tool capital" (Vallet 2017). Taxation and redistribution went hand in hand, and were needed to promote equality of opportunity while building a new kind of capitalism and democracy in the United States.

In spite of evident historical, political and economic differences between today and Small's period, we stress in the last section that Small's ideas still ring true in modern day capitalism.

5.   WHAT SMALL CAN TELL US ABOUT TODAY'S CAPITALISM

Comparing different historical periods can be a difficult exercise, and one that may produce few relevant results. This is clearly true of Small's ideas, in particular because two major events have occurred with comparison to the period of his writings:

1.   The state is now a key actor of the economy, and has had a growing role in the economy through public policy.
2.   Since the collapse of the Soviet Union, capitalism as an economic system has no rival – which does not mean it is not questioned. When Small wrote in his late years, the Soviet Union had already come into existence and constituted a framework for implementing communist ideas.

I believe that Small's thought deserves more attention today, since his views on the dynamics of inequalities could be relevant to the current framework of capitalism. There are two major concerns which will be addressed here.

First, Small warns us against excessive inequality and its negative impact on democracy. Such a view has found an echo in Piketty's more recent work on the long-term dynamics of inequalities in contemporary capitalism (Piketty 2014). Not only does such inequality have a negative impact on global demand – whose level is too low, since the wealthiest prefer saving and even hoarding money – but it is also harmful to democracy. Inequalities are unfair because they reflect a form of power which is out of the reach of those at the bottom of the social scale. In particular, some low-income workers experience growing difficulties in accessing home ownership, unlike the wealthiest who have the possibility to accumulate more wealth.

Moreover, in addition to the opposition between capitalists and workers addressed by Small, the current labor market situation is also characterized by the growth of inequalities inside the working class. Globalization has increased the gap between high-skilled and low-skilled workers. In some countries, this gap can even be seen as a rift, creating resentment. Among others, Chauvel (2006) has clearly stressed that in addition to the decrease of inter-deciles ratio in developed countries, the time required for low-skilled workers to reach the situation of high-skilled workers has risen incredibly. This may be observed in the shrinking middle-class in most developed countries.

The problem is, as Simmel underlined, that middle-class is not relevant from the point of view of consumption; it embodies also the social mobility within a given society, reflecting in particular the aspirations of the lower class to climb up the social ladder (Vallet 2011). When the middle-class shrinks, a split occurs within society and the existence of democracy is put at risk. The rise of extremist parties' influence exemplifies such a trend.

Small was aware of that threat, and entrusted the state to implement the above policies. Today's governments ought to be more aware of that and should devise new types of taxation policies in order to avoid such cumulative effects of inequalities. To some extent, the recent *gilets jaunes* (yellow vests) social movement in France is evidence of that process. In our view, recent policies aiming to tax real estate ownership for speculative purposes, although insufficient, should be applauded.

Building on the first of Small's "lessons," a second one may be drawn. Borrowing from Small's ideas, we believe that the root of the problem lies in the productive organizations of firms. Indeed, productive organizations in firms are the framework in which the above three types of capital described by Small interrelate. Small's views could be helpful in rebuilding the governance of firms in order to link more efficiently the capital of workers and the owners of production, especially through the use of "management capital."

Small was certainly correct in asserting the right of each individual to own "tool capital" since the latter participates in carving one's identity. Individual work enables people to understand the ontological meaning of their work and allows them to earn an associated personal income.

But challenges toward "management capital" within firms are more acute. Small's ideas regarding the fairer use of "management capital" refer to the idea of a firm that is neither merely a bundle of contracts nor the property of stockholders. The economic, and also democratic, functioning of firms depends on the ability of the different stakeholders to devise new rules improving their cooperation (Chassagnon 2011; Chassagnon and Hollandts 2014).

Power within firms must be redistributed on a fairer basis. This implies both reducing inequalities in earnings and also increasing one's participation in the organizations. Therefore, firms must be ontologically considered as a real social entity functioning principally through cooperative social relationships. In the age of modern capitalism dealing with knowledge and cognitive models, firms must be seen as structures of human capital, stemming from all the individuals involved in their organizations. Firms only exist through the willingness of individuals to be involved together in a legal structure, implying that shareholders own only the shares of the firm, not the firm itself.

With his own words, I argue that Small was close to such an approach, because he stressed that the firm is not merely a structure of property rights. On the contrary, Small shed light on the necessity of cooperation between workers and capitalists because the workplace is like a socio-economic chain whose each part is important for the whole. Without getting rid of vertical ties – and then on stockholders and managers' *de jure* power – Small believed in a new type of stakeholder-based framework through the different use of "management capital."

Such an approach seems highly relevant in the aftermath of the "Great Recession," which cast doubts on firms' functioning and the social impact of their actions. Many reforms have already been passed, and more is yet to come, with a view to improving the relationships between capitalists and workers. The "loi PACTE" bill, which came into force in France is evidence of this, even though its real content has largely been questioned since then.

6.   CONCLUSION

This chapter has intended to shed light on Albion W. Small's views on the issue of inequality, in particular inequalities stemming from the concentration of capital. The latter are a threat to the functioning of both the economic system and democracy, since they prevent individuals from realizing their own selves. At stake is the ability for each society to be able to promote equality of opportunity for all. This is a key challenge for democracy; otherwise, class warfare will threaten its existence. Therefore, the treatment of inequality is not an individual but a real social concern, associated with morals.

Against this backdrop, I do believe that Small's thoughts deserve more attention. As one of the prominent intellectual leaders of the Progressive Era, he put forward innovative ideas with a view to improving social well-being while preserving the positive aspects of the capitalistic order without sacrificing the efficient economic functioning of capitalism. His stance attracted vehement criticism on both sides of the political spectrum: conservatives viewed him as a radical, while his Marxist contemporaries saw him as a vassal to capitalism. Regardless, no work dealing with the Progressive Era would be complete without a mention of Small, whose pioneering ideas are simply "too big to fail."

NOTES

1.   The *Verein für Socialpolitik* was founded in Germany in 1872 as a response to the "social question." Its founders sought a middle path between socialist and *laissez-faire* economic policies.
2.   See this volume, Chapter 8.

REFERENCES

Abbott, Andrew. 1999. *Department and Discipline*. Chicago, IL: University of Chicago Press.

Chassagnon, Virgile. 2011. "The Law and Economics of the Modern Firm: A New Governance Structure of Power Relationships." *Revue d'Economie Industrielle* 134, June: 25–50.

Chassagnon, Virgile and Xavier Hollandts. 2014. "Who Are the Owners of the Firm: Shareholders, Employees or No One?." *Journal of Institutional Economics* 10, no. 1: 47–69.

Chassagnon, Virgile and Guillaume Vallet. 2019. "Albion W. Small's Neglected Progressive Views: Reducing Inequalities for a 'Reasonable' Capitalism." *Journal of the History of Economic Thought* 41, no. 1: 77–98.

Chauvel, Louis. 2006. "Are Social Classes Really Dead? A French Paradox in Class Dynamics." In *Inequalities of the World*, edited by Göran Therborn. London: Verso, pp. 295–317.

Christakes, Georges. 1978. *Albion W. Small*. Boston, MA: Twayne Publishers.

Dibble, Vernon K. 1975. *The Legacy of Albion Small*. Chicago, IL: University of Chicago Press.

Diner, Steven J. 1998. *A Very Different Age: Americans of the Progressive Era*. New York: Hill and Wang.

Fine, Sydney. 1951. "Richard T. Ely, Forerunner of Progressivism, 1880–1901." *The Mississippi Valley Historical Review* 37, no. 4: 599–624.

Lindert, Peter. 2000. "Three Centuries of Inequality in Britain and America." In *Handbook of Income Distribution*, edited by Anthony Atkinson and François Bourguignon. Amsterdam: North Holland, pp. 167–216.

Lindert, Peter and Jeffrey Williamson. 1985. "Growth, Equality, and History." *Explorations in Economic History* 22: 341–77.

Glaeser, Edward, José Scheinkman and Andrei Shleifer. 2002. "The Injustice of Inequality." *NBER Working Paper Series* 9150.

Piketty, Thomas. 2014. *Capital in the Twenty-First Century*. Cambridge, MA and London: The Belknap Press of Harvard University Press.

Ross, Dorothy. 1991. *The Origins of American Social Science*. Cambridge: Cambridge University Press.

Shackel, Paul A. and Matthew M. Palus. 2006. "The Gilded Age and Working-Class Industrial Communities." *American Anthropologist* 108, no. 4: 828–41.

Small, Albion Woodbury. 1899. "On the Capita Lent the Trusts." *Chicago Telegraph*, March 10.

Small, Albion Woodbury. 1905. *General Sociology*. Chicago, IL: University of Chicago Press.

Small, Albion Woodbury. 1907. *Adam Smith and Modern Sociology: A Study in the Methodology of the Social Sciences*. Chicago, IL: University of Chicago Press [Kindle edition].

Small, Albion Woodbury. 1912. "Socialism in the Light of Social Science." *American Journal of Sociology* 17, no. 6: 804–19.

Small, Albion Woodbury. 1913. *Between Eras: From Capitalism to Democracy*. Kansas City, KS: Inter Collegiate Press [Kindle edition].

Small, Albion Woodbury. 1914. "The Social Gradations of Capital." *American Journal of Sociology* 9, no. 6: 721–52.

Small, Albion Woodbury. 1925. "The Sociology of Profits." *American Journal of Sociology* 30, no. 4: 439–61.

Small, Albion Woodbury and George Vincent. 1894. *An Introduction to the Study of Society*. New York: American Book Company.

Tocqueville, Alexis de. 1961 [1840]. *De la Démocratie en Amérique*. Volume 2. Paris: Gallimard.

Vallet, Guillaume. 2011. *Petit Manuel de Sociologie à l'Usage des Economistes*. Grenoble: Presses Universitaires de Grenoble.

Vallet, Guillaume. 2017. "Cooperation Rather than Competition in Industrial Organisations: Albion W. Small's Underestimated View." *Business History* 59, no. 3: 453–70.

Williamson, Jeffrey. 1997. "Globalization and Inequality: Past and Present." *World Bank Research Observer* 12, no. 2: 117–35.

4. Forgetting and remembering the Chicago School of Columbus, Ohio: Roderick D. Mckenzie, neighborhoods and inequality

Jeffrey Nathaniel Parker

1. INTRODUCTION

Between 1921 and 1922, Roderick D. McKenzie published his dissertation, completed for his PhD in sociology at University of Chicago, in its entirety over five issue of the *American Journal of Sociology* (AJS). Entitled "The Neighborhood: A Study of Local Life in the City of Columbus, Ohio," the document took up 107 pages of the journal in the five editions printed between September 1921 and May 1922, which translates to over 15% of 678 pages of total material printed in the journal over that time period. Each segment, minus the last one, ends with "[*To be continued*]" like a Dickens novel printed out serially. A sprawling study of Columbus, McKenzie completed it when he was an instructor at Ohio State University, after spending just two years in residence as a graduate student at the University of Chicago (Hawley, in McKenzie 1968: x).

Although he would only complete his PhD when he was an associate professor at West Virginia (Hawley, in McKenzie 1968: xi), the monograph drew from his years in Columbus, and consisted of all the characteristics we have come to associate with early Chicago School urbanism: maps of ethnic group settlement, population information drawn from the census, household surveys, cognitive maps, discussion of the urban landscape in terms of population distributions and economic status, historical accounts of social institutions and, most crucially, attention to the neighborhood level as a significant unit of sociological analysis.

For the most part, this research has been ignored, or rather "collectively forgotten" (Schwartz 2009). A citation analysis using Web of Science reveals that the five articles have been cited a combined 38 times, by 32 citing articles, in the almost one hundred years since they have been published. Compare this to a roughly contemporaneous treatment of the same subject like Park's (Park 1915) "The City: Suggestions for the Investigation of Human Behavior in the Urban Environment", which has been cited 211 times.[1]

While "The Neighborhood" has received *some* scholarly attention, it has mostly consisted of perfunctory or ceremonial citations. Scholars have discussed McKenzie in terms of what he says about planning (Mitchell-Weaver 1990; Talen 2017), the heterogeneity of conceptions of neighborhoods (Moon 1990), delinquency (Taylor et al. 2011), slums (Lee 1945; Winchester and Costello 1995; Gaspare 2011), disenfranchised neighborhoods (Johnson and Halegoua 2014), neighborhood analysis (Rey et al. 2011; Talen 2018a; Williams and Hipp 2019), and urban mobility (Browning et al. 2017). Molotch (1976: 311) references McKenzie's discussion of "that 'we feeling' (McKenzie 1921) which bespeaks of community," as do Johnson and Halegoua (2015: 350) on the "'we' sentiment." Similarly, Madden quotes him on how "loyalty, self-sacrifice, and service are the natural products of the intimate personal neighborhood groups" (McKenzie 1921: 349, cited in Madden 2014: 474). A fairly commonly cited passage from the dissertation is about the difficulty of defining the neighborhood as a concept, where in the second serialized article McKenzie says "probably no other term is used so loosely or with such changing content as the term neighborhood, and very few concepts are more difficult to define" (McKenzie 1921: 344–5, cited in Looker 2010: 352; Sampson 2013: 8), and others cite McKenzie on the difficulty of defining the neighborhood without including the passage (Yabiku 2004, 2006a, 2006b).

Gaziano (1996) discusses McKenzie extensively, but mostly in terms of his work with Park on human ecology. When he does mention McKenzie's dissertation, all he says is "This empirical study was conducted squarely within the parameters of human ecology (concerns with mobility and segregation), but McKenzie relied exclusively on Park's 1915 version of *The City* with its emphasis on institutional urban analysis rather than an explicit ecological analysis for theoretical support" (881). Similarly, Nikolaev (2009) discusses McKenzie in an article about ecology, and Guest (2001) includes a citation of "The Neighborhood" in a footnote about ecology.

There are a few notable exceptions that identify work from "The Neighborhood" as significant. Talen notes that "R. D. McKenzie's four-part [*sic*] series The Neighborhood, published in the *American Journal of Sociology* in 1921 and 1922, defined neighborhoods as places that functioned as 'the universal nursery of primary human ideals' like 'loyalty, truth, service and kindness' (McKenzie 1921: 344)" (Talen 2017: 351). Arnold (1979: 25) recognizes McKenzie as "one of the few classic urban ecologists to give attention to the role of local associations in neighborhood stability," and Hayward (2013: 55) discusses McKenzie's findings about segregation and black Columbus.

Finally, there is a Heritage of Sociology volume about McKenzie entitled *Roderick D. McKenzie on Human Ecology: Selected Writings*, with an introduction by Amos H. Hawley. It includes the first two sections of the dissertation, and Hawley discusses it briefly in his introduction. Even here, though, McKenzie's contribution gets undercut. In his introduction, Hawley claims that

> It is of interest to note that the report of the neighborhood study shows no traces of E. W. Burgess' later formulation of a general growth pattern of cities. That there were no foreshadowings of that ingenious hypothesis cannot be attributed to the fact that McKenzie, having already embarked upon his teaching career, wrote the dissertation in absentia. For the two men were close friends and colleagues on the faculty of Ohio State University. Apparently the idea had not yet occurred to Burgess, or, if it had, he kept it quietly to himself. There seems to be little doubt, however, that Burgess consulted the neighborhood study among other research reports prepared by students and colleagues in the course of crystalizing his thoughts on the development and form of the city. (Hawley, in McKenzie 1968: xvi)

While it is true that no concentric circles show up, it is difficult not to read a precursor to the model in statements like "the population of any city is distributed according to economic status into residential areas of various rental or real estate values. Family income tends to segregate the population of a city into different economically districts much the same as the price of tickets at a theater divides the audience into several different strata of economic and social distinction" (McKenzie 1921: 152).

2.   REASONS WE FORGET

McKenzie wrote a piece focused on a key theoretical component of urban sociology at a time when the early American canon of urban sociology was developing, and it received prominent placement in the discipline's flagship journal.[2] And yet, there are no extant citations to the work before 1945, the five articles collectively reached their peak of annual citations with four in 1990, and today McKenzie is known for his work on human ecology and being the third name listed on *The City* but not as a foundational figure of neighborhood studies. Why?

I suggest that there are two primary reasons, the first a matter of timing, and the second a matter of politics. In terms of timing, McKenzie had the misfortune to publish his dissertation immediately before the University of Chicago Press began a serious enterprise of publishing student dissertations that formed much of the canon that emerged from the first Chicago School. In terms of politics, the dissertation is a strange beast when situated within debates about early urban sociology, insofar as it is a Chicago School dissertation that happens to not be about Chicago.

Timing

One likely reason "The Neighborhood" has not received more attention is because it was never published as a book. A contemporary of many of the more famous sociologists associated with the first Chicago School, McKenzie wrote his dissertation before a period when the University of Chicago Press began releasing a succession of dissertations as popular standalone monographs. Canons are most likely to form around what gets published, or in this case, what gets published in book form, and "The Neighborhood" did not get this treatment. While it was published by the press, it was as a reprint from *AJS*.

The University of Chicago Press had published dissertations from the Department of Sociology as far back as 1897, when it released both Annie Marion MacLean's *Factory Legislation for Women in the United States* and W. I. Thomas' *On a Difference in the Metabolism of the Sexes*, and would continue to do so throughout the early twentieth century. That said, the press seemed to ramp up the enterprise in the 1920s, when they put out dissertations-turned-into-books like Nels Anderson's *The Hobo: The Sociology of the Homeless Man* (1923), Frederic M. Thrasher's *The Gang: A Study of 1,313 Gangs in Chicago* (1927), Ruth Cavan's *Suicide* (1928), Louis Wirth's *The Ghetto* (1928), Walter C. Reckless' *Vice in Chicago* (1933), and E. Franklin Frazier's *The Negro Family in Chicago* (1932). Many, though not all, of these books were released under the auspices of the Chicago Sociology Series, overseen by McKenzie's professor, co-author, and lifelong collaborator Robert Park. Not part of that series, but released around the same time by the University of Chicago Press was *The City* by Park, Burgess and McKenzie (1925), although McKenzie's contribution was limited to a chapter on human ecology. The ideas McKenzie laid out in "The Neighborhood" are better associated with scholars more famous than him – notably Park, Burgess, Wirth and Zorbaugh – and the fact that "The Neighborhood" predates and suggests directions for much of this other work is less consequential than the contingency of McKenzie having finished his dissertation perhaps a few years too early to get wider attention.

Disciplinary Debate Mismatch

Much has been written, of course, about the Chicago School of Sociology. Some of it analyzes the school's relationship to subdisciplines in sociology like criminology (Short 2002), subculture (Colosi 2010), and urban studies (Gieryn 2006), or suggest lessons we might take from it in application to contemporary research (Merriman 2015). Still others consist of reflections of those who were involved in one way or another (Anderson 1983), or treat the "schoolness" of the Chicago School as a social object to be studied (Bulmer 1984; Fine 1995; Abbott 1997, 1999). The genre of writing I am interested in for the purposes of this chapter, though, is that which utilizes the Chicago School as a rhetorical object in partisan debates. This is what Abbott (1999: 5) refers to when he says that, in addition to descriptive histories of the department, "there is also much work chronicling the Chicago school in the process of invoking it in current substantive and methodological arguments, sometimes for its intellectual content, sometimes for its halo of legitimacy, sometimes for its utility as a target." Even more specifically, I am interested in the way people have discussed the Chicago School's relationship to urban sociology and the study of the city more broadly, in which Abbott (1999: 23) contends "usually the Chicago school figures as a tradition to be transcended or an orthodoxy to be overthrown."

Chicago has had a reputation as an urban sociological object dating back at least as far as 1904, when Weber visited Chicago and declared that "with the exception of some exclusive residential districts, the whole gigantic city, more extensive than London, is like a man whose skin has been peeled off and whose entrails one sees at work" (Weber 1946: 15). The idea of Chicago as an urban laboratory took hold, and has persisted across the decades as scholars of all sorts have used the city as the site of their studies. Of course, much of this persistent reputation has to do with the presence of the University of Chicago's Department of Sociology and the early work done there by Park and his students, but there was also a great deal of work emerging from places like Hull House and other settlement houses where Jane Addams and her colleagues worked (Deegan 1988). Nevertheless, it is fair to say that Chicago's urban sociological reputation rests primarily on Park, Burgess, and their students, and is crystalized in *The City* (1925), the dissertations mentioned in the previous section, and in later years by the Morris Janowitz helmed book series Heritage of Sociology at the University of Chicago Press (Abbott 1999: 18–19).

This reputation has been challenged on a number of fronts. In recent years, scholars have done a great deal of work bringing attention to the pioneering work of Du Bois[3] and the Atlanta School, discussing the ways the writer of *The Philadelphia Negro* has been systematically excluded from canonization processes (Wright 2002; Hunter 2013; Morris 2017), to the benefit of the mostly white scholars associated with the first Chicago School. A different strand of criticism is founded not on the idea that other people got to these crucial urban ideas first, but rather that Chicago is held up as the urban sociological object par excellence when it should not be. Scholars point out that Chicago is a unique case that is not necessarily generalizable to other places (e.g. Small 2007). Dear (2002) takes it a step further in the inaugural issue of

City & Community – the American Sociological Association's dedicated urban journal – by not only suggesting that Chicago is not the model of urbanism we should be looking at to understand other places, but that Los Angeles *is*, and that we should dispose of the Chicago School in favor of the Los Angeles School as we look "to map the intellectual terrain surrounding a long-overdue revision of our perspective on 21st century cities" (Dear 2002: 28).

Without adjudicating among the competing claims about the legitimacy of taking Chicago as a model for understanding urban life, I propose two statements that help us make sense of McKenzie's work on Columbus in the context of this disciplinary debate. First, the Chicago School is a socially meaningful category that scholars have found useful, whether in a parochial sense that suggests something about the right way to study cities, or just a descriptive sense that usefully groups together a set of scholars and ideas about the city. Second, the Chicago School has also been an anti-model, a sort of bogeyman to point to when lamenting something wrong with sociology, whether it is racism or urban ecology or over-reliance on a dominant specific case to describe urban life everywhere. It is in these statements that we can see the rhetorical awkwardness of McKenzie's work in Columbus in the terms of this debate.

To be brief, McKenzie's dissertation is too Chicago to be useful to critics of the lionization of the School, and not Chicago enough to be held up as a prototypical work in discussing work from the period. That is to say, "The Neighborhood" offers many of the characteristics we have come to associate with the Chicago School. Abbott (1999: 6) offers a specific description of the Chicago School, saying

> It is often about the city and, if so, nearly always about Chicago. It is processual-examining organization and disorganization, conflict and accommodation, social movements and cultural change. It imagines society in terms of groups and interaction rather than in terms of independent individuals with varying characteristics. Methodologically it is quite diverse, but it always has a certain empirical, even observational flavor, whether it is counting psychotics in neighborhoods, reading immigrants' letters to the old country, or watching the languid luxuries of the taxi-dance hall.

McKenzie's dissertation ticks off all these categories except for one: it is not a study of Chicago. McKenzie laid down the foundations of urban ecology (1921: 147–50) that Burgess became famous for with his concentric circle model,[4] described ethnic neighborhood settlement (154) before Zorbaugh wrote *The Gold Coast and the Slum*, counted juvenile delinquents (165) before Thrasher did his work on gangs or Reckless did his work on vice, discussed urban instability (157) before Wirth wrote "Urbanism as a Way of Life," and identified "a city of blacks within the larger community" (155) before Drake and Cayton (1945) wrote *Black Metropolis*. Most crucially, he offers an early attempt at a systematic theorization of the concept of the neighborhood, arguably the most important social category in all of urban sociology and one with a direct through-line to many of the dominant strands of urban scholarship in the twentieth century, including Firey (1945) and Suttles' (1972) cultural ecology and the neighborhood effects agenda spearheaded by Sampson (2013). But McKenzie wrote about all this in Columbus, Ohio, where he was an instructor at Ohio State University, and not in Chicago, which means it is not as easy to shoehorn into the story of the first Chicago School as are the ethnographies of Chicago that took that particular city as its site and subject.

That said, neither is it an appropriate bludgeon against the hegemony of the Chicago School given McKenzie's training, commitment to an ecological understanding of urbanism and methodological pluralism. As mentioned above, the contemporary reader of McKenzie finds connections to the Chicago School constantly, even if the dissertation is a treatment of somewhere farther East. Betwixt and between, "The Neighborhood" exists in a liminal space, as it relocates the Chicago School to Columbus, Ohio, meaning neither boosters nor critics of the first Chicago School have really known what to do with it, rhetorically.

3.   CONCLUSION

Why does it matter that this dissertation written early in the last century did not become famous, and what does it teach us? I suggest that there are three primary lessons: one about canonization, one about the debates over the Chicago School and, most importantly, one about how we think about neighborhoods and inequality.

Canonization

The collective forgetting of "The Neighborhood" provides a case for how canonization works, or more specifically how it does not work. Specifically, I have argued that McKenzie's dissertation did not enter the urban sociological canon for two specific reasons, having to do with timing and politics. This suggests that when we think about how canons are formed, we must take into account both historical contingency and questions of categorization.

Regarding historical contingency, it is appropriate that this chapter deals with the Chicago School, as Abbott (1999: 3) holds that "the fundamental insight of the Chicago tradition has been to take the location of social facts seriously, to see all social life as situated in time and place." McKenzie certainly does this – the dissertation takes seriously the contingency of place in particular, describing in great detail the social and economic world of

Columbus – but the story of the non-canonization of "The Neighborhood" is also a lesson in situating social life temporally and spatially. Specifically, McKenzie's dissertation might have gained more purchase – and perhaps he would have been mentioned in the list of prominent students of the Chicago School in Abbott's book about the department (1999: 6), which he is not – if it had been written a little bit later, or about a different place.

As to the place, this is the root of the question of disciplinary politics, of course. McKenzie wrote a Chicago School dissertation that was not about Chicago, and thus it served no rhetorical use in the debate about the primacy of Chicago in urban sociology. Organizations scholars have long told us about the importance of being able to categorize objects for their social legibility in markets (e.g. DiMaggio and Powell 1983; Podolny 1993; Zuckerman 1999). The story of "The Neighborhood" reveals that objects need to be categorizable in intellectual markets as well. Otherwise actors do not know what to do with them, and they are not utilized to their full potential.

Debates about the Chicago School

A second lesson has to do with the way we think about the Chicago School and the debate surrounding it. Put simply, for the same reason that "The Neighborhood" is not useful in historical and contemporary debates about the Chicago School, it *could* be incredibly useful in thinking more clearly about what the Chicago School was actually about. In the aforementioned inaugural issue of *City & Community*, a number of scholars quite ably responded to Dear's (2002) call to let the Chicago School go by pointing out that all too often what people mean when they talk about the Chicago School is an over-simplified straw man, or in this case, a straw concentric circle model (Abbott 2002; Clark 2002; Molotch 2002; Sampson 2002; Sassen 2002). A careful consideration of exactly what "The Neighborhood" is, is a further call to complicate how we think about the Chicago School, for those who champion it and those who abhor it. Here we have a description of urban life steeped in the intellectual traditions associated with the Chicago School, but it has nothing to do with Chicago, thus dodging the accusation that it is parochial and non-generalizable to all other cities.[5] By moving the focus to a different city, we are forced to grapple with the actual theoretical and methodological contributions and drawbacks of the Chicago School, instead of arguing about whether or not it is annoying that there is so much written about a single city.

Neighborhoods and Inequality

Finally, and most importantly, McKenzie's dissertation offers lessons about urban sociology that we would do well to consider. As has been established, many of his contributions were later formulated by others, often in more thoughtful or complete ways. Therefore, while it is notable that McKenzie covered the ecological model of the city before Burgess, juvenile delinquency before Thrasher, and urban instability before Wirth, we have not necessarily collectively lost something because that has not been adequately recognized, as the ideas did emerge soon after.

That said, McKenzie's singular focus on the concept of the neighborhood as a social object is worth recovering as contemporary urbanists. Interest in exactly how neighborhoods come into being is a perennial concern (Hunter 1974; Talen 2018b), and McKenzie provides us with a solid foundation for the multiple epistemological bases of neighborhoods.

He is not doctrinaire about it, and in fact expresses ambivalence about how neighborhoods might be defined. In the most theoretically oriented part of the dissertation, printed as the second of the five articles, the first sentence of the abstract, following *Meaning of the concept neighborhood*, reads "It is difficult to define the neighborhood in the modern city." He then goes through a number of different ways of conceiving of the idea of a neighborhood, noting that "the word neighborhood has two general connotations: physical proximity to a given object of attention, and intimacy of association among people living in close proximity to each other" (McKenzie 1921: 345), but also that crucially these two connotations do not always overlap. McKenzie anticipates the general disciplinary discussion about the relative importance of physical proximity vs. network ties (Wellman and Leighton 1979), but instead of coming down on one side or another, he quite sensibly documents the different ways in which different definitions are used. Noting that "the concept of neighborhood has come down to us from a distant past and therefore has connotations which scarcely fit the facts when applied to a patch of life in modern large city" (McKenzie 1921: 346), he draws out the history of the concept across different social science disciplines (346–9).

McKenzie had his students draw their neighborhoods with explanations of why they chose to draw what they did (350), anticipating Suttles' (1972) cognitive maps. What he found when he did this is that "the conception which the average city dweller holds of his own neighborhood is that of a very small area within the immediate vicinity of his home, the limits of which seem to be determined by the extent of his personal observations and daily contacts," which he contrasts with the simultaneous observation that "in referring to neighborhoods in general in Columbus much larger areas seem to be implied, spatial proximity to some central focus of attention being the determining feature" (351). He concludes that "for certain administrative purposes it is important to consider these larger geographical expressions as units of neighborhood interest, while for other purposes, where intensity of social opinion counts, the smaller nuclei of common life may prove more effective units" (351–2).

This will sound familiar to any social scientist trying to make sense of the incongruousness of neighborhoods, community areas, police districts and wards. Beyond being an academic question, questions over how different social objects have different boundaries have been shown to be relevant to questions of safety and political power (Vargas 2016). McKenzie offers us the language to probe the ambiguity of neighborhoods, a subject as crucial today as it has ever been. That he also documents instances of territoriality (McKenzie 1921: 353), boosterism (354, 357), and what amounts to collective efficacy (355) makes it even more conversant with contemporary concerns of urban sociologists, and suggests new directions for thinking about how the social process of defining neighborhoods is productive in itself of inequality.

NOTES

1. This essay was of course reproduced in *The City* (1925) by Park, Burgess and McKenzie, and served as an influence on the work of McKenzie (Hawley, in McKenzie 1968: xv), but it was first published in the *American Journal of Sociology* ten years earlier. The citation numbers mentioned are for the journal publication, not the book.
2. While it became the official journal of the American Sociological Association, the *American Sociological Review* was not even founded until 1936, fifteen years after the serialized publication of "The Neighborhood".
3. See this volume, Chapter 16.
4. While McKenzie alludes to a shape that would come to stand in for the Chicago School when he says "most of our great cities are circular or star shaped unless directly modified by geographic peculiarities," he tells us that "Columbus is shaped like a Greek cross" (147).
5. No city is generalizable to all other cities, and I will not be making a brave call to found the Columbus School of Sociology at the end of this chapter.

REFERENCES

Abbott, Andrew. 1997. "Of Time and Space: The Contemporary Relevance of the Chicago School." *Social Forces* 75, no. 4: 1149–82.
Abbott, Andrew. 1999. *Department and Discipline: Chicago Sociology at One Hundred*. Chicago, IL: University of Chicago Press.
Abbott, Andrew. 2002. "Los Angeles and the Chicago School: A Comment on Michael Dear." *City & Community* 1, no. 1: 33–8.
Anderson, Nels. 1923. *The Hobo: The Sociology of the Homeless Man*. Chicago: University of Chicago Press.
Anderson, Nels. 1983. "A Stranger at the Gate – Reflections on the Chicago-School-of-Sociology." *Urban Life* 11, no. 4: 396–406.
Arnold, Joseph L. 1979. "Neighborhood and City Hall – Origin of Neighborhood Associations in Baltimore, 1880–1911." *Journal of Urban History* 6, no. 1: 3–30.

Browning, Christopher R., Catherine A. Calder, Brian Soller, Aubrey L. Jackson and Jonathan Dirlam. 2017. "Ecological Networks and Neighborhood Social Organization." *American Journal of Sociology* 122, no. 6: 1939–88.

Bulmer, Martin. 1984. *The Chicago School of Sociology: Institutionalization, Diversity and the Rise of Sociological Research.* Chicago, IL: University of Chicago Press.

Cavan, Ruth Shonle. 1928. *Suicide.* Chicago: University of Chicago Press.

Clark, Terry Nichols. 2002. "Codifying LA Chaos." *City & Community* 1, no. 1: 51–7.

Colosi, Rachela. 2010. "A Return to the Chicago School? From the 'subculture' of Taxi Dancers to the Contemporary Lap Dancer." *Journal of Youth Studies* 13, no. 1: 1–16.

Dear, Michael. 2002. "Los Angeles and the Chicago School: Invitation to a Debate." *City & Community* 1, no. 1: 5–32.

Deegan, Mary Jo. 1988. *Jane Addams and the Men of the Chicago School, 1892–1918.* New Brunswick, NJ: Transaction Books.

DiMaggio, Paul and Walter W. Powell. 1983. "The Iron Cage Revisited: Collective Rationality and Institutional Isomorphism in Organizational Fields." *American Sociological Review* 48, no. 2: 147–60.

Drake, St. Clair and Horace R. Cayton. 1945. *Black Metropolis: A Study of Negro Life in a Northern City.* New York: Harcourt Brace and Company.

Fine, Gary A. 1995. *A Second Chicago School?: The Development of a Postwar American Sociology.* Chicago, IL: University of Chicago Press.

Firey, Walter I. 1945. "Sentiment and Symbolism as Ecological Variables." *American Sociological Review* 10: 140–48.

Frazier, Edward Franklin. 1932. *The Negro Family in Chicago.* Chicago: University of Chicago Press.

Gaspare, Angelo. 2011. "Emerging Networks of Organized Urban Poor: Restructuring the Engagement with Government toward the Inclusion of the Excluded." *Voluntas* 22, no. 4: 779–810.

Gaziano, Emanuel. 1996. "Ecological Metaphors as Scientific Boundary Work: Innovation and Authority in Interwar Sociology and Biology." *American Journal of Sociology* 101, no. 4: 874–907.

Gieryn, Thomas. F. 2006. "City as Truth-Spot: Laboratories and Field-Sites in Urban Studies." *Social Studies of Science* 36, no. 1: 5–38.

Guest, A. M. 2001. "Some Evolving Thoughts on Leo F. Schnore as a Social Scientist." *Journal of Urban History* 27, no. 4: 387–404.

Hayward, Clarissa Rile. 2013. *Black Places.* Cambridge: Cambridge University Press.

Hunter, Albert. 1974. *Symbolic Communities: The Persistence and Change of Chicago's Local Communities.* Chicago, IL: University of Chicago Press.

Hunter, Marcus Anthony. 2013. *Black Citymakers: How the Philadelphia Negro Changed Urban America.* Oxford: Oxford University Press.

Johnson, Bonnie J. and Germaine R. Halegoua. 2014. "Potential and Challenges for Social Media in the Neighborhood Context." *Journal of Urban Technology* 21, no. 4: 51–75.

Johnson, Bonnie J. and Germaine R. Halegoua. 2015. "Can Social Media Save a Neighborhood Organization?." *Planning Practice and Research* 30, no. 3: 248–69.

Lee, Alfred McClung. 1945. "Interest Criteria in Propaganda Analysis." *American Sociological Review* 10, no. 2: 282–8.

Looker, Benjamin. 2010. "Microcosms of Democracy: Imagining the City Neighborhood in World War II-Era America." *Journal of Social History* 44, no. 2: 351–78.

Madden, David J. 2014. "Neighborhood as Spatial Project: Making the Urban Order on the Downtown Brooklyn Waterfront." *International Journal of Urban and Regional Research* 38, no. 2: 471–97.

McKenzie, Roderick D. 1921. "The Neighborhood: A Study of Local Life in the City of Columbus, Ohio." *American Journal of Sociology* 2, no. 7: 145–68, 344–63, 486–509, 588–610, 780–99.

McKenzie, Roderick D. 1968. *On Human Ecology: Selected Writings.* Ed. Amos H. Hawley. Chicago, IL: University of Chicago Press.

Merriman, Ben. 2015. "Three Conceptions of Spatial Locality in Chicago School Sociology (and their Significance Today)." *The American Sociologist* 46, no. 2: 269–87.

Mitchell-Weaver, Clyde. 1990. "Community Development in North America: Survey and Prospect for the 1990s." *Community Development Journal* 25, no. 4: 345–55.

Molotch, Harvey. 1976. "City as a Growth Machine – Toward a Political-Economy of Place." *American Journal of Sociology* 82, no. 2: 309–32.

Molotch, Harvey. 2002. "School's Out: A Response to Michael Dear." *City & Community* 1, no. 1: 39–43.

Moon, Graham. 1990. "Conceptions of Space and Community in British Health-Policy." *Social Science & Medicine* 30, no. 1: 165–71.

Morris, Aldon. 2017. *The Scholar Denied.* Chicago, IL: University of Chicago Press.

Nikolaev, V. G. 2009. "Multidimensional and Reductionist Strategies in Chicagoan Sociology: The Case of Human Ecology." *Sotsiologicheskii zhurnal*, no. 2: 18–55.

Park, Robert E. and Ernest W. Burgess. 1915. *The City: Suggestions for Investigation of Human Behavior in the Urban Environment.* Chicago, IL: University of Chicago Press.

Park, Robert E., Ernest W. Burgess and Roderick D. McKenzie. 1925. *The City: Suggestions for Investigation of Human Behavior in the Urban Environment.* Chicago, IL: University of Chicago Press.

Podolny, Joel M. 1993. "A Status-Based Model of Market Competition." *American Journal of Sociology* 98, no. 4: 829–72.

Reckless, Walter C. 1933. *Vice in Chicago.* Chicago: University of Chicago Press.

Rey, Sergio J., Luc Anselin, David C. Folch, Daniel Arribas-Bel, Myrna L. Sastre Gutierrez and Lindsey Interlante. 2011. "Measuring Spatial Dynamics in Metropolitan Areas." *Economic Development Quarterly* 25, no. 1: 54–64.

Sampson, Robert J. 2002. "Studying Modern Chicago." *City & Community* 1, no. 1: 45–8.

Sampson, Robert J. 2013. "The Place of Context: A Theory and Strategy for Criminology's Hard Problems." *Criminology* 51, no. 1: 1–31.

Sassen, Saskia. 2002. "Scales and Spaces." *City & Community* 1, no. 1: 48–50.

Schwartz, Barry. 2009. "Collective Forgetting and the Symbolic Power of Oneness: The Strange Apotheosis of Rosa Parks." *Social Psychology Quarterly* 72, no. 2: 123–42.

Short, James F. 2002. "Criminology, the Chicago School, and Sociological Theory." *Crime Law and Social Change* 37, no. 2: 107–15.

Small, Mario L. 2007. "Is There Such a Thing as 'The Ghetto'? The Perils of Assuming that the South Side of Chicago Represents Poor Black Neighborhoods." *City* 11, no. 3: 413–21.

Suttles, Gerald D. 1972. *The Social Construction of Communities.* Chicago, IL: University of Chicago Press.

Talen, Emily. 2017. "Social Science and the Planned Neighbourhood." *Town Planning Review* 88, no. 3: 349–72.

Talen, Emily. 2018a. *Neighborhood*. Oxford, New York: Oxford University Press.

Talen, Emily. 2018b. "The Relentless Link between Neighbourhoods and Segregation: What Are the Alternatives?." *Town Planning Review* 89, no. 5: 443–62.

Taylor, Ralph B., Phillip W. Harris, Peter R. Jones, R. Marie Garcia and Eric S. McCord. 2011. "Ecological Origins of Shared Perceptions of Troublesome Teen Groups: Implications for the Basic Systemic Model of Crime, the Incivilities Thesis, and Political Economy." *Journal of Research in Crime and Delinquency* 48, no. 2: 298–324.

Thrasher, Frederic Milton. 1927. *The Gang: A Study of 1,313 Gangs in Chicago*. Chicago: University of Chicago Press.

Vargas, Robert. 2016. *Wounded City: Violent Turf Wars in a Chicago Barrio*. Oxford: Oxford University Press.

Weber, Max. 1946. *From Max Weber: Essays in Sociology*. Ed. Hans Heinrich Gerth and Charles Wright Mills. New York: Oxford University Press.

Wellman, Barry and Barry Leighton. 1979. "Networks, Neighborhoods, and Communities: Approaches to the Study of the Community Question." *Urban Affairs Quarterly* 14, no. 3: 363–90.

Williams, Seth A. and John R. Hipp. 2019. "How Great and How Good?: Third Places, Neighbor Interaction, and Cohesion in the Neighborhood Context." *Social Science Research* 77 (January): 68–78.

Winchester, Hilary P. M. and Lauren N. Costello. 1995. "Living on the Street – Social-Organization and Gender Relations of Australian Street Kids." *Environment and Planning D-Society & Space* 13, no. 3: 329–48.

Wirth, Louis. 1928. *The Ghetto*. Chicago: University of Chicago Press.

Wright, Earl. 2002. "Using the Master's Tools: The Atlanta Sociological Laboratory and American Sociology, 1896–1924." *Sociological Spectrum* 22, no. 1: 15–39.

Yabiku, Scott T. 2004. "Marriage Timing in Nepal: Organizational Effects and Individual Mechanisms." *Social Forces* 83, no. 2: 559–86.

Yabiku, Scott T. 2006a. "Land Use and Marriage Timing in Nepal." *Population and Environment* 27, nos 5–6: 445–61.

Yabiku, Scott T. 2006b. "Neighbors and Neighborhoods: Effects on Marriage Timing." *Population Research and Policy Review* 25, no. 4: 305–27.

Zorbaugh, Harvey Warren. 1929. *The Gold Coast and the Slum. A Sociological Study of Chicago's Near North Side*. Chicago: University of Chicago Press.

Zuckerman, Ezra W. 1999. "The Categorical Imperative: Securities Analysts and the Illegitimacy Discount." *American Journal of Sociology* 104, no. 5: 1398–1438.

5. Progressive values and institutional realities at The New School for Social Research

Cherry Schrecker

1. INTRODUCTION

Nearly 30 years after Albion Small was named to build the university department we now know as the Chicago School of Sociology,[1] dedicated to research in the social sciences (Bulmer 1984; Chapoulie 2001), another school, The New School for Social Research,[2] was founded in New York. As was the case with the Chicago School, the founders intended The New School to be integrated into the town, conceived of as a research object: ". . . this is the hour for experiment; and New York is the place, because it is the greatest social science laboratory in the world and of its own force attracts scholars and leaders in educational work."[3] The object of this research in both universities, which clearly integrated progressive ideas, was that of social improvement. Some of the intellectuals who had been involved with the University of Chicago (such as Alvin Johnson, John Dewey and Thorstein Veblen) were to be among the founders and members of The New School; others were to navigate between the two institutions.

In this chapter I will present The New School, its founders and the progressive values on which the idea of the school was based, before discussing the way in which the school interpreted and integrated these values at its foundation and over time.

2. ON THE FOUNDERS AND ORIGINS OF THE NEW SCHOOL

The origins of the school are the work of several progressive thinkers, and can be attributed to a series of events. These begin with a dispute opposing the University of Columbia and several members of its teaching staff. In 1917, two members of the faculty spoke up in opposition to the involvement of

American troops in Europe. In response to this their contract was terminated by the trustees of Columbia, represented by the president of the university Nicolas Murray Butler. Charles Austin Beard and James Harvey Robinson, both historians, handed in their notice in protest, not because they were in agreement with the positions taken by their colleagues, but in defense of academic freedom which involves the right to speak one's own opinion within a university setting. This they felt had been flouted in Columbia and in many other American universities (Hofstadter and Metzger 1955; McCaughey 2003). After the incident, other professors, such as the philosopher, psychologist and educational reformer, John Dewey and the anthropologist Franz Boas, remained on the Columbia university staff, whilst distancing themselves from the academic life of the university; Boas, like Dewey, was later to give courses at The New School.

Judging that Butler's attitude was characteristic of the majority of university presidents, Beard and Robinson set out to found a teaching and research institution whose values would be compatible with theirs. They believed that academic freedom in a university setting was the only possible basis for the reconstruction of American society and for the furtherance of democracy. They developed their project under the auspices of the progressive and liberal journal *The New Republic*. As well as Beard, the organization committee (as described in the 1918 *Proposal for an Independent School of Social Science*) includes 18 people, among them the two founders of *The New Republic*, Mrs. Willard Straight (the married name of the heiress and social activist Dorothy Payne Whitney) and Herbert Croly (journalist). Several of those named, including Caroline Bacon (historian) and Alvin Johnson (economist), were later to become members of the board of directors of The New School.

The first members of the teaching staff, named in the catalogue of preliminary lectures, which preceded the official inauguration in September 1919 (NSA 1918), include Thorstein Veblen (economist), James Harvey Robinson (historian), Charles Austin Beard (historian), Emily James Putnam (author and educator), Wesley Clair Mitchell (economist), Ordway Tead (business and administration), Harold J. Laski (political theorist and economist) and Frederic J. Ellis (psychologist). Among other names appearing in this preliminary list are Herbert Croly (director of the journal *The New Republic*), Alvin Johnson (later to become director of The New School) and Winston Churchill. In October 1919, when the school officially opened, the staff list had grown to 24 instructors including, among others, Harry E. Barnes (historian), John Dewey (psychologist and philosopher), Horace Kallen (culture and civilization) and Roscoe Pound (law). In the fall of 1920 their number was down to 12. This development, and a subsequent increase, is very illustrative of the changing fortunes of The New School over time; periods of great activity were to alternate with more difficult times, mainly in the form of financial crises.

3.   PROGRESSIVE VALUES, RESEARCH AND
        EDUCATION

Progressive thinkers in New York and elsewhere were connected by multiple
links. In publishing, for example, over and above their membership of *The New
Republic*, Robinson was on the editorial board of *Political Science Quarterly*,
edited by the Faculty of Political Science at Columbia University from 1896,
which Johnson joined in 1905 as assistant managing editor. Johnson also published in the *American Journal of Sociology* (Commons 1908) where Dewey's
and Robinson's books were reviewed.

The ideas circulating among progressive thinkers on the importance of
social science research and education as a means of social improvement were
already largely accepted and put into practice by the time The New School
opened. Links with the University of Chicago have already been mentioned.
On a more local count, many of the founders of The New School had been
members of the staff at Columbia where a drive for the resolution of social
problems via social science teaching, and that of New York as a place in which
to put these ideas into practice, had long been in vogue. John Recchuitti names
the "Report on a Department of Social Science at Columbia College" as a place
where activist values were made explicit:

> [The department] would seek to ease the grinding poverty of industrial capitalism,
> and renew democracy at an age when wealth was in the hands of a few. They would
> begin with work on the city in which they lived (Recchiutti 2007: 30).

As was the case in Chicago, the city is thus conceived as a "natural laboratory
of Social Science" (Recchiutti 2007: 31).[4] What did The New School bring to
this effort that was new? The idea of a school was that of a place in which students came to learn skills which would be useful for their own future and that
of society, not to accumulate disembodied knowledge on past events with little
or no value other than academic knowledge. The documents consulted in the
New School Archives put great emphasis on academic freedom and on further
education for adults far from the constraints weighing on many universities of
the time.

4.   THE NEW SCHOOL AS A PROGRESSIVE
        INSTITUTION

As is shown by the documents issued by the group of founders, and emphasized in the catalogues announcing the courses for the preliminary session
and during the first year of its existence, The New School was conceived,
right from the start, as a progressive institution. Great importance was placed

on world peace and on the furtherance of democracy both in America and abroad. In an article published in *The New Republic*, Croly (1918) particularly emphasizes the "pursuit of truth" and the need for "practical experimentation" (171). He stresses the need for a science of society which would be an element of social progress, transcending social particularisms and individual interests:

> The school is born in general of the conception of a modern nation as a political group which proposes candidly and thoroughly to learn the lessons of its own experience and which gains experience by testing its ideals in practice. (Croly 1918: 171)

The graduates of the school should be informed experts able to initiate and accompany social reform taking into account the needs and desires of ordinary people (which he argues that experts did not do at the time of writing) and disseminate the ideas learned at the school. The means to achieve this were to provide continuing education for adults, enabling them to develop a critical attitude toward society and social and political institutions. Great importance was placed on the social sciences as a means of understanding and improving society. This hope was shared by many social scientists of the time, as is demonstrated by William I. Thomas and Florian Znaniecki, who affirm in their introduction to the *Polish Peasant* that

> The marvellous results obtained by a rational technique in the sphere of material reality invite us to apply some analogous procedure to social reality. Our success in controlling nature gives us confidence that we shall eventually be able to control the social world in the same measure. (Thomas and Znaniecki 1918: 1)

However, a look at the titles of the classes taught at The New School over the first four years of its existence reveals the predominance of theoretical discussion over more applied or activist teaching. To name just the first three entries, the catalogue of preliminary lectures includes titles such as "The Industrial Transition from the Eighteenth Century to the Twentieth" (Veblen), "The Relation of Education to Social Progress" (Robinson), and "Problems of American Government" (Beard). Alongside historical and analytic classes, the first full-year catalogue includes courses on qualitative and quantitative methods, such as Dewey's "Method in the Social Sciences" in which he analyzed some of the notions employed in social theory and social discussion, and drew attention to "The chief obstacles to impartial inquiry and application of its results."[5] Human interests and emotions were also addressed theoretically in this section. A third type of course are those dedicated to contemporary problems, such as "Problems of Tax Reform in America" (Roscoe Pound), "Problems of Work and Wages" (Leon Ardzrooni) and lectures on the question of the finance of war reform (Thomas Adams) or business cycles (Wesley Clair Mitchell[6]). All these subjects and many others are tackled mainly from a theoretical point of view, and the question of the reduction of inequality, though it can be assumed to be a constituent element of social progress, is rarely explicitly mentioned.

Two categories of students were to be admitted: regular students who wished to improve their knowledge and analysis of society, and graduate students approved by the instructors for their academic credentials and who wished attend smaller, more specialized classes. The level of tuition was to be postgraduate, but the school would not issue diplomas; this was another means of guaranteeing academic independence. It is also important to note that, though the majority of the instructors were male, the school was proposed explicitly as an educational establishment for "MEN AND WOMEN" (NSA 1918, capitals in the original). The inequalities the founders sought to fight were clearly set out. A later anonymous document bearing the address of the first building occupied by The New School and found in the Roscoe Pound papers, indicates the importance of the study and interpretation of "the ideals problems and methods of all classes" and argues that the "the extension of women's interest into new and important spheres of public life will lead them to seek a better equipment both for power and service" (4). Racial inequalities are not mentioned in these early documents.

As means of ensuring institutional independence, the founders of The New School decided not to seek state subsidy or support from foundations. The main source of revenue was to be student fees. Private donations were also accepted from disinterested benefactors wishing to support the institution and sympathetic to its aims and values. Many of these benefactors figure in an "Advisory Committee," which appears in the New School Announcement for the year 1925–26. They include Eleanor Roosevelt, "already a well-known activist for progressive causes" (Friedlander 2019: 74) and the judge and judicial philosopher Bennington Learned Hand, who in 1913 had co-founded *The New Republic* with Herbert Croly (Purcell 1995). Edward Purcell also refers to Hand's progressive convictions in his early years (which were to weaken in later life) and to his links with Theodore Roosevelt to whom he had sent Croly's book, *A Promise of American Life*, which Roosevelt had greatly appreciated. We can see again the importance of the network composed of progressive thinkers.

Two other examples of long-standing benefactors are Daniel Cranford Smith and Clara Woollie Mayer. Smith, a business man and student of The New School, known as "Uncle Dan," donated land for the construction of a new building, which was finally inaugurated in 1931.[7] As part of the deal, an apartment was constructed on the last floor, which was to be his home as long as he lived. He also donated money to The New School on several occasions and became a member of the Board of Trustees.[8] Woollie Mayer was a rich heiress whose family donated a large sum of money toward the construction of the new building.[9] She was to bail out the institution in times of financial crisis on several occasions, and served as assistant director from 1931.[10]

5.   CLOUDS ON THE HORIZON

But let us move back in time to the years just after the founding period. As was to occur regularly over a hundred years of existence (The New School celebrated its centenary in 2019), the school was rapidly beset by financial difficulties. These were to bring to light or exacerbate differences of approach and attitude which divided the founders. Divisions were particularly rife with reference to the relationship between knowledge and public life. Robinson and Dewey insisted on the importance of the applicability of knowledge, whereas Veblen supported by Croly, argued that research should be independent from social life; he also believed that researchers should be free from everyday constraints enabling them to dedicate their time to their studies. This tension between science as an "elitist enterprise" and science as a "democratising force" is evoked by Recchiutti (2007: 13) as a dividing factor more globally in progressive thought.

Thus, at the start of the university year 1921–22, a difficult choice faced the members of The New School. If they wished the school to survive, they could either give priority to research and reduce teaching to a minimum, which would involve finding other sources of finance, or develop the educational offer whilst maintaining a small research department whose main function would be to advise students carrying out research projects (Johnson 1952). Without consulting the majority of the members, the Board of Directors set up a publicity campaign promoting the classes which brought in the most money. This initiative brought protest both from those who put an accent on pedagogical excellence and those who wished to give priority to research, the former in view of what they considered as a threat to academic liberty, whilst the latter feared that the school was prepared to trade its intellectual excellence and become a center for adult education. A vote was organized among the members who came out in favor of the second solution. But it was too late and a large number of the founders resigned in protest. Though many agreed with the outcome of the vote, they were outraged by the way in which the Board had handled the question.

6.   NEW DIRECTIONS OR RENEWING OLD THEMES?

It was at this point that Alvin Johnson, an economist, took over the running of The New School, becoming its official director in 1923 (Johnson 1952). In order to improve the financial situation, he gave priority to teaching and suspended research activities until such time as financial stability could be re-established. As stated above, he was soon to be seconded by Clara Mayer; member of the Board of Directors from 1924, she became assistant director in 1931.[11] After Johnson's arrival as president the teaching program was to change over time, showing the ever greater influence of Mayer; more courses linked to the arts and architecture and others, such as psychoanalysis, were introduced. The arts as a subject area in its own right is mentioned in the 1923 Summer Catalogue. By 1927, courses pertaining to mental health and artistic questions had become an important aspect of the agenda. We observe a gradual diminution of courses on economic and political questions and of those relating to work, which had previously been dominant. It would seem that the accent was shifting from structural problems toward individuals, their mental health, and their more immediate surroundings. Had Johnson, as certain critics were to affirm later, moved away from the original purposes of The New School and transformed it into an "Aladdin's Lecture Palace" (Wilson 1931)? This question will be examined in the last section of this chapter.

It is interesting to observe, also in the 1923 catalogue, the arrival of the sociologist W. I. Thomas of the University of Chicago. This addition to the pedagogical team is illustrative of Johnson's ideals and of the public image of The New School over the years: that of a place in which misfits, be they academic or political, would be welcome. Thomas had been suspended from his functions in Chicago after being accused of having an affair with the wife of an army officer. Though the facts were never proven, Thomas' reputation and academic career were ruined; he taught at The New School until 1926. During this time, he taught a course named "Races and Culture," which reinforced a course taught as from the academic year 1921–22: "Race and Race Problems." As a development of this, several courses on race were proposed by the anthropologist Alexander A. Goldenweiser, who had been an instructor at the school since 1919, under the main title "Problems of Race". The courses (1) "Theories of Race"; (2) "Race and Culture"; and (3) "Race and Politics," were spread over the three academic terms. The question of race was a moot point among progressives, some seeing Negros as inferior to Northern types, whilst others affirmed that they should be considered as politically equal (Recchiuti 2007: 177 *et seq.*). Judging from the brief descriptions in the catalogues, it would seem that the classes at The New School aimed to examine in a scholarly manner the principles behind the different affirmations on race current at that time.

Another occasion on which those unwanted elsewhere were welcomed at The New School was the setting up of the Graduate Faculty in 1933, with the express purpose of saving Jewish intellectuals threatened by the Nazi regime. With one exception (Horace Kallen), the Graduate Faculty was composed of academics (mainly Jews) exiled from Europe. Johnson's initiative accented freedom of speech and of action, and the refusal to tolerate oppression. Over and above the saving of a large number of academics who would have been condemned had they remained in Europe, the Graduate Faculty (with the financial support of the Rockefeller Foundation[12]) was also the means of bringing research back onto The New School's agenda.

In 1934, a provisional charter (which became absolute in 1941) gave the Graduate Faculty the right to dispense diplomas at Master and PhD level, undergraduate diplomas, dispensed by the adult education department, were to follow in 1944. These were all steps toward a more academically based course offering, although adult education classes continue to the present day, The New School was becoming, and is now, a university with a university curriculum which enters into competition with similar institutions for students, finance and renown. The ideal of dispensing knowledge in its own right, and with the unique purpose of social improvement, was a thing of the past.

7.   HOW FAR DID THE NEW SCHOOL LIVE UP TO ITS PROGRESSIVE IDEALS?

Though the desire to improve society is clearly stated, The New School's quest for equality is not a central element of discourse in what, in many ways, seems to have been a fairly elite institution. The original objective of the founders as stated in the first New School Catalogue, was "to seek an unbiased understanding of the existing order, its genesis, growth and present working, as well as those exigent circumstances which are making for its revision."[13] Johnson confirmed this aim in the 1924– 25 catalogues, adding that "its point of view is intellectual liberalism, seeking to understand existing institutions and institutional trends rather that to defend them or to subject them to destructive criticism".[14]

Who Were the Students?

A more precise idea of the desired composition of the student body is given in the New School Catalogue issued in spring 1925: "not primarily young men and women who find themselves in the college stage of development, but persons of maturity with an intellectual interest, graduates of colleges engaged in the professions or in business, and men and women who by reading and discussion have prepared themselves for the serious study of social problems." That is to say, mature students. We learn in the 1926–27 New School Catalogue that of these students only 20% did not hold a university degree or professional qualification and that between 5% and 10% had no paid employment. As to the professions represented, teachers and social workers constituted about a third of the student body.

The standard of work is described as "postgraduate" (even though no diploma was required to prove this level), and the price of classes for the first year of study is $20,[15] which, converted to present day rates (2020) gives the sum of $299, far more than most working class or poorer populations would be able to afford at the time. Some of the documents insist on the importance of the situation in New York City, and though links with various bodies in the city do exist, the geographical situation seems to have provided an attractive and convenient setting rather than a laboratory for social experimentation. Originally then, the classes were designed to train a socially conscious elite who could take charge of the social problems the progressives felt were endangering social progress and stability.

How Should Social Improvement Be Brought About?

The top-down approach to the resolution of social problems seems to have been a current procedure in the early years of the twentieth century. We find a suggestion in this sense in Harvey Zorbaugh's (1929) *The Gold Coast and the Slum*. Based on a study carried out during the 1920s, the author offers a solution to the social problems encountered. Having affirmed that the social organization of the upper classes is the most stable, Zorbaugh argues that the members of this class could have a positive influence on those below them, thus helping to promote a sense of community in the area.

Social improvement is envisaged by most progressive thinkers as a peaceful and gradual evolution. Johnson states his own point of view on the role to be attributed to the working classes in a commentary on a paper on class conflict (Commons 1908) published in the *American Journal of Sociology*. At the end of his commentary, he gives the example of a young man he had known who came to San Francisco to study labor conditions in the city. This young man, who had been sympathetic to the labor movement, was attacked by unionists and, as a result, changed his attitude. In the last paragraph, Johnson (1952: 174) affirms:

> If ever the working class becomes strongly organized throughout the country, we who are not directly engaged in the class conflict will meet with many unpleasant experiences and we shall find our impartiality somewhat impaired. . . There will be no impartial jury to whom the questions at issue may be submitted.

This would seem to support the idea that Johnson's priority was the training of professional people able to accompany social reform and to help to promote social justice. Like many other progressive thinkers, he was not favorable to the idea of a revolution. The solution to inequality was thus not that of abolishing hierarchies, but rather the training of an intelligentsia who would deal with social problems. In line with this, the preoccupations of The New School, as announced in the catalogues, pertain more to academic freedom (the possibility to state one's opinions and to educate as one sees fit), and social justice as academic themes, than to direct intervention vis-à-vis underprivileged groups.

The links with outside bodies such as the Workers' Educational Bureau[16] seem to be similarly oriented to the idea of social reform rather than that of direct social action. This was not necessarily the case for all members of the progressive movement; other progressive thinkers such as Jane Addams in Chicago, founder of the settlement Hull House, became far more directly involved with social welfare on a concrete and everyday basis, whilst continuing to fight for equality on a political level and via academic publications (Hamington 2018).

Transforming the Objectives

But even the education of the administrators of today and tomorrow seems to have lowered in the priorities of The New School by the end of the 1920s, to such an extent that in the 1926–27 catalogue the educational need is presented in the following manner:

> The New School for Social Research was founded with the object of providing persons of mature intelligence with facilities for instruction and research in the vital problems of contemporary life. It was recognized that there is a great and growing body of men and women, engaged for the most part in the professions, business and industry, who feel the need of continuous and systematic study, chiefly *as a means of keeping mentally fit.* (5, emphasis added)

Should we understand from this quotation that the desires expressed by students were not those which had been central for the founders? Again in 1927–28, we learn that the majority of students "come to the New School primarily to satisfy purely intellectual needs" (5). It would not be true to say that the original objectives have been entirely put aside at this period, but individual and personal development is far higher on the agenda than at the time of the foundation with its emphasis on the need for social improvement.

8.   HAS THE NEW SCHOOL PRESERVED ITS IDEALS?

Over the years, The New School has experienced several periods of great financial difficulty during which questions similar to that posed in 1921 came to a head: Where should the priority lie, in the continuity of the institution or in the perpetuation of its original values? The questions went hand in hand with differences as to the means of implementing these values. Those who took charge at these points and saved the institution affirmed that both objectives had been attained. Others, who left, claimed that the basic values had been traded against institutional survival. Many of those on both sides referred to the history of the institution to prove their point (Schrecker 2014). Still today, we can read on the website in the "About us" section: "The New School is a progressive university with its main campus in New York City."[17]

As was the case with the Chicago School, as described by Lee Harvey (1986, 1987), different myths have grown up around The New School and the people who have been there, either as staff or as students. External accounts, which have been relatively limited, include three books (Rutkoff and Scott 1986; Krohn 1987; Friedlander 2019), a few articles in social scientific reviews (Luckmann 1981; Zolberg and Callemard 1998), and a larger number of news-paper articles, many of which can be found in diverse archives (New School, New York Public Library, Rockefeller, Albany, Nebraska, etc.). Many, but not all, of these accounts rely on facts related by members of the institution and on documents found in the archives, some of which were produced as publicity.

To a great extent, the school seems to have been a guardian of its own history. Johnson, for one, was a great communicator; he includes chapters about The New School in his autobiography (Johnson 1952) and his actions and publicity events were widely diffused in the press. Diverse historical accounts have been included in brochures and later on the website. Thus, many of these myths seem to have been built up inside the school and have become common knowledge, often relayed by people connected with the school. As is the case with the Chicago School, they are in many cases not completely divorced from reality. They have served to reinforce the image of a non-conventional educational establishment whose teaching and research programs are pragmatic in their practical applicability, devoted to forwarding justice and democracy and the making of a better world.

Julia Foulkes (2017) argues that popular ideas about The New School, such as its founding, sometimes attributed to John Dewey, who never in fact left Columbia, the role of famous members of staff, the presence of James Baldwin as a student, or its defense of equality, though coherent with its stated aims have not always been brought about in reality. Publicity campaigns have claimed legitimacy with reference to the links with well-known activists or members of minority groups, such as James Baldwin and Martin Luther King, "both of whom made, literally, one-time appearances on the school's stage" (Foulkes 2017) to mask its shortcomings and the difficulties encountered in the concretization of the values it has defended as principles.

9. CONCLUSION

Two statements can be made then with relation to The New School as a progressive institution. Firstly, we have seen that though the founders and generations of those who succeeded them largely agreed on the values on which The New School was founded, they have differed over time on the best way to put these values into practice. Secondly, the facts related during this chapter illustrate how institutions may be transformed over time, compromising the ideals which inspired their founding in order to ensure their own continuity. This paradox has been discussed, for example, by Everett Hughes (1971). As Foulkes (2017) affirms:

> The New School has increasingly become more university than school. . . At the same time, there has been a renewed interest in the university's past. The valorization of the institution's history and the desire to re-think everything may have more to do with wanting to believe the university remains progressive when, in fact, it has become more conventional than ever.

In this sense, The New School's present use of its history could be described as a means of "saving face" (Goffman 1959; Schrecker 2014).

Ambiguities similar to those found in the history of The New School can be observed in the history of the progressive movement, many of whose members gradually moved away from their progressive ideals and adopted a rather more conservative vision of society. Rechiutti (2007) suggests that those who brought about social change and prevented stagnation were not the original proponents, but the social scientists trained in progressive institutions who fought to transform the principles they had learned into activity and activism in the public realm. In this sense, progressives ideals flourished outside the institutions the "great thinkers" set up to promote them.[18]

NOTES

1. See this volume, Chapters 3 and 4.
2. The name of the school has varied over time; in the rest of this chapter I will use its present name: The New School.
3. *Proposal for an Independent School of Social Science* (1918, 10), New School Archives (NSA).
4. Not all members of the university departments held such activist views of government and many, such as John W. Burgess, founder of the department at Columbia, held a much more *laissez-faire* view of government activity.
5. New School Catalogue (NSC), 1919–20, pages are not numbered.
6. Graduate of Chicago, also present in the preliminary catalogue.
7. NSC, winter (1931), 5, NSA.
8. Clara Woollie Mayer, undated untitled typescript, 4–5.

9.   Clara Woollie Mayer, undated untitled typescript, 10–11 and NSC winter (1931), 5.
10. New School Announcement (1931), NSA.
11. New School Announcement (course catalogue) (1924–25), Announcement Winter Term (1931), NSA.
12. The Rockefeller Foundation financially supported a large number of actions in favor of the "well-being of mankind throughout the world." These actions include numerous projects related to education and health, such as the founding of the General Education Board (GEB) in 1903 before the official incorporation of the Foundation in 1913. The objective of the GEB was to improve education throughout the United States: see https://www.rockefellerfoundation.org/ (accessed 03/23/19).
13. NSC 1919–20 (pages are not numbered).
14. NSC 1924–25 (5).
15. NSC 1919–20, NSA.
16. NSC 1921–22 (19).
17. See https://www.newschool.edu/about/ (accessed April 1, 2019).
18. I would like to thank The New School for Social Research and the members of staff who have helped and encouraged me in many ways during my research. Special thanks go to The New School Archives (NSA) for having opened their doors to me and to Carmen Hendershot who accompanied me throughout my research. Thank you also to the Rockefeller Archives for a grant which covered many of the costs of my first stay in New York and for access to the archives during and after the period of research. The archives at the New York Public Library, the Leo Baeck archives and the archives at the University of Albany were also precious sources of documentation. Last but not least, I would like to express my gratitude to all of those who agreed to share their experience to The New School with me, via interviews and informal exchanges, during my research.

REFERENCES

Bulmer, Martin. 1984. *The Chicago School of Sociology*. Chicago, IL and London: University of Chicago Press.
Chapoulie, Jean-Michel. 2001. *La Tradition Sociologique de Chicago*. Paris: Seuil.
Commons, John R. 1908. "Is Class Conflict in America Growing and Is It Inevitable?." *American Journal of Sociology* 13, no. 6: 756–83.
Croly, Herbert. 1918. "A School of Social Research." *The New Republic* June 8: 167V171.
Foulkes, Julia. 2017. "On James Baldwin and The New School: What It Means to be a Progressive University." Public Seminar, December 28, available at http://www.publicseminar.org/2017/12/on-james-baldwin-and-the-new-school/.
Friedlander, Judith. 2019. *A Light in Dark Times*. New York: Columbia University Press.
Goffman, Erving. 1959. *The Presentation of Self in Everyday Life*. New York: Doubleday Anchor.
Hamington, Maurice. 2018. "Jane Addams." *The Stanford Encyclopedia of Philosophy* (summer 2018 edition), edited by Edward N. Zalta, available at https://plato.stanford.edu/archives/sum2018/entries/addams-jane/.

Harvey, Lee. 1986. "The Myths of the Chicago School." *Quality and Quantity* 20, nos 2–3: 191–217.

Harvey Lee. 1987. *Myths of the Chicago School of Sociology*. Aldershot: Gower Publishing Company.

Hofstadter, Richard and Walter Metzger. 1955. *The Development of Academic Freedom in the United States*. New York: Columbia University Press.

Hughes, Everett C. 1971. *The Sociological Eye*. Chicago, IL: Adline-Atherton.

Johnson, Alvin. 1952. *Pioneer's Progress*. New York: The Viking Press.

Krohn, Claus-Dieter. 1987. *Intellectuals in Exile*. Amherst: University of Massachusetts Press [translated from German by Rita Kimber and Robert Kimber, 1993].

Luckmann, Benita. 1981. "Eine Deutsche Universität im Exil." *Kölner Zeitschrift für Soziologie und Sozialpsychologie* Special issue 23: 427–39.

McCaughey, Robert A. 2003. *Stand Columbia: A History of Columbia University in the City of New York, 1754–2004*. New York: Columbia University Press.

NSA [New School Archives]. 1918. *Proposal for an Independent School of Social Science*. New York: The Marchbanks Press [document attributed to Charles Beard].

Purcell, Edward A. 1995. "Learned Hand: The Jurisprudential Trajectory of an Old Progressive." *Buffalo Law Review* 43, no. 3: 873–926.

Recchiuti, John Lewis. 2007. *Civic Engagement*. Philadelphia: University of Pennsylvania Press.

Rutkoff, Peter M. and Willima B. Scott. 1986. *The New School: A History of the New School for Social Research*. New York: The Free Press.

Schrecker, Cherry. 2014. "Les Enjeux du Passé dans la Construction d'une Façade. La New School for Social Research au Prisme de son Histoire." *Sociologies Pratiques* 29, no. 2: 39– 49.

Thomas, William Isaac and Florian Znaniecki. 1918. *The Polish Peasant in Europe and in America*. Chicago, IL: University of Chicago Press.

Wilson, Edmund. 1931. "Aladdin's Lecture Palace." *The New Republic*, June 10.

Zolberg, Aristide and Agnès Callemard. 1998. "The École Libre at the New School, 1941–1946." *Social Research* 65, no. 4: 921–51.

Zorbaugh, Harvey W. 1929. *The Gold Coast and the Slum*. Chicago, IL: University of Chicago Press.

6. Progressive economic thought in interwar Australia

Alex Millmow

1. INTRODUCTION

As part of its tercentennial celebrations in 1936, Harvard University arranged a week-long Conference of Science and Letters and invited some of the world's leading scholars to attend. Two or three scholars, drawn from the social sciences, were asked to present papers on the state of their discipline. The topic chosen for the economics symposium was "Authority and the Individual." The three chosen speakers were Wesley Clair Mitchell from the National Bureau of Economic Research, Dennis Robertson from Cambridge and, perhaps an unfamiliar name to some, Douglas Copland from the University of Melbourne. Introducing Copland to the podium, Robertson (1940) hailed him as "that skill-ful designer of cunningly mixed cordials for depressed economic systems"; it was a reference to Copland's role in designing an economic recovery package for the depression-hit Australian economy in 1931; a plan which Keynes rec-ognized had saved the economic structure of Australia. It had also put Copland on the world map for economists.

In his address he spoke on *The State and the Entrepreneur*, focusing on the relationship between public and private sectors and of the need for greater social control in the allocation of resources. He argued that the old-style entre-preneurial economy was being replaced by what he called the mixed economy. He took heart that both Robertson and Mitchell had arrived at a similar conclu-sion, namely, that "unfettered enterprise would not produce an economic and social order that would satisfy the aspirations of the common man."[1]

While delighted by the reception, Copland made an interesting observation about his hosts; he was bemused at how resistant American economists were to the idea of state control: "To a visitor from a country which had long ago gone far in this direction the controversies about state control in the US appear a little unreal."[2] In other words, Australia had gone further down the road of economic progressivism than America, not least when it came to economic stabilization and recovery policies.

Apart from being a significant figure in world economics, Copland was Australia's leading interwar economist and also the one most likely to express and advance progressive views. He was also the most internationally well-connected Australian economist, given his appointment as the Australasian representative for the Rockefeller Foundation of New York.

This chapter will focus, therefore, upon Copland as the figurehead of progressive economics within Australia. Systematically this chapter will quickly look over his contributions on economic stabilization and trade theory as well as his evolving economic philosophy. We will also touch upon his role as the great builder of the economics profession in Australia and how it became a distinctive and empirically inclined school of economics. This inclination attracted one of Keynes's most treasured colleagues to settle in Australia. Most importantly, the chapter will explain how Australian economists applied theory and practice to fit in with Australia's unique institutional settings that were compatible with a progressive economics paradigm. Before all this, a brief overview of the main institutional features of Australia at the time of Federation is warranted.

2.   THE AUSTRALIAN FEDERATION

The Commonwealth of Australia was established following Federation in 1901. As a new nation, Australia consisted of six states and two territories. Since its time as a penal settlement, Australia had always had some significant role for the public sector, particularly at the state level. Now, following Federation, there was an added layer of government at the federal level based in Canberra. However, the Commonwealth government's footprint upon the Australian economy was relatively modest since most spending and taxing powers still lay with the states.

Nonetheless, by the 1920s the Commonwealth government had four extra-parliamentary agencies; namely, the Arbitration Court, the Tariff Board, the Commonwealth Bank and the Australian Loan Council. They exercised a "quadripartite control of industrial and financial circumstances" (cited in Brown 1994: 91). The Tariff Board examined issue concerning advice on industry assistance including bounties and duties. The Commonwealth Bank was established in 1912 not just as a people's bank but with aspirations to become, in time, an effective central bank. The Commonwealth Grants Commission was established in 1933 with a formula for distributing the tariff and customs revenue on the basis of each state and territory's taxable capacity. This enshrined the principle of fiscal equalization, or, put simply, that the living standards of every Australian be roughly equal in terms of the provision of government services.

A considerable part of this economic architecture had come about due to the legacy of the 1890s depression which reached a climax in 1893 with a number of bank crashes (Merrett 2013). Indeed, that depression and the class conflict that percolated through it proved to be the "dominant economic influence" behind the establishment of compulsory wage arbitration (Kelly 1992: 7). In 1904 the Commonwealth Parliament established the Court of Conciliation and Arbitration to arbitrate over interstate industrial disputes and bring to an end industrial disorder. The ethos of this new compulsory arbitration system was to deliver equitable wage outcomes or, in Australian parlance, the pursuit of "the fair go." It was true that as a system of national wage regulation, arbitration was the "greatest institutional monument to Australian egalitarianism . . . and social order" (Kelly 1992: 9). In 1907 the Harvester judgement was handed down by Justice H. B. Higgins denoting that a fair and reasonable wage for an unskilled worker would need to be sufficient for him to furnish a wife and three children in basic comfort. Manufacturers paying that wage would not find their tariff protection stripped away from them. This meant that arbitration moved in concert with protection and this dynamic became known as New Protection (Kelly 1992).

In 1910 a Labour government led by Andrew Fisher introduced social security legislation including pensions for those over 65 years of age as well as disability pensions; it also introduced a maternity allowance scheme. These reforms meant that Australia moved toward reclaiming its nineteenth-century status as the working man's paradise. However, by the late 1920s that paradise was becoming economically unsustainable; Australian tariff levels had reached unsustainable levels and put pressure on Australia's export industries. The fact was that Australian wages were way out of kilter with productivity. Arbitration came under some scrutiny; Copland told Justice Higgins: "Arbitration, like any other institution, has its defects but it seems to me to be the height of absurdity and wickedness to insist upon all our troubles being due to this institution."[3]

With Australia's economic fortunes slipping as early as 1928, attention switched to the Australian tariff. The Australian prime minister, S. M. Bruce, set up a committee of economists led by James Brigden to investigate whether protection had indeed gone too far. It was the first time the Commonwealth government had turned to academic economists but Bruce was receptive to the idea of scientific administration. The economists presented their report in 1929 and while concluding that tariff protection had been a good thing for Australia's economic development they cautioned that it had reached its limits. That latter advice was overruled when tariffs were further raised in 1930 as the Great Depression swept over Australia. More stringent action was needed once the Depression hit Australian shores and it fell to Copland to be both the architect and engineer of a plan that would save Australia. Before all that some background on the nature of the Australian economic profession is warranted.

3. THE ESTABLISHMENT OF THE AUSTRALIAN ECONOMICS PROFESSION

In the Roaring Twenties Australian economics was a fledgling, scattered university discipline; a Cinderella science (Cain 1973: 2). Of course, there had been earlier political economy courses in Australia with the first chair in economics established at the University of Sydney. The occupant, Robert Francis Irvine, had also visited America to witness economics instruction there. But it was something of a false start since Irvine never considered himself a full-fledged economist and indeed was suspicious of academic economists and their methodology. He was critical, too, of their preoccupation with static theory and minimizing the role of the state (Goodwin 1966: 563).

According to his biographer, Marjorie Harper (2013), it was Douglas Copland who was the man behind the establishment of the academic economics profession in Australia. In that sense he was more a man of action and institution-builder than he was a theorist. Neville Cain called him "the public relations man of university economics selling its 'practical usefulness' to city men . . . and to politicians" (Cain 1980: 2). The Canadian economist, Wynne Plumptre (1934: 490), marveled at Copland's gifts as an economic theorist, propagandist and financial expert all in one. It was those qualities that led to him being elected as Foundation Dean of the Faculty of Commerce at the University of Melbourne. A year later, in 1925, he proved the driving force, along with the business community, in establishing the Economic Society of Australia and New Zealand along with its flagship journal, the *Economic Record*. It has been argued that the Economic Society, sponsored by the business community, was one means to isolate and suppress radical views from economic heretics (McFarlane 1966: 17; Clark 1974, 1976).

Further recognition of Copland's vitality and position within the local economics profession was revealed when he was appointed as the Australian representative of the Laura Spelman Memorial Fund, with the Rockefeller Foundation of New York. This would allow local economists and social scientists to go overseas to undertake postgraduate study or field work and then return home. Over the next decade the Foundation, under Copland's watch, would allow nearly ten Australian economists to study abroad, mostly at European and British universities. The Foundation allowed Copland to make a world tour of universities to see how economics and commerce were taught elsewhere. This experience allowed him to make contact with a number of leading American economists including John Commons, Wesley Mitchell, Allyn Young and Frank Taussig. Copland also met Herbert Hoover, then Secretary for Commerce under the Coolidge administration, who told him that the American public service was "honeycombed with economists."[4] Copland coveted similar ideas about expanding economics education in his own county so that, in time, Australia's civil servants might be so qualified. At the time Australia's civil service only gave preference to hiring returned servicemen.

4.   THE NATURE OF AUSTRALIAN ECONOMICS DISCOURSE DURING THE INTERWAR PERIOD

The Australian economic profession was Anglocentric in orientation with the works of Edwin Cannan and Alfred Marshall particularly influential; while American economists were on their radar, none were on their pedestal. Herbert Heaton (1926: 245–7) told an American audience that the predominant research interests of Australian economists were the economics of federation, wage fixation, and banking and currency policy. Australia possessed a centralized wage-fixing system that gave an independent but trusted body, the Conciliation and Arbitration Court, a direct lever over wage levels (Copland 1930). Australian economists supported the apparatus, seeing it as another form of control. However, as mentioned, there were growing concerns about the link between tariffs and wage arbitration. Tariff walls had been sanctioned by the fathers of Federation because it advanced the development of the Commonwealth and dispersed a growing population. Economists saw protection as a means to redistribute income from rich landowners to factory workers living in the cities.

The theoretic justification for this was advanced by James Brigden (1925) in the first issue of the *Economic Record*, arguing that labor working in agriculture was subject to diminishing marginal returns whereas, in the manufacturing sector, labor enjoyed constant marginal returns. A tariff for domestic manufactures would therefore induce a flow of labor from agriculture to manufacturing which meant that the marginal product of labor in agriculture would rise. The upshot was that tariff would lift real wages at the expense of agricultural rents (Coleman 2015: 285). This would become internationally known as the Australian case for protection. Later Copland (1931) regaled American audiences about what the Brigden committee had discovered in its deliberations.

The decision to justify protection and indeed compulsory arbitration revealed something about the nature of the Australian economics profession. Besides being progressive by inclination, it showed how it lent itself to giving practical advice rather than engaging in purely scientific research. Lyndhurst Giblin, who held the Ritchie research chair in economics at the University of Melbourne and had been a member of the Brigden committee, reflected upon the values and axioms that characterized the local profession:

> In Australia economists are a peculiar tribe. Rarely are they nourished by the pure milk of the word. Mostly they have been advisers to governments for many years –

permanently or intermittently, publicly or privately. Governments do not love them but are inclined to believe they are honest . . . They are frequently more practical and realistic than businessmen . . . They are resented of course by sectional business interests. The word of complaint or abuse is "academic"; but, in truth, they are the least academic of God's creatures. (cited in Hytten 1960: 154)

Copland corroborated this when he told the American economist, Edmund Day that ". . . it is true to say that the economists in Australia have a common limitation in respect of their training and interest in pure theory."[5] Despite their relative lack of professionalism Australian economists were, however, quick in acclimatizing to new theory and indeed pioneering new theoretical innovations. The policies they advocated during the Depression and thereafter sprang from the very latest theoretical and applied research (Copland 1951: 17).

Besides developing a new theoretic case for protection, Giblin's export multiplier, first articulated in 1930, showed how a fall in export revenue delivered a direct and amplified effect upon domestic output (Cain 1980: 10). This insight gave Australian economists an economy-wide perspective of the costs and benefits of external economic shocks. Giblin's multiplier analysis preceded that of Richard Kahn's (1931) but the Australian was never given due acknowledgment for it. His analysis would prove extremely useful when the Commonwealth confronted an economic test that threatened its very survival.

5. AUSTRALIAN PROGRESSIVISM UNDER THREAT

In 1929 Australia was caught in the twin vice of huge deficits in both its trade account and public accounts. It also had to honor a huge foreign debt at a time when the prices of her major exports, wool and wheat, had plummeted in international markets. Defaulting upon its loans from London was seen as unacceptable. In short, Australia faced an economic plight not unlike Weimar Germany.

The traditional responses of deflation and austerity, along with maintaining the link with sterling, meant unemployment and squalor. It also meant pressure upon wages that would lead to social unrest, especially where rentiers, benefiting from the deflation, increased their hold over consumption. Australian economists agreed that this form of relative cost adjustment was too draconian. One alternative was to defy London and break with sterling.

Facing a political stalemate, the Commonwealth government asked Copland to chair a committee of economists and treasury officials and come up with a plan. It was the economists, however, who did all the formulations. The committee included Giblin, Melville, the chief economist at the Commonwealth Bank, and Edward Shann who held the chair in history and economics at the

University of Western Australia. While the latter two were conservatively inclined, the Melbourne duo of Copland and Giblin were liberal and pragmatic. Together, after much deliberation, they fashioned a plan that would be acceptable to all political parties. Initially called the Copland plan, it was retitled the Premiers' Plan after the six state premiers who were expected to carry out its measures, including proportionate cuts to public expenditure.

It was Copland who had been the first to argue for devaluation, coupled with wage cuts and fiscal consolidation as a way out of the economic trap. That policy, "a middle way" between inflation and deflation also had a strong emphasis on sharing the loss across all economic classes, including rentiers and landlords. These measures would also allow Australia to find a more appropriate relationship between her export prices and domestic cost structure. Devaluation would give Australia's export- and import-competing sectors a fillip allowing the country to trade out of its difficulties. It was Copland himself who drew further controversy and opprobrium upon himself by giving expert evidence before the Arbitration Court supporting the employers' call for a ten percent wage cut for all Australian workers. Keynes communicated his support when he received an article from Copland on his proposed comprehensive package of measures for the Australian economy: "I only hope that you, and those who are thinking and working with you, will be able to steer your country along a wise middle course between the impracticable demands of the too orthodox and the dangerous demands of the too heretic."[6] Copland's recipe of economic adjustment was inspired by Keynes's *Treatise on Money* dealing with an open economy's adjustment to disequilibrium. It also drew upon Copland's own work, *Credit and Currency Control* (1930). His scheme entailed money wage cuts coupled with devaluation and some Treasury bill finance to tide over budget deficits but also to slightly raise the price level. The cuts to government expenditure were premised on the belief that Commonwealth and state budgets had to be balanced before business confidence would return.

Given all these drastic adjustments, Copland reminded Keynes that Australia was lucky that a Labour government had carried the program through since it would never have been achieved had the conservatives been in power.[7] When Copland wrote another note to the *Economic Journal* informing its readers about the latest developments in Australia, Keynes replied: "You seemed to have been working wonders, and it has been very gratifying to see what a prominent part the Economists have been able to play."[8]

Frank Taussig also saluted him: "Your own part gives one hope that after all, we economists are not so entirely useless as some of the critics allege."[9] Two years later Copland told Taussig that the Australian economists' ingenuity in masterminding their country's economic rehabilitation was only one part of the story:

> It has been uncommonly successful, but it has been greatly helped by a run of good seasons. Whether we shall continue . . . depends more upon the courage we show and the psychology of the people than upon the actual economic efforts themselves. If it succeeds it will at least establish the principle that 'intelligent economic control' is capable of handling a difficult situation with great advantage to all concerned.[10]

Copland told Irving Fisher about how much latitude the economists had been given: "our economists and monetary advisors knew pretty well what they wanted, but I am quite sure that neither the Treasury authorities nor the Central Bank quite appreciated the nature and importance of the experiment they were conducting."[11]

Copland therefore always took an extremely positive view of what the package actually achieved and the role of economists in carrying it through. He was aware that politicians were prepared to embrace the cover of "expert" advice as their ambit of action was constrained. Nonetheless, no other country had done as much as Australia in its economic readjustment to the Depression (Copland 1931: 549). "Australia," he claimed, "came out of the depression earlier than most other countries because of the approach that was made under the Premiers' Plan."[12]

The educational aspect of the Premiers' Plan was interesting; by departing from classical economic prescriptions, the Australian economists were far ahead of their peers overseas. They had engaged in a nationwide effort to bring some social equity into economic planning with every class enduring a cut in income. Keynes was impressed at how Australian economists laid stress on the facts and then tried to fit the theory to the facts. That mixture of pragmatism and "a certain native wisdom" had saved Australian progressivism from dissolution (Cain 1982).

The last word in all this adulation of Australia should go to Keynes who put out a statement to members of the Royal Economic Society promoting subscriptions to the *Economic Record* and, in doing so, praising the achievement of the Australian economists behind the Premiers' Plan:

> Experience seems to show that when countries are plunged into economic difficulties they either, as a rule, do nothing whatever or else proceed to extravagant extremes. The advice of those counsellors who believe that reasonable remedial measures within the existing structure of society will not be in vain are generally ignored. But Australia has given the rest of us a lesson in accepting and positively carrying into effect advice which was experimental and unorthodox and at the same time a severe dose to swallow down, yet was not violent or revolutionary or destructive. We all know how satisfactory the results have been. Their colleagues in the rest of the world are envious and proud of Australia's economists who have not

only been successful in getting their advice accepted but have been shown, in the event, to have been lacking neither in practical wisdom nor in scientific insight.[13]

6.   BASKING IN THE LIMELIGHT

Despite Copland's rhetoric and showmanship about the united voice of Australian economists, not all were supportive of pragmatic intervention or the pursuit of economic equality. Edward Shann was a classical liberal who raged against the forces of economic restriction, particularly arbitration and protection. He was apprehensive, too, of the encroachment of government into economic affairs and of the idea of more public works. Melville agreed, consoling Shann with the thought that "can we really expect a democracy in a hurry to spend its way out of depression, to exercise any discrimination in the works on which it spends its money? To encourage Governments to spend money on public works is, I think, to encourage them to spend it more or less indiscriminately."[14] These two voices against progressivism faded away; Shann died early from misadventure while Melville became consumed by the affairs of the Commonwealth Bank.

Exhausted from his rigors, Copland enjoyed a sabbatical in 1933 where he regaled the world about Australia's achievement. At Cambridge he was invited to give the Alfred Marshall Memorial Lectures where he spoke on Australia's readjustment and rehabilitation from depression. They were subsequently published as *Australia in the World Crisis 1929–1933* (Copland 1934). The book aroused such attention in America that a second print run for the American market was justified. The New Dealers and a group called The Committee for the Nation would give its author a warm welcome when he visited America in November 1933. Drawing on what Keynes was then saying, Copland (1934: 145) admitted that the lack of a stronger stimulus in the form of public works during 1931–32 had been an error. He remained adamant, however, that the Australian focus upon adjusting relative costs "was a mistake in degree rather than principle" (Copland 1951).

Besides meeting "the right people" at Harvard and elsewhere, Copland gave lectures on Australian monetary policy at Cornell.[15] In his own mind Copland was intrigued by Roosevelt's "unorthodox" attempts at recovery but complained that he could not "get any line on the point of view of American economists" in tackling the slump. Copland felt it was critical for the American administration to engage in public spending which would deliver a fillip to the global economy.[16] In fact, he concluded that the United States at the time did not have much experience in depression policy-making which would be useful to Australia.

Having seen at first hand the breakdown in attempts to revive global trade, Copland launched a campaign via syndicated newspaper articles to maintain

Australian tariff levels. To some this was an apostasy since Copland earlier had led the campaign for some degree of tariff revision and, further back, had started his career as a committed free trader.[17] Arguing, à la Keynes, that the circumstances had changed, Copland defended his new position stating that tariff protection had made a substantial contribution to Australian economic welfare. Economic nationalism was the new mantra and he criticized those for whom "The tariff problem is unfortunately a test of faith and not of reasoning for most people."[18]

The work done by this small band of economists both during the Premiers' Plan and, later, in the mobilization of economics expertise that would prepare Australia's war effort from 1939 won high recognition when Prime Minister Robert Menzies (1942) noted how "[i]n the economic history of the last fifteen years nothing will be more notable than the rise to influence and authority of the professional economist."

7.   AN ADMIRING VISITOR

After Copland visited Harvard in 1936 he journeyed to the other Cambridge in England, intent upon recruiting an economist to come out to Melbourne to do some teaching. It was Colin Clark, who Keynes considered "a bit of a genius" at economics statistics, who took up Copland's invitation (Patinkin 1976: 231). He was already interested in Australia because they had an unemployment benefits scheme. As a lecturer in statistics at Cambridge, Clark was asked to teach the same in Melbourne. It went well, with Clark relishing the informality of Australian life. Copland was delighted, telling Keynes how "Colin Clark is a great success here and we would like to keep him."[19] When Keynes heard this he wrote back: "I hope very much you will fail in taking away Colin Clark from us. He is too much needed here."[20] Copland replied with a tinge of prophecy: "At the moment you need not fear for Colin Clark. He is going to Western Australia for part of the next academic year prior to returning to Cambridge. In the course of time, however changes may occur in the personnel of the Schools of Economics and I should not be surprised if Clark turned his eyes to Australia, if a suitable opportunity occurred."[21]

For his own part, Clark who regarded Keynes as one of his mentors told him that he was having "an excellent time" in Australia "where economics ranks after cricket as a topic of interest." It was, however, the latter part of Clark's letter that unsettled Keynes: "I am reaching the conclusion I want to stay in Australia. People have minds which are not closed to new truths . . . and with all the mistakes Australia has made in the past, I still think she may show the world, in economics, politics, education, and technology in the next twenty years" (Keynes 1983: 799).

At the time Clark was an ardent socialist and British Labour party member who had run three times, unsuccessfully, for a parliamentary seat. Before Keynes could intercede from Cambridge, Clark decided to take up a job offer from the Queensland premier, John Forgan Smith, as an economic advisor as well as the state statistician. Clark defended his career switch, telling Keynes:

> I thought it was too remarkable an opportunity to be missed for putting economics into practice. My job is to advise the Premier on practically everything connected with economic matters, to plan the public works programmes, and to manage the state statistical office . . . I believe you yourself would have thought twice before rejecting an opportunity like that for putting some of your conclusions into practice. (Keynes 1983: 801)

It would be Clark's brief to provide the statistical analysis and theoretical argument to underpin the state's economic strategy. Clark explained to the local press why given his new-found eminence in statistical economics and national accounting he had decided to turn his back on Cambridge:

> Australia was a country where economics was being developed as a practical science and not as a server of theoretical speculations . . . Australian people deserve credit for their keen and intelligent interest in economics. I have not been in any other country where the people and the press discuss economic questions so widely and intelligently. And I think Australia will be one of the first countries to solve the very complex economic problems that confront the world.[22]

A few years later Keynes told Clark, "we have not totally forgiven you for your desertion" and asked him to reconsider coming back to Cambridge.[23] In response, Clark gave a fuller explanation why Queensland, and indeed Australia, had secured his services:

> When you leave England for Australia you get a strange feeling you have somehow jumped ten years into the future, and when you come to Queensland you jump ten years further. It will be twenty years before Britain is as socially advanced as Queensland, however high the Labour Party's aspirations. Queensland is a predominantly rural and small enterprise economy, with a very equalitarian distribution of income and property, very generous social services, compulsory Trade Unionism, and all matters of wages, hours and working conditions judicially controlled by the Arbitration Court, which now has such prestige that both sides always accept its decision. Unlike the other states, Queensland is practically free of strikes. Once a year the Arbitration Court reviews all the statistics of the state, hears arguments from both sides and then determines the basic wage which controls all other wage rates. Queensland has a more or less permanent Labour Government. Between 1915 and 1920 they undertook a series of strange experiments in State ownership. The result was to leave the Queensland Labour Party much more intellectually mature than the British Labour Party or the other Australian labour parties. Many of these

ventures continue today as producer co-operatives, which is the form of most of the key industries in Queensland.[24]

Here was the defining truth that Australia was still a beacon of economic pro-gressivism. Another attraction was the way Australian economists went about their work, practicing their art to be "of practical value to the human race . . . with a respect for observed facts in preference to long chains of theoretical reasoning" (Clark 1940: ix).

In August 1938 Clark was invited to give the Joseph Fisher Lecture at the University of Adelaide. It was entitled "Australian Economic Progress against a World Background." In concluding his lecture he paid tribute to his new colleagues and voiced optimism about Australia's future:

> As a returning migrant from the old world, and knowing many European countries, I would say that, other than Sweden, I know of no country in the world for which I have such high hopes as I have for Australia, as a country in which the resources of economic science should suffice to counter depression. In Australian universities, economics is taught and studied as a true applied science, seeking practical remedies for depression and other ills which confront us, eschewing on the other hand the theoretical scholasticism of European universities, or any partisan adherence on the other. In no other country is the public so well informed and so critical on economic questions as in Australia. (Clark 1938: 38)

Despite overtures to return to England, Clark would remain in Australia with his young family.

7.   CONCLUSION

Australia was known as an early exponent of pioneering comprehensive welfare and assisted immigration, building a nation that espoused equality and containing class divisions. This chapter has shown the role Australian econo-mists played in enabling that society to come to fruition. When the Australian economics profession was established it gave approval to both protection and wage arbitration. That same band of economists formulated a package of measures to mitigate the effects of the Great Depression upon Australia. Those measures, built around the theme of spreading the burden of adjustment, helped to preserve the progressive society Australia then was.

NOTES

1. Harvard Notes, 1936, Faculty of Economics and Commerce (FECC), University of Melbourne Archives (UMA).
2. Harvard Material, 1936, FECC, UMA.
3. Copland to Higgins, July 6, 1928, FECC, UMA.

4.   Douglas Copland travel diary, entry May 29, 1927, *Copland Papers*, National
     Library of Australia (NLA).
5.   D. B. Copland to E. D. Day, April 20, 1928, FECC, UMA.
6.   Keynes to Copland, November 19, 1930, *Copland Papers*, NLA.
7.   Copland to Keynes, July 3, 1932, *Copland Papers*, NLA.
8.   Keynes to Copland, August 12, 1931, *Copland Papers*, NLA.
9.   Taussig to Copland, October 19, 1931, FECC, UMA.
10. D. B. Copland to F. Taussig, February 28, 1933, FECC, UMA.
11. Copland to Irving Fisher, November 23, 1935, FECC, UMA.
12. *Sir Douglas Copland Oral Transcript*, 2019b: NLA.
13. Statement by Keynes, April 11, 1934, *Sir Douglas Copland Papers*, 2019a: NLA.
14. L. G. Melville to E. O. G. Shann, November 27, 1934, Reserve Bank of Australia
     (RBA) archives, 2019, GGM-35-2.
15. W. S. Robinson to D. B. Copland, August 28, 1933, NLA.
16. D. B. Copland to T. Balogh, October 23, 1934, NLA.
17. "The Tariff; Burdens and Benefits: The Need for Revision," August 17, 1931, *The
     Argus*.
18. "Is our Tariff a Handicap? Effects on Australia's recovery," August 1934,
     University of Melbourne pamphlet.
19. Copland to Keynes, September 14, 1937, FECC, UMA.
20. Keynes to Copland, October 28, 1937, FECC, UMA.
21. Copland to Keynes, November 1937, FECC, UMA.
22. "Depression can be avoided says Colin Clark, new industry bureau chief," May 6,
     1938, *The Brisbane Telegraph*.
23. Keynes to Clark, February 28, 1940, *Clark Papers*, Clark (2019), University of
     Queensland.
24. Clark to Keynes, November 10, 1941, *Clark Papers*, Clark (2019), University of
     Queensland.

REFERENCES

Brigden, James Bristock. 1925. "The Australian Tariff and the Standard of Living."
    Economic Record 1, no. 1: 29–49.
Brown, Nicholas. 1994. *Governing Prosperity*. Melbourne: Cambridge University
    Press.
Cain, Neville. 1973. "Political Economy and the Tariff: Australia in the 1920's."
    Australian Economic Papers 12, no. 20: 1–20.
Cain, Neville. 1980. "Monetary Thought in the Twenties and its Depression Legacy:
    An Australian Illustration." *Australian Economic History Review* 20, no. 1: 1–27.
Cain, Neville. 1982. "Recovery Policy in Australia 1930–33: Certain Native Wisdom."
    Working Papers in Economic History, no. 1, Canberra: Australian National
    University.
Clark, Colin. 1938. "Australian Economic Progress against a World Background."
    Joseph Fisher Lecture in Commerce, Adelaide.
Clark, Colin. 1940. *The Conditions of Economic Progress*. London: Macmillan.
Clark, Colin. 2019. *Colin Clark Papers*. Fryer Library: University of Queensland.
Clark, David L. 1974. "The Great Depression in Australia: Some Controversial
    Aspects." *Economics* 9, no. 3: 45–53.

Clark, David L. 1976. "The Keynesian Revolution and the Battle of the Plans." *Economics* 11, no. 2: 22–30.

Coleman, William. 2015. "A Young Tree Dead? The Story of Economics in Australia and New Zealand." In *Routledge Handbook of the History of Global Economic Thought*, ed. Vincent Barnett. London: Routledge, pp. 281–93.

Copland, Douglas B. 1930. *Credit and Currency Control*. Melbourne: Melbourne University Press.

Copland, Douglas B. 1931. "A Neglected Phase of Tariff Controversy." *Quarterly Journal of Economics*, 45, no. 2: 289–308.

Copland, Douglas B. 1934. *Australia in the World Crisis 1929–1933*. Cambridge: Cambridge University Press.

Copland, Douglas B. 1951. *Inflation and Expansion: Essays on the Australian Economy*. Melbourne: Cheshire.

Copland, Douglas B. 2019a. *Sir Douglas Copland Papers*. National Library of Australia, Canberra.

Copland, Douglas B. 2019b. *Sir Douglas Copland Oral Transcript*. National Library of Australia, Canberra.

Faculty of Economics and Commerce Papers (FECC): Relating to Professor D. B. Copland 1928–1939. 2019. University of Melbourne Archives.

Goodwin, Craufurd D.W. 1966. *Economic Enquiry in Australia*. Durham, NC: Duke University Press.

Harper, Marjorie. 2013. *Douglas Copland: Scholar, Economist, Diplomat*. Melbourne: Melbourne University Press.

Heaton, Herbert. 1926. "Progress and Problems of Australian Economists." *American Economic Review*, 16, no. 2: 235–48.

Hytten, Torliev. 1960. "Giblin as an Economist." In *Giblin: The Scholar and the Man*, ed. Douglas B. Copland. Melbourne: Cheshire, pp. 153–63.

Kahn, Richard F. 1931. "The relation of home investment to unemployment." *Economic Journal* 41, no.162: 173–198.

Kelly, Paul. 1992. *The End of Certainty*. Sydney: Allen and Unwin.

Keynes, John Maynard. 1983. *Volume XXII of the Collected Works of John Maynard Keynes, Economic Articles and Correspondence*, ed. Donald Moggridge. London: Macmillan and Cambridge University Press for the Royal Economic Society.

McFarlane, Bruce. 1966. *Professor Irvine's Economics in Australian Labour History 1913–1933*. Canberra: Australian Society for the Study of Labour History.

Menzies, Robert G. 1942. "The Australian Economy during War." *Joseph Fisher Lecture in Commerce*, Adelaide.

Merrett, David T. 2013. "The Australian Bank Crashes of the 1890s Revisited." *Business History Review* 87, no. 3: 407–29.

Patinkin, Don. 1976. "Keynes and Econometrics: On the Interaction between the Macroeconomic Revolutions of the Interwar Period." *Econometrica* 44, no. 6: 1091–123.

Plumptre, Arthur FitzWalter Wynne. 1934. "Review of Australia in the World Crisis 1929–1933 by Douglas B. Copland." *American Economic Review* 24, no. 3: 490–91.

Reserve Bank of Australia. 2019. *Lesley Melville Papers*. Reserve Bank of Australia Archives, Sydney.

Robertson, Dennis H. 1940. *Essays in Monetary Theory*. London: Staples Press.

7. Repeated disappearance: why was progressivism forgotten in Japanese economics?

Hidetomi Tanaka

1. INTRODUCTION

One cannot fully comprehend the history of Japanese economic thought without understanding the impact of Progressivism on Japanese economists and social reformers.

Here, Progressivism is the social reform movement and its philosophy that grew in the United States from the 1890s to the 1920s. From the viewpoint of economics, Progressivism assumes that the market would not function as an autonomous self-adjusting system if proper laws or institutions were not in place.

Contemporaneous Japanese economists and social activists were aware of some of the new waves of social reform in the United States. The achievements of Progressive economists such as Richard T. Ely, John R. Commons, Henry R. Seager, Irving Fisher, Frank Taussig, Frank A. Fetter and others were known, and their representative works had been translated into Japanese. The Association for Social Policy Studies, which was the first academic society of economists in Japan, was modeled on the German Association for Social Policy Studies. Its main members were also those who had studied abroad in Germany. Considering that the American Economic Association, which was led by Progressivism economists, was also modeled on the German Association, both the Japanese and American Economic Associations could be considered twins with the German Association as a mother figure. However, exchanges between academic societies in Japan and the United States were not officially held at that time. In addition, the Japan Association for Social Policy Studies disappeared in the middle of the 1920s.

Looking at individual economics contributors, Katayama Sen (1859–1933), the labor-management cooperative activist that studied under Ely, turned to Marxism soon after political repression in Japan. Kawakami Hajime

(1879–1946), who was the pioneer at the time, was actively trying to translate and explain Progressive economics in his writings. However, Kawakami also turned to Marxism, which attracted both attention and praise in some quarters, but also resulted in his being ignored by American economists. Kawakami's rival, Fukuda Tokuzo (1874–1930), incorporated the economics of Fisher and Fetter into his system but, following his death, his economics, with the exception of some of his disciples, were soon forgotten. The fact that Fukuda himself did not succeed in systematizing the Progressivism policy view was also the cause of the demise of his significance. In short, the influence of American Progressive economics has disappeared several times in Japan, and as a result, it has not attracted much attention in Japanese history of economic thought.

The main purpose of this chapter is to confirm the effects of Progressivism and its disappearance in Japanese economics by following the relationship between the Japan Association for Social Policy Studies and Katayama Sen, the relationship between Kawakami Hajime's acceptance of American economists and his shift to Marxism, and the relationship between Fukuda Tokuzo's Welfare Economics and the liquidization principle. It also points out that the effects of repeated disappearances of Progressivism in Japanese economics continues to give rise to a new deal-like stimulus to policy and reflation policy, and misunderstandings in building a system that allows the market to function properly.

2.   JAPAN ASSOCIATION FOR SOCIAL POLICY STUDIES AND PROGRESSIVISM

Policy debates using Western economic knowledge were already underway in the first half of the Meiji Era. However, the economic policy debate from the perspective of social reforms took shape only after the rise of the labor movement and the growing criticism of the poor employment environment of female workers at spinning mills.

The organization of Japanese economics professionals originally started as a social policy society. In 1897, the Association for Social Policy Studies (ASPS) began with a small number of scholars who had returned from studying abroad. The ASPS was actively involved in labor issues, debates over trade liberalization, immigration and the urban environment until its natural disappearance in the 1920s. In particular, the ASPS became active after the Russo-Japanese War (1904–05). In conventional form, it proceeded in a public report and question/answer format while involving scholars, policy makers, business people, and so on.

The Japan ASPS was modeled on its sister organization in Germany, the main destination for those who studied abroad. The German ASPS aimed to initiate reforms within the framework of the existing system, influenced by its leader, Gustav Schmoller's new historical school. Specifically, the main point was to engage in institutional reform to allow the labor market to function smoothly with the cooperation of both capitalists and workers. The reforms of institutions included the right to organize workers and the introduction of a health insurance system. Many members of the German ASPS emphasized the economic consequences that would follow from an autonomously functioning market operating in a well-developed system. Schmoller, Lujo Brentano, Werner Sombart and others were major members of the German ASPS.

The American Economic Association, led by some Progressivism economists such as Ely, was also established using the German ASPS as a model. However, there was no exchange between Japanese and American academic societies.

The Japan ASPS further emphasized that reforms of the market mechanism should take place within the existing social order. The ASPS prospectus of 1899 gives a good representation of the basic character of the association:

> We oppose liberalism, because extreme selfishness and unrestricted free competition widen the disparity between rich and poor. We also oppose socialism. It destroys economic organization and the extinction of capitalists is harmful to the progress of the nation. Our principle is to maintain the current privately owned economic organization and its economic order. Within the scope of this principle, it aims to prevent class antagonism and to harmonize society with personal activities and national power. (Shakai Seisaku Gakkai 1978: 37–8)

The denial of "socialism" here was a particularly important point of view. The repression of the labor movement in 1897 urged the socialist movement in the middle of the Meiji Era into the opposite directions of more radical system reform and a labor–management cooperation line. It is particularly important that Kanai Noburu (1865–1933), a professor at Tokyo Imperial University who was the leader of the ASPS, argued with Katayama Sen in a public debate in 1899.

Katayama was enlightened by Ely's Christian social reforms while studying in the United States.[1] At that time, Ely contributed a discussion on social issues to the Christian Union, and his *Social Aspects of Christianity* had just been published (Ely 1889). Katayama read both works and was strongly influenced by Ely's views on poverty and labor issues, and his belief, propounded in *Social Aspects*, that the commandment to love your neighbor would create a fairer society. In particular, the 1891 Homestead strike and the 1894 Pullman strike, which both occurred when Katayama was in the United States, reinforced the importance of labor issues in his thinking.

Katayama's Christian social reform beliefs were further reinforced by observing the social work of the Salvation Army in Britain. After returning to Japan, Katayama formed a trade union meeting (Rodo Kumiai Kiseikai) with Takano Fusataro (1869–1904), who was supported by the American Federation of Labor (AFL) led by Samuel Gompers. Based on this trade union meeting, they established the first trade union movement in Japan, the Steel Workers Union (1897), followed by the Nippon Steel Correction Association (1898), and the Letterpress Workers Union (1899). Both Katayama and Takano advocated modest labor market reforms aimed at a labor–capital cooperation route. However, the government at that time discerned a sense of crisis in the excitement of the labor movement. Therefore, it enforced the Security Police Law (1900), and dismantled these labor unions. Takano died young in the United States, greatly affected by the government repression of the labor movement. Katayama also abandoned the traditional labor–capital cooperation route by affirming the right of workers to strike – gradually adopting a more radical stance, he eventually became a Marxist.

Kanai was one of the earliest students to study economics at Tokyo Imperial University. After graduation, he studied in Germany, where he attended a lecture by Schmoller and some of his colleagues from the German Historical School. During a stay in England, he also conducted a survey of poverty in the East End of London. After returning to Japan, he took lectures at Tokyo Imperial University and became a leading figure in Japanese economics.

Kanai advocated social policy from the viewpoint of labor–management cooperation, but Katayama criticized this relationship as one between "master and slave." Katayama's own socialist position was still to deny the labor–management cooperation line at this stage and aggressively launch a strike. On the other hand, the ideas of Kotoku Shusui's group (he was regarded as a representative socialist), were anarchist, and affirmed terrorism that would destroy the regime. The differences between Katayama's and Kotoku's positions were obvious, but were not considered so from the perspectives of central members like Kanai and his colleagues.

Kanai's social policy represented the typical framework of the ASPS. Taking social policy as the maximization of national interests, individual benefits depended on national interests. The denial of Katayama's labor–management cooperation line and the active use of strike were distinct from the mainstream tenets of the Association. In fact, at the first meeting of the Japan ASPS, Takano Fusataro, who invented labor–management cooperation as a pioneering stance of Japanese social policy, was sent an academic compliment. However, there was no room for a positive evaluation of Katayama-like practical activities in the ASPS.

The industrialization of the Japanese economy reached full-scale development after the Sino-Japanese War. Exports to developed countries were strong and received government protection and assistance. Industrial sectors such as spinning, shipbuilding, steel and machinery production expanded rapidly. With this modern sector takeoff, the government and modern capitalists had become interested in the development and securing of a modern workforce. However, typically, there was a factory law problem.

There was no legal system to protect workers until the establishment of the Factory Law (1911). The factory law mainly focused on the prohibition of child labor under 10 years of age, restrictions on long working hours for girls under 15 years of age, and the provision of holidays and breaks. The majority of factory workers received limited protection, such as administrative supervision for safety and health matters, the business owner's assistance and responsibility for occupational accidents, wage payments and employment rules. The factory law itself was first drafted in 1897 by the government of the Imperial Parliament. However, plans for the new legislation were repeatedly delayed due to the outbreak of the Sino-Japanese War, resistance from the capitalist class, and ignorance of politicians. It is noteworthy that the government was trying to promote a worker protection policy in order to develop and secure the workforce while suppressing the labor movement under the Security Police Law. This is a Japanese style of carrot-and-stick policy.

That being said, there was general agreement between the national government and the ASPS of the need for the establishment of a factory law. The theme of the 1907 first meeting of the ASPS was "Factory Law and Labor Issues."

The purpose of social policy is to define the personality of all people "through the nation." Kanai and other members of the ASPS aimed to eliminate class conflict between capitalists and workers in the interests of the whole country, and then to complete personality as a member of the nation. They also tried to contribute to the development of national culture through social policy, in which both individuals and society themselves were inextricably linked with the state. In this sense, their social policy should be considered a national organic theory. Their social policy was not for society or individuals, but for the state.

It was from the next generation of economists that a different view to Kanai-like social policy emerged in earnest in Japan, epitomized by Kawakami Hajime, who is particularly notable in the context of the importance of American economics in the Progressive Era.

3.   KAWAKAMI HAJIME AS A TYPICAL PROGRESSIVIST IN JAPAN AND ITS DISAPPEARANCE

Kawakami Hajime (1879–1946) was a multi-faceted economist, although at times his nature was so complex that it gave people a contradictory impression.[2] Kawakami was famous as the representative Marxist economist of Japan. In Marxism, it is common to deny religious truth. However, Kawakami defined himself as believing in "unification of religious and scientific truth." His position seemed likely to deviate from the "common sense" of Marxism. Sumiya Etuji named Kawakami as a "special Marxist" or "Kawakami Marxist" (Tanaka 2001). No one is supposed to be "Kawakami Marxist" other than Kawakami Hajime, and no Marxist economist has actually sought "unification of religious and scientific truth" after Kawakami. And in the history of Japanese economics as well as Marxian economics, Kawakami Hajime is in a position of isolation due to his turbulent way of life, passionate spirituality and ideological plurality.

As for Kawakami's multi-facetedness, one should first consider the spiritual circumstances of his hometown of Yamaguchi Prefecture. From an early age, he was influenced by Yoshida Shoin (1830–1859) and cultivated a spirit of passion and nationalism. This spiritual nationalism remained throughout his life as a non-selfish attitude of devoting himself to his home country. Many scholars have described this aspect as "the spirit of seeking."

This spiritual nationalism moved to an absolute non-selfish position when Kawakami went to Tokyo and came under the influence of Christian Uchimura Kanzo (1861–1930). Kawakami had donated all of his personal belongings to the Salvation Army after he attended a lecture on the Ashio Copper Mine environmental disaster. Also, after graduation, despite gaining popularity in journalism, he abandoned his fame and joined an emerging religious organization to try to gain absolute non-selfish enlightenment. Through these experiences and ideological fights, Kawakami gradually became himself a "general public organ," that is, he was only a means with a mission to fundamentally reform society. He seemed to have realized that he had received such a mission from Heaven.

So how should society be reformed? Kawakami became a faculty member at Kyoto Imperial University and engaged in economics research. His purpose was first to solve social poverty. He began by learning the doctrine of the German Historical School, which was the mainstream economics in Japan at the time. He eventually gained a position at an academic society as an introducer of American Progressive Era economics. His understanding of Marxism was initially deepened through Seligman's translation. The fact that Kawakami Hajime absorbed the thoughts of the German Historical School, American neoclassical economics and Marxian economics one after another, supported his ideological multi-facetedness from economic viewpoints.

Dividing Kawakami's career into two periods, the first is prominent for the introduction of American economists and many works based on them. Kawakami's immersion in US economics is unique because many Japanese economists were influenced by European economics such as in the UK, France and Germany. Especially from the beginning of the twentieth century to the early 1910s, it can be said that the Progressive Era's economics was almost exclusively imported to Japan by Kawakami.

He actively translated works by Seligman (1902), Fisher (1906, 1907), Fetter (1905), and briefly introduced works by Ely, Laughlin, Commons, Patten and others. Based on the work of Taussig (1911) and Fisher (1910), he lectured at Kyoto Imperial University and later compiled his thoughts in *Economic Principles* (Kawakami 1983 [1913]). *Economic Principles* comprises four chapters in total: an introduction, demand and price, supply and price, and money and general prices. In particular, the utility, marginal utility diminishing law, and the relationship between marginal utility and demand were briefly summarized. Kawakami particularly learned the translation of utility and its meaning from Taussig's and Fisher's economic writings. There was a dispute with Fukuda Tokuzo about the translation and meaning of the utility, and there are multiple rounds of letters between Kawakami and Fisher. In terms of content, they are mainly clerical relating to the translation of Fisher's work and the preface of the original author, although Kawakami's translations of Fisher's two works (Fisher 1906; Fisher and Fisk 1915) are also mentioned. I would like to pay attention to the latter in two ways. One is the appreciation of Fisher's health promotion method in the context of John Ruskin. Kawakami's economics was greatly influenced by Ruskin and added a humanitarian perspective. Another point is that Kawakami introduced eugenics here. This is examined later in the chapter.

From an economic point of view, the biggest influence American economics had on Kawakami was related to Fisher's monetary theory, a subject on which Takagi Senjirou and others actively wrote translations and explanatory papers in Japan. Kawakami, unlike those scholars, severely criticized Fisher's monetary theory in his *Gold, Credit and Prices* of 1913 (Kawakami 1982 [1913]). He questioned Fisher's theory of monetary quantity, which is based on a stable relationship between the circulation of money and the current account balance. Kawakami insisted that it was doubtful that the central bank in particular was able to control the money supply. Kawakami rather emphasized a Credit Channel and thought that crediting a bank would affect employment, wages and prices. In addition, he emphasized that rising prices itself was not a problem, but that they made peoples' lives harder by lowering workers' real wages. After this price controversy, Kawakami's perspective shifted to distribution theory to improve workers' living difficulties.

Changes in Kawakami's interest in distribution theory were revealed in his masterpiece *The Poverty Story* (Kawakami 1917). This economic story was written at the beginning of the twentieth century based on Kawakami's awareness of the crisis that "poverty in abundance," a common scene in Europe and the United States, would soon come to Japan. "Poverty in abundance" here refers to the situation of people in advanced countries who fall into "economic shortages." Kawakami defines economic shortage as "being poor in the sense of not enjoying the necessities of life." Moreover, his problem consciousness was that this kind of poverty was steadily progressing, hidden behind the rich appearances of the city. He named the boundary of the economic situation in which people could not live a life as a "poverty line," which included food, clothing, housing, fuel and miscellaneous expenses. In this sense, the poverty line is the "minimum cost of living expenses." There is no doubt that the problem of being "poor" in Kawakami's time can be related to the welfare philosophy corresponding to today's national minimum wage. At the same time, his purpose was to propose a solution to why many people who are below the "poverty line" exist in rich economic powers.

It is interesting to examine why *The Poverty Story* has the word "story" in the title. Of course, it was not written as non-fiction. It is an academic work, but it is also a "work" that shows the true value of the "literary man Kawakami Hajime." The work is written in a magnificent style, with extensive references to ancient and modern East–West classics and historical materials. His work is profound and gives readers a warning from a civilizational perspective. In that sense, "the story of poverty" may have been more appropriate than "the economics of poverty."

The warp weaving this "story" is a life-history perspective, and the weft is East–West culture theory. In the former, Kawakami first explains the society of ants, then goes back to the primitive era and explains the origin and characteristics of humans. Advanced progress can be observed in the ant society. But humans have had one unique ability since primitive times. Kawakami points out that it is the use of tools. As the use of tools progresses, human society has gained a richness that is completely different from ant society. The horizontal thread reflects the experience of studying abroad several years ago. This is a comparison of East and West cultures in which Japan is not based on individualism and has a nation-centered "national character" while Europe and the United States are individual-centered "personality" countries. The warp (biological perspective) and weft (East and West culture theory) add interesting features to the analysis of "poverty" in *The Poverty Story*.

Mankind has gained productivity that is incomparable to other creatures through the use of tools, and it seemed that it was able to realize richness. However, in reality, there are many people currently in Western countries that are below the "poverty line." Why? According to Kawakami, the daily necessities of the poor have become scarce and their prices have increased due to the luxury lifestyles of the wealthy. In other words, the economic disparity itself is creating Kawakami's "poor." Kawakami's expectation was that the "poor" that luxury brings would soon come to Japan. The specific poverty alleviation proposed by Kawakami was mainly an ethical requirement for the wealthy to quit their luxury existence.

From his perspective of East–West culture, this measure for "poor" was different in Europe and Japan. European and American policy was designed to save the lives of individuals. On the other hand, Japan would be required to eliminate the "poor" from the nation so as not to damage healthy people who contribute to the growth of national power. Kawakami believed that healthy and productive people were the foundation of the country. His recognition was a eugenics point of view, and more of a nationalist point of view. The country is the center, and individuals come after that. In this respect, Kawakami was clearly Kanai's successor.

While his rival Fukuda Tokuzo appealed for the need for a social policy that allowed the socially vulnerable to survive, Kawakami was in a negative position on such a social policy. Kawakami demanded improvement in the treatment of vulnerable groups just to contribute to national productivity. However, Kawakami's multi-facetedness comes to the fore here. The basis of his economic system was humanitarian. This, of course, leads to absolute non-selfishness, which was the basic idea behind the rescuing of people who had been abused in the Ashio Copper Mine incident.

Such a humanitarian aspect would be at odds with the ruthless nationalist poverty reduction mentioned above. This confrontation became a more serious problem as Kawakami Hajime inclined to Marxism more radically following the Rice Riots of 1918. The ideals of humanitarian economic thought and nationalist policy should be "unified" by thorough Marxism. At least Kawakami might have understood that way.

It is well known that Kushida Tamizo's criticism encouraged this "unification." Kushida particularly criticized Kawakami's humanitarian aspect. As a result, Kawakami strived to study Marxist literature extensively as well as Marx's *Capital*. At the same time, he endeavored to conduct political activities so that he could resign from Kyoto University. His full-time training period of Marxism also overlapped with the Showa Depression period.

During the Showa Depression, Kawakami argued with Ishibashi Tanzan (1884–1973) about countermeasures to the depression effects. At that time, Ishibashi, who was the owner of the economic magazine *Toyo Keizai Shinpo*, insisted on a reflation policy (to overcome deflation and shift to low inflation to achieve economic stabilization). Kawakami, on the other hand, was critical of this approach, believing that aggressive fiscal spending and monetary easing policies were ineffective or could even lead to hyperinflation. Kawakami's basic position was that the depression was an unavoidable phenomenon in a capitalist economy, and it was necessary to shift to a communist regime to cure it fundamentally. Tanzan claimed that Kawakami's position would be detrimental in causing a delay to institutional transformation. Here again, Kawakami's multi-facetedness appeared. He asked, can we abandon those who are in need now until the future system changes? Kawakami's political radicalism was accelerating.

Kawakami worked to translate and popularize the Comintern in 1932 and eventually became a member of the Japanese Communist Party. He was arrested and convicted after developing "underground activities" and was held in prison from 1933 to 1937. During this time, he began writing his autobiography and wrote various articles on the theme of "unification of religious and scientific truth." This religious truth was a system of complex beliefs consisting of his scholarly nationalism, anti-selfishness and humanitarianism. On the other hand, scientific truth refers to Marxist doctrine. He regarded the "plurality of identities," which was advocated by Amartya Sen, as his uniqueness. They settle in one personality without contradicting these two truths. By now, the influence of Progressivist economists followed by Kawakami in his academic career has completely disappeared.

4.   FUKUDA TOKUZO'S INCOMPLETE WELFARE ECONOMICS AND PROGRESSIVISM

With Kawakami Hajime turning to Marxism, it looked as though the full-scale introduction of Progressive Era economics into Japan had retreated, but this is only half of the picture. An unexpected person inherited the Progressive Era's economics and incorporated it into his own economic thought. That person is Fukuda Tokuzo, a rival of Kawakami, who has appeared many times.

Fukuda's position in economics was strongly influenced by the New Historical School influenced by Lujo Brentano and Karl Bücher, who were his early teachers. Later, as the "Taisho Democracy" went into full swing, his focus shifted to the theories of Alfred Marshall, Arthur Cecil Pigou, John A. Hobson and others. Eventually, Fukuda distinguished traditional economics as "Price Economics" and his position as "Welfare Economics."

This distinction between the two is not unique to Fukuda. He does not specify the authority, but it is Fetter's paper (Fetter 1920a, 1920b). Fetter represented Price Economics, particularly British classical economics, and criticized them for subjective economics against a background of specific class interests. In contrast, Fetter thought that through Welfare Economics, outcomes of the market's autonomous adjustments improve social well-being.[3] Before comparing Fukuda and Fetter's economics, I would like to briefly explain how Fukuda understood the economics of the Progressive Era.

Fukuda's interest in American economics was expansive, but initially it was not profound. His first systematic book, *Economics Lecture* (Fukuda 1907–09), contains references to many books written by American economists. The names of Carver, Clark, Davenport, Fetter, Seager, Seligman, Taussig and so on, can be found.

Fisher's theory of money quantity was the first time Fukuda applied American economics in earnest. Immediately after the First World War, Fukuda was in opposition to the lifting of the gold embargo. At that time, Fukuda thought that the distribution of national income had been the most important thing, and that the distortion of assets between the upper class and the lower class had been prominent since the mid-1910s. And, as a cause of promoting this economic disparity, the inflation that continued from the First World War was regarded as a problem. He and Kawakami had exactly the same opinion that inflation was a problem from a distribution theory perspective. However, they adopted opposite policies. Fukuda thought that inflation could be adjusted by the government and the Bank of Japan (BOJ). He supported Fisher's monetary theory and thought that the BOJ should control the money supply in order to curb inflation. On the other hand, economists such as Kawakami, the government and BOJ policy makers insisted that the money supply could not be controlled.

The rising price of rice had been a problem since the First World War, but if you look at Fukuda's view of this issue, you can understand his basic view of money. At that time, the Ministry of Agriculture and Commerce tried to regulate buying and selling with a ban on free bargaining in order to prevent prices from rising, but Fukuda decided that it was impossible to control rice prices with such regulations. This is because not only the price of rice but also the general price level had risen, and it was stated that such a general price level could be controlled by "currency reduction."

However, Fukuda abandoned this Fisherian position in the mid-1920s. Fukuda thought that Japan in the 1920s had experienced long-term deflation, and that inefficient economic activity should be eliminated in order to cure this deflation. Fukuda adopted a so-called liquidation theory, which states that the market should be left to self-adjust even in a recession. Aggressive fiscal and monetary easing policies by the government and the BOJ would instead delay this liquidation. Like Kawakami, Fukuda also argued with Ishibashi Tanzan during the Showa Depression and criticized his reflation policy.[4] Fukuda and Kawakami were lifelong rivals, but in the Showa Depression they were working together by adopting a de facto austerity policy. When faced with a harsh environment, as Katayama used to do, they also considered extreme remedies such as system change rather than gradual social reform. This trend of Japanese economists has been repeated here.

However, Fukuda was not as extreme as Kawakami, who moved to Marxist practice. Fukuda now separated himself from Progressive Era economists in the area of macroeconomics by moving to a liquidation principle. On the other hand, in the area corresponding to microeconomics, Fukuda introduced the above-mentioned distinction between Fetter's Price Economics and Welfare

Economics into his own economics. Fukuda adopted this distinction in the late 1920s (Fukuda 1930). However, there was not much time left in his life.

According to Fukuda, Price Economics targets only the degree of subjective desire, not the level of satisfaction at the social level. Social satisfaction and subjective satisfaction do not always coincide. The subject of Welfare Economics is about social-level satisfaction. This definition is almost the same as Fetter's.[5] At present, utility is a term that expresses subjective satisfaction, but Fukuda used it as a term that expresses social satisfaction. This led to controversy, including the selection of translations with Kawakami. Kawakami regarded utility as a word that expresses subjective satisfaction. Fukuda's terminology is similar to V. Pareto's distinction between ophelimity and utility. Pareto's utility is also something that meets social and basic needs. Ophelimity, on the other hand, means subjective desire. Pareto used a famous metaphor that states that "bitter medicine has utility for sick children but no ophelimity" (Pareto 2014 [1906]).

The central theme of Fukuda's Welfare Economics was to rescue those who were excluded from the market. It was to build an institutional framework in which socially vulnerable people, such as children, women, the elderly and the sick, could meet the greatest utility under the capitalist economy. Fukuda's achievements in this aspect were also called the "social policy of the right to survival." Maximizing the utility of workers was also an issue. Negotiations over the employment between workers and capitalists have always been disadvantaged by capitalists. This is because they have enough assets to live without work, but workers lose their food to live without work. Fukuda referred to Adam Smith and Marx for the image of this labor-management negotiation. Fukuda argued that the government must actively encourage the formation of trade unions and, at the same time, ensure the legal institution of labor contracts to compensate for the lack of workers' negotiating power. Fukuda said that if such institutional arrangements were not made, the maximization of the utility of workers would not be achieved. This perspective is similar to John Rogers Commons' early labor economics. However, the name of Commons cannot be found in Fukuda's works.

Progressive Era economics was found in Fukuda's Welfare Economics, but he did not live long enough to complete his work. Fukuda was blessed with a large number of disciples, but his Welfare Economics never succeeded in earnest in the context of Japanese economics after his death. Again, the disappearance was repeated.

5. CONCLUSION

The Progressive Era's American economics has been introduced into Japan almost contemporaneously since the end of the nineteenth century. Its introduction to Japan was attempted by Katayama Sen, Kawakami Hajime and

Fukuda Tokuzo, but their contributions did not take root in Japanese economics. They moved to more radical Marxist activities (Katayama, Kawakami),
or Progressive economics survived in barely one generation (Fukuda) without
finding a successor. The disappearance was always repeated. This led to a lack
of economists who supported stimulus policy or understood appropriate market
designs, and so on, until the end of the Second World War. Exceptions are
non-academic economists, such as Ishibashi Tanzan and others, who argued
with Kawakami and Fukuda and insisted on a reflation policy. They used, for
example, Fisher's Debt Deflation Theory to combat Japan's deflationary recession. But their contribution was an exception to Japanese economics. After the
country's defeat in the Second World War, Japan imported the achievements
of American economics one after another, mainly in mathematical economics.
Over time, the number of Japanese economists who are active in international
academia has steadily increased and continues to do so today. However, there
is also a negative legacy – stimulus policies, reflation policies and appropriate
market design are still not fully understood in Japan. It might be true to say that
this is due to the "repeated disappearance" of progressivism in Japan.

NOTES

1.　For the relationship between Katayama Sen and R. T. Ely, see Sumiya (1960).
2.　See Bernstein (1970) and Tanaka (2001) for the versatile and multi-faceted life of
　　Kawakami Hajime.
3.　Nishizawa (2014) first pointed out the relationship between Fukuda's and Fetter's
　　Price Economics and Welfare Economics.
4.　See Tanaka (2004) for the controversy of the Showa Era between Tokuzo Fukuda,
　　Hajime Kawakami and Mt. Ishibashi.
5.　Although Fukuda does not explicitly refer to it, Fisher's (1918) distinction
　　between Ophelimity and Wantability is the same view as Fetter's.

REFERENCES

Bernstein, Gail L. 1970. *Japanese Marxist: A Portrait of Kawakami Hajime, 1879–1946*.
　　Cambridge, MA: Harvard University Press.
Ely, Richard Theodore. 1889. *Social Aspects of Christianity, and Other Essays*. New
　　York: T. Y. Crowell & Company.
Fetter, Frank A. 1905. *The Principles of Economics*. New York: The Century Co.
　　[translation and critical examination in Japanese by Kawami, Hajime. 1911. *Butuzai
　　no Kachi*. Tokyo: Yuhikaku].
Fetter, Frank A. 1920a. "Price Economics versus Welfare Economics." *American
　　Economic Review* 10, no. 3: 467–87.
Fetter, Frank A. 1920b. "Price Economics versus Welfare Economics: Contemporary
　　Opinion." *American Economic Review* 10, no. 4: 719–37.

Fisher, Irving. 1906. *The Nature of Capital and Income*. New York: Macmillan [abridged, translated and commentary by Kawakami, Hajime. 1912. *Shihon Oyobi Rishi-buai*. Tokyo: Hakubunkan].

Fisher, Irving. 1907. *The Rate of Interest*. New York: Macmillan [abridged, translated and commentary by Kawakami, Hajime. 1912. *Shihon Oyobi Rishi-buai*. Tokyo: Hakubunkan].

Fisher, Irving. 1910. *Introduction to Economic Science*. New York: Macmillan.

Fisher, Irving. 1918. "Is 'Utility' the Most Suitable Term for the Concept It is Used to Denote?." *American Economic Review* 8, no. 2: 335–7.

Fisher, Irving and Eugene Lyon Fisk. 1915. *How to Live: Rules for Healthful Living Based on Modern Science*. New York and London: Funk & Wagnalls [translated by Kawakami, Hajime. 1917. *Ikani Ikiru Bekika*. Kyoto: Kobundo].

Fukuda, Tokuzo. 1907–09. *Keizaigaku Kougi* [*Economic Lecture*]. Tokyo: Okura Shoten.

Fukuda, Tokuzo. 1930. *Kosei Keizai Kenkyu* [*Welfare Economic Studies*]. Tokyo: Tokoshoin.

Kawakami, Hajime. 1917. *Binbo monogatari* [*The Poverty Story*] Reprinted in 1982. *Kawakami Hajime zenshu* [*The Complete Works of Kawakami Hajime*], Vol. 9. Tokyo: Iwanami Shoten.

Kawakami, Hajime. 1982 [1913]. *Kin to Shinyo to Buttka; Bankin Buttka no Ichi-kenkyu* [*Gold, Credit and Prices: A Study of Recent General Price Increase*] Reprinted in 1982. *Kawakami Hajime zenshu* [*The Complete Works of Kawakami Hajime*], Vol. 6. Tokyo: Iwanami Shoten.

Kawakami, Hajime. 1983 [1913]. *Keizai Genron* [*Economic Principles*] Reprinted in 1983. *Kawakami Hajime Zenshu* [*The Complete Works of Kawakami Hajime*], Vol. 7. Tokyo: Iwanami Shoten.

Nishizawa, Tamotsu. 2014. "Kousei-keizaigaku no Genryu: Marshall, Ruskin, Fukuda Tokuzo" ["Origins of Welfare Economics: Marshall, Ruskin, Fukuda Tokuzo"]. *Keizai Kenkyu* 65, no. 2: 97–112.

Pareto, Vilfredo. 2014 [1906]. *Manuale di Economia Politica con una Introduzione alla Scienza Sociale*, translated in English by Aldo Montesano, Alberto Zanni, Luigino Bruni, John Chipman and Michael McLure (Eds). 2014. *Manual of Political Economy: A Critical and Variorum Edition*. Oxford: Oxford University Press.

Seligman, Edwin Robert Anderson. 1902. *The Economic Interpretation of History*. New York: Columbia University Press [translated by Kawakami Hajime. 1905. *Shin-Shikan*. Tokyo: Shoheido-Kawaoka shoten].

Shakai Seisaku Gakkai. 1898. "Skakai-Seisaku-gakai-shuisho" ["Association for Social Policy Studies Prospectus"] Reprinted in Shakai Seisaku Gakkai (Ed.) 1978. *Sahakai-seisaku gakai shiroyu-shusei* [*Historical Materials for Association for Social Policy Studies*]. Tokyo: Ochanomizu Shobo].

Sumiya, Mikio. 1960. *Katayama Sen*. Tokyo: University Press of Tokyo.

Tanaka, Hidetomi. 2001. *Chinmoku to Teikou aru Chisekijiin no Shougai Hyouden Sumiya Etuji* [*Silence and Resistance: Sumiya Etuji, a Life Story of an Intellectual*]. Tokyo: Fujiwara Shoten.

Tanaka, Hidetomi. 2004. "Keizai-mondai ni Kakawaru Zatushi-janarizumu no Tenkai" ["Development of Magazine Journalism Related to Economic Problems"]. In *Showa-kyokou no Kenkyu* [*Studies of Showa Depression*], ed. Iwata Kikyo. Tokyo: Toyo Keizai Shinpo, pp. 143–66.

Taussig, Frank William. 1911. *Principles of Economics*. New York: Macmillan.

PART II

Fighting income, capital and land inequalities

8.   Income inequality: a turning point, 1880–1930

Christian Morrisson

1.   INTRODUCTION

The 1880–1930 period witnessed unprecedented change with regard to income distribution worldwide, both at the national scale and at the individual scale. Studying this change requires some preliminary remarks on the notion of inequality and the tools making an appraisal of it possible. In every country, income distribution can be looked at through various different prisms: the first approach is that of production factors, which requires measurement of all the shares of revenue derived either from capital, work or both. A second approach would be to measure the distribution of revenue derived from capital, work or both by active individuals and allocating to each the total sum of their overall revenue,[1] regardless of the factor of production. This distribution relates to primary revenue. Third, one can alternatively measure household or individual distribution by focusing exclusively on disposable income, by which is meant factor-derived income, after taxation and state benefits are deducted. The world index is the aggregate of the figures obtained for the income distribution of all the countries examined.

In the nineteenth century, as had been the case in earlier times, the figures for the distribution of individual (and household) disposable income closely matched the figures for primary revenue. State spending accounted for only a small portion of GDP and was for the most part directed toward the military sector – in theory for the equal benefit of all.

A shift occurred as early as 1930 as the budget of several developed countries grew to as much as two or three times their 1900 GDP figures. Among the chief factors were the rapid growth of education spending (e.g. Lindert 1994), as well as social and unemployment benefits. Simultaneously, the widespread enforcement of progressive taxation – levied on a minority of households – affected the distribution of disposable income.

By 1900, the income distribution for active people – taken in its broad sense to include pensioners and people of independent means – was chiefly determined by markets. During the nineteenth century state intervention in the economy was minimal, which resulted in the markets driving the distribution of wages and capital revenue. If there were, for example, an epidemic outbreak which caused many fatalities among the labor force, the resulting shortage of laborers would automatically drive up wages. A similar scenario played out in France, as the high number of casualties caused by the Revolutionary Wars and Napoleonic Wars brought about a sharp increase in salaries. Likewise, a downturn in agricultural production caused by inclement weather would push up prices, thereby benefiting farmers who had been spared from disaster.

Only in the event of such exogenous shocks as epidemics or wars would the distribution of income be affected. Of course, in those cases the state would have played no significant role, and the income distribution would gradually revert back to its pre-shock levels within a few years. Changes had set in by 1930, as states gradually regulated markets, notably by passing minimum wage legislation. In France, policies were introduced to freeze rents on properties during inflationary periods like the First World War. This legislation remained in place in the postwar period and would not be repealed until the 1950s. This had a lasting impact on property distribution, since only rented property, whose ownership was for the most part in the hands of the 10th decile, was discouraged, not other holdings.

Consequently, landlords suffered a drop in their income. In Russia, the brutality of the Bolshevik Revolution of 1917 was unprecedented, as non-operating property owners saw their properties being seized by the state, and all forms of income were suppressed, with the sole exception of legitimately earned wages.

In the following sections of the chapter, I will shed light on relevant data and facts related to the Progressive Era (1880–1930), dealing with the issue of inequality and income distribution in particular. In our view, as I shall explain, the 1880–1930 period was a turning point for income inequality in many Western countries.

2.   THE PRE-1880 FREE MARKET MODEL AND THE KUZNETS CURVE

Among the chief features of the free market model is the relative absence of government intervention in the economy, limited to dispensing justice and protecting its territory. The state would only be involved in the factors of production, wages, or savings, and would only be prepared to protect the most vulnerable groups in society (e.g. children and pregnant women) in drastic circumstances such as war. Primary school teaching would be publicly funded on the grounds that some fundamental knowledge would be necessary to join the labor force. This principle of "minimal intervention" can be clearly seen in the relatively low level of (non-military) public spending that remained low – 15% at the time, as opposed to 30% to 50% these days – as progressive taxation had a negligible impact on income distribution. These traits illustrate the gap separating nineteenth-century economic structures from those in place today.

As industrialization and urbanization swept across England, and France, America and Germany later on, inequality became more noticeable than at the turn of the nineteenth century, when the poor were concentrated in rural areas.

Most blue-collar workers could be found in the cities. In the first decades, they were drawn there by the rapid growth in industries such as textiles and food, which offered low-wage work to laborers with few formal qualifications. However, as the influx of rural workers toward the cities stalled, these industries were forced to raise wages. The discrepancy between low wages and higher labor productivity decreased, with the effect of reducing profits, sometimes leaving firms with little choice but to rely on investment to increase their profit.

To that extent, increases in wages can be said to have been a crucial factor in income distribution. *Ceteris paribus*, it matches the rise in salaries for the first deciles and the fall in income of the 10th decile. This pattern was first seen in England in 1870, before reaching France, and Germany around the start of the twentieth century.

A pioneering insight by the American economist Simon Kuznets tells us that if the average urban income is double that of the average rural income, and that the percentage of rural population declines from 80% to 20% around the same time period, we can surmise that income inequality will first rise steadily, only to fall when the rural population reaches less than 60% of the total population (Kuznets 1972).

An alternative model which includes other factors such as agriculture, industry and services in the overall growth has been suggested in recent years (Duarte and Restuccia 2010). In developing countries, the productivity of the non-agricultural workforce far exceeded that of the agricultural workforce, but the former involved half of the population. The overall rise in incomes is to a large extent caused by farmhands being redirected toward non-agricultural sectors. An estimate based on a sample of one hundred countries revealed that 85% of the productivity gap between advanced countries and developing countries was due to two main factors: (1) dramatic productivity gaps between various sectors, (2) largely agriculturally based employment. This is a clear vindication of Kuznets' insight.

The Kuznets hypothesis has been widely debated in recent decades. Indeed, trends in income distribution are determined by numerous factors and not all of them are economic. The validity of the hypothesis has therefore varied according to the particular case study in question.

All case studies show that the key parameter in econometric studies – that is, per capita income, often represented in the quadratic shape of an inverted U-curve – is not always relevant. Higgins and Williamson (1999) provided a plausible explanation for this: the mechanism identified by Kuznets only applies insofar as other variables, such as education or demographics, are accounted for.

This outcome has been validated by a series of tests, the first of which were carried out in the 1970s and 1980s, and relied upon cross-sectional data. However, the hypothesis was only authoritatively accepted by Higgins and Williamson's longitudinal study (1999), which gave positive results by including complementary factors such as demography. Yet, other studies fail to arrive at similar conclusions.

Piketty (2014) cites the case of the United States as a robust counterexample to the Kuznets hypothesis. Income inequality in the USA was at a moderate level around 1850, rose steadily until the 1910s, fell from 1920 to the postwar period and remained stable from the 1950s to the 1980s, only to rise again as a result of deregulations and privatizations.

It might be argued that the Kuznets hypothesis fails to account for the peak in inequality starting from the 1980s onwards. But Piketty pays closer attention to capital, the central theme of his work. Inequality, he argues, is related to the capitalist order; the decline of inequality in the 1920s is the direct consequence of new fiscal policies, and it is therefore not caused by any mechanism inherent to a dualist market economy such as labor force shifts. Thus, for Piketty the 1920s constitutes a new socio-economic context.

To test the Kuznets hypothesis using longitudinal data, it is necessary to select a time range corresponding to a historical period which is both long and stable, such as the period 1800–1913. My sample includes countries which together experienced the first signs of declining inequality before 1914. Among those, I have paid special attention to three countries of Northern Europe, which share numerous crucial features and are statistically congruent, as well as to the three leading European countries of the day: Germany, France and the United Kingdom.f

Denmark, Norway and Sweden all went down a similar path, with industrialization and urbanization coming into being in the nineteenth century. Growth was relatively swift (+40% in Denmark and Sweden within 20 years between 1880 and 1900), as they avoided going to war. Of the three countries, Denmark had the highest GDP per capita as of 1850. According to fiscal data, the share of the 10th decile decreased from 59% (1870) to 30% (1903). Although these are net salaries – which was unusual for the period – taxation levels were low, which means that the data we have constitute an accurate picture.

In Norway, fiscal data in several cities suggest a pattern compatible with the Kuznets hypothesis. Indeed, we find a Gini of 0.57 in 1840, 0.68 in 1855, 0.49

in 1870 and 0.40 in 1905. But whether this validates Kuznets' theory or not is uncertain as Norway's GDP per capita was still low in 1900 – approximately 60% of that in Sweden or Denmark. Norwegian economists offered other explanations. Sweden, however, fits Kuznets' curve more closely. Between 1750 and 1850 inequality peaked, in both rural and urban environments, whilst the average income gap between the two rose only moderately. The combination of these two phenomena points to rising inequality in Sweden for the period in question. There is evidence that income inequality increased in cities, for the most part, due to rising numbers of employed skilled workers. In rural areas, the job market became increasingly smaller as a result of the industrialization which occurred from 1860 to 1914. Transfers of labor from agriculture to industry led to a widening gap between the average income in the agricultural sector and the average income in the industrial sector, and in turn to a rise in inequality at a national level. For Swedish economists, that trend reversed around 1900–10.

As regards the German case, according to Prussian and Saxon statistical evidence from both before and after 1871 (at a time when industrialization and urbanization were at a more advanced stage in Saxony), inequality rose in the nineteenth century, before declining a little at the onset of the twentieth century. In Saxony, the shares of the 10th decile and the 100th centile also varied substantially (43.3 and 17.1 respectively as of 1875; 44 and 19.6 in 1898; and 42.9 and 19.3 for the year 1913). The figures for Prussia at the same dates with regard to share of the last ventile are 27.8, 32.6 and 30.6. These data match the hypothesis laid out by Kuznets, who even used them as an illustration of his inverted U-curve diagram.

France presents an unusual case. As early as the eighteenth century, income inequalities were high and would only decrease as a consequence of the upheaval of the French Revolution. France thus began to industrialize around 1830, after the United Kingdom, but ahead of most other European countries. In the period 1830–70, French urbanization and industrialization accelerated at a faster pace than at any other time between 1780 and 1914. Income inequality increased and capital revenue doubled – in fact might even have trebled – while wages remained low.

The following period (1870–1914) saw gradual wage increases: wages doubled for unskilled laborers, farmhands and servants (accounting for almost 30% of all active workers and belonging to the poorest 40%) between 1864 and 1894, despite GDP per head only rising by about a third. This rise was caused by rapid urbanization which diverted redundant farmhands toward the cities. Hence there was a 5% fall in income of the 10th decile (from 49% to 44%), along with a rise in the overall share of the poor (quintiles 1 and 2) from 13.5% to 15%. As was the case with Germany and the Nordic countries, the evolution of inequality from 1830 to 1914 validates Kuznets' hypothesis.

France's uniqueness lies in its above-average rate of inequality, whether in the eighteenth century or in the 1830–70 period. Such income gaps come at a price: the country suffered a series of civil wars: first in 1789–94, then in June 1848 and finally in 1871. Such a high degree of inequality is unquestionably one of the factors which triggered such conflicts, and also explains the emergence of a reform-avert, even revolutionary, brand of French-style socialism, quite different from German social democracy.

The United Kingdom also follows Kuznets' curve. As the cradle of the Industrial Revolution in the mid eighteenth century, the aggregate result of Lindert's (2000) distribution estimate unsurprisingly reveals a rise in the last ventile until the year 1867, followed by a decline (41.1% to 38.7% in 1867). As far as the timeframe of 1867–1911 is concerned, it is widely accepted that there is a fall in both cases.

In most cases, results match the Kuznets hypothesis. What can be observed in this case are results that seem to coincide with Kuznets' hypothesis, but do not confirm it. Although the data he collected was apparently irrefutable, Lindert expressed skepticism, acknowledging the weakness of his evidence. In my view, however, I find this data to be of great value, as it concerns the pre-1914 period. This is before significant state intervention began to complicate any assessment of the impact that the *takeoff* stage (as mentioned in Rostow's theory of the stages of growth) might have had on economies characterized by the dual-sector model of capitalist and subsistence production. Among the various cases cited above, only France experienced changes in capital distribution, the result of mass confiscation of Church property. From 1815 onward, the owners of such assets received compensation, and France reverted back to the free-market environment that had been in place in the early 1830s – that is, until August 1914 when a new economic model set in, and would shape most of the twentieth century.

Economic development under a socialist regime no longer appeared far-fetched, and was presented as the best solution for the problems caused by the takeoff process. This model was backed by effective propaganda, one that conveniently concealed both the economic and the human toll this choice would entail. Some parts of the general public opposed socialism for reasons unrelated to the economic issues, yet also opposed the free market on entirely economic grounds. Resorting to State corporatism as a way out of this dilemma proved ineffective due to excessive protectionism and a rent-based economy. Free-marketeers condemned both corporatism and socialism alike, but a liberal economic policy could not be pursued and the 1929 crisis explains the success of Keynesian policies.

The Second World War and the period that followed required a great deal of state supervision until the 1960s. Victorian *laissez-faire* principles were no longer relevant for solving the ills of the new world and free-marketeers were in need of a new policy. The upheavals of the nineteenth century were consigned to history. The foregoing examples constitute solid evidence of the potential for growth inherent in a free-market economy. Yet this should be balanced against widening disparities in income over the initial three or four decades of growth before poverty finally begins to decline. Whether or not the Kuznets hypothesis is confirmed, the similarities between its premises and the two phases of economic growth just described above can hardly be in doubt.

On this issue, much of the case against international organizations on the grounds that they allegedly espoused free-market principles is invalid. But in the second half of the twentieth century, no such free market model like in the nineteenth century has been advocated and even less applied by international organizations. Since 1945, no such organization has advocated measures such as wage freezes or significant raises in capital income, as was the case in France over the period 1830–70. Instead of letting markets dictate the income trends for decades to come, new ways of improving labor conditions were constantly on the government agenda. This account of the first decades of growth reveals the extent to which 1914 was a sea change. It also explains Bismarck's system of social insurance – funded exclusively by wage-earners and private firms – which would act as a safety net against hardship. Bismarck had become aware that capitalist market economies called for social reforms in order to influence disposable income. Such reforms, which were the exception before 1914, gradually proved the rule in most European countries.

3.   THE FACTORIAL INCOME DISTRIBUTION

In the context of an unsophisticated agrarian economy, let us assume two factors of production: land controlled by a single owner and labor produced by many workers. In this model, income inequality is determined by the rent/wage ratio. Such a simplistic mechanism had some relevance in the early nineteenth century for advocates of classical economics. Population distribution between landowners and farm workers rather faithfully reflected the social order in an overwhelmingly rural society. Hence, classical economists tended to approach the question of income inequalities from a factorial standpoint. The shift from factorial distribution to individual distribution seemed inevitable. In reality, this change has raised much skepticism recently, as shown by Atkinson and Bourguignon (2000).

The main objection concerns occupational differences within the labor force as a function of their education. In other words, manual workers undergoing extensive training are significantly more productive than their unskilled counterparts. Their increased knowledge should rightly be viewed as a form of investment, on a par with physical capital. Additionally, whereas eighteenth-century workers could only earn money from their wages, most of today's wage-earners have diverse sources of income, which they derive from private assets – however scant – such as bank deposits, rents if they own property or share dividends handed out by their respective employers as incentives. A final objection involves the state, which significantly altered income distribution by imposing progressive taxation measures, particularly on high-income households.

In sum, we should take into account measurements of the income distribution both prior to state redistribution and after redistributive transfers (for example disabled people eligible for state benefits). Shifting from a macro-economic approach – appraising agricultural workers' total wage share and land rent – to a micro-economic one – appraising each worker's income in a given rural environment – was feasible, since most rural laborers did not have any source of income beside their wages; likewise, landowners usually derived the entirety of their income from their land.

However, in the period 1880–1914 such an approach became increasingly inadequate for the reasons mentioned above. It appears that factorial income distribution does not yield results as satisfactory as in the past if we want to understand income inequalities between individuals. Yet, significant changes have occurred since the early nineteenth century, and the years between 1880 and 1930 deserve some scrutiny as a transitional period. A striking example is the rising number of savings accounts in France, from 566,000 in 1850 to 3.8 million in 1880 (14.1 million if we include national savings banks). This figure would from then on continue to rise slowly. The savings accounts per capita ratio stood at 20 to 1,000 in 1850 (excluding minors), then at 130 to 1,000 in 1880, and finally at 250 to 1,000 in 1910 (in fact as high as 310 to 1,000 if one includes national savings banks).

Both the number of people holding savings accounts as well as the value they held on average – equivalent to approximately four months of a work-er's wages – constitute evidence that this was a widespread phenomenon which affected society as far as individuals in the 5th quintile. Yearly interest derived from these savings (which equaled four days' worth of wages) merely accounted for a very low share of citizens' annual income, which justifies the use of a factorial approach in this case. It was only in the 1920s, and even more so in the postwar period, that taxation and transfer payments to households began reshaping primary income distribution in such a way as to create an insurmountable disconnect between inequalities in income and disparities in living standards.

There are two approaches for comparing factorial income distribution with disposable income distribution. One consists in surveying those in higher income brackets, for example by contrasting the share of capital income in the aggregate of factorial income, based on the percentage of the last ventile or centile in the income distribution.

Another approach focuses on those in lower income brackets, by contrasting the income share of urban wage-earners (factorial distribution) with that of the bottom 80% of society. Only in an urban context can the wages of the bottom 80% be clearly identified. For clarity's sake, we will distinguish between the concepts of "sectoral distribution" and "income distribution."

In Sweden, the share of capital income in the distribution of sectoral income remained stable from 1900 to 1920, before steadily declining until 1980. The share of the richest centile in the distribution of disposable income declined more substantially: falling from 35% to 15% as opposed to a decrease from 53% to 28% in gross income distribution. This trend in the period 1930–80 reflects the socialist policies of the time. In the post-1950 era, the correlation between these two variables is far less certain. This result should not come as a surprise: indeed, the nearer we are to the present day, the more the distribution of disposable income deviates from the factorial distribution. But in 1800, the percentage of one, two or three centiles in income distribution could equal the share of capital income relative to factorial income. This suggests that capital was the exclusive possession of individuals comprised in centiles which did not relate to any other factor. In such economies, any slight variation in the capital price/wage ratio will affect income distribution. Conversely, in the twentieth century income distribution and factorial distribution became increasingly less interdependent.

A study based on a sample of ten countries (Bengtsson and Waldenstrom 2018) exemplifies the relationship between capital income (share in factorial income) and the percentage of the 100th centile in disposable income. This corresponds to post-depreciation capital income. While a third of independent wage-earner income was derived from capital, two thirds were derived from labor. Among the countries surveyed (Denmark, France, Finland, Germany, Japan, Spain, the United Kingdom and Sweden), this pattern typically sets in around 1900 or some time earlier (1880).

For the majority of these countries, the two indicators rose between 1880 (or 1900) and 1914, as European savings – French and British in particular – boosted growth. These savings are significant in that they were concentrated in countries with high levels of capital exports outside Europe. Such investments gradually increased the share of the wealthy in aggregate disposable income, a sign that the group made up of the most wealthy (100th centile or 99th and 100th centile) was confident in European economies, despite some serious political crises. This wave of optimism in the business world was created by growth (the GDP of countries such as Germany, the USA, France and the United Kingdom rose by 180%, 220%, 75% and 88%, respectively, between 1880 and 1914) and a boom in trade volumes. The prospect of a long and protracted conflict which would seriously disrupt trade seemed unthinkable. Yet the inconceivable occurred, which caused the share of capital and of the 100th decile in the aggregate income distribution to plummet. Later, countries which remained neutral during the First World War suffered a similar slump during the 1929 crisis and the subsequent Great Depression.

4.   INCOME DISTRIBUTION

I will now explain how income distribution between individuals is affected by intervention from either the state, private individuals or organizations – cases of relatives in economic hardship have sometimes led to significant cash transfers among families. The impact of such intervention had had a limited impact before 1930, but it paved the way for more comprehensive policy measures after 1945, when the ratio of the average income of the highest centile to that of the first quintile was cut twofold.

The shift from per capita primary income for active individuals to individual disposable income implies a different picture of inequality. If we compare the case of a single wage-earner on a monthly wage of 10,000 euros to that of 5,000 for a couple with two children (each counting as half a share), the disparity per wage-earner is moderate (2 to 1), while the disparity in income per individual is high – 10,000 to [5,000/3] 1,660, a ratio of 6 to 1. Such a scenario was typical of an European country devoid of income tax and social benefits in the 1900s. If the state deducts 2,000 out of 10,000 and redistributes 500 to households with two children and a €5,000 income, this ratio falls from 8,000 to 1,830 – that is 4.3 to 1 instead of 6 to 1. It is therefore clear that family structures and public transfers have affected inequalities in income between wage-earners.

The 1880–1930 timeframe presents us with interesting signs of changes to come. As of 1880, family-oriented government spending was insignificant: it amounted to between 0.1% and 1% of GDP in several countries and was non-existent in the others. As of 1930, this spending exceeded 2% in eight countries and 1% in four others. This figure is more meaningful than it seems at first hand in a context of low state expenditure in the 1930s (usually below 20% of GDP). It is therefore accurate to say that the foundations of our contemporary post-1945 welfare states were laid around our period of interest, especially after 1914.

Although the First World War created the conditions for a break from the early nineteenth-century free-market model and the establishment of a new society, the architecture of modern social policy had already come into being in the *Belle Époque* era (1871–1914).

5.   WORLD INCOME DISTRIBUTION

This research theme only started attracting interest around forty years ago. Quantitative historical studies first focused on advanced countries before widening their scope to include several more. In the 2000s, the first estimates of world income distribution since the early nineteenth century enhanced our understanding of the patterns and changes occurring before and after 1914. The results of the first estimate by Bourguignon and Morrisson (2002) (on the period 1820–1992) were later confirmed by van Zanden et al. (2014) (on the 1820–2000 era) as both studies arrived at similar Gini figures through different sources and methods.

Both studies show a break between the nineteenth century and the twentieth century, through recourse to two different estimates for the same data. Each study combined GDP per capita with income distribution in a single country. The first study relied exclusively on Maddison's estimates (in 1990's value of the dollar) (Maddison 2003) while the second one used 2000's value of the dollar in International Comparison Program (ICP) terms. It should be noted that estimates produced by the World Bank tend to differ considerably from those produced by Maddison.

The data most worth considering is the inequality index. From 1820 to 1910, that is a 90-year time span, the Gini index rose from 0.492 to 0.610 – a 0.118 difference – and continued to increase by 0.025 between 1910 and 1960. From then onwards, the Gini index remained stagnant. Its rise in the nineteenth century is unusual compared to the eighteenth and twentieth centuries, marked by only slight variations of + 0.015. The data on eighteenth-century GDP per capita are lacking, with only records of upward trends in England and the Netherlands which bore little impact as these two countries accounted for only 1.6% of the world's population as of 1700. The Theil index,[2] which is more efficient at capturing increases in high incomes, rose by 0.284 from 1820 (0.513) to 1910 (0.797), against a 0.021 fall in the 1910–60 interval. These results concur with van Zanden's (2014) survey, which found that the Gini index rose from 0.490 to 0.605 on average for the period 1910–29.

Statistics for quantiles further reinforce the uniqueness of the twentieth century. According to Morrisson and Murtin (2012), the share of the tenth decile increased from 42% (1820) to 50.9% (1910), a similar figure to that obtained for the year 1960 (50%). The share of the poorest 60% (from 26.2% in 1820 to 17.7%) decreased at the same rate as the increase of that of the 10th decile. There is sharp contrast between the 9th and 10th deciles and all other deciles which lost out.

Using a decomposable inequality index such as the Theil index allows us to more fully appreciate the break between the nineteenth and twentieth centuries with regard to domestic inequality – I posit that the average income of each country is the same. National inequality, which was high from the start, widened slowly between 1820 and 1910. From 1914 onward, however, it would begin rapidly decreasing, from 0.498 (1910) to 0.318 as of 1960. The figure would not rise again before the twenty-first century, when increasing inequalities in China and in the USA in particular bear a disproportionate impact on the index. The previous narrowing in inequality was caused by two events: one was Russia's adoption of socialism, followed by Eastern Europe (after 1945) and many Asian countries (such as China); another was the electoral success of social democratic parties in advanced economies. This led to the widespread enforcement of redistributive fiscal policies, which became partly accepted by opposition political forces.

Few countries then pursued a pre-1914 *laissez-faire* path. It is obvious that domestic inequality – concerning individuals within the same country – had a deeper electoral impact than global inequality – inequality between average incomes in different countries. The latter is only significant for exporters, investors or international philanthropists.

The trends of national inequality can be easily forecast as long as the political regime in place is democratic in nature and the citizenry is informed about the national state of affairs. Yet a phenomenon of equal significance was taking place between 1820 and 2000: the rapid growth of inequalities between countries. The Theil index records a tenfold increase for this period. Only after 2000 would inequality decrease, as the behemoths of the developing world like China and India grew at a faster rate than advanced economies.

In 1820, inequality between countries only accounted for 10% of global economic disparity. Indeed, international inequality rose from 38% in 1910 to 65% in 2000. This was the dominant trend for two centuries. There are, however, reasons for believing that the world has entered a second phase since 1990–2000, with decreases in inequality between countries and in world inequality. More recent studies on the period (including Morrisson and Murtin 2012) vindicate this view.

6.   LONG-TERM INEQUALITIES IN WELL-BEING

The inequality separating an illiterate from a literate person is as substantial as a twofold increase in income. Inequalities pertaining to education, health and living environment matter as much as income inequality in the global appraisal of welfare inequality. These can be measured by tools such as literacy rates, school enrollment rates, the length of time spent in formal education, or life expectancy. This is particularly striking when one notices high GDP per capita countries ranking below underdeveloped or poor countries in this respect. This is true of some areas in the USA, where life expectancy is below Bangladeshi standards.

Estimating the distribution for public healthcare and education within one country is an impossible task, which is why I have retained each country's average figures for each variable and measured international inequality only.

Among the results worth discussing is the drop in world inequality in terms of well-being (excluding GDP per capita) in the early twentieth century, despite disparities in income distribution only beginning to decrease from the 2000s, that is, a century later. With regard to literacy, the Gini index remained stable from 1870 (0.67) to 1913 (0.66), but fell by 50% between 1913 and 2000. The Gini index for school attendance steadily decreased until 1929 and after. Overall, educational inequality followed a similar downward trend starting in 1870 with regard to the two variables of literacy and school attendance.

Life expectancy is a crucial aspect of well-being. From 1870 to 1913, inequality in life expectancy rose but returned to its previous levels in 1929. Its rapid decline thereafter was due to a combination of several factors: economic growth, which gave rise to improvements in nutrition, science, and in the fields of medicine and public health, with preventive medicine at school and protective measures for new-born children. Also worth noting is that mortality rates plummeted in the 1930s as new cures and medicine spread to developing countries while GDP per capita remained stagnant or decreased.

The United Nations Development Programme's (UNDP) well-being index combines several aspects of well-being, namely life expectancy, length of schooling and income. With regard to these criteria, the Gini index remained stable from 1870 to 1913, before declining from 52 (1913) to 44 (1929), and even reaching a low of 22 in 2000. The Theil index indicates an even sharper decline, from 53 to 31 in 1929 and 0.08 in 2000. In both cases, in the context of generally stable income disparities, the period 1913–29 would set a trend of decreased inequality in well-being.

Such results undermine the arguments in favor of GDP per capita as the most appropriate index for estimating well-being. Other variables might also be included, such as the environment, by taking into account pollution levels. Such an approach would make the concept of global inequality more comprehensive by widening the scope of its definition beyond GDP per capita.

Unlike the nineteenth century, the twentieth century experienced significant declines in national inequality as a result of political factors such as socialist revolutions and socio-democratic regimes. This drop compensates for the average rise in inequality between countries, so that the aggregate figure remains at its turn-of-the-century level, and did not follow the trend set by global well-being.

What also sharply demarcates the twentieth century from the previous century is the dramatic decline in inequalities in global well-being, caused by wider access to primary schooling on the one hand, and improvements in life expectancy (made possible by public health services and vaccines) on the other. As far as raised living standards are concerned, such breakthroughs played a role comparable to that of rising incomes.

7.   CONCLUSION

This study has aimed to provide an analytical account of the income fluctuations during the period 1880–1930. Should these evolutions be understood along the lines of the great nineteenth-century economists who were greatly concerned by income distribution? Or should they be construed as part of a transitional period, containing the seeds of change to come about after 1930?

A defining feature of the 1880–1930 era is the split, particularly with regard to income inequality within countries, a highly sensitive issue at the time. In the most developed European countries, rises in inequality would not halt until the 1850–80 period.

Inequality could even be seen as continuing to worsen until 1910 if one considers the European continent as a whole, which would include the late-comers to industrialization. The twentieth century is characterized by declines in domestic inequality, coupled with increasing inequality between economies since 1820. It is for that reason that the 1880–1910 period saw a rise in inequality both between and within countries.

In the pre-industrial eighteenth-century economies, macro-economic approaches and micro-economic approaches were interchangeable. As for our period of interest, however, interconnections have reached a level of complexity which makes a sectoral approach impracticable without a comprehensive appraisal of capital revenue or social benefits in addition to a worker's income. This would not apply in the pre-1880 state of affairs.

The late nineteenth-century poor, whether they suffered from ailment, aging or unemployment, rarely if ever could count on state benefits. With a few minor exceptions, statistics do not ascertain the existence of any significant state spending to that effect. As early as 1910, however, about a dozen countries are listed as being actively involved in social spending, which in effect became solidly entrenched in government budgets by 1930. This period saw the gradual introduction of the modern welfare state, underpinned by social legislation, overseen by new administrative departments and supported by an adequate budget. Although such policies only concerned a handful of countries at the time, the necessary factors to ensure their wider uptake were already in place.

Lastly, welfare inequality between countries started to decrease in the early twentieth century, while income inequality between people was still rising. This drop fostered economic growth and contributed to bring about a decrease in income inequality between countries in the 1990s. The first two decades of the twenty-first century have seen a steady decline in both well-being and income inequality which bodes well for the future.

NOTES

1. By active individuals we refer to anyone who controls a factor of production, be it labor, capital or land.
2. The Theil index measures the gap between the significance of an individual or group within the overall population and also its significance within the aggregate income. The more spread out the income or the wider the gap, the higher the index. One of the key features of this index is that it may be easily disaggregated.

REFERENCES

Atkinson, Anthony and François Bourguignon. 2000. "Income Distribution and Economics." In *Handbook of Income Distribution* (Vol. 1), ed. Anthony Atkinson and François Bourguignon. Amsterdam: Elsevier, pp. 1–58.

Bengtsson Erik and Daniel Waldenstrom. 2018. "Capital Shares and Income Inequality: Evidence from the Long Run." *The Journal of Economic History* 78, no. 3: 712–43.

Bourguignon, François and Christian Morrisson. 2002. "Inequality among World Citizens." *American Economic Review* 92, no. 4: 727–44.

Duarte, Margarida and Diego Restuccia. 2010. "The Role of the Structural Transformation in Aggregate Productivity." *Quarterly Journal of Economics* 125, no. 1: 129–73.

Higgins, Matthew and Jeffrey Williamson. 1999. "Explaining Inequality the World Round: Cohort Size, Kuznets Curves, and Openness." *NBER Working Papers* 7224.

Kuznets, Simon. 1972. *Croissance et Structures Economiques*. Paris: Calmann-Lévy.

Lindert, Peter. 1994. "The Rising of Social Spending 1880–1930." *Exploration in Economic History* 31, no. 1: 1–36.

Lindert, Peter. 2000. "Three Centuries of Inequality in Britain and America." In *Handbook of Income Distribution* (Vol. 1), ed. Anthony Atkinson and François Bourguignon. Amsterdam: Elsevier, pp. 167–216.

Maddison, Angus. 2003. *The World Economy: Historical Statistics*. Paris: OECD.

Morrisson, Christian and Fabrice Murtin. 2012. "Vers un Monde plus Egal?", *Revue d'Economie du Développement* 20, no. 2: 5–30.

Piketty, Thomas. 2014 [2013]. *Capital in the 21st Century*. Cambridge, MA: Harvard University Press.

van Zanden, Jan Luiten, Joerg Baten, Peter Foldari and Bas van Leeuwen. 2014. "The Changing Shape of Global Inequality, 1820–2000: Exploring a New Dataset." *Review of Income and Wealth* 60, no. 2: 279–97.

9. Inequalities in the United Kingdom: the "Progressive" Era, 1890s–1920s

Patricia Thane

1. INTRODUCTION

A number of inequalities became politically prominent in the United Kingdom (UK) in the 1890s and early 1900s and remained so throughout the twentieth century and beyond, though they waxed and waned over time in their intensity and as sources of concern and protest. Significantly, the Labour Party was founded in 1900 with a central mission to improve the lives of working-class people and reduce income and wealth inequalities. The party was supported, indeed established and funded, by the growing trade unions who had a similar mission and were very active in demanding better pay and working conditions throughout these years (Thorpe 2014).

The three most prominent areas of inequality to arouse public debate and controversy at the turn of the century, and for much longer, were inequalities of income and wealth, the gulf between rich and poor; of gender, as women protested ever more explicitly about the many inequalities they endured compared with men; and racial inequalities as racism, especially directed against Jews, was more evident and the government responded with the first laws restricting access to British nationality rights. This chapter discusses each of these three areas in turn.

2. POVERTY AND WEALTH

Labour's concerns were reinforced by a succession of poverty surveys whose findings aroused widespread shock. First, Charles Booth conducted a massive survey of social conditions in London and concluded that about 30% of Londoners lived "in poverty or in want" (Booth 1903). But London was known to have a complex economy and to attract needy people seeking work and some thought/hoped its level of poverty might be exceptional. Then Seebohm Rowntree, like Booth a businessman who became committed to social investigation and social reform, studied poverty in York, a town he knew well because the family chocolate firm was based there. He believed it was worth studying because it was a fairly typical English town, unlike sprawling London, so might better indicate what conditions were like across the country.

Using a more precise measure of poverty than Booth (whose approach was largely impressionistic) he was shocked to discover that even in York 28% of the population lived "in obvious want and squalor" (Rowntree 1902). A more precise and stringent measurement of "primary poverty" in five representative English towns between 1912 and 1914, was undertaken by the academic statistician A. L. Bowley, using innovative sample survey techniques. This produced more variable, somewhat lower, but still significant numbers in poverty (Bowley and Burnet-Hurst 1905; Gazeley 2003: 30–31).

The surveys, including Bowley's, also revealed that most of the poverty was not, as often suspected, due to feckless shirking by the irresponsible lower classes but to low pay for full-time work, or to under-employment or an inability to obtain regular full-time work despite best efforts to do so, both resulting in incomes insufficient, as Rowntree (1902) put it, "to maintain a moderate family (i.e. not more than four children) in a state of physical efficiency." He found that in York this was true of 52% of households in poverty. They worked hard but for inadequate incomes. In 22% of households the main cause of poverty was "largeness of family," i.e. more than four children; in 16% of cases it was the "death of the chief wage-earner," usually the man, leaving a lone mother to support the family on low wages or the inadequate poor relief available to women.

Low pay and insecure employment became a major concern at this time of William Beveridge, who influenced UK social policy throughout the first half of the twentieth century. He encountered poverty in East London in the early 1900s when, as a young Oxford graduate, he was active in voluntary social work as a resident at Toynbee Hall, the pioneering East London settlement house. He saw workers clustering at the dock gates each morning, never sure how many hours' work, if any, they would get, rarely receiving a full week's work and pay. Employers took advantage of excess labor supply and the numbers desperate to work to feed their families and offered only insecure work and low pay. There were growing numbers of protest demonstrations in periods of economic downturn and especially high unemployment, in the late 1880s, mid 1890s and 1902–05. Beveridge became convinced that only state intervention could regulate the labor market and reduce poverty by ensuring regular work at decent pay. He became an advisor to Winston Churchill, minister responsible for labor affairs in the Liberal government from 1908, and, as a first step, instigated the introduction of Labour Exchanges in 1909. These were offices in every district providing information about permanent job vacancies for the first time, and advice on work and training to school-leavers and the unemployed, assisting escape from casual labor (Harris 1997: 138–97).

This was followed by the introduction in 1911 of the first Unemployment Insurance system in the world, also designed by Beveridge, another step toward regulating the labor market and reducing poverty by supporting (mostly more secure and better paid, skilled) workers through periods of involuntary unemployment due to cyclical and seasonal swings in the labor market. This was one of several innovative early measures of what became the UK Welfare State, including free school meals for needy children, introduced in 1906; state old age pensions in 1908; and National Health Insurance in 1911. They were direct results of the shock and furor following the poverty revelations, combined with pressure from the growing labor movement on a progressive Liberal government in office from 1906 to 1916 (Thane 1996: 49–118). Whatever the uncertainty about the exact numbers in poverty, the conclusion of all research, including further surveys in town and country (Gazeley 2003: 34–64; Freeman 2003), was that it was excessive.

Alongside the poverty surveys, a study of income and wealth in the UK in 1900 by the radical Liberal politician and economist, Sir Leo George Chiozza Money, found serious income and wealth inequality:

UK Income and Wealth c. 1900
Total UK population 1901: 41,438,700
20% employees earned above the income tax threshold of £150 pa.
0.5% earned above £5,000.
87% private property owned by 882,690 persons; 4,400,000 including families.
13% shared among 38,600,000.
17,000 property holders owned c. two-thirds private wealth.
90% of population left no recorded property at death. (Harris 1993: 99; Money 2012)

The sources of wealth and status in the UK were changing. From 1870 to 1914 the value of shares grew fourfold. Landed wealth declined along with the value of rural land, much of which ceased cultivation as Britain imported more food from abroad, made cheaper by modern forms of transport (Harris 1993: 97–8). Many landed estates were sold but wealthy landholders were not pauperized. Some invested in land abroad, often in the British Empire, while others profited from owning urban land, notably the Dukes of Westminster who inherited what became the richest districts of central London and remained one of the wealthiest families in Britain a century later. Or, like Lord Londonderry in north-east England, rich coal deposits under their land yielded fortunes. Others transferred their assets into finance and businesses at home and abroad. Sons of landowners moved into the finance houses of the City of London and business families increasingly intermarried with those of wealthy landowners and financiers. In 1896, a quarter of the landed peerage (by 1910 half) were company directors, many of several companies.

But still, in 1914, the greatest wealth was held by landowners, rivaled only by some leading City financiers. This was because the largest landowners had built up great wealth over many generations and, as land declined in value, many, though not all, successfully reinvested their accumulated assets in a variety of other forms of profitable enterprise, as described above. Parallel with the declining value of land, the City of London, always a major financial center, became the undisputed major capital market of the world, especially following the collapse of the rival Paris money market in the Franco-Prussian war. The City dominated international financial markets and loans to governments throughout the world, making some financiers very rich (Harris 1993: 19–20, 100–106).

Increasingly, business wealth was concentrated in London rather than the industrial North and Midlands, increasing regional inequalities. With the growth of public companies more people lived wholly or partly on investment income. The middle classes continued their nineteenth-century expansion in numbers and diversity while the gap between middling and great wealth grew. In 1905, 861,150 people in the UK owned assets worth £500 to £50,000. They can be assumed to constitute the middle class (Harris 1993: 106–10). The lower middle class grew as clerical and lower level managerial work increased with the expansion of central and local government and large business firms. Most of this new "white-collar" class were upwardly mobile from the skilled working class, to whom they were perceived to be socially superior, the inequalities signified by greater job security though not always higher pay, "respectable" dress (suits and ties for men), living in different neighborhoods, and following different leisure pursuits, though many kept contact with their working-class families.

During the early months of the First World War unemployment rose as the economy adjusted to war needs, and the government was slow to introduce adequate allowances for the families of recruits to the services, further increasing poverty. Thereafter poverty fell and working-class living standards rose due to unprecedented full employment, in the services and essential war work, at adequate pay, despite inflation. This was secured by growing trade unions taking advantage of their exceptional bargaining power in occupations essential to wartime production (Winter 1985; Reid 2004: 221–34).

"White collar" workers were less well protected against inflation. Poverty continued among those unable to work due to age or disability, for whom pensions and poor relief did not keep pace with prices, which rose by 40% in 1914–15 due to shortage of supplies, including food. It rose further thereafter but more gradually as management of the war economy improved. Many businessmen did well from booming demand, causing so much resentment among workers that profits were capped in 1916 at 20% above prewar levels. Also taxes rose and income tax became more progressive, arousing less opposition when required to fund the war than the tentative first moves from a flat-rate income tax which accompanied the early welfare measures from 1908. From 1914 to 1918 the "basic," lowest, rate of income tax rose from 1*s*. 2*d*. to 6*s*. in the pound, and the threshold income at which taxation started to be levied was reduced from £160 to £130 p.a. Higher rate taxes rose from 13% on earned incomes above £500 p.a. to 43% at £10,000 and above, slightly narrowing the gap between higher and lower incomes. The number of direct taxpayers rose by 350% through the war (Daunton 2002: 47–9). Some landed wealth was depleted by death duties following the death of heirs at war.

The government anticipated the return of insecure employment after the war and feared the political impact on a population now accustomed to higher living standards. Advised by Beveridge, they introduced much improved unemployment benefits as the war ended, and also significant improvements to state education, housing and healthcare (Thane 1996: 128–45; Thane 2018: 56–8, 68–71, 73–6). In fact, unemployment was much lower than feared and the economy adjusted smoothly in the two years following the war, due mainly to high levels of international demand arising from postwar reconstruction. Again, trade unions took advantage of the situation to demand and achieve improved pay and working conditions. They expanded from 16% of the labor force in 1910 to 48% by 1920, representing 6.5 million workers (Reid 2004: 182–5).

Then in late 1920 the international economy went into decline bringing high unemployment in Britain which continued until 1940 (Stevenson and Cook 2009). Hardest hit were the industries central to Britain's nineteenth-century development: shipbuilding, engineering, textiles, and coalmining, concentrated in northern England, southern Scotland and South Wales, whose export markets contracted. The government's response to the downturn was to cut much of the postwar welfare expansion, while retaining basic (rather than generous) benefits for the unemployed, to prevent unrest (Thane 2018: 87–117). There was resistance, leading to the only general strike in British history in 1926 in support of miners experiencing wage cuts and unemployment. But unions were weakened by unemployment in their centers of strength and the strike was short-lived, its main outcome legal restrictions on future union activity (Reid 2004: 314–16).

In the 1920s new industries developed supplying electricity, motor vehicles, cycles, chemicals, aircraft, consumer goods (including newly invented household appliances), cigarettes, and cosmetics, generally supplying home rather than export demand which expanded in response to growing employment in these new sectors and in expanding services. Economic development, like decline, was regional. The new industries were concentrated in the Midlands and South of England, further increasing regional inequality (Broadberry 2014: 330–61; Nicolas 2014: 181–204; Offer 2014: 205–25). Unemployed workers from the old industries could not easily transfer to the new. Employers were suspicious of former workers in unionized industries and preferred to employ younger men and, whenever possible, lower-paid women.

Through the 1920s the income share of the top 1% fell fractionally from 20% to approximately 18% of total incomes, and the share of wealth of the top 1% of wealth-holders from 40% to approximately 38% (Atkinson and Morelli 2014). Signifying shifts in popular consumption, two of the largest fortunes left at death in the 1920s were by the first Earl of Iveagh, of the Guinness brewing family, who left £13.5 million in 1927, and Bernhard Barron, inventor of the cigarette slot machine and founder of Carreras cigarettes, who was upwardly mobile from a humble background and a major benefactor of the Labour Party and left £4 million in 1930 (McKibbin 1998: 22–37).

There were more surveys of poverty as the social sciences expanded in universities. They revealed less desperate destitution than before the war, but it had not disappeared and there was considerable variation across the country. In 1924 Bowley repeated the five towns study, adjusting the poverty measure to allow for a slightly more generous average diet. He found alarming levels of child poverty, mainly caused by low pay or the death, disability or absence of the father. A Social Survey of Merseyside in 1929–30, conducted by researchers at Liverpool University, used a similar but more stringent poverty measure and found 16% of the population in poverty, mainly due to inadequate earnings, though unemployment was increasingly significant.

In 1929–31, H. Llewellyn Smith, retired Ministry of Labour civil servant and former researcher on Booth's London survey, headed a team at the London School of Economics, advised by Bowley and using a similar poverty measure, aiming to repeat Booth's survey in selected areas. They concluded that 14% of the population of east London were "subject to conditions of privation which, if long continued, would deny them all but the barest necessities and cut them off from access to many of the incidental and cultural benefits of modern progress." In the whole London County Council area 9.6% were in poverty, though the level was 24% in the poor East London borough of Poplar and 16% of all children in East London. There was acute inequality in London. New industries, especially the manufacture of electrical goods, developed in West London while the East remained depressed and areas of central London were among the richest in the country. The survey concluded that inadequate wages caused 38.5% of London poverty, lack of a male earner 37%, and old age 16.5% (Gazeley 2003: 65–89).

3.   GENDER INEQUALITY

From the 1890s, and still more so in the first years of the twentieth century, women campaigned more militantly than ever before for equality. Campaigners focused especially on demanding the national vote, from which women were excluded. A minority of property holding women (mainly unmarried or widowed) could vote in local government elections from 1869 because the concerns of local government with education, poor relief, public health and other social issues were deemed by influential men, and some women, to lie within women's sphere of interest and competence as major affairs of state did not (Hollis 1987). Women now demanded the national vote for its own sake, since lacking it was a gross symbol of inequality, but they also wanted it as the key to improving social conditions generally which they believed were being neglected by an all-male parliament. Other inequalities women suffered also needed to be eliminated; examples include: access to work and pay; it was easier for a man to get a divorce than a woman (in England and Wales, though not in Scotland where divorce rights were equal, another regional inequality) (see Cretney 2003: 161–318); if a couple did divorce or separate only the father had the right to custody of children over age 10; and women had very limited property rights after marriage. Women believed that the vote would give them the political influence to achieve change (Liddington and Norris 1978).

After campaigning in larger numbers and more openly than before – some militantly, others more quietly – before the First World War, the women suspended activism during the war since it was unlikely to be effective and might be interpreted as unpatriotic to their disadvantage. Then, toward the end of the war, the government began to plan franchise reform and peaceable campaigning revived (Holton 1986). The Representation of the People Act was passed in February 1918, before the end of the war, partially enfranchising women. It removed another longstanding inequality more decisively: it also enfranchised for the first time all adult men. Previously 40% of adult men were excluded by a 12-month residence qualification and the requirement to hold property of a certain value. Most, but not all, of those excluded were working class. Middle- and upper-class men, mostly unmarried, who did not own or rent their own property but lived in parental property or rented lodgings were also excluded (Tanner 1990).

The 1918 Act was a move toward class equality among men which the Labour Party had demanded from its foundation. It came about because the wartime coalition government felt it necessary to enfranchise men who were fighting in a war of unprecedented violence, often involuntarily because from 1915 they were conscripted, required to fight, for the first time in modern British history. Conscription had been previously fiercely resisted, especially by Liberals, as an infringement of freedom. Nevertheless, politicians found the prospect of millions more working-class male voters alarming, especially because the Labour Party was growing in strength, while the Russian Revolution of 1917 brought the specter of socialism still closer. One means to counter this danger, it was believed, was to give women the vote – but not all adult women. Women were enfranchised only at age 30, men at 21, or younger if they had served in the war (though conscientious objectors were banned from voting for five years after the conflict ended). This inequality came about because another alarming prospect for male politicians was that women were a majority of the adult population and so would become a majority of voters if enfranchised on the same terms as men. This was not just due to male deaths during the war, as is sometimes believed. The 1911 UK census recorded 107 females to every 100 males; that of 1921 110/100; an increased majority but not massively so. Women had possibly always been a majority because on average women lived longer than men, and still do.

The other reason why women were enfranchised only at age 30 was politicians' beliefs that older women were more mature and stable, less likely to be attracted to socialism than irresponsible younger women. They made this more certain by further restricting the female vote by imposing on women the property qualification which the same law removed from men: female voters must be property-holders or married to property holders. This excluded most working-class women over age 30.

Women university graduates could also vote: male and female graduates could vote for candidates for nine parliamentary seats representing UK universities, though women formed only 25% of all graduates. Also, under the new law the right of businessmen to vote twice if their residence and business premises were in different constituencies did not apply to businesswomen. Equally irrationally, three single men "jointly occupying" a ratable property each had the vote, whereas if three women did so, only two could vote. The local government franchise was extended to the wives of male electors at age 30; suitably qualified single women continued to vote from age 21. The 1918 Act narrowed class and gender inequalities in some respects while reinforcing them in others. It tripled the electorate from 7 million to 21 million and women represented 43% of voters (Pugh 1978).

Once women had the vote they used it, often less conservatively than the politicians had hoped, to achieve greater equalities, including campaigning for an equal franchise. Few women were elected to parliament. From November 1918 they could stand for election from age 21, before they could vote. Women had not campaigned for this and it was not mentioned significantly in the debates on the Representation of the People Act. The change came about because it was unclear whether, now that many women could vote, they, like male voters, automatically gained the right to seek election to parliament. There were concerns that, unless the law was clarified, it would be left to local returning officers to decide whether women were qualified to stand.

The reform started with a parliamentary resolution submitted by Liberal MP Herbert Samuel, who regretted he had not supported suffragism more enthusiastically (his wife was a suffragist). He presented the reform as a logical consequence of the 1918 Act, arguing for 21 as the age limit since the objection that the adult franchise would make women a majority of voters would not apply to candidates. Also, he and other MPs pointed out that they had been elected before they could vote, before they met the property qualification, so the same right could not be denied to women (Takayanagi 2012: 16–37). It was also suggested that women should be allowed to join the House of Lords. This was rejected by the Lords but the campaign continued until women were at last admitted in 1958 (Sutherland 2000). Samuel's proposal passed easily though parliament, but it created new anomalies. Ellen Wilkinson was elected in 1924 as Labour's first female MP, aged 33 but was unable to vote because, she said, she had "neither a husband nor furniture" (Takayanagi 2012: 131).

Perhaps parliament expected few women to be elected. If so, they were right. In the December 1918 election 17 women stood but only one was elected, Countess Constance Markiewicz, Irish nationalist and feminist, in Holloway prison at the time for her role in the Easter Rising. Like other Sinn Feiners she refused to take her seat in Westminster. The first woman to be elected was Conservative Nancy Astor in 1919, joining 706 male MPs. She succeeded her husband in his seat when he was elevated to the House of Lords after inheriting a peerage on his father's death. She found the Commons a lonely, often hostile, place. She later recalled: "When I stood up and asked questions affecting women and children, social and moral questions, I used to be shouted at for 5 or 10 minutes at a time" (Takayanagi 2012: 137). In 1920 she was joined by Liberal Margaret Wintringham, a former suffragist, who also replaced her husband, on his death. Many women lacking the advantage of a husband's reflected glory wanted to stand for parliament but for decades sexist prejudice prevented their selection for winnable seats for any party (Childs et al. 2005: 18–47). The largest number of women elected between the wars was 15 in 1931, when 62 women stood.

Feminists were dubious about Astor because she had no record of supporting women's causes, but she was responsive to their briefings, perhaps grateful for support in a hostile political world and worked to support many of their campaigns, as did a small group of male MPs. She cooperated with Wintringham and other female MPs across parties. Women voters demanded her attention, sending her up to 2,000 letters each week. They similarly bombarded male MPs on policy issues, reminding them that women's votes mattered, achieving a degree of influence over politicians, who needed their votes. Women certainly used the vote and the flourishing women's organizations of the period campaigned, with some success, for legal changes promoting gender equality (Thane 2001). Astor supported the campaign for equal voting rights which they achieved in 1928, after considerable foot-dragging by Stanley Baldwin's Conservative government leading to threats to revive suffragette militancy (Law 1997: 202–18). Women then represented 53% of the electorate.

They kept campaigning for equality through the interwar years and after. It used to be thought that once women got the vote they became much less active until the women's movement revived in the 1960s. They did not; indeed, probably more women were active, campaigning on more fronts, between the wars than in the suffrage campaigns before 1914. They were less flamboyant and they fought for a number of different issues, not just the single demand for the vote. Very gradually they achieved some moves toward gender equality; for example, access to a wider range of occupations, including the legal profession, accountancy and architecture from 1919, though true equal opportunities within those professions would involve a still longer struggle. The same legislation, the Sex Disqualification (Removal) Act, granted women the right to sit on juries for the first time in their long history, partially ending the terrifying situation whereby women faced court proceedings alone in a wholly male courtroom. However, again, there was a property qualification for jury members which excluded most women. And judges could exclude female jurors from "unsuitable" trials thought offensive to their "delicacy," e.g. rape trials, a situation that continued until 1972. Women could also join the police force, though by 1939 only 174 were admitted to a force of 65,000 (Jackson 2006).

The Act also allowed women to become magistrates, administering justice unpaid at the lowest but indispensable level of the system. By 1927 there were 1,600 female magistrates in a total of 25,000. But here, too, inequality was sustained. Three justices sat together in every magistrates' court; it was permissible for two, the majority, to be male but not female (Logan 2008: 55–63, 86–95). Women were also admitted to the highest grade of the civil service, though few succeeded for many decades, and they were excluded from representing their country in the diplomatic service until 1973 (McCarthy 2014). In posts they were allowed to enter they were disadvantaged not only by prejudice but by the "marriage bar" which excluded married women from work anywhere in the public sector. Women in the civil service, teaching and elsewhere campaigned unsuccessfully against this inequality throughout the interwar years. And while they worked they were paid less than men even for the same work, another cause of persistent campaigning which took even longer to overcome (Glew 2016).

More successfully, in the 1920s, women campaigners, with the help of female and male MPs, achieved gender equality in divorce rights and child custody. When divorce was re-established in England and Wales in 1857, for the first time since the Reformation, husbands could divorce their wives for adultery, but, in keeping with the prevailing sexual double standard, wives had to prove an "aggravation" in addition to adultery, such as extreme violence. The reformed law from 1923 abolished this inequality and included provision of adequate alimony, to avoid trapping women in unhappy marriages for fear of poverty, given the continuing limited work opportunities and low pay of women. But divorce was still expensive, which ruled it out for poorer women and men. In principle, women in England and Wales gained equality in divorce with Scotland, but no divorce was possible in Northern Ireland where the churches opposed it, except by the expensive process of private Act of Parliament. Inequalities across the countries of the UK continued (Cretney 2003: 196–318).

Women were also trapped in unhappy marriages by fear of losing their children, since only fathers had rights to custody of children from age 10. A change in the law from 1924 allowed women to request custody after divorce or legal separation, though it required an expensive legal process and judges were still inclined to favor fathers.

4.   RACE INEQUALITY

Another equality issue that became prominent in Britain in the 1900s (and which has never disappeared) concerns race. In 1900, immigration to Britain was unrestricted. One large group of potential immigrants, people born anywhere within the vast British Empire, were British with identical rights to people born in the UK. In law, since at least the seventeenth century, anyone born within the Empire was a British "subject" of the Crown (not a "citizen," a term reserved for republics, like France) with full rights of British nationality, including the right to remain in the UK for as long as they wished and to vote if suitably qualified. This remained the case in law until 1962 (Dummett and Nicol 1990; Thane 1998: 29–46). Many colonial-born seamen, especially, settled in Britain in the nineteenth and early twentieth centuries creating multicultural communities in the major port cities, including London, Bristol, Liverpool and Glasgow.

But, at all times, if colonial migrants aroused official suspicion for any reason they could be asked to provide evidence of their birthplace, a birth certificate or equivalent, which many poorer colonial people could not. They could then be excluded from the UK. This became especially prevalent amid the unemployment of the 1920s if people of colonial origin applied for unemployment benefit, and more so after 1925 when the Home Office introduced the Coloured Alien Seamen's Order defining all "colored" seamen as "aliens," i.e. not British, unless they proved otherwise, as few could (Tabili 1994: 2011). Wealthy colonials who came to Britain as students, for business or for any other reason, as many did, could be sure of equal rights as poorer migrants could not, though all people of color faced everyday racist discrimination.

In 1900 the situation was different and already becoming difficult for immigrants from outside the Empire, "aliens" as they were officially termed, who had no automatic right to remain in Britain or to other nationality rights. They could buy British nationality for a payment of £3, without other conditions, but this was expensive for poor people. How many non-colonials migrated to Britain, for how long, is uncertain because there were no passports or border checks. Around 1900, there were substantial numbers of Italians, Germans and others, mainly from Europe, in London and other cities who were generally accepted and tolerated (Tabili 2011). Immigrants might be fleeing persecution or seeking work, including poor Italians and wealthy men of many countries attracted to the City of London, the world's financial center. Another dimension of gender inequality was that from 1870 British-born women who married "aliens" lost their nationality and all associated rights and were required to adopt that of their husband, though they could apply for British nationality five years after widowhood or divorce; from 1914, following protests, immediately upon widowhood. This unequal treatment of women in nationality law was international and a cause of international women's protest between the wars. It survived in Britain until 1948.

Despite persistent hostility to "coloreds," racist antagonism to immigrants was not a significant issue in the UK until thousands of Jews fled Russia from the 1880s, mostly escaping vicious pogroms, but also severe poverty. Perhaps 250,000 reached Britain by 1914 – the number is uncertain – often impoverished, settling in particularly large numbers in East London. Like poor immigrants throughout the century, they were accused of taking jobs and homes from British people, disrupting their communities and culture, and lowering living standards. To avoid accusations that Jews were abusing public welfare services, and to protect them against intensified anti-Semitic discrimination, the established Jewish community, including wealthy businessmen and financiers, set up institutions to support them, including Jewish schools and a Jewish Board of Guardians providing welfare aid. They helped immigrants establish themselves in employment or small businesses, contributing valuably to the economy.

They received little thanks and racist protests led to Britain's first immigration restrictions: the Aliens Act, 1905. Conservative Prime Minister Arthur Balfour told parliament: "We have the right to keep out everybody who does not add to . . . the industrial, social and intellectual strength of the community." To remain, immigrants must show they could support themselves and their dependents "decently" and could "speak, read and write English reasonably well." Criminals, the insane and those thought likely to apply for poor relief were excluded. No "alien" could apply for naturalization before five years' residence. Following parliamentary pressure, the Act granted asylum to refugees who could prove they were escaping "persecution involving danger of imprisonment or danger to life or limb on account of religious belief'" (Feldman 1994: 287–90).

The law was reinforced in 1914 based on the principle, as a Home Office circular put it,

> That, save in very exceptional circumstances a person can have no claim to be invested with the full rights of British nationality if he has not identified with the life and habits of the country to the extent of becoming reasonably proficient in the language . . . [and] . . . cannot read the language . . . Mere conversational facility when he meets a Gentile does not suffice to show that a Jew is identifying himself with English life . . . if the only newspapers he can read are Jewish ones, the likelihood is that his ideas are kept widely apart from those of the ordinary English citizen (Feldman 1994: 372).

A clear statement of which migrant group it was aimed at. Jewish immigration from Russia declined by 1914, but antisemitism and unequal treatment of Jews did not disappear. It was strong during the war when Jews were, quite unjustly, accused of cowardly evasion of military service, while Germans, or people with German names, were vilified and attacked. The German-origin royal family changed its name from Saxe-Coburg-Gotha to the very English Windsor in response. Antisemitism and the discrimination and inequalities which went with it peaked in fascist attacks in the early 1930s, though these were strongly resisted by British anti-fascists (Skidelsky 1975; Stevenson and Cook 2009: 195–217; Gottlieb 2003).

5.   CONCLUSION

In conclusion, inequalities were a pervasive feature of British culture from the 1890s to the 1920s. This chapter has focused upon inequalities of income, gender and race, which were very different in their manifestations but all politically and culturally significant. Nor were they new. There had always between a large gulf between the incomes and life chances of rich and poor, in the rights and opportunities of women compared with men, and anti-Semitism is age-old and international. They became politically prominent at this time due to campaigns and protests by a range of political and social movements. This gradually led to changes in the law: gender inequalities were somewhat diminished following demands by women after they partially gained the vote; inequalities of wealth and income narrowed slightly following protests especially by the labor movement and the birth of a welfare state; race inequalities, on the other hand were intensified by new restrictions on Jewish and other immigrants of non-British nationalities.

Since the 1920s these same inequalities have waxed and waned but have persisted despite repeated movements challenging them, though the continuance of race inequalities, unlike those of income and gender, owes much to a succession of pro-racist movements. The same long period has seen other inequalities brought to public notice by protest campaigns, including concerning homosexuality, old age and disability, and some measures of variable success to mitigate them (Thane 2010). The history of Britain since the 1890s, in this as in other respects, is a story of change but not of uncomplicated progress toward all-pervasive equality.

REFERENCES

Atkinson, Tony and Salvatore Morelli. 2014. *The New Chartbook of Economic Inequality*, available at http://www.chartbookofeconomicinequality.com/inequality-by-country/united-kingdom.

Booth, Charles. 1903. *Life and Labour of the People of London: First Series, Poverty, Volume 2*. London: Macmillan.

Bowley, Arthur Lyon and Alexander Robert Burnett-Hurst. 1905. *Livelihood and Poverty*. London: G. Bell and Sons.

Broadberry, Stephen. 2014. "The Rise of the Service Sector." In *The Cambridge Economic History of Modern Britain. Volume 2. 1870 to the Present*, ed. Roderick Floud, Jane Humphries and Paul Johnson. Cambridge: Cambridge University Press, pp. 330–61.

Childs, Sarah, Joni Lovenduski and Rosie Campbell. 2005. *Women at the Top 2005: Changing Numbers, Changing Politics?* London: Hansard Society.

Cretney, Stephen. 2003. *Family Law in the Twentieth Century: A History*. Oxford: Oxford University Press.

Daunton, Martin. 2002. *Just Taxes: The Politics of Taxation in Britain 1914–1979*. Cambridge: Cambridge University Press.

Dummett, Ann and Andrew Nicol. 1990. *Subjects, Citizens, Aliens and Others: Nationality and Immigration Law*. Chicago, IL: Northwestern University Press.

Feldman, David. 1994. *Englishmen and Jews: Social Relations and Political Culture, 1840–1914*. New Haven, CT: Yale University Press.

Freeman, Mark. 2003. *Social Investigation and Rural England, 1870–1914*. Rochester, NY: Boydell and Brewer.

Gazeley, Ian. 2003. *Poverty in Britain, 1900–1965*. London: Palgrave.

Glew, Helen. 2016. *Gender, Rhetoric and Regulation: Women's Work in the Civil Service and the London County Council, 1900–55*. Manchester: Manchester University Press.

Gottlieb, Julie V. 2003. *Feminine Fascism: Women in Britain's Fascist Movement 1923–1945*. London: I. B. Tauris.

Harris, Jose. 1993. *Private Lives, Public Spirit*. Oxford: Oxford University Press.

Harris, Jose. 1997. *William Beveridge: A Biography*. Oxford: Oxford University Press.

Hollis, Patricia. 1987. *Ladies Elect: Women in English Local Government, 1865–1914*. Oxford: Oxford University Press.

Holton, Sandra Stanley. 1986. *Feminism and Democracy: Women's Suffrage and Reform Politics in Britain 1900–1918*. Cambridge: Cambridge University Press.

Jackson, Louise. 2006. *Women Police: Gender, Welfare and Surveillance in the Twentieth Century*. Manchester: Manchester University Press.

Law, Cheryl. 1997. *Suffrage and Power: The Women's Movement, 1918–28*. London: I. B. Tauris.

Liddington, Jill and Jill Norris. 1978. *One Hand Tied Behind Us: The Rise of the Women's Suffrage Movement*. London: Virago.

Logan, Ann. 2008. *Feminism and Criminal Justice: A Historical Perspective*. London: Palgrave.

McCarthy, Helen. 2014. *Women of the World: The Rise of the Female Diplomat*. London: Bloomsbury.

McKibbin, Ross. 1998. *Classes and Cultures: England 1918–51*. Oxford: Oxford University Press.

Money, Leo George Chiozza. 2012 [1905]. *Riches and Poverty*. London: Nabu Press.

Nicolas, Tom. 2014. "Technology, Innovation and Economic Growth in Britain since 1870." In *The Cambridge Economic History of Modern Britain. Volume 2. 1870 to the Present*, ed. Roderick Floud, Jane Humphries and Paul Johnson. Cambridge: Cambridge University Press, pp. 181–204.

Offer, Avner. 2014. "Consumption and Affluence: 1870–2010." In *The Cambridge Economic History of Modern Britain. Volume 2. 1870 to the Present*, ed. Roderick Floud, Jane Humphries and Paul Johnson. Cambridge: Cambridge University Press, pp. 205–28.

Pugh, Martin. 1978. *Electoral Reform in War and Peace 1906–1918*. London: Routledge.

Reid, Alastair J. 2004. *United We Stand: A History of Britain's Trade Unions*. London: Allen Lane.

Rowntree, Benjamin S. 1902. *Poverty: A Study of Town Life*. London: Macmillan.

Skidelsky, Robert. 1975. *Oswald Mosley*. New York: Holt, Rinehart and Winston.

Stevenson, John and Chris Cook. 2009. *The Slump: Britain in the Great Depression*. London: Routledge.

Sutherland, Duncan. 2000. "Peeresses, Parliament and Prejudice: The Admission of Women to the House of Lords, 1900–1963." Unpublished PhD thesis. University of Cambridge.

Tabili, Laura. 1994. "The Construction of Racial Difference in Twentieth Century Britain: The Special Restriction [Coloured Alien Seamen] Order, 1925." *Journal of British Studies* 33, no. 1: 54–98.

Tabili, Laura. 2011. *Global Migrants and Local Culture: Natives and Newcomers in Provincial England, 1841–1919*. London: Palgrave Macmillan.

Takayanagi, Mari. 2012. "Parliament and Women, 1900–1945". Unpublished PhD thesis. King's College London.

Tanner, Duncan. 1990. *Political Change and the Labour Party, 1900–1918*. Cambridge: Cambridge University Press.

Thane, Patricia. 1996. *Foundations of the Welfare State*. London: Longman.

Thane, Patricia. 1998. "The British Imperial State and National Identities." In *Borderlines, Genders and Identities in War and Peace, 1870–1930*, ed. Billie Melman. London: Routledge, pp. 29–46.

Thane, Patricia. 2001. "What Difference did the Vote Make?." In *Women, Privilege and Power: British Politics 1750 to the Present*, ed. Amanda Vickery. Stanford, CA: Stanford University Press, pp. 253–88.

Thane, Patricia (ed.). 2010. *Unequal Britain: Inequalities in Britain since 1945*. London: Bloomsbury.

Thane, Patricia. 2018. *Divided Kingdom: A History of Britain, 1900 to the Present*. Cambridge: Cambridge University Press.

Thorpe, Andrew. 2014. *A History of the British Labour Party*. London: Palgrave.

Winter, Jay R. 1985. *The Great War and the British People*. London: Macmillan.

10. Distribution as a macroeconomic problem

Robert Skidelsky

1. INTRODUCTION

John Maynard Keynes (1883–1946) introduced chapter 24 of the *General Theory of Employment, Interest and Money* (*GT*) with the words: "The outstanding faults of the economic society in which we live are its failure to provide for full employment and its arbitrary and inequitable distribution of wealth and incomes." His *magnum opus*, he wrote, was directed to the first, but his theory had an important bearing on the second, in two respects. First, it denied that saving was the engine of investment. Up to full employment, "the growth of capital depends not at all on the low propensity to consume but is, on the contrary, held back by it." Secondly, whereas investment was promoted by a low rate of interest, the belief that it was necessary to provide a sufficient inducement to save, kept interest rates high. A full employment policy would require, and would lead to, "the euthanasia of the rentier" (Keynes 1964: 372– 6).

Keynes was *relatively* indifferent to questions of inequality and distribution. For this there were three main reasons. Keynes was a macro-economist. His economics came out of the theory of money, not out of the theory of value, which was then, as indeed it has reverted to being, the core of economic theory. In the *GT*, he provided a short-run equilibrium theory which took the "distribution of the national income" as given (Keynes 1964: 245).

Second, he was concerned to limit his attack on orthodox economic theory and the social structure which it supported to the minimum needed to secure intellectual and political support for his full employment policy. His attack, he emphasized, was not on the way the capitalist system allocated a given volume of resources, but its failure to secure the full utilization of potential resources (Keynes 1964: 379). In his politics, Keynes was a liberal, not a socialist or social democrat.

Third, Keynes was personally not much moved by the existence of "poverty in the midst of plenty." Consider the distinctly complacent picture he paints of the class structure of Victorian England in *Economic Consequences of the Peace (ECP)*:

> The greater part of the population, it is true, worked hard and lived at a low standard of comfort, yet were to all appearances, reasonably content with this lot. But escape was possible, for any man of capacity or character at all exceeding the average, into the middle and upper classes . . . (Keynes 1919: 6)[1]

It is possible to find much more critical passages in Keynes's writing,[2] but these were incidental to the main thrust of his ideas.

Thus Keynes stood apart from the attempt of his Cambridge colleague, Arthur Pigou, to use neoclassical economics to make the case for income redistribution,[3] and, more generally, from left-wing attempts to pin the malfunctioning of capitalist economies on the unequal distribution of wealth and incomes. Indeed, he attributed the triumph of *laissez-faire* to the "poor quality" and "scientific deficiency" of the "opponent proposals," especially Marxist socialism (Keynes 1926).[4] It was not until he started to work on the *GT* in the early 1930s that he saw the affinity between his own account of capitalist malfunction and the distributional questions raised by its left-wing critics. The meeting point was class differences in the propensity to consume.

2. THE THEORY OF UNDER-CONSUMPTION

Under-consumption theories – which might just as well be called over-saving theories – have a long lineage, starting in the early nineteenth century and featuring such names as Sismondi, Malthus, Karl Marx, and Rosa Luxemburg.[5]

Under-consumptionists were impressed by the fact that part of the income generated by production is saved. They then concluded (too hastily) that saving reduces aggregate demand relative to aggregate supply.

Their reasoning went something like this. Imagine an economy which uses money, in which everything produced is consumed, including the machines which wear out at a steady rate. Say's Law holds: demand equals supply.

But now suppose people decide to invest an extra 10% of their earnings in new machines rather than just replace old ones. There will then be a simultaneous fall in demand for consumption goods and an increase in capacity to produce them. We have over-saving or over-investment in relation to demand: Say's Law is breached, a depression ensues.

Orthodox economists pointed out that this chain of reasoning neglects the fact that real incomes rise with the new investment to enable the purchase of the enlarged flow of consumer goods. No excess stocks of capital accumulate.

The more sophisticated under-consumptionists understood that saving was not a simple subtraction from demand. They were not against saving as such, but against over-saving. Over-saving existed when it led to more investment in new machines than any expected demand for consumables in the future would justify.

They thought this could happen if saving is divorced from the desire for more consumption goods, but is an automatic consequence of some people having too much money. The rich have more surplus income than the poor; so the more concentrated wealth becomes, the more over-saving, and over-investing, there will be.

By far the most influential under-consumptionist writer was the English liberal thinker J. A. Hobson (1858–1940), who can claim to have influenced both Keynes and Lenin.[6] His argument is summarized in his book *The Physiology of Industry* (1889), which he co-authored with a businessman, A. F. Mummery:

> Saving, while it increases the existing aggregate of Capital, simultaneously reduces the quantity of utilities and conveniences consumed; any undue exercise of this habit must, therefore cause an accumulation of Capital in excess of that which is required for use, and this excess will exist in the form of general overproduction. (Hobson and Mummery 1889: v)

Hobson uses his theory to explain the business cycle. In the boom phase, the saving to income ratio rises, leading to over-saving and the collapse of the boom. As the depression deepens, the saving class reduces its saving to conserve its consumption, and the saving/income ratio falls back to a "normal" rate, before the chronic tendency to over-save starts the whole process again (Hobson 1910: 303; 1922: 12).

In a subsequent book, *Imperialism* (1902), Hobson applied his theory to explaining imperialism; imperialism provided a vent for surplus capital and thus a method for overcoming periodic crises of overproduction (Hobson 1902). Domestic under-consumption was thus the "taproot" of imperialism. The surplus savings which reduce consumption at home earn an income for capitalists when invested abroad. In a similar vein, the German Marxist Rosa Luxemburg thought that capitalism required external markets, such as afforded by colonies or government spending on armaments, to offset the deficiency of domestic consumption. Lenin's theory of the inevitability of wars between competing capitalist states, each seeking to export its surplus capital, derives directly from Hobson.[7]

How does Hobson explain the "undue exercise" of the saving habit? In his books *The Problem of the Unemployed* (1896) and *the Economics of Distribution* (1900), he locates it in the class distribution of wealth and income.

Hobson rejected the marginal productivity theory of rewards to the factors of production. Rather, he generalized Ricardo's theory of rent to cover the surplus of return over cost which capitalists were able to extract from the workers.

This surplus was derived from their ability to monopolize the "requisites of production," i.e. to get "rents" or super-profits from the ownership of scarce factors of production like land, skills, raw materials and techniques. This put them in a superior bargaining position to labor; in every market the right of the economically stronger prevailed. The more monopolized the ownership of scarce resources, the more opportunities there would be to extract rent. The inequalities of wealth thus created were perpetuated and increased by inheritance. Ever alert to the existence of monopoly firms, economists were blind to the existence of monopoly conferred by ownership of the means of production.

The ownership of productive tools by the class of capitalists was at the heart of under-consumption theory. This meant that the fruits of productivity growth went unduly to the saving, not the consuming class. Since Hobson assumed that savings were automatically invested, this resulted in periodic gluts of production which led to periodic slumps. The remedy was to tax "surplus" wealth through a graduated income tax and high death duties, and redistribute it to those with a high propensity to consume. That would end crises of overproduction and the need to export surplus capital abroad.[8] Hobson attacked low wages as detrimental to both productivity and quality of life, and the high earnings of directors as vastly in excess of their economic contribution.

Hobson thus emphasized class power, but as a contingent, rather than a necessary, feature of a capitalist system. This was in contrast to Karl Marx, who saw "exploitation" of the worker – paying workers less than they produced – as necessary for profit. For Hobson, only part of profit was rent: for Marx, the whole of it. Marx's labor theory of value was an attempt to isolate that part of the price of a product which simply provided a free lunch for the owner of capital. Competitive capitalism was driven by the quest for profit, profit derived from exploitation – extracting "surplus value" from workers. But exploitation left workers unable to buy all they had produced. Here was capitalism's great contradiction: "The last cause of all real crises," Marx wrote, "always remains the poverty and restricted consumption of the masses as compared to the tendency of capitalist production to develop the productive forces" (Blaug 1996: 270).[9] His followers regarded social democratic schemes like Hobson's for redistributing wealth within capitalism as utopian. Exploitation could be ended only by abolishing "surplus value" – extinguishing capitalists as a class.

The Hobson–Marx under-consumption theory of capitalist crisis is at the opposite pole of the Austrian "overconsumption" theory. According to Hayek it is not over-saving but under-saving which is the problem. The crisis which produces the slump is a crisis of over-investment relative to the amount of consumption people want to postpone, financed by credit-creation by the banking system. The slump is merely the process of eliminating the "malinvestments," those not financed by genuine savings. Slumps can be prevented by stopping banks from creating more credit than people want to save. As the rap put it: "You must save to invest, don't use the printing press. Or a bust will surely follow, an economy depressed."[10]

Keynes was notoriously tone-deaf to Marx, but he was much more sympathetic to Hobson than to Hayek.[11] In the *GT* he made handsome amends for his previous neglect of him, enlisting him in the "brave army of heretics, who, following their intuitions, have preferred to see the truth obscurely and imperfectly rather than maintain error, reached indeed with clearness and consistency and by easy logic, but on hypotheses inappropriate to the facts" (Keynes 1964: 371). His criticism of Hobson was based on what he saw as a technical mistake in Hobson's reasoning: it was to suppose that

> it is a case of excessive saving causing the *actual* accumulation of capital in excess of what is required, which is, in fact, a secondary evil which only occurs through mistakes of foresight; whereas the primary evil is a propensity to save in conditions of full employment more than the equivalent of the capital which is required, thus preventing full employment except when there is a mistake of foresight. (Keynes 1964: 367–8)

Hobson's problem, Keynes thought, was that he lacked an "independent theory of the rate of interest" (Keynes 1964: 370). He assumed that changes in interest rates automatically equalized saving and investment, giving rise, on his over-saving theory to systemic over-investment, interrupted by crises, whereas for Keynes, the rate of interest being the price of money, not saving, the only equalizing mechanism was a change in income. Thus Hobson's was a theory of over-investment: Keynes's a theory of under-investment.

Keynes thought that the most important short-run remedy for unemployment was to raise the rate of investment, not reduce it. This would require, in addition to public investment, keeping the long-term rate of interest permanently low, resulting in the "euthanasia of the rentier, and, consequently the euthanasia of the power of the capitalist to exploit the scarcity value of capital." For "interest today rewards no genuine sacrifice, and more than does the rent of land" (Keynes 1964: 376). This was a return to Ricardo.

Though he never identified "over-saving" as the main *cause* of unemployment, which he thought, rather, lay in the weakness of the inducement to invest at any given level of saving, he did believe that the marginal efficiency of capital would fall as capital became more abundant, making it increasingly difficult to maintain a full employment level of investment. In this sense he was a long-term under-consumptionist. As communities became richer, they should consume more and save less: savings habits appropriate to the accumulation of wealth became dysfunctional when accumulation was no longer a priority. At this point schemes for the "higher taxation of large incomes and inheritance" would come into their own, though Keynes was doubtful about how far or fast they should go (Keynes 1964: 376–7). He was only moderately sympathetic to the ethical case for income distribution, writing that "there is social and psychological justification for significant inequalities of income and wealth, but not such large disparities as exist today" (Keynes 1964: 374).

Under-consumptionist theory influenced left-wing explanations of the Great Depression of the 1930s, both at the time and subsequently. The explosion of consumer credit kept consumer demand buoyant in the United States up to 1929; its withdrawal amplified the slump. Typical in its under-consumptionist reasoning is this passage from Marriner Eccles, chairman of the US Federal Reserve Board from 1934 to 1948:

> A mass production economy has to be accompanied by mass consumption. Mass consumption in turn implies a distribution of wealth to provide men with buying power. Instead of achieving that kind of distribution, a giant suction pump had by 1929 drawn into a few hands an increasing proportion of currently produced wealth. This served them as capital accumulation. But by taking purchasing power out of the hands of mass consumers, the savers denied to themselves the kind of effective demand for their products that would justify a reinvestment of their capital accumulations in new plants. In consequences, as in a poker game when the chips were concentrated in fewer and fewer hands, the other fellows could stay in the game only by borrowing. When their credit ran out, the game stopped. (Eccles 1951: 76)

Under-consumption also featured in Marxian explanations of the Great Depression of the 1930s. For example, James Devine argued that, in the USA, stagnant wages (relative to labor productivity) meant that increases in working-class consumption could only be financed by debt. Eventually (in 1929), the over-investment boom ended, leaving unused industrial capacity and debt obligations. Once the depression occurred, recovery of private investment and consumption was blocked by falling prices which increased the real debt burden. Trying to restore the profit rate by cutting wages only reduced prices and consumer demand further. Devine called this the under-consumption trap (Devine 1994).

3.   THE MODERN UNDER-CONSUMPTIONIST STORY

The modern under-consumptionist story starts with the big increase in inequality, noticeable in all developed countries since the 1970s.

Thomas Piketty's *Capital in the Twenty-First Century* documented in exhaustive detail the increase in inequality over the last forty years (Piketty 2014). Coming on top of the crash of 2008, it rekindled interest in distributional issues in both their moral and efficiency aspects. Piketty restated the familiar social democratic charge against capitalism: that its ownership system offended the principle of distributive justice. But his analysis also led people, eager to explore causes of the Great Recession of 2008–09 deeper than the familiar tale of predatory bankers, to wonder whether the patchy and unbalanced performance of market economies in recent years was not somehow the result of growing inequality.

The fact that inequality has increased is not in dispute. Median real incomes have stagnated, or fallen, throughout the Western world even as economies have continued to grow. Egregious examples are legion. A frequently cited US statistic is that over the past two decades, the ratio of the pay of CEOs to the average pay of their workforces has increased from 20:1 in 1961 to 231:1 in 2011 (Mishel et al. 2012). (For some companies, it is over 1,000 to 1.) Atkinson, Piketty and Saez (2011) show that inequality in the USA fell for decades after the Wall Street crash of 1929 before starting to rise again in the 1970s. Now the top 1% own over 20% of US wealth. The same pattern is seen in the UK and Italy. This coincides with the transfer of wealth from the public to the private sector. Cross-country studies show that practically all the increase in advanced country wealth in the last twenty years has gone to the top 1%. The rich have raced away from the poor; and the very rich have raced away from the rich.

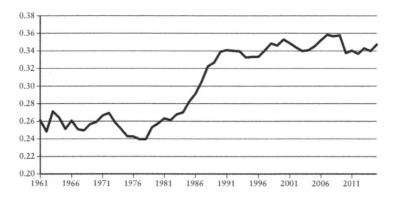

Figure 10.1   UK Gini coefficient, 1961–2016

Note: Absolute equality is zero; absolute inequality (one person owning all the income) is 1.
Source: Gini coefficient data calculated using net equivalized household income before deduction of housing costs (Institute for Fiscal Studies 2016), graph my own.

Edward Luttwak, writing in the *Times Literary Supplement*, claims that the service economy is in fact becoming a servant economy: "too-busy-to-live live high-techies employ retinues of nannies, housekeepers, dog walkers, cat-minders, pool boys and personal shoppers" (Luttwak 2015). Automation of manufacturing will release more and more servants to serve the rich. The Gini coefficient for the UK shows the spurt in inequality from 1979 to 1990 (Figure 10.1).

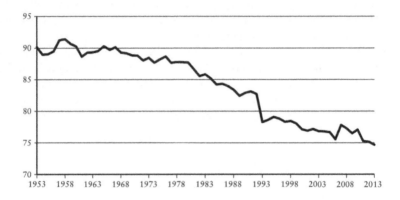

Figure 10.2   *Median family income as proportion of mean family income in the USA, 1953–2013 (%)*

Source: Data from Federal Reserve Bank of St. Louis (2015), graph my own.

A second chart from the USA shows the growing gap between mean and median income (Figure 10.2). (If only the rich are getting richer, mean incomes will rise while median incomes stagnate.)

An important reason for this divergence has been the fall in wage share of national income. Steady at about two-thirds for most of the postwar period, it has fallen to 55% in the last two decades (Figure 10.3).

The causes of disequalization have been disputed. One of the commonest explanations is the information revolution: the technologically agile have benefited at the expense of the rest. Another is globalization: cheap labor competition from Asian countries has driven down the median wage of Western workers. A third is the shift in the balance of power from workers to employers.

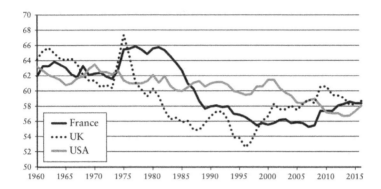

Figure 10.3   Labor income share in GDP, 1960–2016 (%)

Source: Data from ILOSTAT (2017), graph my own.

All three might explain widening inequality; only the first might plausibly explain the exorbitant gains of the top 1%.

Piketty's argument is straightforward. The growing concentration of capital in fewer hands, for whatever reason, has enabled its owners to keep it relatively scarce and thus valuable. Urban real estate has taken the place of land as the main source of rent.

Piketty argues that tendency to increased inequality, inherent in a capitalist system, was suppressed in the period between 1910 and 1960, as the two world wars and the Great Depression destroyed a mass of inherited capital, while trade union pressure, progressive taxation and welfare prevented its reconstitution. But from the late 1970s, with the decay of these countervailing forces, the natural inequality of the system has reasserted itself, so that today it is almost as great as it was before 1914.[12]

The historical record so painstakingly dissected can be summarized by what Piketty calls the "fundamental force of divergence," which he represents by the equation r > g. When the return on capital continuously exceeds the growth of the economy, inherited wealth continues to grow faster than output and income, meaning that inequality continues to increase, since there is nothing to stop the children of today's super-salary earners becoming the rentiers of tomorrow. And the return to low growth, partly caused by an aging population, means that inequality will rise even more. Piketty predicts that growth will not exceed 1% to 1.5% in the long run, whereas the average return on capital will be 4% to 5%.

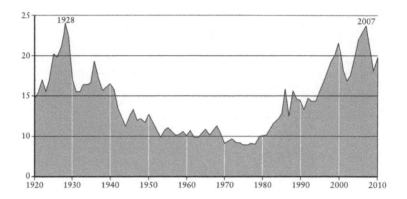

Figure 10.4   Share of US income going to richest 1 percent (%)

Source: Picketty 2014: 292.

This contrasts with the predictions of the American statistician Simon Kuznets, whose data – dating from 1955 – showed inequality naturally diminishing over time. Using large data sets, Piketty presented a U-shaped curve running from the late nineteenth century to today, with a "compression" of inequality between 1914 and 1970 (Figure 10.4).

It is a sign of the importance of Piketty's intervention that it has provoked a furious debate. This has centered on two issues: (a) his use of data, and (b) his theoretical framework.

Chris Giles of the *Financial Times* led the empirical assault, asserting that the raw data used by Piketty do not show any increase in the share of wealth going to the top 1% and the top 10% in the UK from 1960 to 2010, rather the reverse.[13] His attempt to discredit Piketty failed to run, but it shows Piketty had hit a raw nerve (Reed 2014).

The second assault was not on Piketty's data, but on his theoretical framework. It was led by left-wing economists who accused him of using a neoclassical framework to explain the returns to capital. American economist Thomas Palley writes:

> Using a conventional marginal productivity framework, Piketty provides an explanation of rising inequality based on increases in the gap between the marginal product of capital, which determines the rate of profit (r), and the rate of growth (g). Because capital ownership is so concentrated, a higher profit rate or slower growth rate increases inequality as the incomes of the wealthy grow faster than the overall economy. (Palley 2014: 144)

But power and monopoly, the left-wing critics assert, is absent from Piketty's theoretical account:

> Mainstream economists will assert the conventional story about the profit rate being technologically determined. However, as Piketty occasionally hints, in reality the profit rate is politically and socially determined by factors influencing the distribution of economic and political power. Growth is also influenced by policy and institutional choices. That is the place to push the argument, which is what critics of mainstream economics have been doing (unsuccessfully) for decades. The deep contribution of Piketty's book is it creates a fresh opportunity in this direction. (Palley 2014: 145)

James Galbraith, who had been working on long-run trends in inequality long before Piketty published *Capital in the Twenty-First Century*,[14] criticized Piketty's claim that the wage share in national income is technologically determined, leaving governments with scope for intervention only in the post-tax distribution of earnings. Piketty's mistake had been to treat capital as an independent "factor of production" – confounding physical and financial accounts of capital in doing so – when a "social" analysis of capital would be more appropriate, its determinants including infrastructure spending, education, regulation, social insurance, globalization and much else (Galbraith 2014).[15]

Orthodox theorists attribute the build-up of debt, leverage and financial fragility before the crash to "misperceptions" by households, businesses, and banks about the sustainable level of lending and borrowing. This is true, of course, but banal. One really wants to know about the source of these misconceptions. Under-consumptionist theory provides one answer: the growth of inequality. Households increase their debt because wages have fallen, but they still wish to consume as much as before. Banks and firms become "over-leveraged" because they exaggerate the profits they expect to make from consumers' debt-enlarged incomes. Governments borrow too much because they over-estimate the revenues they will get from over-borrowed financial systems. Thus excessive credit creation, which the Hayekians see as *the* cause of the financial collapse of 2008–09, can, on further analysis, be rooted in the stagnation or decline of consumption from earnings.

While the upsurge and withdrawal of consumer credit played an important role in under-consumptionist explanations of the Great Depression of 1929–32, it has become the main under-consumptionist explanation for the collapse of 2008–09.

Cheap credit, leading to asset bubbles, and collapses, have been central to Thomas Palley's writings. Palley restates the under-consumptionist concern with finding a balance between consumption and saving, which boils down to the balance between wages and profits: "The perennial challenge is to find the right balance, avoiding a profit-squeeze that undercuts investment and a wage-squeeze that undercuts consumer demand" (Palley 2015: 31).

A key argument in this tradition is that a balance between capital and labor existed in the Keynesian era of the 1950s to 1970s – in fact, it was what made Keynesian policy possible. Strong trade unions were able to push wages up in line with productivity; extensive government transfers kept up mass purchasing power. Commitment to full employment created a favorable climate for business investment and hence improvements in productivity, and the state's own capital spending policies maintained a steadiness of investment across the cycle. As a result, business cycles were dampened, and economies enjoyed unprecedented rates of economic growth.

However, this benign capitalist environment unraveled in the 1970s. First, wage-push by unions led to rising inflation. Attempts by governments to control inflation by prices and incomes policy broke down. With wage inflation pushing ahead of profit inflation, the only solution available under capitalism was to recreate the Marxist "reserve army of the unemployed." This was done through downsizing and off-shoring: opening up domestic economies to global competition. Higher unemployment simultaneously shifted income from wages to profits and brought down inflation; but at the cost of a secular stagnation punctuated by asset bubbles.

According to Palley, the collapse of the dot-com bubble in 2001 reflected deep-seated contradictions in the existing process of aggregate demand generation. He saw these as resulting from a deterioration in income distribution. The resulting depressive forces were held at bay for almost two decades by a range of different demand compensation mechanisms: steadily rising consumer debt, a stock market boom, and rising profit rates. However, these mechanisms were now exhausted. Fiscal policy would help only temporarily unless measures were taken "to rectify the structural imbalances at the root of the current impasse . . . Absent this, the problem of deficient demand will reassert itself, and the next time around public sector finances may not be in such a favorable position to deal with it" (Palley 2001).[16]

Written in 2001, this was a prescient forecast of the disablement of fiscal policy following the crash of 2008.

In February 2008 – just before the US economy collapsed – Palley wrote that ". . . the US economy relies upon asset price inflation and rising indebtedness to fuel growth. Therein lies a profound contradiction. On one hand, policy must fuel asset bubbles to keep the economy growing. On the other hand, such bubbles inevitably create financial crises when they eventually implode." The need, he said, was to "[restore] the link between wages and productivity. That way, wage income, not debt and asset price inflation, can again provide the engine of demand growth" (Palley 2001).

The new under-consumptionism attaches great causal importance to the "financialization" which serves to "redistribute income from productive activities to non-productive finance. The rich alone are the winners in that transfer, because it involves no productive activity that might possibly 'trickle down' to the rest of us" (Weeks 2011). "Financialization" is a necessary part of the neoliberal model, its function being to "fuel demand growth by making ever larger amounts of credit easily available . . . The old post-World War II growth model based on rising middle-class incomes has been dismantled, while the new neoliberal growth model has imploded" (Palley 2009).

4.   CONCLUSION

The argument of this chapter is that distribution is a macroeconomic question, because a distribution of purchasing power heavily skewed toward the owners of capital assets creates a problem of deficient demand. The "financialization" of the economy increases this instability by allowing debt to replace earnings from work. Quantitative easing increases it still further by creating asset bubbles.

The problem to which the older generation of under-consumptionists drew attention was the failure of real wages to keep pace with productivity. But a striking feature of the post-crash years has been the decline in productivity as workers have moved to less productive jobs. Flexible labor markets, greatly lauded by the conventional wisdom, are bound to slow down productivity growth, because it is more efficient for employers to hire cheap labor than invest in capital, physical or human. This has been a job-rich, productivity poor, recovery.

The fall in worker productivity must lead to even greater income inequality, and, therefore, on the under-consumptionist argument, to even greater macroeconomic instability in future, as the economy relies even more heavily on debt.

In Keynesian terms, a situation in which the inducement to invest is falling, but income inequality is rising, is the worst possible basis for both stability and growth. This is the situation in which we find ourselves today.

NOTES

1. In *Collected Writings* (*CW*) II: 6. Note, all references to *CW* are to Keynes (1971– 89).
2. e.g. in *Indian Currency and Reform* (1913: 192), he wondered for "how long it will be found necessary to pay city men so entirely out of proportion" to the services they rendered.
3. Notably in Pigou's *Wealth and Welfare* (1912).
4. In *CW* IX: 285.
5. Though Michael Bleaney (1976) denies that Malthus and Luxemburg were truly under-consumptionists.
6. On Hobson, see Nemmers 1956.
7. See Lenin 1970.
8. The most detailed examination of Hobson's doctrines is to be found in Lee (1970). D. K. Fieldhouse finds that of the big four capital exporters before 1914 (the UK, France, Germany, and the USA), only the USA and Germany showed marked signs of capital concentration; see Fieldhouse (1973), 47–53.
9. Marx's *Das Kapital* (vol. III, ch. 30) quoted in Blaug (1996), 270.
10. "Fear the Boom and Bust," a Hayek vs Keynes rap anthem (2010), quoted in Durand (2017), 43. For Hayek's position, see e.g. Butler (1983), 58–61.
11. See Skidelsky (1992), 454–9. "The wildest farrago of nonsense yet" was Keynes's comment on a draft of Hayek's paper "Capital Consumption," published in German in 1932. See also Durand (2017), 46–8.
12. This is also the argument of Walter Scheidel (2017), for whom war is history's "Great Leveller."
13. Giles (2014). See also the critique of the way Piketty presents his data in his graphs by Noah Wright (2015).
14. Ferguson and Galbraith (1999) cover 1920–47, and Galbraith (1998) covers 1950 to the early 1990s. See also Skidelsky (2009), 124–5.
15. More specifically, Piketty (2014) glosses over and mischaracterizes the Cambridge capital controversies.
16. See https://ideas.repec.org/p/lev/wrkpap/wp_332.html.

REFERENCES

Atkinson, Anthony B., Thomas Piketty and Emmanuel Saez. 2011. "Top Incomes in the Long Run of History." *Journal of Economic Literature* 49, no. 1: 3–71.

Blaug, Mark. 1996. *Economic Theory in Retrospect*. Cambridge: Cambridge University Press [5th Edition].

Bleanney, Michael. 1976. *Under-Consumption Theories: A History and Critical Analysis*. New York: International Publishers.

Butler, Eamonn. 1983. *Hayek: His Contribution to the Political and Economic Thought of Our Time*. London: Temple Smith.

Devine, James. 1994. "The Causes of the 1929–33 Great Collapse: A Marxian Interpretation." *Research in Political Economy* 14: 119–94.

Durand, Cédric. 2017. *Fictitious Capital: How Finance is Appropriating Our Future*. London: Verso.

Eccles, Marriner. 1951. *Beckoning Frontiers: Public and Personal Recollections*. New York: Alfred A. Knopf.

Federal Reserve Bank of St. Louis. 2015. *The Mean vs the Median of Family Income: FRED blog*, available at https://fredblog.stlouisfed.org/2015/05/the-mean-vs-the-median-of-family-income/ (accessed July 28, 2017).

Ferguson, Thomas and James K. Galbraith. 1999. "The American Wage Structure, 1920–1947." *Research in Economic History* 19: 205–57.

Fieldhouse, David K. 1973. *Economics and Empire 1830–1914*. Ithaca, NY: Cornell University Press.

Galbraith, James K. 1998. *Created Unequal: The Crisis in American Pay*. New York: Free Press.

Galbraith, James K. 2014. "'Kapital' for the Twenty-First Century," *Dissent Magazine*, spring.

Giles, Chris. 2014. "Data Problems with Capital in the 21st Century." *Financial Times*, available at http://blogs.ft.com/money-supply/2014/05/23/data-problems-with-capital-in-the-21st-century/ (accessed July 28, 2017).

Hobson, John A. 1896. *The Problem of the Unemployed*. London: Methuen & Co.

Hobson, John A. 1900. *The Economics of Distribution*. London: Macmillan.

Hobson, John A. 1902. *Imperialism*. New York: James Pott and Co.

Hobson, John A. 1910 [1909]. *The Industrial System: An Inquiry into Earned and Unearned Income*. London: Longman, Green & Co.

Hobson, John A. 1922. *The Economics of Unemployment*. London: George Allen and Unwin.

Hobson, John A. and Albert F. Mummery. 1889. *The Physiology of Industry*. London: John Murray.

ILOSTAT. 2017. *SDG Labour Market Indicators*, available at http://www.ilo.org/ilostat/faces/ilostat-home/home?_adf.ctrl.
state=c04kb9iu4_4&_afrLoop=196666878792954#! (accessed November 23, 2017).

Institute for Fiscal Studies. 2016. *Institute for Fiscal Studies: Living Standards, Inequality and Poverty Spreadsheet*, available at https://www.ifs.org.uk/tools_and_resources/incomes_in_uk (accessed July 28, 2017).

Keynes, John Maynard. 1913. *Indian Currency and Finance*. London: Macmillan.

Keynes, John Maynard. 1964 [1936]. *The General Theory of Employment, Interest, and Money*. Orlando, FL: Harcourt.

Keynes, John Maynard. 1971–89. *The Collected Writings of John Maynard Keynes*, 30 volumes. Cambridge: Cambridge University Press for the Royal Economic Society.

Lee, Alan J. 1970. "The Social and Economic Thought of J. A. Hobson." PhD Dissertation. University of London.

Lenin, Vladimir Ilitich. 1970 [1917]. "Imperialism, the Highest Stage of Capitalilsm." *In V. I. Lenin, Selected Works (I)*. Moscow: Progress Publishers, pp. 667–768.

Luttwak, Edward N. 2015. "Too High a Bill." *Times Literary Supplement*, 23 September.

Mishel, Lawrence, Josh Bivens, Elise Gould and Heidi Shierholz. 2012. *The State of Working America*. Ithaca, NY: Cornell University Press [12th Edition].

Nemmers, Erwin Esser. 1956. *Hobson and Underconsumption*. Amsterdam: North Holland.

Palley, Thomas I. 2001. "Contradictions Coming Home to Roost? Income Distribution and the Return of the Aggregate Demand Problem." *Levy Economics Institute Working Paper* 332, available at https://econpapers.repec.org/paper/levwrkpap/wp_5f332.htm (accessed December 12, 2017).

Palley, Thomas I. 2009. "America's Exhausted Paradigm: Macroeconomic Causes of the Financial Crisis and Great Recession." *Institute for International Political Economy Berlin Working Paper* 02.

Palley, Thomas I. 2014. "The Accidental Controversialist: Deeper Reflections on Thomas Piketty's 'Capital'." *Real-World Economics Review* 67: 143–6.

Palley, Thomas I. 2015. "Policy Issues and Institutional Challenges." *Real-World Economics Review* 70: 27–48.

Pigou, Arthur Cecil. 1912. *Wealth and Welfare*. London: Macmillan.

Piketty, Thomas. 2014 [2013]. *Capital in the Twenty-First Century*. Cambridge, MA: Harvard University Press.

Reed, Howard. 2014. "Piketty, Chris Giles and Wealth Inequality: It's All about the Discontinuities." *The Guardian*, available at https://www.theguardian.com/news/datablog/2014/may/29/piketty-chris-giles-and-wealth-inequality-its-all-about-the-discontinuities (accessed July 28, 2017).

Scheidel, Walter. 2017. *The Great Leveler: Violence and the History of Inequality from the Stone Age to the Twenty-First Century*. Princeton, NJ: Princeton University Press.

Skidelsky, Robert. 1992. *John Maynard Keynes: The Economist as Saviour 1920–1937*. London: Macmillan.

Skidelsky, Robert. 2009. *Keynes: The Return of the Master*. London: Allen Lane.

Weeks, John. 2011. "Mean, Median and Mode of Impoverishment: Why to Occupy Wall Street." *Social Europe*, available at https://www.socialeurope.eu/mean-median-and-mode-of-impoverishment-why-to-occupy-wall-street. (accessed July 28, 2017).

Wright, Noah. 2015. "Data Visualization in 'Capital in the Twenty-First Century'." *The University of Texas Inequality Project Working Paper* 70.

11. Land ownership as a mechanism for the reproduction of inequality in Ecuador from 1895 to the 1920s

Francisca Granda

1. INTRODUCTION

The Latin American region has been characterized by great inequality throughout its history, a factor that is still present today, and Ecuador is not an exception. To understand the mechanisms that reproduce inequality in Ecuador, it is crucial to reflect on how the processes of social integration have been promoted throughout the country's history. The study of these processes at the beginning of the twentieth century is particularly interesting. The Liberal Revolution of 1895 brought great expectations for the integration of subaltern populations, mainly indigenous and Afro-Ecuadorian communities. Indigenous communities (the main population of the Sierra region) had great expectations that the revolution would free them from domination by the *hacendados* (owners of vast landholdings). However, the first decades of the twentieth century showed an expansion of a system of domination called *concertaje* and its land concentration processes. In this chapter, I describe how race inequality is reproduced by exploitation processes through land ownership institutions in Ecuador during this period.

   I have resorted to three main sources to cover the processes of social integration. First, *Seven Interpretative Essays on Peruvian Reality* (1973), a classical paper by the Peruvian José Carlos Mariátegui la Chira, one of the most prominent Marxist political thinkers of the time. I also review, *Essay of the Original Accumulation in Ecuador: Hacendados, cacaoteros, bankers, exporters and merchants in Guayaquil (1890–1910)* by the Ecuadorian Marxist political thinker Andres Guerrero (1977).[1] The third source I analyze is the doctoral dissertation of Adriana Valeria Coronel, "A Revolution in Stages: Subaltern Politics, Nation-State Formation, and the Origins of Social Rights in Ecuador, 1834–1943" (2011).

In order to give some background to the organization of agriculture in the colonial period, I describe the system of domination throughout the first decades of the twentieth century. I then show how the *hacienda* system was the intermediary between the local economy and the capitalist mode of production and its insertion into global capitalist relations. I present the production of exports in the coastal region and the hacienda system in the Sierra region, inhabited by indigenous communities. In this section, I also examine how the *hacienda* system was based on racial division. Finally, I briefly cover the role of Christianization and its approach to social integration in the country.

2.   LAND OWNERSHIP IN THE COLONIAL PERIOD

Spanish settlers landed in Ecuador in 1531 and it officially became a Spanish colony in September 1532, after Francisco Pizarro ousted the new Incan emperor, Atahualpa (Murra 2002). The colonial period extended from this date until the first call for independence, led by a republican group in Quito, on August 10, 1809. By 1821, after the decisive Battle of Pichincha, military forces beat royalist forces and subjugation to the Spanish crown became history.

During colonial times, Ecuador was a country of abundant land which was cultivated exclusively by the indigenous population. Mariátegui (1973) explains that under the Incan empire, agricultural production was characterized by an agrarian communist organization named "ayllu," which was not completely dismantled after the Spanish settled. During the initial phase of conquest and settlement, one of the main institutions that the Spanish created were the "encomiendas"; these allocated vast areas to a relatively small number of settlers. Under the rule of the "encomiendas," each colonist owned the labor and tributes from the indigenous communities inside an established territory. The value of their production was eroded over time, mainly due to the rapid decline of the native population in the sixteenth century. Over time, "encomiendas" gave way to large-scale landholdings called *latifundios* or *haciendas*; these also derived their income from indigenous communities via their labor activities carried out for the *hacendados* and their families. The *latifundios'* grocery and hardware stores also generated income for landowners.

The organization of the agrarian production through *haciendas* was an effective mechanism for the control of the indigenous population. The chief of the *hacienda* collected taxes, organized indigenous labor and was in charge of their Christianization in order to "civilize" them. The *Laws of the Indies* protected the indigenous communities' lands and recognized their own rules of organization, but these progressively changed over time. Outside the territories included in the *hacienda*, the indigenous communities held both communal and individual land, on each of which they were obliged to pay taxes. The individual lands provided subsistence consumption for the family and were too small to permit substantial production and income outside of the *hacienda* system.

When the chief of an indigenous family died, his sons inherited his lands and debts, the latter being very common in the indigenous population (a practice that continued later on to be called *concertaje*, discussed below). Thus, through the indebtedness of the indigenous communities, the *hacienda* system was also effective in preventing migration. Additionally, the land rules favored landowners – employing an argument that they were "vacant," communal lands were permanently at risk of expropriation. In sum, the allocation of lands and their production originated what can be characterized as "a feudal agrarian system" based on indigenous labor and owned by the descendants of settlers, mostly aristocratic landowners.

3. ECUADOR'S TRANSITION FROM A COLONIZED ECONOMY TO A CAPITALIST MODE OF PRODUCTION

During the middle of the nineteenth century, the main exports of Ecuador were concentrated in four products: cacao, tobacco, toquilla straw hats (more commonly known as Panama hats) and husk. These items accounted for 90% of Ecuadorian exports and by the 1880s cacao production had increased greatly in the Guayas river basin in the coastal region. In 1904, Ecuador was the greatest cacao producer in the world.

Despite the fact that land ownership records were not clear during that time, several authors agree that cacao production was concentrated on properties owned by just a few families and that small, independent growers disappeared (Guerrero 1977). The production system rested on the sharing of lands between two types of workforce: the sowers and the laborers. The sowers would take care of the cacao plants during their unproductive phase that could last from 4 to 7 years. During the productive period of the plants, the sower gave the *hacienda* the plants which became part of its regular production.

For subsistence, the sowers had access to a consumption fund during the unproductive period of the plants. The *terrateniente* (the owner of the *hacienda*, also called *hacendado*) made successive contributions to support the plantation and supplemented the means of subsistence of its workers. Additionally, the sowers' families had small plots of land for self-production, usually for vegetable crops, hens, and grassland if they owned a cow or a horse. The "advances" received by the peasant families allowed them to enter a sphere of mercantile circulation that enabled them to acquire other products from the *hacienda* grocery and hardware stores.

Table 11.1   *Cacao production by province, 1901*

Provinces on the Coast	Number of farms	Number of trees
Los Ríos	1594	30,634,761
Guayas	546	14,530,300
EL Oro	977	6,618,00
Manabí	1440	6,532,170
Esmeraldas	270	235,781
Total	4837	58,551,142

Source: From Guerrero 1977: 5

The laborers were responsible for the majority of cacao production. Their main duties were weeding, pruning and harvesting, for which they received a daily payment that did not vary between 1901 and 1920. Usually, cacao production was not based on individual laborers, but on the laborer and his family. Table 11.1 shows some figures of cacao production by province in the coastal region in 1901.

Guerrero (1977) examines the main features of Ecuadorian capitalist development and the nature of social classes during this period. Based on the author's findings, we know that Ecuador's insertion in the capitalist mode of production was not achieved by the dissolution of the social structures built during the colonial period. Few transformations were made on the structures maintained by the *hacienda* system. For Guerrero, such a system was an inter-mediary form linking the capitalist production sphere with other social spheres. In other words, the extension of *haciendas cacaoteras* was not a process of proletarianization, but one designed to forcefully maintain the workforce and their families on the vast landholdings. The proletarianization paradoxically occurred later on, when the workforce was freed from the *hacienda* system and also after the Great Depression in the 1930s.

Cacao production was highly relevant for the Ecuadorian economy, since it produced enough rent to create a local market in both rural and urban areas. In the cities, some capitalist relations of production emerged, building a financial and commercial bourgeoisie. However, the local capitalist production concen-trated on those activities that could not be supplied by imports and that were profitable locally. According to Guerrero, the capitalist mode of production developed in Ecuador, as in other countries in the region, shows "the trace of its tangential origin to the insertion of social formation to the world's capitalist relations of the twentieth century" (Guerrero 1977: 51). In Ecuador the pecu-liarity of local capitalist accumulation is that it is related to the non-capitalist production of income (in the *hacienda* system) and the division of international labor. Thus, such a process leads to a blocked capitalist development lacking an autonomous social formation. Moreover, Ecuador entered into global capitalist relations based on a social class structure that was the root of Ecuadorian social and economic development (usually mistakenly called underdevelopment).

The *terrateniente* social class, based on cacao rents, began as a regional class, but it could not become a national capitalist class since it depended on the non-capitalist relations of rent appropriation in their *haciendas*. The financial and commercial capitalists that did become established, mainly in Guayaquil (the main city on the Ecuadorian coast), were the ones that represented the "national bourgeoisie," and that looked to expand the ideology of capitalism and its social and economic domination throughout the country. This class tried to maintain its domination through compromise between the non-capitalists relations on the coast and pre-capitalist relations in the Sierra. In the end, they maintained social relations similar to those of the colonial period (instead of dissolving them) and were highly dependent on the world market's demand for cacao production.

This financial and commercial capitalist class is the one that supported the Liberal Revolution of General Eloy Alfaro in 1895. This occurred after a series of conservative governments, and had the support of liberal financial and commercial capitalists in the coastal regions and the indigenous communities in the Sierra. According to Guerrero, when this class came to power, capitalist domination expanded to a national scale and sealed the political and economic unification of the country. Others described this process as the beginning of a modernization process led by the state.

The Liberal Revolution brought great expectations and perspectives to the indigenous communities. Indeed, the Liberal Revolution seemed to be sympathetic with their historic struggles such as the abolition of *concertaje*, the restitution of communal lands and, more broadly, changes of certain legal processes in their favor. For the revolution to succeed, the political participation of radicals, peasants and indigenous communities was crucial. However, the period between 1900 and 1922 was particularly difficult for indigenous communities in the Sierra region – conservative and liberal elites, and the state, retreated from negotiations with indigenous communities, hampering their political expectations and exacerbating division and the fragile nature of the Ecuadorian state.

Coronel (2011) explains that in the context of the celebrations of Ecuador's centennial of independence, it is clear to see the differences between the place indigenous communities had to negotiate after the Liberal Revolution and the place they had before, under the conservative government of García Moreno (1860–1865), one of the most difficult periods for indigenous communities. In these celebrations, General Eloy Alfaro's discourse mentioned that under García Moreno's government "in order to sell our territory, he asked for two hundred *sucres*[2] for a lot for a poor family . . . that is a hurdle for their work

(Coronel 2011:342). Whereas Alfaro proposed to distribute national lands freely,

> ten hectares at a time to each individual that belonged to an agricultural society and 50 hectares to each family that would establish itself in the mountains. He would charge five times the price of lands to rich people who wanted to become owners of this vast region. (Coronel 2011: 342)

At the inauguration of the centennial Exposition, Alfaro called for compromise and a national peace that required questions to be asked about the causes of the revolution. According to Alfaro, the three principal sources of conflict were the formation of capital, servitude and a lack of productivity, and political problems. As far as the work was concerned, Alfaro pointed out "the concentration of unproductive lands in the hands of the *terratenientes* and the lack of liberty guarantees for the peasantry as obstacles to productive work" (Coronel 2011: 340–41).

During his second term in office, Alfaro (1907–1911) sought to enter into a democratic national system, by recovering the hegemony of liberalism on the coast and ceasing conflict with conservatives in the Sierra. Under the peace negotiations between both parties, a civilizing discourse arose, replacing the discourse of popular sovereignty prominent during the civil war period. There was a shift, as well, in the concept of reparations, which were no longer to be considered as positive discrimination or negotiations about ethnic citizenship, but simply as reparations. This created a new kind of "colonial frontier." The frontier discursively defined a division between actors prepared for integration and "actors subject to tutelage for their moral flaws and uncivilized nature" (Coronel 2011: 318). Coronel also points out that modern civilization in Ecuador was characterized by a co-existence between instrumental rationalism and subjective autonomy. By this she means that social institutions were integrated into a single religious, economic and political entity. As a result, this closed the space to integrate indigenous communities' struggles.

4.   THE *HACIENDA* SYSTEM AND RACE DIFFERENTIATIONS

The feudal system established in Ecuador was related to the *hacienda* system. As a parallel to the European feudal system, the feudal lord was acknowledged as superior to his servants. However, since the colonial period in Latin America, Spanish settlers and, later on, aristocratic landowners, were considered superior: this was not only justified with reference to their resources, but also on a racial basis. The *terrateniente*, who exercised his power through different religious and moral practices that forged the conviction of white superiority over the dark-skinned population, was also regarded as the owner of indigenous families. In fact, the indigenous populations were effectively controlled by the alliance between the *terrateniente* representing the *hacienda*, the priest representing the Catholic Church and the *teniente politico* representing the national state at local levels.

The work contract in the *hacienda* system, called *concertaje*, clearly institutionalized a system of domination of *terratenientes* over the indigenous population (or any peasant). Various authors describe it as a reinforcement of internal colonialism. This system of domination operated through the administration of labor. It consisted of lifelong work contracts at low-subsistence salaries for peasants and their families. Any extra "advances" became a debt that was inherited by peasants' families and their descendants in case of disease or death. No release from work contracts existed, and supervision was carried out either by the administration of the *hacienda* directly, or the *teniente politico* and priest representing the state and the Church. As Mariátegui (1973) points out for the Peruvian case, the conditions needed to develop a capitalist system did not exist: there was no market competition, and labor was not exchanged for a free salary, but operated under an aristocratic political and feudal economic system.

Jijón y Caamaño, a politician who represented the landholding elite of Pichincha province during the mid-twentieth century, described the salary of the *concierto*:

> In a sum of money, the least important portion, in the income from a piece of land, if it be well cultivated, should give him what is sufficient to not die of hunger, he and his family; in a periodic quantity of goods; in the right to graze their animals in determined areas; in the interest of the advances received. (Coronel 2011: 387)

It was not until 1917 that the *concertaje* was called into question. By that time, many liberal thinkers had promoted a debate to eliminate *concertaje* and two discourses came to the forefront. The liberals argued in favor of the abolition of *concertaje* based on the constitutional guarantee of equality and the role of the state to protect workers. They claimed that in contrast to the *indios conciertos*, the "free indigenous" had demonstrated the capacity to control their lives by themselves, to show dignity and a will to become better citizens. This ethic could be compared, in contrast, to the *indios conciertos*, who because of servitude were prone to vices and laziness. The liberals were aware of the risks that abolition of *concertaje* entailed; however, they claimed that bringing a labor market, higher salaries in the Sierra, and the covering of daily needs would urge the indigenous to fulfill their contracts. In contrast, for the conservatists the *indios conciertos* did not have the moral capacity to self-fulfill their duties; they had a mentality that did not make them fit for the values of equality and freedom established in the constitution. Finally, by the 1920s, debt constraint was abolished and gradually *concertaje* came to an end, lasting longer where indigenous communities resided (Maiguashca 1994; Prieto 2004).[3]

5.   THE *HACIENDA* SYSTEM IN THE SIERRA REGION

As mentioned earlier, in the coastal region a *hacienda* system developed for the production of exports, whereas in the Sierra, the *hacienda* system produced mainly for the local market or for businesses such as the textile industry. An expansion of *concertaje* and land concentration processes took place in the 1910s and 1920s. In the rural areas of the Sierra, the *hacienda* itself was perceived as a cultural institution whose function was to achieve the "civilization" of indigenous communities and reinforce Ecuador as a Catholic nation (Tobar Donoso 1974; Coronel 2011). This division renewed the concept of racial difference and new frontiers emerged between cities and rural areas, and the conforming of the *mestizo* and indigenous population.

As Pfaff-Czarnecka shows:

> The exclusion of ethnic groups from public representations, their pejorative descriptions, the barriers of integration in political and administrative positions to the members of minorities, that lacked social and cultural capital or whose political capacity was denied by the elites, became in the Andean region (. . .), a matrix of exclusion. In [the region], the ethnic minorities were notably excluded from political communication in the national sphere. (cited in Büschges 2007: 24)

The land concentration process occurred by a gradual attack on indigenous communal lands. Coronel (2011) presents several cases in the central and northern Sierra, that show the contentious situations indigenous communities experienced as a result of the pressure of conservative-led attempts at modernization. The trials that communities and *haciendas* experienced included entire communities being captured after they were surrounded by the *haciendas* territory, and denied access to local markets and roads.

The reduction of communal lands was promoted by legislation in favor of the aristocratic landowners, leaving the indigenous population to manage small subsistence plots or to farm certain communal lands that lacked sufficient irrigation, thus making indigenous living conditions harder still. Nonetheless, indigenous people's willingness for communism persisted, with their claims over communal lands continuing to be the primary dispute against *hacendados* – in spite of their difficulties they persisted.

Moreover, between 1910 and 1925 various models of production existed based on the *hacienda* system. One model was where successful *hacendados* affiliated with the Conservative party and promoted a system of patronal administration for productive units of rural and urban areas. For instance, the Jijón family moved laborers from the *hacienda* in Imbabura province into textile industries in Quito. Furthermore, one of the most extensive models also tied rural and urban areas, where laborer members of the family were moved between the *hacienda* and the family's own production lot, enacted by pre-capitalist relationships that were a *distorted form of proletarianization.* This allowed the *hacendado* to keep the peasant tied to his parcel of land and, thus, prevented migration.

In sum, in the first two decades of the twentieth century, the justice system disappointed communities. It protected the *hacendados'* interests and it did not correspond to the ideals of the Liberal Revolution indigenous communities had fought for. The indigenous were not recognized as small landowners with a free salary until the late 1920s, excluding them as citizens of the Ecuadorian state and maintaining them in servitude. In testimonies of the 1930s, the process of concentration of land led to the fragmentation of indigenous communities in several provinces. These struggles also led to the formation of the first political organizations such as the Federación Ecuatoriana de Indios (FEI) in the 1940s, that was affiliated with the Communist Party (Coronel 2011).

Additionally, under these conditions, the origin of the Ecuadorian state was fragile, and had a complex relation with regional elites divided between the coast and the Sierra landlords, who disputed control over territory and resources. Coronel points out that landlords maintained an advantageous position: "their privileges included the evasion of fiscal payments, the use of force to appropriate resources and pretensions of administering the population in a personalized way instead of throughout public functionaries" (Coronel 2011: 979).

6.   THE ROLE OF CHRISTIANIZATION OF INDIGENOUS COMMUNITIES

It is well known that from the colonization of Latin America onward, a social division was created between Spanish settlers and their descendants, the population of mixed indigenous and Spanish ancestry *mestizos*, and the indigenous population itself. As has been shown, different colonial institutions were established for the subordination and gradual integration particularly of the subaltern population. Christianization was a main mechanism to "civilize" the population, carried out by religious art, collective manifestations of culture, and Jesuit brotherhoods and religious missions, such as the Jesuit and Salesian orders' missions to the Amazon region (Coronel 2011).

After the Liberal Revolution (1895), two different integration processes occurred. A political integration promoted by Alfaro's first administration, who tried to extend political rights to the subaltern populations in urban and rural areas, one that is usually described as an integration from above. Under the Alfaro government, the idea was to attenuate the differences between liberal and conservative elites, and engage them to "integrate" workers; however, a real integration did not occur. Catholic archbishops promoted another integration effort, one inspired by the preaching of popes Pious IX and Leo XIII, characterized within the traditional philosophies of social authority of the Hispanic world. The idea was to continue the evangelizing missions internally to promote an integration without a political discourse and as a pacific process (Coronel 2011; Larrea and North 2016).

During this time, new concepts inspired by social Darwinism justified the establishment of modern institutions as a response for the integration of the subaltern population. At this time, Coronel states that:

> As an effect of the agreement of no aggression between the Church and the state, the *patronal* elite was constituted into a political vanguard cloaked under a series of cultural and economic institutions that promoted the internal conquest of the Indigenous as a moral mission. (Coronel 2009: 347–8)

Around 1909, the liberal President General Eloy Alfaro promoted munici-palities for social administration, and thus promoted the civilization of the population. Liberal and Conservative parties administered the municipalities, and both received guarantees confirming the institutionalization of the liberal state. In urban centers, both parties sponsored the creation of workers' unions in alliance with the Church. Consequently, several institutions dedicated to private charity were created. Through such institutions, the idea was to smooth the contradictions of the modern world and avoid the formation of antagonistic class identities. As a result, liberal and conservative elites welcomed gradual integration for artisans and workers, but their political integration did not come to be.

Moreover, state health and education agencies promoted policies with new concepts of integration. However, as Coronel states "the discourse of the liberal redemption was displaced from the sphere of political negotiation by a civilizing discourse, according to which the working classes needed to be prepared for their future integration as citizens" (Coronel 2011: 370). According to several authors, ministers of government, health and education promoted policies for social integration in urban and rural areas, through notions of health, hygiene, civilization, enlightenment and technical formation in liberal arts schools (Kingman 2009; Prieto 2004). Nonetheless, such policies showed tensions between a will for integration and pessimistic views based on racial differences.

7. CONCLUSION

In this chapter, I have described the failed process of social integration after the Liberal Revolution in 1895 until the 1920s in Ecuador, responsible to a great extent for the country's social and economic inequality. I have shown that the particular expectations and perspectives held by indigenous communities at the time were not met. During this period, the conservative and liberal elites and the state retreated from negotiations with indigenous communities, who were not considered a sovereign population with rights. Just as in the colonial period, they were regarded as an uncivilized community that needed to be under tutelage of the *hacendados*. Also, the Church came to an agreement with the state, to reconfigure a type of internal colonialism established through cultural, political and economic institutions.

In the 1910s and 1920s, peasant conditions were exacerbated. The *concertaje* deepened the means by which peasants were tied inextricably to their parcels of land, communal lands were permanently at risk of expropriation, and the justice system favored the *hacendados'* interests. In this context, pre-capitalist relations extended throughout the territory, and promoted a feudal agrarian system based on peasants' and indigenous communities' labor. This process of accumulation was the root of Ecuadorian social and economic development, promising low improvements for the years to come. Under these conditions, Ecuador deepened a clear social division, based on race differences and peasants' unpaid labor that in time built a fragile state. Thus, social and economic inequality were expected outcomes.

It was not until the *hacienda* system declined around the 1930s that peasants and indigenous communities could gradually become small landowners. In addition, only after their continued resistance to the established internal colonial system could they develop political organizations to enter into dialogue with the state and fight for a social integration that recognized their claims (Szaszdi 1964).

Indigenous organizations were able to participate in politics after the first indigenous uprising in 1990; however, many of their demands and aspirations have still not been achieved. According to the Urban Survey of Employment and Unemployment (INEC 2017), the poverty rate of the indigenous population is 65.2%, whereas the national rate is 32.1%. Also, the indigenous population's illiteracy rating is 19.2%, against the national figure of 5.9%. Both rates are the highest among ethnic groups in Ecuador. A report from the World Bank (2015) shows that an indigenous person has 13% more probability of being poor due to his ethnic condition, regardless of gender, education, place of residence, and other factors. These high levels of inequality will be maintained unless the government addresses the unfavorable conditions of the indigenous population.

Undoubtedly, the political participation of indigenous populations is a big step toward more equality; nonetheless, structural responses are required to transform the historical unfavorable conditions of indigenous communities.

NOTES

1. The Spanish book title is *Ensayo sobre la acumulación originaria en el Ecuador: Hacendados, cacaoteros, banqueros exportadores y comerciantes en Guayaquil (1890–1910)*.
2. *Sucre* was the currency of Ecuador from 1884 to 2000.
3. Despite the fact that the Ecuador constitution had formally eliminated imprisonment for debt in 1906.

REFERENCES

Büschges, Christian. 2007. "La Etnincidad Como Recurso Político. Etnizaciones y De-etnizaciones de lo Político en América Andina y Asia del Sur." In *Etnicidad y Poder en los Países Andinos*, ed. Christian Büschges, Guillermo Bustos, and Olaf Kalmeier. Quito: Corporación Editora Nacional, pp. 5–30.

Coronel, Adriana Valeria. 2009. "Orígenes de una Democracia Corporativa: Estrategias para la Ciudadanización del Campsinado Indígena, Partidos Políticos y Reforma Territorial en Ecuador (1925–1944)". In *Historia social urbana. Espacios y flujos*, ed. Eduardo Kingman. Quito: Flacso y Ministerio de Cultura, pp. 323–64.

Coronel, Adriana Valeria. 2011. "A Revolution in Stages: Subaltern Politics, Nation-State Formation, and the Origins of Social Rights in Ecuador, 1834–1943." Unpublished PhD thesis. New York University.

Guerrero, Andrés. 1977. *Ensayo Sobre La Acumulación Originaria en El Ecuador: Hacendados Cacaoteros, Banqueros Exportadores y Comerciantes en Guayaquil (1890–1910)*. Lima: Congreso de Historia Latinoamericana.

Instituto Nacional de Estadísticas y Censos (INEC), 2017, Encuesta de Empleo y Desempleo, Quito.

Kingman, Eduardo. 2009. "Estudio Introductorio. Lo Urbano, Lo Social: La Historia Social Urbana." In *Historia social urbana. Espacios y flujos*, ed. Eduardo Kingman. Quito: Flacso y Ministerio de Cultura, pp. 11–36.

Larrea, Carlos and North, Liisa. 2016. "Reformas Agrarias Bloqueadas y Alternativas Posibles: Ecuador a La Luz De Casos Comparativos, Latinoamericanos y Asiáticos." In *50 años de Reforma Agraria*, ed. Francisco Rhon and Carlos Pástor. Quito: Ediciones La Tierra, pp. 189–212.

Maiguashca, Juan. 1994. *Historia y región en el Ecuador 1830–1930*. Quito: Corporación Editora Nacional.

Mariátegui, José Carlos. 1973 [1928]. *Siete Ensayos De Interpretación De La Realidad Peruana*. Lima: Biblioteca Amauta.

Murra, John. 2002. *América Latina en la época colonial*. Barcelona: Critica.

Prieto, Mercedes. 2004. *Liberalismo y temor: Imaginando los sujetos indígenas en el Ecuador postcolonial 1895–1950*. Quito: Abya Ayala.

Szaszdi, Adam. 1964. "The Historiography of the Republic of Ecuador." *The Hispanic American Historical Review* 44, no. 4: 503–50.

Tobar Donoso, Julio. 1974. *Las Instituciones Del Periodo Hispanico, Especialmente En La Presidencia de Quito*. Quito: Editorial Ecuatoriana.
World Bank. 2015. *Indigenous Latin America in the Twenty-First Century*. Washington, DC: World Bank.

12. Peasants, inequality and progress in the research of Alexander Chayanov: Russia and the world

Vladimir Babashkin and Alexander Nikulin

1.   INTRODUCTION

Comprehending Chayanov's heritage has been a task for social science that is connected to the history and prospects of inequality and the global progress of rural development. Both Russian and foreign scholars have attempted this, but there remains an obvious need for further investigations. Of the publications touching on this topic in a general or fragmented way, the works by V. Danilov, B. Kerblay, T. Shanin and J. D. van der Ploeg (Ploeg 2014) are noteworthy.

Kerblay was perhaps the first to rediscover Chayanov's heritage abroad in the 1960s. He drew attention to Chayanov's vast interdisciplinary scientific erudition, and emphasized its importance for the study of not only the peasant household economy and agricultural cooperation but also a wide range of different social problems (Kerblay 1966: 26–7).

Danilov's article "The Russian Revolution in Chayanov's fate" pays special attention to the foreign period that marked the beginning of the scholarly career of the young researcher. Chayanov's internship at European agricultural centers began when he was still a student and continued into his postgraduate years. In 1909–12 he published around twenty texts on the analysis of reforms in European agriculture, stressing the importance of learning from this experience in rural Russia. Danilov especially noted that the original foreign materials accumulated by Chayanov were widely used in his later works, which have become classics of the genre. To corroborate this, the historian draws upon the following argument:

> In Belgium Chayanov was interested, first of all, in the interaction of cooperation, public agronomy and state policy in the process of radical commodity modernization of agriculture arising inevitably from the aggravation of struggle between large and small forms of production which was harmful for peasantry . . . It was in those very Belgian essays where some initial explanations of the importance of peasant

cooperation appeared, formulating it as "the ability to organize some of its individual technical, economic processes in which large-scale production has an undoubted advantage to the extent of this large-scale production without any changes in the economic balance, without a major breakdown of the organizational plan of the household. By technical separation and merging them with similar processes of neighbors in a cooperative" (Chayanov 1909, 2, b, 8–9). The words given here will move from work to work including the latest of Chayanov's publications. (Danilov 2011: 155)

Shanin noted the importance of Chayanov's basic principles for understanding the progress of agrarian reforms in various regions of the world in the twentieth century:

Many experiments having both positive and negative results, carried out in Europe, Asia, Africa, Latin America showed the value of A. Chayanov's hypotheses on the nature of agriculture, and to a certain extent of his more general theoretical constructs . . . and also on the way the production is connected with the relations between peasants and bureaucracy, with resource availability and issues of agricultural branches. Researching these issues Chayanov and his colleagues with their excellent knowledge of agriculture and rural society were unique. (Shanin 1989: 153)

The remainder of the chapter is structured as follows. The second section deals with Chayanov's study of peasantry in prewar Europe. The third section stresses the paradoxes of the autarkical economy in Russia. The fourth section compares the situation of Russia with other countries, and the fifth section deals with collectivization and Soviet–American agro-giants. Finally, the sixth section offers a brief conclusion.

2.   CHAYANOV'S STUDY OF PREWAR EUROPE: PEASANTRY AND PROGRESS

In his early works, primarily devoted to the study of agriculture in European countries, Chayanov provided samples of fascinating phenomenological descriptions of the countries he was able to visit. Against this background he characterized the agricultural phenomena that he investigated: the features of national organization of farms; types and forms of agricultural cooperative in Italy; the peculiarities of cooperative cattle breeding in Belgium and France; sugar-beet farming in Germany; dairy farming in Switzerland; and so on.

For example, Chayanov's work about the success of public agronomy and agricultural cooperation in Italy opens with an amusing historical and statistical excursion into the rapid economic development of the country in the late nineteenth and early twentieth centuries. The author especially notes that agricultural production in Italy ". . . was not artificially inflated, detached from the masses . . . but, on the contrary, was born from the depths of the popular economy, and being a real economic revival of the whole nation strongly contributed to the welfare of the masses" (Chayanov 1909: 1–4).

In another example of this approach, Chayanov begins his analysis of the success of Belgian peasant cooperation with a description of a cozy cafe owned by Belgian cooperatives, where they hold their meetings. This helps him to proceed to the presentation of the organizational principles of Belgian cooperatives (Chayanov 1909: 2, a, 8).

We find the same approach in his brochure describing Swiss agriculture. First, the author offers a brief, though mobilizing, picture of the socio-economic coexistence of the "two Switzerlands" in one country: the first is the world-famous Switzerland of famous resorts; and the second country, situated away from the tourist attractions, is the Swiss peasant village, reliably providing high-quality meat and dairy products to Swiss cities and tourist resorts (Chayanov 1912: 1).

Among Chayanov's international publications of the prewar period, one short article deserves special attention. It was published in 1914 in an influential Petersburg journal, *Sovremennik*,[1] entitled "On the Question of National Welfare in Europe" (Chayanov 1914: 2). In this article he goes beyond his agrarian specialization to undertake some reasoning on broad issues of political and social economy.

The article begins with a generally optimistic anti-Malthusian passage:

> At the beginning of the last century the English economist Malthus foreshadowed gloomy future of contemporary humanity. He argued that the human population of the globe had been increasing uncontrollably in number, and that growth surpassed the possible growth of livelihoods. In his opinion, with the further increase in the density of the world's population, it will be increasingly difficult for mankind to produce their daily bread . . . But he misses the fact that in parallel with the growth of population human knowledge has been growing extremely fast, and technical methods of obtaining livelihoods improve no less quickly. The gains of the human mind multiply the capacities of man to the extent that allows him to deal successfully with the consequences of the growing population density . . . (Chayanov 1914: 78)

Then Chayanov turns to the statistics of mass consumption in England and France. In both major European countries the long-term dynamics of consumption of basic agricultural products (e.g. meat, bread, sugar, cotton) obviously indicated the primacy of anti-Malthusian trends. Thus, Chayanov concludes:

> We can undoubtedly establish that England . . . has managed to increase the production of means of subsistence so much that, despite a significant increase in the population, the level of welfare of the masses not only has not decreased, but, on the contrary, has increased tremendously. The increase in the level of well-being is especially clearly seen when studying France . . . (Chayanov 1914: 79)

At the same time, Chayanov refers to the social aspects of inequality in the distribution of benefits in Europe: for example, in France, 86.5% of the population received 54% of the national income, while the remaining 13.5% received 46%. He demonstrates that, although historically the welfare of the working classes of France had been growing, the increase was slower than the rapidly growing wealth of the richest classes of the country.

The article ends with a conclusion that is somewhat characteristic of a progressive thinker of the early twentieth century:

> So, contrary to the forecast of Malthus, popular welfare in advanced countries has been growing, not falling. For their spiritual culture they have a solid material base, which is growing stronger, not weaker, with the growth of the population. The problem of *production* is not faced by modern humanity; and the attention of the masses is rightly moved towards a different problem – *distribution*. (Chayanov 1914: 82)

The Eurocentric optimism of this article is bewildering. Chayanov seems to forget that in other parts of the globe, less developed and more agrarian, Malthusianism does not yield its position so readily. Never mind the problem of *distribution* mentioned by Chayanov, which concerned not only the goods between social strata in Europe but also world territories to be divided between the European imperialist powers. It is also perplexing that Chayanov believed the expanding European food base to be sufficient for the prosperity of the spiritual culture of Europe.

In a treacherous twist of fate, the issue of *Sovremennik* containing Chayanov's reformist–progressive forecast was published just at the time when an unprecedented and cruel war broke out in Europe, awakening the darkest forebodings of Malthusianism.

3.   THE FIRST WORLD WAR AND THE CIVIL WAR: SOME PARADOXES OF AUTARKICAL ECONOMY

The very outbreak of war and the conflict's protracted nature were completely unpredictable for Chayanov and his contemporaries, which he noted in 1914 (Chayanov 1914: 1–5). Later, he wrote that "no one could have predicted that the war would drag on for years . . . It had been widely believed that the global clash of nations would result in a bloody battle, and within 2 or 3 months everything would be over. That kind of belief was universal both in the military world and among the economists" (Chayanov 1917: 6–7).

The war caused a break in long-standing international trade and economic relations. Rural Russia had been involved in the international trade of food production for several decades. With the closure of rail links with Europe and

sea routes through the Black and Baltic Seas the country seemed bound to suf-
focate from the inability to sell bread, butter, flax, poultry and other products
on global markets.

However, the expected sharp drop in prices for agricultural products did
not happen, for various reasons. On the contrary, from 1915 food prices in
Russia were at their highest, a result of making the Russian agrarian economy
increasingly natural and autarkical. Similar processes of naturalization and
disintegration of the economy were taking place in other belligerent nations.
Furthermore, in 1915 Chayanov undertook some abstract mathematical mod-
eling, based on the concept of the German economist I. Thünen, in an attempt
to address the problems of the autarkical agrarian economy. The results
were published in "The Problem of Population in an Isolated State-Island"
(Chayanov 1915: 42–56).

Chayanov was one of the first to draw the attention of his contemporaries to the importance of macro-autarkical trends (the isolated state) and
micro-autarkical processes (the natural economy of households). He tried to
analyze the interrelation of these processes in the long term, not only in mankind's past but also the present and possibly the future.

Nowadays, we often use words such as "globalist" or "anti-globalist,"
which do not relate to Chayanov, who sought to be a realist, recognizing the
mutual work of the processes of economic integration and autarkization under
the specific conditions of historical place and time. He considered the art of
economic policy to be the skillful conducting of various economic structures
in their financial and natural manifestations.

During the First World War Chayanov not only undertook tremendous work
analyzing a variety of socio-economic phenomena in the world crises; being on
the board of various all-Russian cooperative bodies he also personally participated in the organization of food and material supplies for the army and cities.
In 1917 he took an active part in preparing agrarian reform, and in October he
was appointed Minister of Agriculture of the provisional government.

In the Civil War years Chayanov maintained and established the network of
Russian cooperative organizations, seeking to defend their independence in the
face of total Bolshevik nationalization.

It was a unique experience of theoretical comprehension and administrative
management in the "time of troubles." Chayanov reflected this in the form
of an ironic liberal–populist parable, writing in 1919 a futuristic fantasy, *My
Brother Alexei's Journey to the Country of Peasant Utopia*. The hero of the
story, an old intellectual Bolshevik, mysteriously finds himself in Moscow in
1984. While reading a book on the world and Russian history of the twentieth
century he discovers that even after the rapid victory of the World Communist
Revolution there is no ". . . end of history." Human history continues to bring

about an unpredictable revenge of diversity of social alternatives over the universal dogmas of any shades of progressivism.

Many parts of Chayanov's utopia are now being read as prophecies that have been strikingly fulfilled or are still coming true, for example: "The world unity of the socialist system did not last long, and centrifugal social forces very soon broke the reigning consent . . . The oligarchy of Soviet employees degenerated into a capitalist regime . . . Europe again broke up into component parts. The building of world unity collapsed . . ." (Chayanov 1989: 204). The social globe in this utopia is multi-polar and multi-layered, its regional forms are various, whimsically diverse, and evolution is concentrated on the human personality.

Four years later Chayanov developed some ideas from this fiction in a strict treatise on political economy entitled *On the Theory of Non-Capitalist Economic Systems*. It was published in German in Berlin since Soviet censorship prevented issues of the kind (Tschajanow 1924: 577–613). The author admits the global dominance of the capitalist economy, primarily in the form of financial capital. However, he draws attention to other economic systems coexisting with capitalism – the family economy or, for example, the Soviet economic system. Chayanov denotes the latter as "state collectivism," and he calls for comprehension of its place and role in the diversity of global economic life.

Chayanov summed up the principle conclusions of this research as follows:

> It seems . . . appropriate to develop in political economy a special theory for each economic regime. The only difficulty in implementing this idea is that in real economic life we very seldom deal with an economic system as a "pure culture" if we borrow the term from biology. Typically, economic systems coexist side by side forming complex conglomerates . . . Today, when our world gradually ceases to be only the European world, and Africa and Asia with their specific economic formations will more and more interfere in the circle of our life and culture [. . .] the future of economic science will consist not in constructing a universal theory of economic life, but in creating a number of theoretical systems which would be adequate to a number of present and past socio-economic structures and which would reveal the forms of their coexistence and evolution. (Chayanov 1991: 195–6)

Chayanov's principles remain relevant in modern, interdisciplinary, social and economic regional studies.

4.   INTERNATIONAL AGRARIAN REVIEW: RUSSIA BETWEEN THE POLES OF RURAL EVOLUTION

Early in October 1927 Chayanov submitted to the government an analytical report containing the quintessence of the international agricultural experience of the 1920s. The postwar period of economic development of the USSR was over, and it was high time to start discussing the prospects of the country's agricultural development in the context of the first five-year plan.

The text opens with a survey of the evolution of world agriculture over the previous few decades. Chayanov highlights two poles of that evolution: the Western pole (North America and, to a large extent, South America, as well as South Africa and Australia); and the Eastern pole (Indian and Chinese, also characteristic of countries with agrarian overpopulation).

The American type of rural development is typically an extensive, highly mechanized farm, where the farmer employs just two or three laborers, his or her enterprise being tightly controlled by an unfolded vertical system of capitalist concentration (e.g. bank loans, elevator, land-improvement, trading companies extracting significant profits from farming).

The Indian and Chinese pole is, first of all, agrarian overpopulation where peasantry remains under the continuing domination of the feudal–communal system, extreme labor intensity, widespread conditions of servitude in land tenure, credit and employment.

Chayanov placed the rest of the world between these two poles, describing Russia of the late nineteenth to early twentieth century as an incredibly paradoxical "district mixture" of these polar types. The Russian village of the period, disentangled from the remnants of feudal relations, in his opinion was undergoing the "*most severe turning-point* caused by the transition from feudal to commodity system" (Chayanov 2003: 207, emphasis added).

From the point of view of the market economy, the process of settling in the USA had been rational from the very beginning. Zones of economic intensity were determined by market conditions. And in Russia, from the seventeenth to the end of the nineteenth century, the population was primarily determined by such factors as land fertility and the strategic safety of the regions. Thus, by the beginning of the twentieth century the Russian population was regionally located "in flagrant discrepancy . . . with market requirements" (Chayanov 2003: 207). The regional map of Russia included areas of severe agricultural overpopulation in fertile areas of the Central Black Earth region – "similarly to the Chinese land regime" (Chayanov 2003: 208). In the non-Black Earth areas, the crisis of agrarian overpopulation was both softened and aggravated by the mass seasonal work in the cities of the industrial center. And in the steppe and under-populated southeast of the Volga region, the North Caucasus and Siberia, there was a rapid Americanization of Russia with the growth of mechanized farming and capitalist socio-economic differentiation.

Chayanov noted that those polarizing agrarian Russian worlds determined the debate at the beginning of the twentieth century in Russian agrarian science between agronomists – "southerners" and "northerners" – on the strategy of rural development. While the former offered characteristics of "pure

America," forcing individual farming, the latter insisted on relying upon the middle peasantry and its own vertical rural cooperation to prevent the village from being captured by trade and financial capital.

Returning to the late 1920s, Chayanov described the intrigue of the polarized and uneven world of rural development as follows:

> Cooperated farmer involved through contact with the Bank in the system of capitalist economy – that's the hero of the day of agriculture of both Americas, Australia and South Africa . . . In contrast, in agriculturally overpopulated countries, with the exception of Japan, the situation remained almost the same as before the war. (Chayanov 2003: 208)

As for Soviet Russia, its agriculture had recovered to the prewar level, and Chayanov emphasized that the country had reached a crossroads. Again, there was increasing potential for rural capitalist development based on the pattern of American farmers, especially in the southeast, while most of the country was still an ocean of semi-natural peasant households. However, these households only seemed to be the same as in prewar times.

In reality, the postwar, post-revolutionary village had changed significantly. A comparatively young generation of peasants, who had experienced the Great War and the Russian Revolution, became most authoritative and influential in the villages. They had a broader outlook, and they were open to further change. The traditional power of conservative elderly men was mostly a thing of the past. Another factor of change was the agronomic science and rural cooperation of the 1920s. Such institutions had their own prewar experience; therefore, in the 1920s they promoted real progress in farming. These were the conditions in which Soviet Russia had the chance to determine its own effective way of development, avoiding the Scylla of American-farmer dependence on financial capital and the Charybdis of Indian–Chinese stagnation and peasant overpopulation. Instead of American vertical integration through the dominance of banking capital in agriculture, Soviet agricultural vertical integration developed as a variety of market-based forms of agricultural cooperation, constructed and controlled by the socialist government. Chayanov outlined a number of gradual steps in the governmental agrarian policy leading to ". . . accumulation of socialist elements in our village . . .," which ". . . alone can resist the development of farmer-type trends" (Chayanov 2003: 219).

Chayanov especially noted that even farmer-type developments may well exist in such conditions, their capitalist potential not being dangerous when peasant cooperation is predominant and the socialist state controls all the key economic positions.

The final part of the analytical paper is devoted to the probable challenges of impending Soviet industrialization and the possible answers to it. Of course, industrialization could not be limited to the accelerated development of urban manufacturing. The next five years would inevitably be related to some dramatic manifestations of the upcoming agricultural industrialization. For this reason, Chayanov called on party leaders "to anticipate *the turning-point* in question" (Chayanov 2003: 219, emphasis added).[2]

Indeed, the "turning-point" was not far off. A new round of stormy Soviet political debates on agricultural industrialization took place in the following year, 1928. Moreover, when calling for investigation of the international agricultural experience, the participants mostly did not consider typical American farmers; indeed, they were more interested in unique American agricultural factories.

5.   COLLECTIVIZATION AND SOVIET–AMERICAN AGRO-GIANTS

In 1928 the grain-procurement campaign of the Soviet power faced serious difficulties, which finally resulted in the policy of de-kulakization and collectivization. Of all the possible explanations, the party leadership chose the reason that the peasantry was unwilling to sell bread at state procurement prices, being led by wealthy peasants (*the kulaks*) who were class enemies and counter-revolutionaries. To obtain enough bread from the peasants to meet the needs of industrialization and urbanization, Stalin insisted on the use of repressive non-economic measures at village level. At the same time, Stalin initiated an ambitious plan of creating a network of giant state farms in the southern steppe regions of the USSR. These state agricultural factories were supposed to have 100% mechanization (How they broke the NEP 2000, 453–524).

The policy of pressure on the peasantry in the late 1920s created resistance, not only among the peasants but also among party members and other intellectuals. However, the idea of accelerated "sovkhozization" (agro-giants) created no less skepticism among intellectual and political circles than that of forced collectivization. Nonetheless, there was an important exception: the cohort of young Marxist agrarians dreaming of the advent of highly mechanized socialism in the village (Proceedings 1930). When Stalin put forward the idea of creating numerous grain farms at the plenum of the Party Central Committee, a few party leaders objected strongly (Proceedings 1930: 453–524, 482–5, 513–16).

At a special party meeting with experts on agriculture, professors of the old agronomic school spoke at length about the danger of forced creation of agro-giants in arid steppes, where unpredictable weather conditions, imperfections of transport and warehouse infrastructure, underdeveloped agricultural technologies and the impossibility of 100% mechanization could lead to a fatal failure (Meeting of Experts 1930). Stalin was adamant. He even used these agro-giant projects as an argument against the opponents of non-economic pressure on the peasantry. He claimed that he did not care where the missing millions of tons of grain that were so badly needed for industrialization would be taken, and if the required grain resulted from implementation of the agro-giants project it would be possible to slow down the excesses of collectivization and de-kulakization (How they broke the NEP 2000: 17–18).

Through the events described, Chayanov had been removed from all his official academic positions, including Head of the Chair at university. He and his colleagues were subjected to ideological harassment by agrarian Marxists. Any studies of independent peasant households were brutally criticized and terminated. All forms of peasant cooperation, except collective farms (*kolkhozy*), were declared kulaks and "petit bourgeois" (Proceedings 1930).

At the same time, the campaign of achieving 100% "Americanization" of agriculture was on the run, meaning that it was borrowing the experience of the agro-giants from the USA. In 1929 the famous American agricultural entrepreneur Thomas Campbell was invited to the USSR for consultations on state-farm (*sovkhozy*) construction. He owned the world's largest 100% mechanized agricultural factory covering an area of 36,000 hectares in Montana. His nickname was "Agro-Ford" because of his experiments in the conveyor mechanization of agriculture (Nikulin 2008).

In 1928 Chayanov took the decision to support the official plans of new *sovkhozy* construction. Up to his arrest in June 1930, he had focused on the development of Americanized agro-giants. Many of Chayanov's contemporaries, critics and colleagues reasonably believed that Chayanov was trying to avoid political threats, not just to him personally but to all his scientific school.

It is therefore evident that Chayanov had no choice. His study of agricultural cooperation was declared an enemy's (*kulak*) theory. Justifying the newly created collective farms (*kolkhozy*) was not for him. In his previous works he had comprehensively described what a problematic and contradictory economic model *kolkhoz* was. However, to start with a "clean slate," or rather with an empty virgin soil field where the highly mechanized agro-giants were to emerge, it was worth trying. Perhaps the super-ambitious state project would indeed partly compensate for the enormous costs and failures of collectivization.

So Chayanov took up the challenge. From 1928 to 1930 he published a dozen articles devoted to large grain farms, which could be designed in the USSR based on the model of American large agricultural enterprises. He was the first Soviet economist to raise the fundamental question of the similarities, differences and prospects of the American and Soviet ways of development of large-scale agricultural production. He did this in 1928 in an article named "*Sovkhozy*-giants. – Degor Integrated Plant, – What Can We Borrow from America? – The Problem of Elimination of Agricultural Overpopulation."

Chayanov was skeptical about the euphoria of directly borrowing the American experience when organizing state farms in the southeastern steppes of the USSR:

> Many people tend to believe that these initiatives are simply an attempt to transfer the American technique of tractor farming to our arid zone. A kind of borrowing Ford's conveyor system by our enterprises. It is worth, however, to take a closer look at the projects being debated now, to make sure that the problem is not in America . . . (Chayanov 1928: 3)

He stressed that the highly mechanized America of the 1920s was not a country of large agricultural enterprises. The average size of a farm in 1925 was only 38 acres, or 16 hectares. Of 6,371,640 US farms, only 7,455, or approximately 0.1%, exceeded 2,000 hectares. And the vast majority of them were not grain farms, but pasture cattle farms in Texas. In fact, there was just one example in the whole of the United States of a highly mechanized giant agricultural factory, which was Thomas Campbell's farm, covering 36,000 hectares. Moreover, the Soviet reformers were dreaming of hundreds of American-style *sovkhozy*, each exceeding Campbell's structure in area and other parameters!

Therefore, in Chayanov's opinion, it was possible that some of the technical elements of large farms could be borrowed from the Americans, while the organizational forms of the Soviet agricultural giants were still to be invented. Chayanov thought the same about the experience of other regions of the world: "We won't be given much in this regard by other countries like Uruguay and South Africa where the size of farms is incomparably larger than in the U.S., but the type of agriculture is mainly cattle-breeding" (Chayanov 1928: 3).

While inventing these organizational forms many circumstances had to be taken into consideration. Sparsely populated Soviet steppes and, for example, the foothills of the Caucasus set different tasks for scholars. The latter case created the most complex social problem, which Chayanov described while observing the situation in Digor (North Ossetia), where a widely advertised experiment to create an agricultural giant was taking place:

> 12,000 people (including about 6,000 working age) live in the densely populated territory of the future Digor plant. Suffocating of the lack of land, they keep to ultra-intensive forms of economy, forcing the development of labor-intensive crops, and their contribution to high gross income of the area is reduced labor productivity. There is no sense involving this situation in the plant.
>
> What is more, just introduction of American machinery in harvesting and processing immediately make redundant over half of manpower. Selection of crops according to higher labor productivity, rather than gross income, will reduce it to 30–40 percent of the current index. Therefore, withdrawing this labor from farming we have to provide its application with an equally high performance factor. Hence, the

inevitable idea of the integrated plant, that is, integrating agriculture with industrial production and special industries able to absorb the released labor.

It goes without saying that such approach to organization at Digor plant relates to the most important, most acute and most urgent problem of our national economy – *the problem of the elimination of agrarian overpopulation*. Neither America nor other countries can give us anything concerning the solution of this problem. The whole work and responsibility for the results is up to us. (Chayanov 1928: 3)

6.   CONCLUSION

Chayanov wrote "*Sovkhozy*-giants" two-and-a-half years before his arrest on charges of anti-Soviet conspiracy. In those years he was completely absorbed in designing optimal plans and forms of giant *sovkhozy* and integrated agricultural plants. On the eve of his arrest, he had even prepared for publication a special monograph on the prospects of super-large-scale Soviet agriculture, which was lost among his seized documents (Nikulin 2004).

Chayanov believed in the possibility of implementing the ambitious plan of super-large-scale agricultural production in the USSR, which was unprecedented in world history. However, in 1930 he warned that there were two difficult problems to resolve as necessary conditions for making the plan feasible: adequate financial support of large state farms, and personnel. Chayanov realized the crucial importance of the personnel issue, and in December 1929 he wrote:

> Our old agronomic staff is insignificant in number and educated on the skills of a completely different type of farms and other equipment. The question of personnel for us, therefore, is not a question of selection, but a question of creation. We think that the network of our universities and technical schools will be unable to give the necessary giant amounts of personnel in the shortest possible time we have at our disposal. (Chayanov 1929: 101)

He also wrote about the danger of bureaucratization of the work involved in creating *sovkhozy*, nullifying the economic efficiency of that type of state-owned enterprise. His last articles before his arrest were devoted to training new personnel for Soviet agriculture (Chayanov 1930).

Furthermore, the Soviet authorities invited a number of qualified American agricultural machine operators to cope with the state-farm personnel shortage (Nikulin 2008). However, these foreign specialists were just a drop in the ocean in terms of the hastily created *sovkhozy* and giant integrated state farms of the early 1930s. And, of course, the fundamental state-farm reform required enormous financial resources. The Soviet government, with all the disarray and miscalculations of the first five-year plan, proved unable to issue anything of the kind.

By 1932 state-farm construction had suffered a severe economic, techno-logical and environmental crisis. The fields of agro-giants were overgrown with weeds, the demoralized manpower had run away, and the great famine was impending (Zelenin 1996). By that time, Chayanov was in prison; and in 1937 he was shot.

In the 1930s the initial *sovkhozy* were disaggregated. However, the Soviet government never abandoned the idea of a super-large-state agricultural enterprise. It was considered the crown of progressive agricultural evolution. However, most of the subsequent attempts in this direction under Stalin, Khrushchev and Brezhnev turned out to be costly, bureaucratic and inefficient.

Peculiar heirs of Soviet state-owned agricultural enterprises can be found in modern Russia. State–capitalist agro-holdings of the day rely on an incom-parably more powerful scientific and technical base of rural development in comparison with the 1930s. Nonetheless, they display similar problems: finan-cial voracity, bureaucratic inflation and personnel shortages. In the United States and other developed countries of the West we still find the dominance of more mobile and economical family farms. They are rather high-tech and have proved to be more appropriate to operate in agriculture itself. As for the heirs of Campbell's agro-giant and Soviet state farms of the early 1930s, their expansion is currently taking place on the semi-peripheries of capitalism, mostly in post-socialist and Latin American countries. Moreover, the peasant economy, which was always the focus of Chayanov's research, struggles to exist on the semi-peripheries and peripheries of the global world.[3]

NOTES

1. Meaning "contemporary" in English.
2. We should bear in mind that both beginning his report and concluding it in October 1927, Chayanov used the word ("turning-point") that Stalin referred to in November 1929 in the article "The Year of the Great Turning-Point" to declare the policy of collectivization.
3. This chapter was prepared using a grant from the President of the Russian Federation "School of A. V. Chayanov and Contemporary Rural Development: Perpetuating the actions of scientists through the updating of their heritage."

REFERENCES

Chayanov, Alexander. 1909. "Cooperation in the Agriculture of Italy: Letters from Agrarian Belgium." *Vestnik Sel'skogo Hozjajstva (Bulletin of Agriculture)* (a) no. 33: 8–11; (b) no. 36: 7–10.

Chayanov, Alexander. 1912. "Peasant Farm in Switzerland." *Vestnik Sel'skogo Hozjajstva (Bulletin of Agriculture)* no. 32–4, M: 24 p.

Chayanov, Alexander. 1914. *War and Peasant Economy*. Moscow: Sovremennik.

Chayanov, Alexander. 1915. "The Problem of Population in an Isolated State-Island." *Agronomicheskii Zhurnal (Journal of Agronomy)* 2, Har'kov: 42–56.

Chayanov, Alexander. 1917. *Food Question: Lectures Read at the Courses on Training Workers in Cultural and Educational Activities at the Council of Student Deputies in April 1917*. M: 1–54.

Chayanov, Alexander. 1928. "*Sovkhozy*-Giants. – Degor Integrated Plant, – What Can We Borrow from America? – The Problem of Elimination of Agricultural Overpopulation." *Ekonomicheskaya Zhizn' (Economic Life)* no. 255, November 15: 5.

Chayanov, Alexander. 1929. "Technical Organization of Grain Factories." *Ekonomicheskoe Obozrenie (Economic Review)* no. 12: 95–101.

Chayanov, Alexander. 1930. "New Personnel for New Agriculture." *Sotsialisticheskoe zemledelie (Socialist Agriculture)* January 5: 4.

Chayanov, Alexander. 1989. *My Brother Alexei's Journey to the Country of Peasant Utopia*. Moscow: Sovremennik.

Chayanov, Alexander. 1991. *On the Theory of Non-Capitalist Economic Systems* [translated from German]. Moscow: INION.

Chayanov, Alexander. 2003. "A. Chayanov's Letter to V. Molotov about the Presentation of a Report on the Current Situation in the USSR Agriculture in Comparison to Its Pre-War Situation and the Situation of Agriculture in the Capitalist Countries." *Unpublished and other Well-Known Works*. Moscow: Dashkov and Co.

Danilov, Viktor P. 2011. *The History of Peasantry in Russia in the 20th Century: Selected Works (Part 2)*. Moscow, ROSSPEHN: 149–77.

How they broke the NEP. 2000. *The Transcripts of Plenums of the Central Committee of the CPSU (b) 1928 and 1929* (5 vols). M, MDF, Volume 1: 1–495.

Kerblay, Basile. 1966. "A. V. Chayanov: Life, Career, Works." In *A. V. Chayanov on the Theory of Peasant Economy*, ed. Daniel Thorner, Basile Kerblay and Ref Smith. Homewood: The American Economic Association, pp. 279–96.

Meeting of Experts on the Organization of Large Soviet Farms (Grain Factories). 1930. May 16. *Russian State Archive of Social and Political History* Fund 78, Inventory 7, File 109, List 174–232.

Nikulin, Alexander. 2004. "Chayanov's Version of Collectivization." *Otechestvennye zapiski (National Notes)* no. 1: 215–30.

Nikulin, Alexander. 2008. "American Agrarians in the USSR: 'You're in the *Sovkhoz* Now!'." *Znamja* no. 10: 178–88.

Ploeg, Jan Douwe van der. 2014. *Peasants and the Art of Farming: A Chayanovian Manifesto*. Halifax, Nova Scotia: Fernwood Publishing.

Proceedings of the First All-Union Conference of Marxist Agrarians. 1930. *Volume 1*. M: 1–534.

Shanin, Teodor. 1989. "Chayanov's Legacy: Theory, Erroneous Interpretations and Modern Theories of Development." *Vestnik Sel'skohozjajstvennoj Nauki (Bulletin of Agricultural Science)* no. 2: 14–18.

Tschajanow, Alexander. 1924. "Zur Frage der Bedeutung der Familienwirtschaft im Gesamtaufbau der Volkswirtschaft." *Weltwirtschaftliches Archiv. Tubingen* (1925) Bd. 22, H. 1: 1–5.

Zelenin, Ilya. 1996. "The First Soviet Program of Developing the Virgin Lands (the Years Late 20s–30s)." *Otechestvennaya Istoria (Russian History)* no. 2: 55–65.

13. Broadacre City: Frank Lloyd Wright's vision of an organic capitalism

Catherine Maumi

1.   INTRODUCTION

In June 1935, a critic, Stephen Alexander, reported in *New Masses* on his visit to the Industrial Arts Exposition of the National Alliance of Art and Industry, which had opened on April 15 at the Rockefeller Center in New York City. Despite stating in his article's introduction that the event was not worth one's time or money, he revealed that he had discovered one particular stand worthy of attention: "The most important display in the exhibition is Frank Lloyd Wright's set of scale models for his 'Broadacre City, A New Community Plan'" (Alexander 1935: 28), he wrote. All the models and panels were accompanied by a brochure explaining the principles the architect stood for and his idea of community planning. Alexander explained at some length how this exhibit by Frank Lloyd Wright (1867–1959)[1] had drawn his attention away from the other more or less utilitarian and functional displays, and he ended up devoting most of his article to him. Although he considered the architect's vision, which he called utopian, staggeringly naive, utterly unrealistic, and likely incapable of solving the major problems posed by the exploitation of the American working class, he admitted it had the advantage of confronting political and economic questions – dimensions that architecture cannot escape. Thus, Alexander acknowledged that:

> Briefly, Mr. Wright offers as a solution, not only for architecture but for everything that's wrong with present-day society, *Decentralization*. (. . .) Despite his badly confused notions of the nature of social forces in our societies – (only a serious and completely sincere person could have written such a naive concoction of adolescent idealism and Wellsian it's-all-done-with-push-buttons fiction) – Frank Lloyd Wright must be regarded as one of the important forces in progressive American architectural thought. (. . .) He is virtually alone among the prominent architects of this country in his approach to the fundamental problems of present-day architecture as primarily socio-economic. (. . .) As far as relevance to an immediate program is concerned, the significance of Mr. Wright's project is that it points inexorably to the necessity for the removal of capitalism and the creation of a socialist society as the primary condition for the progressive development of architecture. (Alexander 1935: 28)

Wright's response to Alexander was not long in coming: it was published the very next month. Besides not being particularly fond of being classified as a dream artist, Wright was upset that his project could be likened to one of a "socialist society" – he rejected any and every kind of *ist* and *ism*. Even if Broadacre City[2] signaled an end to the capitalism that had been imposed on the United States, it did not extol the values of communism or socialism. He was in no way persuaded by the idea of having a "life by 'committee meeting,'" nor was he seduced by the socialist or communist governments of the time, especially because, in his opinion, there was nothing more important than individual freedom. This, the most precious of what humanity had to offer, was what allowed him to develop his "creative individuality." And this was one of Broadacre City's main challenges: to create an environment in which free and equal individuals could flourish, as should be the case in any democratic society. His response to Alexander was as follows:

> I deplore the fact that the present city and the machine that built it and the capitalistic machine that is now trying to maintain it by centralization of every kind but the right kind should find its reflection and counterpart in the struggle for freedom the masses are urged to make, called Communistic. This inversion may be the only way open to labor because it is the only way labor has learned from the very capitalism that has enslaved laborers. (. . .) But Broadacres has proposed a life as anti-capitalistic as it is, in this sense, anti-Communistic. It is anti-socialistic, too, so far as current socialism goes. (. . .) It had nothing to sell. It was a preliminary study for the decentralization that to me seems necessary to human freedom. (. . .) There must be some way of life wherein there is no antagonism between the more developed and the less developed – or even between the rich and poor if each had a fair chance to be what you call "rich and poor." (Wright 1935a: 23)

This "dialogue" between Wright and Alexander is instructive in that it immediately asks us to realize that the Broadacre City project presented by Wright in April 1935 was not just an architectural project as one usually understands the term. It was essentially a project with economic and political dimensions – aspects that were often neglected and the model itself may even have contributed to blur. In fact, most of the public saw it only as a model of what would be constructed in the future, even though its mission, according to Wright, was to lay out the principles of a new, democratic way of life in the United States. Understanding the model as the concept of Broadacre City meant learning to read between the lines because, as Wright put it: "There is more between the lines still than appears in the lines" (Wright 1940a: 18).

Broadacres' aim was to respond to the economic, social, cultural, and ecological crises that the country was experiencing at the time. Some of the panels in the exhibit also offered valuable clues, such as the one entitled "Living in America," on which visitors could read "no private ownership, no landlord and tenant, no 'housing', no slum, no traffic problem," etc. On others, there were the names of the different thinkers and personalities whose thinking had informed the project. For example: "Broadacre City commemorating [among others] Goethe, Mazzini, Count Tolstoi, Prince Peter Kropotkin, Silvio Gesell, Henry Thoreau, Henry George, William Blake, Louis Sullivan, not forgetting Thorstein Veblen, Edward Bellamy"; one could also take note that the "required reading for students of Broadacre City [includes] Spinoza, Voltaire, Walt Whitman, Henry George, William Blake, Louis Sullivan, not forgetting Nietzsche, Thoreau, Emerson." Admittedly, such a pantheon may well have seemed, at the very least, eclectic and original to the activists for the working class, such as Stephen Alexander or the readers of *New Masses*, but it was actually in keeping with the cultural environment and intellectual milieu of Frank Lloyd Wright – both of which help us grasp the roots and the scope of his architectural and urban thinking. In the following sections of the chapter, we will explain the extent to which Wright's Broadacres can be seen as a true progressive project.

2.   A WAY OF THINKING ROOTED IN THE PROGRESSIVE CULTURE OF THE MIDWEST

Frank Lloyd Wright was born June 8, 1867 in Richland Center, Wisconsin. His father, a preacher, and his mother, a school teacher, divorced in 1884. His family on his mother's side, the Lloyd Joneses, had a considerable influence on the young Wright, as evidenced by the architect's autobiographies and his attitude toward the world. After arriving in the United States in 1844, the Lloyd Joneses (originally from Wales) settled in Wisconsin, near the city of Madison, in 1864, and established themselves as a most respectable family. The Lloyd Joneses were members of the Unitarian Church, which Wright's great-great-grandfather had founded in 1726, and shared the ideals of transcendentalist culture. The writings of Ralph Waldo Emerson (1803–1882) inspired the young Wright, as did those of Henry David Thoreau (1817–1862) and the long time he spent every year of his childhood on the farm of his uncle James Lloyd Jones. This education, which he received by way of Emerson and Thoreau but also from his work on the farm, led him to an understanding of and love for nature. This fondness would be inextricably linked with the attention he paid to and the immense respect he had for nature throughout his life.

This world view also matches the one that his aunts, Ellen and Jane Lloyd Jones, sought to convey with the Hillside Home School, a Unitarian establishment they had founded in 1887 on family lands near Spring Green. The place served as a farm, a home, and a school all at once, and the goal was for children to accrue daily experiences and the teaching to develop everyone's individual faculties while they learned to live as part of a community. The Lloyd

Jones sisters' experimental school is often regarded as a forerunner of the progressive reforms that took hold in education early in the twentieth century. Governor Robert La Follette, Sr., visited the Hillside Home School on many occasions, and many of the La Follette children attended school there (Bohrer 1955). Wright himself later used his aunts' educational principles when he founded the Taliesin Fellowship in 1932. At the Taliesin Fellowship, which offered architecture training, members of the community took turns performing all the tasks (working in the field, on the drawing board, and in the kitchen, constructing and maintaining buildings, etc.). Wright was an ardent supporter of the Experimental College that Alexander Meiklejohn (1872–1964) set up in 1927 at the University of Wisconsin. The issue of education was by no means insignificant; for Wright, as for many of his friends, the future of American democracy was at stake, and it was important to support and promote the education of individuals who had a strong and creative individuality at a time when capitalism only favored individualism and, thus, deprived society of its true wealth. This was the cause for which Wright was trying to advocate in 1932 when he said:

> But some 500 years before Jesus the philosophy of the Chinese philosopher, Laotze, had a sense of individuality as achieved organic unity. Our own ideal social state, Democracy, was originally conceived as some such organic unity – that is to say – the free growth of many individuals as units free in themselves, functioning together in a unity of their own making. This is the natural ideal of democracy we now need to emphasize and live up to in order to regain the ground we have lost to the big cities centralization has over built. The "rugged individualism" that now captains our enterprises and becomes the "capitalist" is entirely foreign to this ideal of individuality. (Wright 1932a: 15–16)

The organic unity at the root of American democracy had already been severely weakened by the increasing development of industry during the second half of the nineteenth century, and it was threatened all the more by the power and hegemony that the "big city" (with New York City at the forefront) wielded over the rest of the territory. The soil and its resources were nothing more than objects to be speculated, and man – an anonymous pawn lost among the masses – was dominated by the machine, which had become one of his greatest enemies. In Wright's eyes, this evolution of the industrialized world only confirmed Emerson's cruel assessment – one he could not make peace with, however:

> Man is not a farmer, or a professor, or an engineer, but he is all. Man is priest, and scholar, and statesman, and producer, and soldier. In the *divided* or social state these functions are parceled out to individuals, each of whom aims to do his stint of the joint work, whilst each other performs his. (. . .) But, unfortunately, this original unit, this fountain of power, has been so distributed to multitudes, has been so

minutely subdivided and peddled out, that it is spilled into drops, and cannot be gathered. The state of society is one in which the members have suffered amputation from the trunk, and strut about [like] so many walking monsters – a good finger, a neck, a stomach, an elbow, but never a man. (Emerson 1968: 32)

When the young Frank Lloyd Wright, whose spirit had been shaped by such a view of the world, arrived in Chicago in 1887 looking for work as an architect, his uncle Jenkin Lloyd Jones, the minister at the All Souls Unitarian Church, introduced him to a circle of social reformers he belonged to and among whom he also counted as an authority. Wright became a regular at Hull House, founded in 1889 by Jane Addams (1860–1935) and Ellen Gates Starr. At Addams' request, he delivered an address there in 1901, which has since become famous: "The Art and Craft of the Machine." Among others, he met Thorstein Veblen (1857–1929, also originally from Wisconsin) and John Dewey (1859–1952). Wright was among the intellectuals – such as Carl Sandburg, Vachel Lindsay, and Theodore Dreiser from the world of literature, John Root and Louis H. Sullivan from architecture, and Jens Jensen from landscape architecture – who were working to prove that the Midwest and its capital, Chicago, were the cradle of true American culture. Wright introduced a radically new kind of thinking about architecture, and his influence was felt as far as Europe (the Netherlands and Germany, in particular) following Wasmuth's publication of the first monograph devoted to his work, in 1910–11.

In 1910, Wright left Chicago to settle on family land in Spring Green, where he founded Taliesin, which was both an architecture firm and a home for his family. His friendships with many University of Wisconsin professors, such as John R. Commons (1862–1945), as well as the La Follette family, also help explain his political and economic positions. He was proud as can be of the experiments carried out in his "dear" state of Wisconsin, which were collectively known as the "Wisconsin Idea" (McCarthy 1912). He was fond of the state's landscapes dotted with valleys, farm hills, and red barns: "So 'human' is this countryside in scale and feeling. 'Pastoral' beauty, I believe, the poets call it." And he liked that wherever he went, including overseas, Wisconsin was regarded, time and again, as a "progressive" state: "I have found out, too [he wrote, not without feeling a sense of pride], that we are known abroad as a 'progressive' state. They know about Ross and Commons, Reinsch and Glenn Frank:[3] names that help to make Wisconsin scientific, agrarian and political to the outside world. The name of La Follette distinguishes our political history, I find, wherever I go" (Wright 1993: 134–5).

While it was not until the beginning of the 1930s that his words had such a political inflection, Wright had already expressed his rejection of the big city much earlier, calling it a "monster leviathan, stretching acre upon acre into the far distance" (Wright 1992: 68). He was determined to redefine the domestic space and was simultaneously working to "blow up" the notion of the house as a "box" – which he achieved with the so-called "Prairie houses" – and to develop new urban (or suburban) morphologies. His work evinces the desire he had to preserve each home's "individuality" and intimacy while promoting a spirit of community by studying the size and shape of the plots and the how the houses were positioned on them. Consequently, his research on the typology of the "Prairie house" is inseparable from research conducted in parallel and since the 1890s on the "Quadruple Block Plan."[4] The first outcome of this thinking, at the scale of an entire community, was the answer he formulated for a competition by the Chicago City Club (1912–13). In addition to having integrated all the services the community required (in terms of trade, culture, education, and leisure), he was the only one to offer different housing typologies (single and semi-detached houses, smaller/larger apartments for families, couples, and singles, etc.).

Ten years later, after returning from Japan[5] and while living on the West Coast of the United States, Wright published *Experimenting with Human Lives* (1923); this text ushered in a series of articles, conferences, and books in which Wright condemned the skyscraper – calling it an "immoral expedient" – and the excessive congestion it represented. He also called out the shameless speculation that landowners indulged in and the unworthy ambition of the "commercialized architect." According to him, such a concentration was contrary to the spirit that ought to prevail in a city's development. "Our cities grow more and more a concession to the herd instinct and less and less places for the development and emphasis of the quality of individuality, and they become more and more unfit places for human beings, who value that quality of individuality as the most precious asset of human kind, as the supreme entertainment of life" (Wright 1923).

3. "DECENTRALIZATION IS NOT DISPERSAL – THAT IS WRONG . . . IT IS REINTEGRATION" (WRIGHT 1930)[6]

Wright first described the decentralized city at his "The City" lecture, which he delivered at Princeton University in May 1930. It was based in part on observations he had made while driving across North America and during his long stays in the West, in particular in Los Angeles and Phoenix. The major transformations that the automobile had brought about led him to anticipate that the machine "will enable all that was human in the city to go to the country and grow up with it: enable human life to be based squarely and fairly on the ground" (Wright 1931: 108). However, it was essential to get out in front of such a development and counter the land speculation that saw many territories divided up into narrow parcels – a vestige of "feudal thinking," as Wright lamented. According to him, one acre of land per family was to be the minimum democratic surface. Thereby, it was also a question of fighting against the ruining of landscapes caused by a proliferation of the same buildings, moreover of poor quality, on a continental scale. The machine, Wright protested, ought to be used for other purposes than producing only monotony and mediocrity; mankind is entitled to expect the machine to do more than that.

Decentralization, as Wright saw it, also had another purpose, one that was just as vital because it was economic in nature. One of the main problems that had to be solved – one that had contributed to the increasing imbalance in a number of territories – came from the fact that "Cities are great mouths. New York the greatest mouth in the world" (Wright 1931: 110). Not only was the metropolis a powerful magnet drawing men, activities, powers, and money closer, but, in order to feed itself, it had brought about a change in the modes of agricultural production, which lay at the root of the (economic and ecological) problems that the American countryside was already facing. Decentralization meant dividing up the different activities on the territory in an equal manner. One of the first benefits for the population was that local products, especially food, would be distributed along the shortest route: directly from the producer to the consumer. Everything the locals might need would be easy to access because they would be close. It would apply not only to food but also to goods, services, culture, and so on. Schools would be more fairly distributed and located in pleasant areas, and the same would be true of concert halls, theaters, and cinemas: "I do not wish to 'disperse' any city; decentralization is not dispersal – that is wrong . . . it is reintegration," Wright (1939: 35–6) continued to plead, while also expressing the hope that:

> We should soon have in authority developed minds that comprehend the modern sense of spaciousness so characteristic of today now that scientific mechanization is being made available to everyone, rich or poor. We should soon be able to realize that the door of this cage – this thing we call the great city – is at last – open. The door is open and we can fly. (Wright 1939: 12)

To Wright, it was clear that this freedom that had recently been acquired thanks to new means of communication (telephone, radio, television), mobility (automobile), and energy supply (electricity) had to be utilized and ought not to be wasted, as he observed at the time.

This freedom inevitably brings with it new ways of living and, consequently, of organizing people on the ground, and it was essential that they reflect the principles of American culture and democracy, which up to that point had been betrayed, as was made visible by the serious crisis in which the country had been plunged. Wright was obviously thinking of the economic crisis triggered by the October 1929 stock market crash that had engulfed the world in misery. But he also had in mind the living conditions of American farmers, who had already been facing great hardship since the early 1920s. The development of intensive agriculture during the First World War led, after peace had returned, to a catastrophic drop in prices due to the surplus of products. Besides ruining many farmers' lives, the use of intensive agriculture in the western Great Plains also produced one of the greatest ecological disasters in the United States: the *Dust Bowl*.

Wright considered *The Plow That Broke the Plains* (1936), a short documentary film that condemned the irresponsible exploitation of the Great Plains, "an unforgettable film that will take its place among great films anywhere" (Wright 1941b: 209) and comparable overall to the great Soviet films. On top of these economic and ecological crises, another equally profound cultural or "identity" crisis resulted from the steady progress of metropolization: the expanding reach of the metropolis in territories farther and farther away. This encroachment not only devastated natural resources and landscapes but also erased local cultures and lifestyles forever. "We have neglected our ground as the basis for our culture and tried to get culture from the pavements and factories of the world," Wright (1941a: 207) lamented.

Therefore, the aim of Broadacre City was to defend the idea that it was possible to oppose such destruction, not only of natural resources but also of human beings (those who live in cities, as well as those in the countryside), which ought to be a feature of any democracy worthy of the name. To this end, it was essential to fight the "system" itself, namely capitalism as it had developed since the nineteenth century – a capitalism whose sole aim was to garner the maximum amount of benefits in a minimum amount of time. These were ideas he shared with his friend Lewis Mumford (1895–1990), who published two important articles on the subject: "Regionalism and Irregionalism" (1927) and "The Theory and Practice of Regionalism (continued)" (1928). For Wright, Mumford, and many others at the time, such a waste of human and natural resources was proof that the United States was no longer, and for a long time had not been, the democracy envisioned by the country's Founding Fathers. According to Wright, there was an urgent need to restore the idea of "common sense" – a reference to Thomas Paine (1737–1809) and his pamphlet *Common Sense* (1776), which was another major point of reference.

This was the goal of Broadacre City: the project's aim was to state the principles, an ideal, a vision for a democratic America. Wright was perfectly aware of the visionary nature of his proposal, but, in his opinion, that is precisely what the mission of an architect is. To Howard Scott, an engineer who had brushed off the significance of the Broadacre City model by saying "Just an artist's dream," he responded as follows: "The artist, the 'dreamer', supplies an element which the scientist, the 'expert', the statistician, cannot supply, and that element is '**vision**'. 'Where there is no vision the people perish'" (Wright 1940d: 28, emphasis in original).

4.   "BROADACRE CITY: A NEW COMMUNITY PLAN"

The first lecture to focus on Broadacre City was delivered in February 1932 at the Chicago City Club. In March of the same year, the *New York Times* published "'Broadacre City': An architect's vision," and in May an article appeared in *American Architect* under the headline "America Tomorrow." These articles foreshadowed the work that Wright had undertaken since the winter and that was published shortly thereafter, in September 1932: *The Disappearing City*. The book offers virulent criticism of the great industrial city, this veritable cancer that is the metropolis, as exemplified by New York, because at the time it was recognized as the great financial power of not only the United States but also the world. New York was the physical manifestation of triumphant capitalism. Broadacre City, as described, proposed a new way of organizing people on the ground and of putting an end to the metropolis and its monopoly. Wright used only words to make his point, however, which seems surprising for an architect known for his graphic output. This choice seems to confirm the project's utopian dimension.

And so, on April 15, 1935, a spatial formalization of the Broadacres principles was revealed when the now famous model was unveiled at the Rockefeller Center. The exhibit was a huge success, first in New York and then in Madison, Pittsburgh, and Washington, DC. The documents that were circulated to illustrate the various articles devoted to the project consisted of photographs of the models and of members of the Taliesin Fellowship building them. These photographs were meant to show that Broadacre City was the work of the community as a whole that was mobilized to build it. This was confirmed by the seminal article published in *The Architectural Record* upon the opening of the exhibit: "Broadacre City: A New Community Plan" (Wright 1935b).

In the article, Wright explains that the model depicts a representative sample of "Usonia":[7] four sections[8] of US territory that, for more than four generations, had served as home for a usonian community – that is to say, one that is truly democratic. In this respect, Wright's thinking about architecture draws on the great narrative of United States history and follows in the footsteps of the democratic ideals of Thomas Jefferson (1743–1826). This reference to "section" is crucial: in so doing, Wright recalled the ambition that Jefferson had when he created the National Land Survey grid (Maumi 2007). He had designed it to anchor democracy in the soil of the United States and to prevent men, money and power from being concentrated in whatever way. It was supposed to thwart the creation of large estates owned by rich landowners and, thus, rein in land speculation. It also meant that every inhabitant of the United States had the right to own his own parcel of land, a homestead, on the condition that he live there and maintain it. It should have favored the establishment of free and independent smallholders making a dignified living from the work done on their land. This ideal was at the root of the myth of the middle landscape, or of the pastoral landscape.

The National Land Survey grid that appeared on the model was a reminder of this inherent right of every man, woman and child, according to Wright, to own his or her parcel of land – a homestead of a minimum of one acre. A large family could claim more, as could certain farms. According to the model, about 1,400 families – with an average of five people each – lived in Broadacre City. Wright stressed that the model shows a long-term process and not simply the outcome: it represented the spatial organization of a usonian community that had implemented the Broadacres principles over four generations, that is to say, organic and democratic principles. It illustrated a "transition scheme," a time *t* of this long process that has been implemented "from generation to generation" and would continue into the future. This temporal dimension, essential to Wright's thinking, refers to the cycles of life and nature: Broadacres rose up against the egoism of contemporary societies concerned only with their own well-being and neglecting the long term and, therefore, their children's needs and well-being. Moreover, any culture anchors itself in a territory in which historical depth is essential, because that is where its roots are.

In Broadacre City, man once again became an inhabitant of the Earth; he learned anew how to live in harmony with nature, with his environment. Because each family has the right to live on its acre-sized homestead, it has the opportunity to maintain a vegetable garden and an orchard (even some animals) in order to eat healthy and fresh products at a lower cost. Furthermore, electrical energy makes it possible to anticipate a reduction in working time and, as a result, an increased amount of free time. This time could be devoted to other activities – gardening, home maintenance work – but also to (artistic and cultural) pastimes. Wright knew full well that not everybody would necessarily be interested in agriculture or gardening, and for them, small buildings with comfortable apartments were designed. Another major principle was that it was impossible to make a qualitative distinction between each of the buildings or structures: "In the buildings for Broadacres no distinction exists between much and little, more and less. Quality is in all, for all, alike. The thought entering into the first or last estate is of the best. What differs is only individuality and extent. There is nothing poor or mean in Broadacres" (Wright 1935b: 246). In fact, because the principles of organic architecture were respected, all structures had to be of good quality and respectful of their environment: "In an organic architecture the ground itself predetermines all features; the climate modifies them; available means limit them; function shapes them" (Wright 1935b: 247).

According to Wright, the very idea of designing housing specifically for the poorest people was undemocratic. This refusal to consider different social classes and social housing was the reason for most of the criticisms leveled against him by Meyer Shapiro, Catherine Bauer, and even his friend Lewis Mumford. Wright could not accept the solutions imported from Europe with respect to "minimum" housing that was mass-produced by means of the industrial machine, and he took offense when the Museum of Modern Art promoted them in its *Modern Architecture: International Exhibition* (1932). On this occasion, he circulated a pamphlet in which he stated: "A creative architecture for America can only mean an architecture for the individual" (Wright 1932b: 10). He called mass housing a "slum solution" that only further dehumanized the cities' populations during this "Money Melodrama" period: "They're going to build these cages, these barracks [he objected] and they will find that the birds have flown. I don't believe in regimentation," Wright insisted in an interview with John Gloag (1935: 16). He went on to state that the decentralization in Broadacres resulted in no one being poor anymore: unemployment and poverty levels were reduced to zero by the very nature of the new economic choices.

5.   BROADACRE CITY: TOWARD AN ORGANIC CAPITALISM

Wright explained that the key element of Broadacres was the small farm; small because, given its location and the preferred growing method it used, it respected its environment – unlike intensive agriculture. Its main task was to supply the community with fresh produce. This points to another essential dimension of the project: most of the food and goods were produced locally by small farms, small factories, and small workshops, and they were distributed within the community on a regular basis (the advantage of having electrical power was that there was no longer a pollution problem). Everything was sold at the local cooperative market,[9] which received fresh stock every day. Families could also sell their surplus there if they wanted. Just like his friend John Dewey,[10] Wright condemned *Big Business*, which explains why everything was small in Broadacres: farms, businesses, factories, workshops, schools, universities. This valuing of *Small is Beautiful* (Schumacher 1973) before it was popular meant that the concentration of wealth and speculation – on property, land and money – had been defeated once and for all. Everything was done to counter such concentration and speculation and prevent the "middle-man" from doing any harm. The "middle-man" (i.e. the intermediary enriching himself and speculating on the work of others) no longer had a place in such an organization: "The waste motion, the back and forth haul, that today makes so much idle business is gone. Distribution becomes automatic and direct: taking place mostly in the region of origin. Methods of distribution of everything are simple and direct. From the maker to the consumer by the most direct route" (Wright 1935b: 245). Decentralization meant that the community had learned how to manage the natural resources available to it and that these resources were managed cooperatively. The cooperative economy was essential to Wright; it was the only kind able to fight against all the speculation, prevent the destruction of (natural and human) resources, and preserve natural landscapes and ecosystems. Here we see, in particular, the influence of Baker Brownell[11] and the ideas he developed in the chapter "A Balanced Society" of the book he co-wrote with Wright, *Architecture and Modern Life* (1937).

In order to avoid any monetary speculation, what Wright considered to be one of man's inherent rights was put in place in Broadacres: "His social right to a direct medium of exchange in place of gold as a commodity: some form of social credit" (Wright 1935b: 245). He was familiar with the theories of engineer Clifford Hugh Douglas (1879–1952) on social credit, but also those of Silvio Gesell (1862–1930), to which his friend Owen D. Young had probably introduced him (see March 1981: 200). There is no doubt that the very title of Gesell's book, *The Natural Economic Order* (published in German in 1916, translated into English in 1929), piqued his interest, as well as statements such as this one, which introduced the work: "'Man is the measure of all things' including the economic system under which he lives" (Gesell 1929: 1). Wright explained that he borrowed the idea of "free money" and "free land" from Gesell; the theorist had also bolstered his conviction that, economically speaking, the shortest path – between producer and consumer – was also the cheapest.

This did not mean that Broadacres stood in the way of progress or advocated taking a step backward. Wright was keen to distinguish himself from followers of agrarian or back-to-the-land movements. In simple terms, the idea of progress was incompatible with destroying the environment for the sole purpose of achieving short-term benefits. In the same way, he opposed the standardization of the world as required by the metropolis and the monopoly it enjoys. He described the Broadacres landscape as follows:

> It is true that landscape becomes architecture just as architecture becomes a kind of landscape. But both are integral with the ground and are an orchestration of form according to nature. Right in the midst of the future city we have fields of flowers and grain. Right in the farming section are the buildings of industry, culture, recreation and residence. Right in the midst of all is the market place, a perpetual fair. And anywhere in it all folk may live happily at work. (Wright 1940a: 16)

Such a decentralization of all activities meant, in Wright's view, that it had become impossible to separate the urban and rural worlds from each other. Undoubtedly, this is what has been the most difficult to understand until today. He was accused of advocating sprawl, even though his project was aimed precisely at countering such a development of urbanization – the physical manifestation on the ground of the expanding grip of capitalism. He emphasized this point in the following terms: "To reiterate: the basis of the whole is general Decentralization as an applied principle and a harmonious architectural reintegration of all unit into one fabric: ground held only by use and improvements: Public utilities and government itself directly owned by the people of Broadacre City" (Wright 1940b: 9). Many of the ideas expressed here are important, and they form the foundation on which the project was built. Wright formulated one of them as follows when the architect Mies van der Rohe paid him a visit in 1937: "Broadacre City is the entire country and predicated up on the basis that every man woman and child in America is entitled to 'own' an acre of ground so long as they live on it or use it" (Wright 1940a: 10). A key notion that critics have often overlooked is that while every inhabitant is entitled to his parcel of an acre, it is a matter of having the right to use it according to what Paine called "common sense." The land must be lived on, cultivated, and maintained: "APPROPRIATE LAND IS FREE TO THOSE WHO CAN AND DO CHOOSE TO USE IT CONSISTENTLY WITH THE COMMON GOOD," is how he put it (Wright 1943: 23). He was convinced, however, that as an inhabitant of the Earth, every Broadacres owner would take great care of his property not only for what it could bring him (fruits, vegetables, etc.) but also for what it would represent: his attachment to the soil, to a culture. He often cited Henry George's *Progress and Poverty* (1879), which he regarded as the best point of reference on the subject in English. In his view:

> And here we find Henry George for the ground and Silvio Gesell for the money. The analysis of the basis of human poverty made by Henry George has never been refuted. (. . .). The preface to the **Natural Economic Order** and the preface to **Progress and Poverty** are two of the finest things in recorded English. Both are an exposition of Principle rather than panaceas: both dealing with Land and Money with a simplicity seeming naïve to the prestidigitators of interest: our professional economists." (Wright 1943: 12–13, emphasis in original)

Although Wright did not explicitly refer to the single-tax on land that George was advocating, the idea of joint management was always there: "Communal ownership by way of taxation of all communal resources is not necessarily communism, as Henry George pointed out with complete logic. It may be entirely democratic," he opined (Wright 1932a: 33). The new order proposed by Broadacre City, which Wright called "organic capitalism," meant a return to the true values and riches of the soil, unlike the denatured capitalism of the time that was based solely on exploiting and speculating them. He explained it as follows to Mies van der Rohe: "Broadacre City follows Henry George in the belief that a man should not only hold his land by way of his own use and improvements, but dedicate himself to it in the best sense of the spirit" (Wright 1940a: 13). This question of land ownership was inextricably linked to the issue of democracy.

The same was true of the management of various services to which the entire American population was entitled. All these services were public in Broadacres, and Wright also wanted all the inventions and scientific discoveries to stay in the public domain. The services were managed by the community or the government, including the various infrastructures, schools, colleges, universities, and cultural places (theaters, concert halls, museums, zoo, aquarium, etc.). They were all fairly distributed across the territory so that the whole population could have access to the same level of education and culture. For example, the schools were located at the center of the model, thereby implying they were the heart of the community – or of the neighborhood, as Clarence Perry had proposed a few years earlier. The constant proximity to nature meant that children were trained to observe it and taught to respect it from a very early age. All Broadacres children could walk to school, the swimming pool, zoo, sports field, and so on, on specially designed paths offering protection against cars.

The decentralization of each of these institutions reaffirmed access to education and culture as a fundamental right of every American and not just the privileged few, namely those who live in the big cities. Broadacres stood in stark contrast with the concentration of the best colleges, schools and universities in the richest cities, forcing the children living far from the city to leave their families and their parents to pay considerable fees to study. The same is true of access to theaters, concert halls and museums. Moreover, radio, telephone and television also contributed to the democratization of culture and knowledge: concerts, cultural and educational programs, and conferences could now reach straight into a home. Education and culture were at the root of every democratic society composed of well-rounded, free and creative "individualities." "The 'rugged individualism' that now captains our enterprises and becomes the 'capitalist' is entirely foreign to this ideal of individuality," Wright asserted. "The actual difference between such 'ism' and true individuality is the difference between selfishness and selfhood; the difference between sentiment and sentimentality; the difference between liberty and license." It was just as critical to resist such an "individual 'ism,' literally 'everyman for himself and the devil for the hindmost'" (Wright 1932a: 16), if one wished one day to have a balanced and harmonious American society enriched by the potential of each of the members, or individuals, that comprise it.

This unique "fabric" made up of all of the (urban and rural) activities also meant there was finally an end in sight to the artificial partitioning between city and countryside, between the inhabitants of the city and those in the countryside. All of them benefited equally from the same services, wherever they were on the territory, whether in terms of education, culture or health. This went hand in hand with employment opportunities that have since become equal for all, since employment would be better allocated on a national scale. Broadacres put an end to unemployment and the hell that a majority of American families, both in cities and on the countryside, were facing at the time. "Here the agrarian, the industrialist, the artist, the scientist, and the philosopher meet on the ground itself. It may not be logical. But is the rising sun logical? It is natural and that is better," said Wright (1940a: 10), who was convinced that Broadacres would make it possible to recover this original social unit, the "fountain of power" that Emerson mentioned with such nostalgia.

In other words, this "harmonious architectural reintegration of all units into one fabric" to which Wright referred was not to be understood only as a landscape harmony but also as a coherent, "organic" organization of the many equilibria found on a territory. Wright explained it as follows: "The design of the new city also sees no value in the part except as the part is harmoniously related to the whole in this sense of man and ground as one" (Wright 1940c: 22). Broadacres was promoting a "middle way" between revolutionary socialism and capitalist *laissez-faire* while betting on Dewey's "cooperative intelligence." Wright drew inspiration from – and combined – several social and economic theories that many of his friends and former acquaintances were developing in search of this "third way" between capitalism and communism (Gilbert and Baker 1997).

He could not, therefore, accept being labeled a supporter of Karl Marx because, in his view, Marx "seemed to reduce everything to the level of crowds on hard pavements with a union card in its vest pocket versus the fat paunch of capital, silk-hat on its head and a big cigar in its teeth" (Wright 1943: 5). As a "transition scheme," Broadacres formed part of the irreversible process of evolution that people and society undergo as it suggested returning to the concrete values of the soil instead of staying with the abstract value of money: "This, of course, is not the capitalism we have now, any more than it is communism. Let us call it 'Organic Capitalism'," he stated and emphasized: "genuine Capitalism. Capitalism made organic since it is broadly based upon the ground and the individual upon the ground. (. . .). And that is the promise of true Democracy" (Wright 1940a: 14) – a democracy that was not solely defined by a form of government but was, above all, a way of living.

6.   CONCLUSION: BROADACRE CITY – THE NEW FRONTIER TO REACH FOR

The Broadacre City project, as it was presented in 1935, was an optimistic vision driven by the hope that Roosevelt's New Deal would move toward this third way. Wright gradually became disillusioned, particularly after the US decision to join the Second World War, as he was a pacifist, like many of his friends. His words took on a radical tone as he sharply criticized his country's policies: "Cooperation and Freedom and a great Art are certainly possible to the order of true Capital. But no Capitalism is true or tolerable where cooperation and freedom of the workers and creative-art do not exist and flourish. (. . .) What can be worse than the deification of money by a whole people?" he asked in 1943 (Wright 1943: 7–8). In order to spread his ideas more widely and make his campaign for Broadacres more effective, he self-published two booklets: the Taliesin Fellowship journal, entitled *Taliesin*, "The New Frontier: Broadacre City" (1940), and *Book Six: Broadacre City* (1943), the sixth chapter of his autobiography (not included in the work itself), which was published in 1943. *Book Six: Broadacre City* was a searing indictment of American imperialism, capitalism, and US policy. It also allows us to understand what this new frontier would be to reach for according to Wright: it is neither physical nor geographical but rather economic and political, as he affirmed in *When Democracy Builds* (1945), in whose introduction he wrote the following:

> Once upon a time the conquering of physical or territorial realm was the new frontier. But to conquer sordid and ugly commercialism in this machine age, 'bony fiber of the dry tree'; this conquest is now 'the New Frontier.' Only by growing a healthy aesthetic in the Soul of our polyglot people can we win this victory: the greatest of all victories. (Wright 1945: vi–vii)

This horizon to reach for was all the more important to him because it was a matter of defending "the faith in democracy, faith in the gospel of individuality (. . .). Faith in Man: his faith in himself" (Wright 1945: vii). However, this faith could only be based on a healthy relationship between people and the Earth. In terms of development, the choices made after the Second World War completely crushed the hopes that had been formed in the 1930s. America was handed over to "Big-Production Boys," which Wright viewed as a denial of democracy. The supermarket supplanted the idea of the cooperative market, and suburb sprawl stretched as far as the eye could see, thanks to government subsidies, ravaging farmland and ruining the natural landscape in its path. Wright kept on modifying the Broadacre City model until his death in 1959; in particular, he added all the unfinished or aborted projects he had previously worked on: "By only the few was the City recognized for what it really was –

a relaxed, resilient, fundamentally free structural FORM for the life that will, some day, become one great free City so founded in common sense as to make human life not only more secure but more beautiful," he lamented (Wright 1943: 29).

We believe the message of Broadacre City is still relevant at a time when we have to admit once and for all that we are overexploiting the planet's resources to such a degree that we are mortgaging the future of the next generations; we also have to agree that the disruption we have caused to our environment seriously compromises its future habitability; more and more people are being driven from the land they live on because of what is called "natural" or "climatic" disasters, but in fact they are nothing other than the consequences of human action; and finally, more and more people on Earth are being dispossessed of the ground they live on – in other words, they are being uprooted from their culture – by foreign countries, multinational food companies, and other trusts whose only interest lies in the resources it is home to and the immediate benefits they can reap from them. "Broadacre City has nothing to sell – but it does ask you to think," Wright said (1940d: 25). This invitation is still valid in the twenty-first century as we urgently need to redefine our relationship to the Earth – our common home – so that we may not only preserve our habitat but also bring back a human dimension to our actions.

NOTES

1. Frank Lloyd Wright was one of the greatest architects of the twentieth century. His work had a major impact on the previous century, and countless monographs have been devoted to him. To this day, his works are being rediscovered by new generations of researchers.
2. The Broadacre City project, its context, and the references that underlie it are laid out in detail in Maumi and Wright (2015).
3. Wright is referring to Edward Alsworth Ross (1866–1951), who was one of the founding fathers of sociology, as well as the institutional economist John R. Commons, Paul Samuel Reinsch (1869–1923), and Glenn Frank (1887–1940), president of the University of Wisconsin from 1925 to 1937.
4. Neil Levine (2016) deals specifically with the development of the Quadruple Block Plan since its inception in 1896.
5. Wright had worked on Tokyo's Imperial Hotel project between 1912 and 1922.
6. Frank Lloyd Wright, "The City," lecture delivered at Princeton University in May 1930; a total of six lectures were published under the title *Modern Architecture, Being the Kahn Lectures* (1931).
7. Wright used the term for the first time in reference to the United States in *Experimenting with Human Lives* (1923).
8. A *section* is a cadastral unit in the United States measuring one mile by one mile, or a surface area of 640 acres; in other words, the model illustrated a piece of land two miles in length, or an area of 2,560 acres.
9. Wright designed a cooperative market for Walter V. Davidson in 1932.

10. Dewey published *Liberalism and Social Action* in 1935, which is the same year the Broadacre City model was presented. Wright's stance echoes the words of Dewey.
11. The exchange of letters between Wright and Brownell was particularly intense between 1931 and 1939.

REFERENCES

Alexander, Stephen. 1935. "Frank Lloyd Wright's Utopia." *New Masses*, June 18: 28.
Bohrer, Florence Fifer. 1955. "The Unitarian Hillside Home School." *Wisconsin Magazine of History* 38, no. 3: 151–5.
Brownell, Baker and Frank Lloyd Wright. 1937. *Architecture and Modern Life*. New York: Harper & Brothers.
Dewey, John. 1935. *Liberalism and Social Action*. New York: G. P. Putnam.
Emerson, Ralph Waldo. 1968. "The American Scholar (1837)." In *Ralph Waldo Emerson: Essays and Journals*, ed. Lewis Mumford. Atlanta, GA: Communication & Studies Inc, pp. 31–48.
George, Henry. 1879. *Progress and Poverty; An Inquiry into the Cause of Industrial Depressions, and of Increase of Want with Increase of Wealth –The Remedy*. San Francisco: W. M. Hinton & Co.
Gesell, Silvio. 1929. *The Natural Economic Order* (translated by Philip Pye). Berlin-Frohnau: Neo-verlag.
Gilbert, Jess and Ellen Baker. 1997. "Wisconsin Economists and New Deal Agricultural Policy: The Legacy of Progressive Professors." *The Wisconsin Magazine of History* 80, no. 4: 280–312.
Gloag, John. 1935. "Design in America: VII. Frank Lloyd Wright." *The Architect's Journal* 81, January 3: 16–17, 202.
Levine, Neil. 2016. *The Urbanism of Frank Lloyd Wright*. Princeton, NJ: Princeton University Press.
March, Lionel. 1981. "An Architect in Search of Democracy: Broadacre City (1970)." In *Writings on Wright: Selected Comment on Frank Lloyd Wright*, ed. H. Allen Brooks. Cambridge, MA: The MIT Press, pp. 195–206.
McCarthy, Charles. 1912. *The Wisconsin Idea*. New York: The MacMillan Company.
Maumi, Catherine. 2007. *Thomas Jefferson et le projet du Nouveau Monde*. Paris: Editions de la Villette.
Maumi, Catherine and Frank Lloyd Wright. 2015. *Broadacre City, la Nouvelle Frontière*. Paris: Editions de la Villette.
Mumford, Lewis. 1927. "Regionalism and Irregionalism." *Sociological Review* 19, no. 4: 277–88.
Mumford, Lewis. 1928. "The Theory and Practice of Regionalism (continued)." *Sociological Review* 20, no. 2: 131–41.
Paine, Thomas. 1776. *Common Sense: Addressed to the Inhabitants of America*. Philadelphia: R. Bell.
Schumacher, Ernst Friedrich. 1973. *Small is Beautiful: A Study of Economics as if People Mattered*. London: Blond and Briggs.
Wright, Frank Lloyd. 1923. *Experimenting with Human Lives*. Olive Hill, Hollywood, CA: The Fine Art Society.
Wright, Frank Lloyd. 1931. "The City." In *Modern Architecture, Being the Kahn Lectures*. Princeton, NJ: Princeton University Press, pp. 101–15.

Wright, Frank Lloyd. 1932a. *The Disappearing City*. New York: William Farquhar Payson.

Wright, Frank Lloyd. 1932b. "Of Thee I Sing." *Shelter* 2, no. 3: 10–12.

Wright, Frank Lloyd. 1935a. "Freedom Based on Form." *New Masses*, July 23: 23–4.

Wright, Frank Lloyd. 1935b. "Broadacre City: A New Community Plan." *The Architectural Record* 77, April: 243–54.

Wright, Frank Lloyd. 1939. *An Organic Architecture: The Architecture of Democracy*, London: Lund Humphries & Co.

Wright, Frank Lloyd. 1940a. "Mr. Wright Talks on Broadacre City to Ludwig Mies van der Rohe." In *Taliesin* 1, no. 1, "The New Frontier: Broadacre City," ed. Frank Lloyd Wright. Mineral Point, WI: Democrat-Tribune Press, pp. 10–18.

Wright, Frank Lloyd. 1940b. "A New Success Ideal." In *Taliesin* 1, no. 1, "The New Frontier: Broadacre City," ed. Frank Lloyd Wright. Mineral Point, WI: Democrat-Tribune Press, pp. 4–9.

Wright, Frank Lloyd. 1940c. "Broadacre City Landscape." In *Taliesin* 1, no. 1, "The New Frontier: Broadacre City," ed. Frank Lloyd Wright. Mineral Point, WI: Democrat-Tribune Press, pp. 19–23.

Wright, Frank Lloyd. 1940d. "Broadacres at the Wisconsin State Historical Library, Madison, 1937." In *Taliesin* 1, no. 1, "The New Frontier: Broadacre City," ed. Frank Lloyd Wright. Mineral Point, WI: Democrat-Tribune Press, pp. 25–8.

Wright, Frank Lloyd. 1941a. "An Architect Speaking for Culture (1936)." In *Frank Lloyd Wright on Architecture: Selected Writings (1894–1940)*, ed. Frederick Gutheim. New York: Duell, Sloan & Pearce, Inc., pp. 205–208.

Wright, Frank Lloyd. 1941b. "Room for the Dead (1936)." In *Frank Lloyd Wright on Architecture: Selected Writings (1894–1940)*, ed. Frederick Gutheim. New York: Duell, Sloan & Pearce, Inc., pp. 209–212.

Wright, Frank Lloyd. 1943. *An Autobiography. Book Six: Broadacre City*. Spring Green, WI: Taliesin.

Wright, Frank Lloyd. 1945. *When Democracy Builds*. Chicago, IL: University of Chicago Press.

Wright, Frank Lloyd. 1992. "The Art and Craft of the Machine." In *Frank Lloyd Wright Collected Writings, vol. 1: 1894–1930*, ed. Bruce Brooks Pfeiffer. New York: Rizzoli, Frank Lloyd Wright Foundation, pp. 58–69.

Wright, Frank Lloyd. 1993. "Why I love Wisconsin." In *Frank Lloyd Wright Collected Writings, vol. 3: 1931–1939*, ed. Bruce Brooks Pfeiffer. New York: Rizzoli, Frank Lloyd Wright Foundation, pp. 134–5.

14. The tariff question, the labor question, and Henry George's triangulation

Stephen Meardon

1.   INTRODUCTION

The most cogent contribution to the US tariff controversy in the penultimate decade of the nineteenth century was a book about something else.

In the predawn of the Progressive Era, the impetus for reform of an industrializing country straining against the institutions of a bygone era was building. There were differences of opinion, of course, about what needed reforming. Henry George's 1879 magnum opus, *Progress and Poverty*, presented the conclusion, drawn from his reconstruction of economic theory from Smith to Ricardo to Carey, that the distribution of income and wealth was warped by private appropriation of the annual returns from land. What needed reforming was that; all else was beside the point. But workers in a burgeoning labor union movement saw need for more direct reform of wages and work hours, which they sought to improve, and immigration of contract labor, which they sought to impede. Farmers and traders saw need for reform of the tariff law, which maintained many of the Civil War era's exorbitant duties on imports, especially those competing with domestic manufactures. These different reform agendas dominated the political discussion. So Henry George undertook to change the subject. His 1886 book, *Protection or Free Trade*, was nominally about the "tariff question," and it also considered the "labor question," but what it was really about was why both questions were amiss.

More than a century later "triangulation" entered the political lexicon. US President William Jefferson Clinton won re-election in 1996 on a platform purporting to transcend tired partisan antagonisms. Transcendence was stylized as a position between and above the political left and right, as at the apex of a triangle. Henry George might have liked the notion. His position was situated similarly.

That is not to say that George's position was *merely* political, although it was partly that. He staked out his position in view of its opportuneness for advancing a great principle. What is more, he set his stakes not only in political space. His triangulation was also in the space of economic ideas, above and between the distributive theories informing doctrines of free trade and protection.

This chapter explores Henry George's moral, political, and economic calculus in *Protection or Free Trade*. It aims to show how different is George's free-trade treatise from other contributions to the nineteenth-century US tariff controversy. The difference manifests the link, in the later part of the century, between the longstanding controversy about tariffs and the emerging one about inequalities of income and wealth. Henry George was one of the chief actors forging that link. Yet the nature and method of the reform he proposed sets him apart from the reformers of the emergent Progressive Era.

2.   BACKGROUND

It is hard to disentangle the coincidence of circumstance and talent that produced George's rise to fame in the last quarter of the nineteenth century. Young Henry George quit his formal education at age 13 (George Jr. 1900: 10), but the schooling he did receive, together with his affinity for reading, travel, and observation, prepared him well to learn. By age 16 he had sailed to Australia and India as foremast boy on a merchant ship, noting (if not yet reflecting much upon) the living conditions in both countries (31–4). By 17 he was employed at a Philadelphia printing firm, engaged in setting type (45). By 18 he had worked his way aboard another vessel bound for San Francisco, traveling North from there in search of gold. He returned to California by age 19 to ply again the printing trade (83). Thus, even before age 20 George had uncommon experience of the world, was curious and literate, and was engaged in work that had him reading news and spelling, if not yet writing.

By 1861, George had saved enough money to buy an ownership share in a small San Francisco daily newspaper (110–111). The work of compiling copy for it fell partly on him, and his livelihood depended on it. He became a wordsmith, and a prolific one. He became, too, a man familiar with privation, as that venture and several others in the same line fared poorly. He was familiar even with desperation, as his wife and child depended on his income. His fortunes improved as the creative element of his writing grew. Beginning in 1866, he was first a reporter, then editorial writer, and then managing editor of the San Francisco *Times*. In the pages of that newspaper and a succession of others he commented on political, social, and economic conditions.

There was much to comment on. The political coalition that had formed the Republican Party from the remnants of antebellum Whigs, Democrats, and sundry others, and that had animated the war effort, suffered defections with the war's end. The questions of secession and slavery had been settled; and while black enfranchisement was not settled so effectively, the Fourteenth Amendment notwithstanding, the weight of public attention shifted to other questions. George reassessed his support for the Republican Party and Grant, for whom he voted in 1868 (208). The party, if not the president, seemed to him now a vehicle for special interests not the workingman's interest. George's reassessment was not the majority view but it was commonplace, and not only among the more tepid erstwhile partisans (Unger 1968: 110–111). Republicans of various stripes, including some of the more ardent abolitionists, joined a great many Democrats in a reform movement taking up causes that were tangential, at best, to postbellum Republican priorities.

The impetus for reform came partly from the pressure on wages caused by the release of men from military service, and partly by successive waves of recession. Gross domestic product declined from 1865 to 1867, and again from 1869 to 1870, and yet again from 1873 to 1879 (NBER n.d.) – to name only recession years between the Civil War and *Progress and Poverty*. The impetus came largely, too, from the belief that the workingman's plight was attributable to business combinations bolstered by government favors. Reformers inveighed against "monopoly" in its several manifestations. The protective tariff, by impeding foreign competition for domestic production, was understood by its opponents to be in this category.

The impediment was large: in 1868 the tariff stood on average between 45% and 50%.[1] Of special concern in the West was rent-seeking and abuse of market power by the telegraphs and railroads. George had first-hand experience of it. His briefly successful venture to transmit news from an independent Philadelphia bureau to his San Francisco newspaper was quashed by the Associated Press, which wanted a monopoly of that business, in combination with the Western Union Company, which had a monopoly of its own of the telegraph lines upon which he relied. The venture was sunk (George Jr. 1900: 186).

Taking up work later at another paper, in Sacramento, George aligned himself with the Democratic governor of California in assailing the system of subsidies enjoyed by the Central Pacific Railroad. The railroad used the subsidies to purchase the influence to maintain them – going so far as to engage its friends to buy out the newspaper in which George published his anti-subsidy editorials. George's response, in 1870, was resignation from the paper followed by publication of a pamphlet that the governor saw fit to circulate for his campaign. "Railroad subsidies, like protective duties," said George, "are condemned by the economic principle that the development of industry should be left free to take its natural direction": their effects worked toward "lessening the comforts of the masses, stifling industry with taxation, monopolizing land and corrupting public service in all its branches . . ." (216–17). Here, arrayed succinctly nine years before *Progress and Poverty*, were the raw ingredients of George's reformism: appropriation of orthodox economic theory, up to a point; agreement with the claim that "industry" should be unhindered by taxation; agreement, too, with the doctrine of free trade, but without especial concern about it; greater concern with "monopoly," particularly in land, and the corollary corruption of public institutions preserving monopoly rents; and ultimate concern with the well-being "of the masses."

George's talent was to mix these ingredients with unflagging industry and present them with intelligence and moral fervor. The field for exercise of such talent only widened in the 1870s as conditions worsened. The Panic of 1873 and the ensuing depression of five and a half years fomented labor unrest, strikes, and violence. The panic, which originated in railroad finance and radiated to railroad freight, rolling stock, iron and labor, yielded in 1877 a labor uprising of unprecedented scale. The Great Uprising was a railroad strike involving tens of thousands of workers from the East Coast to the Midwest, destruction of railroad property by the strikers, and bloodshed by the federal troops and state militias that put them down (O'Donnell 2015: 36). Urbanization accelerated: between 1860 and 1870 the urban population share had already risen from 20% to 25%. It continued apace, propelled by European immigration that increased inequality sharply among urban workers. The income share of the top 1% of US earners began an accelerated ascent that lasted until the First World War (Lindert and Williamson 2016: ch. 5). All this was the ferment of *Progress and Poverty*.

George had already professed as early as 1871 that the puzzle of misery amidst societal progress – "the persistence of poverty amid advancing wealth," as he put it later, in the introduction to *Progress and Poverty* – would be solved by investigating land and land policy (George Jr. 1900: 220; George 1942: 12). In the intervening years he had investigated it in detail. He started with Ricardian rent theory and from there made new advances.[2] Population growth, he determined, pushes out the extensive margin of cultivation, as Ricardo believed, with the postulated effects on rent. To wit, constant increments of labor and capital yield less produce on the lower-quality land that is brought under cultivation as population grows; lower yields on the marginal land raise rent on the inframarginal land. But George also saw "other causes which conspire to raise rent, but which seem to have been wholly or partially hidden by the erroneous views as to the functions of capital and genesis of wages which have been current" (George 1942: 228). He denied the proposition that population growth tended to hold real wages to subsistence level (Ricardo 1817: 90, 102, 107). Like the American protectionist writer Henry C. Carey, he extolled the power of association, holding that the concentration of people made them more productive (Carey 1872; cf. George 1942: 235–8). "[T]he efficiency of labor manifestly increases with the number of laborers," averred George, so "the more laborers, other things being equal, the higher should wages be" (George 1942: 88). The trouble was that the efficiency gains from their concentration would be claimed mainly by the owners of the land upon which they concentrated.

Labor's wages depended on its productivity at the extensive margin, where rent was zero: competition in the labor market would cause the general level of wages to vary accordingly (213). It followed that whether wages rose, remained constant, or fell with population growth depended on whether the increased productivity of labor owing to its greater concentration on the inframarginal land exceeded, equaled, or was less than the diminished productivity of labor at the extensive margin owing to settlers pushing it outward (233–4). In any case rent on the inframarginal land would rise. The only question was by how much, and how little labor everywhere would gain. Supposing the opposing effects were exactly balanced, all of labor's productivity gains from population growth would be gobbled up by rentiers.

The upshot was that the material cause of rent was not land's productivity; it was people's collective productivity. Yet the institution of private property in land allowed some people to reap the benefits individually. Landowners cordoned off a resource that was the work of God, and with that putative right appropriated the work of others. "Rent, in short," said George, "is the price of monopoly, arising from the reduction to individual ownership of natural elements which human exertion can neither produce nor increase" (167).

Framing the problem that way pointed to the remedy: "We must substitute for the individual ownership of land a common ownership. Nothing else will go to the cause of the evil, in nothing else is there the slightest hope" (138). Which was not to say that land should be seized from those who held title to it. The remedy could be effected, indeed effected better, by sweeping tax reform. Rather than confiscating land, the state could confiscate rent by way of a 100% tax on the land's annual value (140). The landowner could keep the title, for whatever value it would hold for him – that of security of use, say, or sentimental attachment – but all value given to the land by the community would be appropriated by the community. At the same time, taxes on all other values that were the legitimate fruit of individual labor could be eliminated, preserving the fruits for the laborer (149). License taxes, imposts upon manufactures, duties on imports . . . all these could be scrapped to the betterment of efficiency, morality, equality, and justice (155–6).

Having finished the comprehensive expression of his reform idea, George undertook to put it into practice.

3.   DEVELOPMENT OF THE STRATEGY

The trouble was that George's idea did not rank high on the public agenda. The agenda was changing, and not in a promising way for George. Former Speaker of the House and then Senator James G. Blaine signaled what lay ahead when, in the presidential election year of 1880, he implored fellow Republicans to "fold away the bloody shirt." In the event, Blaine was denied the nomination and the bloody shirt wore well enough: Republicans regained the Senate majority they had lost in 1878, kept their House majority, and James Garfield won the presidency. But with the Civil War already fifteen years in the past, the strategy was nearly spent. "You want to shift the main issue to protection," Blaine argued (cited in Irwin 2017: 232). Not long after his failure to win the nomination, the shift that he proposed succeeded. But Blaine's success was George's obstacle.

Republicans scrambled to justify protective tariffs anew because one of their longstanding justifications was wearing thin. The Treasury had grown flush with revenue. By the estimation of erstwhile Commissioner of the Revenue David Wells, within four years the Treasury would have retired all the remaining debt payable at its option and be forced to purchase at a heavy premium what remained (Wells 1881: 614). Wells's commission had ended in 1870 with his propounding the "true principles of tariff reform," which, as his thinking had evolved, implied deep and broad reductions. A little over a decade later, some reductions had already been implemented, particularly on goods not produced domestically: hence the "free breakfast table," referring to reduced tariffs on goods including coffee, tea, and sugar (Tarbell 1911: 63). The average tariff on all imports had thus fallen by half from its Civil War heights. Even so, the breadth of the reductions was limited, and duties on imports competing with US goods remained high. In 1881 the average tariff on *dutiable* imports was still upward of 40%. Protectionists found the situation most satisfactory. Perhaps some similar method could be found that would assuage once again the public desire for tariff reform without seriously compromising the protective system.

To find that method, President Arthur called for, and the Republicans controlling Congress authorized, a new commission (Stanwood 1903: 202). The objective was a "judicious tariff" without radical revision; the commissioners chosen to achieve it included, as chair, John L. Hayes of Massachusetts, Secretary of the National Association of Wool Manufacturers; joining him, an iron manufacturer, a wool grower, a sugar grower, an officer of the New York Customs House, and three former members of Congress from Ohio, Virginia, and Georgia, all with protectionist sympathies; and for balance a statistician from the Census Office who "had been at one time strongly inclined to free trade" (204). To Wells, such a commission was but a "dodge to prevent any reconstruction or reduction of the existing tariff" (Wells 1881: 620, 622).

The commissioners began work in mid-July 1882, and continued for two and a half months, taking testimony in twenty-five cities from Rochester to Minneapolis to Atlanta to Philadelphia (Hayes 1882: 2–3). In total they interviewed over 600 witnesses, most of them manufacturers and businessmen who testified of the necessity of tariffs in their particular lines of work. Some witnesses did offer an opposing view, however. Among them was Yale professor and political economist William Graham Sumner, whose major works were not yet written but who had already declared his belligerency against "*protection* under any form or in any degree" (Sumner 1881: 242). He did not assail tariffs for revenue purposes only; of these he approved. But he denied any ambiguity or overlap between revenue tariffs and protective ones.

Sumner also disputed the argument heard lately that protective tariffs benefited labor. "I have noticed that in the discussions which have taken place before this Commission there has been a constant reiteration of some false doctrines of theoretical political economy about wages," he began (Hayes 1882: 2313). The tariff, he insisted, is a tax, and while taxes may be necessary to pay for security and peace, they can never increase the total of goods produced because they discourage production by the most efficient producers of the most valued products. With a smaller value of goods produced by existing capital and labor, "until somebody invents an arithmetic according to which 10 will go into 70 more times than it will in 100, it is certain that smaller dividend will give a smaller share to each person" (2316–17). Protection therefore lowers wages. The conclusion, he maintained, is mathematically demonstrable. It could not be escaped by "a thousand commissions, sitting for ten years, and actually engaging in a real study of the industries of this country," let alone by the commissioners facing him.

Wells's apprehensions about the commission proved to be at least partly misplaced, as was Sumner's slight of the commissioners. To the surprise of many, not least the industrial interests placing their hopes in the commission's report, the recommendations therein were distressingly liberal. The commission found that the wartime tariffs were indeed no longer needed as a stimulus to industry: general reductions of 20% on manufactured goods and 25% on all goods were in order. But once the report was issued and the time came to design legislation in view of it, even Hayes, the commission's chairman, retreated from the liberalism of its recommendations (Tarbell 1911: 113). Divisions in Congress engendered further retreat, and a barrage of lobbying by import-competing interests – "closeted in every leisure hour with the representatives in Congress," by one vivid account (131–2) – hastened it. The resulting law, which became known as the Mongrel Tariff of 1883, reduced slightly a few highly protected items (iron and steel, wool and woolens), increased some others (earthenware, glassware, and cotton goods), and reduced the entirety of customs revenue by a little under 10% (131). It satisfied neither the import-competing interests clamoring for more protection nor the public appetite for reduced customs duties and revenue. What it did – together with a failed Democratic attempt at tariff reform in the next Congress, in early 1884 – was prepare the ground for a presidential campaign in 1884 in which the candidates' positions on the tariff were in the public eye with another revision in view.

Henry George's own view was different. It extended well beyond tariff reform. In a pair of speeches in Brooklyn in early 1883, at the climactic moment of the Mongrel Tariff debate, George prophesied that the debate would be the pivot point for a reorientation of American politics, and priorities. At the Brooklyn Revenue Reform Club he sought to explain how the "spectacle in Congress" that was then playing out reflected the close of a great epoch in American politics. The generation previous to the presidential election of 1880 had been marked by engrossing concern with the slavery question. But the passions excited by that question had inevitably to subside. In the election's aftermath protectionists had hastened the effect, focusing the public mind on economic questions – whether for the better or worse for them. And yet, he counseled, "don't imagine [that the] agitation now beginning will end with more reform of the tariff." The great economic question was, why is it so hard for the masses to make a living? How to get my daily bread? To that question all minor ones, including the tariff, ran. George considered himself a "free trader in [the term's] full true meaning" – unlike most professed free traders (George 1883a). If free trade was right, what ultimately did it involve? Tariff reform was only the beginning. The end involved addressing mightier issues.

The next month, at the Thomas Jefferson Club, he explained how they would be addressed. The explanation drew upon past writings including an address he had made, six years before, in California; the politics would be but a reversion to the historical norm of most of the past hundreds of years. Wherever political life had advanced beyond autocracy, there were two great permanent political parties: "the adherents to the House of Have and the adherents to the House of Want." So it was, he continued, with the Right and Left of the French Assembly, Cavaliers and Roundheads of England under Charles I, Tories and Whigs under George III, and Federal and Anti-Federal parties of the post-Revolutionary United States. Alexander Hamilton and Thomas Jefferson were their respective leaders, actually and archetypically: the one representing centralized government, elaborate administration, the protective tariff, national banks, corporate privilege, and, on the whole, the money power; the other, States Rights, strict construction, simple government, free trade, and the power of the people. The Civil War had interrupted the norm. The Republican Party, which inherited the mantle of Hamilton, included free traders whose purpose had been to extinguish slavery; the Democratic Party, of Jeffersonian lineage, included those who would preserve the privileges of slaveowners. But with the war ended and the question of chattel slavery settled, the two permanent political parties would rise again. "One of these great parties is here. Around the Republican party cluster all the great special interests. But the party that should oppose it – the party of popular rights and democratic ideas, where is it?" (George 1883a).

What had been for George's purpose an obstacle now looked like an opportunity for political realignment. The outcome of the election of 1884 was immaterial. Expecting Blaine's victory over Democratic presidential candidate Grover Cleveland, and sketching out notes on the post-election scene for an audience in Great Britain, his destination that November, George wrote that "the campaign through which the country has just passed is evidently the last that can be fought on old lines" (George 1883b). Blaine would win, he imagined wrongly, by putting away at last the bloody shirt and campaigning on protection to American labor. But closing the book on the Civil War ended the one narrative upon which all Republicans agreed. The Northwestern states that were Republican strongholds were also predominantly for free trade. A split was in the making. If it had not happened yet then it would pretty soon. Democrats, on the other hand, had adopted free trade for their platform, but more from tradition than from deep or widespread conviction. Indeed, George saw Southerners as having gone over to protection.

With party loyalties fraying and economic questions dominating the public discussion, the way to answers was "an appeal to popular intelligence instead of to sectional prejudices" (George 1883b). In making the appeal, "political speakers and writers will hasten, if they are wise, to get some little smattering of political economy if they get no more." Thus given intelligent arguments, "the intelligence of the American people can be safely relied upon" to give politicians their marching orders for enactment of reform.

Upon reaching Great Britain, George found his expectation was wrong: Cleveland was elected president. His prognostication remained the same. In an article on "The American Election" for the London *Democrat*, George explained the coming realignment and its significance. The struggle over chattel slavery having ended, a new struggle would begin. Both major political parties would splinter over the tariff issue. Discussion of that issue, "involving, as it must, economic principles, will be of the greatest importance in the education of the people" (George 1884). Education would open their eyes to the *real* issue: "the monopolization of land, the concentration of wealth." A new political coalition would address it.

In effect Henry George had just sketched the rough outline for his next book, *Protection or Free Trade* (1941). He had only to flesh it out.

4. THE ARGUMENT

Protection or Free Trade would be at once theoretical and practical, intellectual and polemical. It would complement his active politicking; it would hasten the splintering of existing parties and align the new coalition for "popular rights and democratic ideas."

George begins it with a compelling metaphor. The working masses suffering from poverty amidst progress, those whose plight he analyzed seven years earlier in his magnum opus, are now like a massive bull in a pasture, tethered to a stake that it has circled around so many times as to immobilize itself. The pasture's grass is close in view but out of reach. If the bull could understand its plight it would know the remedy. To get from hunger to abundance requires no more than going back around the stake in the right way. But which is that? If one way were protective tariffs and the other their abolition, then which should the bull choose?

The aim of the book is to guide the bull, or to teach it to guide itself. Consistent with the metaphor, the task entails traversing a lot of well-known argumentative ground. But George's manner of doing it, painstaking and without missteps or reverses, gives hope of finding the way to freedom. Thus the reader is prepared for a recapitulation of numerous arguments for the right policy.

That policy, George announces early in the book, is free trade. Protection pretends to advance prosperity but is really "the plea of monarchy, of aristocracy, of special privilege of every kind" (George 1941: 21). Even the pretense is incoherent, because it is unimaginable that protection could advance prosperity if it were applied generally (29). The protective doctrine supposes, inconsistently, that impediments to trade between countries fosters prosperity, while impediments between subunits of countries, like states, impedes it (39). The doctrine teaches us "to do to ourselves in time of peace what enemies seek to do to us in time of war" (47). Protection undoes the specialization and exchange that has allowed people to master the mechanical arts, subdue nature, and promote civilization (51).

So reads about half the book. "To ascertain the effect of protective tariffs," writes George, "we must inquire what they are and how they operate" (25), both economically and politically. The text to that end flows in familiar channels, albeit with rhetorical ripples that are distinctively George's. If the purpose of encouraging domestic industry is to be adopted, then tariffs are the most harmful method because by impeding imports they engender scarcity (89). Subsidies would be better. Where tariffs are preferred it is because their operation is more opaque, so the harm to the many and the benefits to the few can be more surely maintained. Such is the true rationale of protective tariffs. It "resembles the theoretical protectionist's idea of what a protective tariff should be about as closely as a bucketful of paint thrown against a wall resembles the fresco of a Raphael" (92).

George entertains the "infant industry" argument for protection – determining that in most instances the argument is risible. Concerning the "infants" of a century before, "though they have grown mightily they claim the benefits of the 'Baby Act' all the more lustily" (98). Anyway, suppose that protectionists like the follower of Carey, Robert Ellis Thompson of the University of Pennsylvania, were right; suppose that after only two more generations of sustained protection the infants would thrive unaided. "When we are told that two generations should tax themselves to establish an industry for the third, well may we ask, 'What has posterity ever done for us?'" (98).

George entertains the "home market" argument for protection – determining that it is notionally "as absurd as it would be to attempt to make a man prosperous by preventing him from buying from other men" (105). Reserving the home market for home producers deprives us all of better opportunities for satisfying our wants: "Economically, what difference is there between restricting the importation of iron to benefit iron-producers and restricting sanitary improvements to benefit undertakers?" (105).

He entertains the "favorable-balance-of-trade" argument for protection – finding the notion that the way to increase a country's wealth is to promote the sending of valued things away, not to bring them in, is "repugnant to reason." Consider Robinson Crusoe alone on his island, offers George, and then imagine him visited by an American protectionist. The latter hears Crusoe's story, tells him of the world's news and remarkable changes, and finally prepares to depart. The protectionist leaves the outcast with a warning: passing ships will find him now; he should prepare for the "deluge of cheap goods" produced abroad; "unless you make it hard to land them I do not see how you will be able to employ your own industry at all." To which Crusoe might reply, "That will suit me completely. . ." (114).

But if the book were no more than a conventional, if uncommonly expressive, articulation of free-trade doctrine, then George would not have bothered to write it. The other half qualifies all of the foregoing. Under prevailing circumstances, he adds, there is cause for the anxiety people feel about an imbalance of trade. After all, "all exporting and importing are not the exchanging of products" (117): where imports of products exceed exports, the difference is reflected by people in the importing country either selling, in net, their assets to foreigners or receiving, in net, income from their holdings of foreign assets. In the United States at the time the position happened to be the reverse. As of 1885 the country had had an export surplus for a decade; in that particular year the difference between exports and imports was upward of 11% of the sum (United States Bureau of the Census 1970: series 213, 219). To explain it George relates an anecdote of two young people he met on a transatlantic voyage, Englishmen drinking champagne and telling him of their appreciation of America: "It was a good country to have an estate in. The land laws were very good, and if a tenant did not pay promptly you could get rid of him without long formality. But they preferred to live in England, and were going back to enjoy their income there . . ." (George 1941: 119). Thus Iowa farms exported much of their crop without products received currently in return.

The "drain of wealth" illustrated by that anecdote, says George, is indeed cause for anxiety. But it "proceeds from a deeper cause than any tariff can touch, and is but part of a general drift" (121). By now the reader gets the drift. The English absentee landowners could just as well be, and more often than not are, from the Eastern cities of the United States. The anxiety of the public is misattributed to the balance of trade. It is attributable really to the simple observation that so long as Western land owned by Easterners increases in value, Westerners have to send ever more of their produce eastward. The Westerner "may work hard, but grow relatively poorer"; the Easterner "may not work at all, but grow relatively richer" (121). The trend is toward owner-ship of all of the land by city people, and in the final accounting the country people have no reason to care whether their landlords are in cities as far east as New York and Boston or farther east in Europe. The trouble lies not in interna-tional trade but in "the most fundamental of our social adjustments, that which makes land private property" (121).

As with the "favorable-balance-of-trade" argument, so too with the "pauper labor" argument. The protectionist commonly holds that the high wages of US labor are threatened insofar as the competing products of cheap foreign labor are imported. Cheaper labor implies a lower cost of production; lower cost implies lower price; consumers prefer products with a lower price to those with a higher price, so they will cease to buy the domestic product so long as the domestic worker gets his high wages. To this George answers, as one would expect, "the truth is, that a low rate of wages does not mean a low cost of production, but the reverse" (138). Less expected is where George puts the onus of the fallacy. Protectionists are not ultimately to blame for it. Why should we suppose they are when we see free traders availing themselves of it too? "Witness the predictions of free-trade economists that trades-unions, if successful in raising wages and shortening hours, would destroy England's ability to sell her goods to other nations, and the similar objections by so-called free traders to similar movements on the part of working-men in the United States" (140).

The general rate of wages, as George explained in *Progress and Poverty* and now repeats, "is determined by the rate in the occupations which require least special skill, and to which the man who has nothing but his labor can most easily resort" (211). In the United States such occupations have tradi-tionally been agricultural (213): the unskilled man in the city can alternatively strike out and make his living on the land – insofar and in whatsoever quality as land is available. But how far and in what quality is that? The motive of appropriating the returns of land leads to the speculative enclosure of land by some and the diminution of opportunities for all others. Back to Crusoe: in

Defoe's account of his "Further Adventures," when the hero is absent, three English rogues lay claim to ownership of the island and demand rent from the inhabitants. In Defoe's telling, their presumption is met with laughter. But what if the rogues had a monopoly of force to back their claim to monopoly of land? "Thus a class of landowners and a class of non-landowners would have been established, to which arrangement the whole population might in a few generations have become so habituated as to think it the natural order" (263). To George this is an apt description of the current arrangement of the United States. The non-landowners toil at the pleasure of the landowners.

What has this to do with protection or free trade as commonly understood? Not much, says George, and that is the point. The non-landowners may be called "free." They may be called upon to choose between policies of protection or free trade that dominate the public discussion – on the grounds that one policy is pernicious and tends to diminish the general wealth, while the other is beneficent and tends to augment it, and if they choose well they will benefit accordingly. It is true that the policies have those different tendencies: George explains at length which does which. But the point is that, under prevailing circumstances, by choosing the "right" policy laborers will *not* benefit accordingly. It follows that if they are befuddled by the public discussion as it currently goes, if they cannot decide between the claims of the protectionists or the free traders, that is perfectly understandable. The befuddlement is because the fundamental claim of both sides is wrong.

George emphasizes the point with reference to William Graham Sumner and his testimony to the Tariff Commission of 1882. The protectionist fallacies that Sumner raves against "arise from the recognition of actual facts." The reader will recall Sumner's argument that tariff protection, as distinguished from a tariff for revenue purposes, decreases the aggregate wealth; therefore protection decreases wages. The argument supposes a direct relationship between aggregate wealth and wages. Under the circumstances, counters George, the supposition is wrong. "To attempt, as do 'free traders' of Professor Sumner's class, to eradicate protectionist ideas while ignoring these facts, is utterly hopeless" (251).

George's putting "free traders" in scare quotes represents as well as any word or phrase the contribution of the book. The free traders have got their political economy wrong. Their error is different from, but no less than, the protectionists': "A political economy that will recognize no deeper social wrong than the framing of tariffs on a protective instead of on a revenue basis, and that, with such trivial exceptions, is but a justification of 'things as they are,' is repellent to the instincts of the masses" (251).

The solution is not only to renounce protectionism; it is to do the same for free trade, as that doctrine is commonly understood. *True* free trade, says George, is the promise of his one big reform, in senses both narrow and broad.

Narrowly, "revenue tariffs," indeed all indirect taxation, should be supplanted by the single tax on the annual value of land. Broadly, absent either taxes on the fruits of one's efforts or their appropriation via rent, everyone may be free to enjoy or trade them without coercion (289).

5.   CONCLUSION

Henry George's campaign for Mayor of New York City in 1886 was the first manifestation of the political program that his new book justified. The Central Labor Union of New York, established in 1882 on principles partly Georgist – "the land of every country is the common inheritance of the people" (cited in O'Donnell 2015: 120) – established in turn a political party, the United Labor Party (ULP). The ULP aimed expressly to transcend the programs of both the Democratic and Republican Parties, "to form a political party opposed to monopoly in all its forms" and thereby to emancipate labor (cited in O'Donnell 2015: 138). In August 1886, the ULP asked George to accept their nomination for the mayorship.

George was not of the ULP, but he knew it well and was well known to its members. They knew him variously from *Progress and Poverty*, his participation for the previous five years in the Land League, labor workshops, and George's own speeches (O'Donnell 2015: 107–108, 203). The nomination was widely supported by the party but its acceptance by George was not a forgone conclusion. If the campaign fared poorly it would not only fail to advance his program but could even set it back.

In the event, he accepted the nomination conditional upon a demonstration of support by the signatures of 30,000 citizens. The condition was met. George's acceptance letter sets out what, given the condition, he planned to do:

> The time has now arrived when the old party lines have lost their meaning, and old party cries their power, and when men are ready to turn from quarrels of the past to grapple with the questions of the present. The party that shall do for the question of industrial slavery what the Republican party did for the question of chattel slavery must, by whatever name it shall be known, be a working-man's party – a party that shall reassert the principles of Thomas Jefferson in their application to the questions of the present day, and be Democratic in aim as well as in name. (George to James P. Archibald, Esq., Secretary, Conference Labor Associations, August 26, 1886; cited in Post and Leubuscher 2014: 11)

The plan was identical to the strategy of triangulation vis-à-vis the Republican and Democratic Parties, and between *protection* or *free trade*, which inspired the book bearing that title.

George's ultimate objective, the remediation of systematic inequality between workers and their masters, and the moment of his proposed remedy, at the pre-dawn of the Progressive Era, present a superficial invitation to read *Protection or Free Trade* as a proto-Progressive text. The treatment given here suggests a different reading. George's intent was popular education and mass political mobilization; his aim was remediation by way of sweeping legislation, not by the fine-tuning of government administrators acting upon the advice of higher experts. *Protection or Free Trade* is the coda of a historical chapter in which political economy and political circumstances pointed momentarily to a peculiar answer to the "labor question." The chapter presents a contrast with chronicles of the years that followed.

NOTES

1. The average tariff measured as total duties collected as a ratio of the value of dutiable imports was 48.7% in 1868; as a ratio of the value of total imports, 46.56%. US Census Bureau, Historical Statistics of the United States.
2. The treatment of *Progress and Poverty* in this and the following paragraphs borrows from and extends that of Meardon (2018).

REFERENCES

Carey, Henry C. 1872 [1847]. *The Past, the Present, and the Future.* Philadelphia, PA: Henry Carey Baird.

George, Henry. *c.*1840–1950. Papers. *Manuscript and Archives Division.* New York: Public Library.

George, Henry. 1883a. *George Papers*, Box 13, "Lecture Notes: Brooklyn Revenue Reform Club, February 14.

George, Henry. 1883b. *George Papers*, Box 13, "Post-Election Politics in America".

George, Henry. 1884. "The American Election." *The Democrat. A Weekly Journal for Men and Women* (London: William George Hackney) 1, November 15: 5.

George, Henry. 1941 [1886]. *Protection or Free Trade: An Examination of the Tariff Question, with Especial Regard to the Interests of Labor.* New York: Robert Schalkenbach Foundation.

George, Henry. 1942 [1879]. *Progress and Poverty: An Inquiry into the Cause of Industrial Depressions and of Increase of Want with Increase of Wealth; The Remedy.* New York: Robert Schalkenbach Foundation.

George Jr., Henry. 1900. *The Life of Henry George.* London: William Reeves.

Hayes, John L. 1882. *Report of the Tariff Commission, Appointed Under Act of Congress Approved May 15, 1882.* Washington, DC: Government Printing Office.

Irwin, Douglas A. 2017. *Clashing Over Commerce: A History of US Trade Policy.* Chicago, IL: University of Chicago Press.

Lindert, Peter and Jeffrey Williamson. 2016. *Unequal Gains: American Growth and Inequality since 1700.* Princeton, NJ: Princeton University Press.

Meardon, Stephen. 2018. "Yankee Ingenuity in Theories of American Economic Development, from the Founding to the Closing of the Frontier." *History of Political Economy* 50, supplement: 41–58.

NBER [National Bureau of Economic Research]. n.d. "U.S. Business Cycle Expansions and Contractions." Available at http://www.nber.org/cycles/cyclesmain.html.

O'Donnell, Edward T. 2015. *Henry George and the Crisis of Inequality: Progress and Poverty in the Gilded Age*. New York: Columbia University Press.

Post, Louis F. and Fred C. Leubuscher. 2014 [1886]. *Henry George's 1886 Campaign: An Account of the George-Hewitt Campaign in the New York Municipal Election of 1886*, annotated by Wyn Achenbaum. New York: Henry George School.

Ricardo, David. 1817. *The Principles of Political Economy and Taxation*. London: John Murray.

Stanwood, Edward. 1903. *American Tariff Controversies in the Nineteenth Century*, 2 vols. Boston, MA and New York: Houghton, Mifflin and Co.

Sumner, William Graham. 1881. "The Argument Against Protective Taxes." *Princeton Review* 1, January: 241–59.

Tarbell, Ida. 1911. *The Tariff in Our Times*. New York: The Macmillan Company.

Unger, Irwin. 1968. *The Greenback Era: A Social and Political History of American Finance, 1865–1879*. Princeton, NJ: Princeton University Press.

United States Bureau of the Census. 1970. *Historical Statistics of the United States*. Washington, DC: Department of Commerce.

Wells, David A. 1881. "Reform in Federal Taxation." *The North American Review* 133, no. 301: 611–30.

PART III

Fighting social inequalities

15. Schumpeter's view of social inequalities

Odile Lakomski-Laguerre

1.   INTRODUCTION

Joseph Alois Schumpeter's ideas are in the discussion agenda of various economists working in different theoretical traditions. At a time when social inequalities as well as innovation have become favorite themes in public or academic debates,[1] Schumpeter's heritage seems to have found some echo in recent economic models, for instance, the ones examining the link between innovations and rising social inequalities (Aghion 2002; Aghion et al. 2015). Notwithstanding the above, it has to be noted that the topic of social inequalities has not been a central focus in the vast literature dedicated to Schumpeter's thought. Then again, several aspects of Schumpeter's work remain unexplored.

From the perspective of a history of ideas, and in order that we could properly assess his thought, two considerations must be taken into account. First of all, the conception of social inequalities must be closely linked to one of the most consistent analytical works ever dedicated to a central "vision": by which we mean Schumpeter's strong conviction of the dynamic character of life in general, and capitalism in particular. And this view means breaking with a core assumption in orthodox economic theory, which supposes that homogeneous actors and individuals must be treated and dealt with equally, as they act with the same hedonistic and instrumental rationality. This analytical equality is also largely coupled with a philosophical tradition of utilitarian type, to which Schumpeter was extremely reluctant to commit. In this perspective, his fierce opposition to the orthodox postulate is not so much to be interpreted in terms of an "analytical inegalitarianism" (Gislain 1991), than in terms of a special stress on different aptitudes and different types of actors.

Schumpeter was convinced that for all aspects of life, two conflicting forces are at play: a hedonistic-adaptive type (which is typical of stationary states and equilibrating tendencies) and an energetic-creative type (which is required for innovative actions that break with routines and help the economic system undergo qualitative change – Schumpeter's dynamics). Secondly, we aim to show that despite what has been largely identified as an "elitist" view of society, Schumpeter's theory (especially his analysis of leadership as a key factor of coordination for both the economic system and the political arena) does not aim to achieve ethical goals or political objectives. We think that more generally, the issue of sense or finality is entirely foreign to Schumpeter's thought: he was mostly interested in analyzing the social process as it works (and it works as an historical process of qualitative change), not as it is supposed to conform to an ideal.

This chapter is organized as follows. In the second section, we expose Schumpeter's view on social "inequalities," social classes and mobility. Although social stratification has to be explained in terms of different individual skills based on innate characteristics and natural dispositions, what is more relevant in Schumpeter's analysis is the articulation and adequacy of such special aptitudes with what appears to be the most important functions in society at any given time. This is a distinctive feature of Schumpeter's work, in the sense that he was interested not only in pure economics but also in social science more generally. It means that we always have to consider economic sociology as a necessary complement to understand social phenomena in a Schumpeterian spirit. This is also an opportunity to gain a precise idea of Schumpeter's conception of methodological individualism. In the third section we deal with a core idea within the Schumpeterian theoretical framework, which is movement as the essence of economic life, what is best suggested by the concept of "creative destruction."

So we stress the inextricable link between qualitative change in society and the existence of entrepreneurs, those abnormal individuals, able to act differently regarding ordinary or routinized ways of doing things and who become leaders as they demonstrate future possibilities and overcome resistance to change. As we show in the fourth section, this antagonism between leaders and the masses, which is a component of both his economic and political analysis, can lead to an interpretation of Schumpeter's theory as an oft-told example of an "elitist" view of society. As a matter of fact, we find in Schumpeter's arguments many concepts (such as power, leadership, herd, command, selection) that are without doubt elitist and deeply rooted in classical sociology, especially that of Weber (Pakulski 2012) and the Italians Pareto, Mosca and Michels. In particular, Schumpeter's theory of democracy developed in *Capitalism, Socialism and Democracy* in 1942 was largely stamped as an "elitist theory of democracy" (Medearis 2001; Mackie 2009). Nevertheless, we think that reducing Schumpeter's thought to elite theory would lead to a neglect of the main impetus of his work: to build a general and alternative theory of social behavior.

2.   SOCIAL STRATIFICATION AND DIFFERENCES IN INDIVIDUAL SKILLS

"(. . .) Why the social whole, as far as our eye can reach, has never been homogeneous, always revealing this particular, obviously organic stratification" (Schumpeter 2007: 107). To this issue raised in his 1927 study on social classes, Schumpeter argues that class structure is the result of a selection process, which is both social and biological (natural): "Class structure is the ranking of such individual families by their social value in accordance, ultimately, with their differing aptitudes" (Schumpeter 2007: 160). This passage clearly illustrates that unequal positions in society are not so much founded on individual aptitudes and sets of talents as on their adequacy to the functions that appear to be decisive for the economic logic of a social order at a given time: "The ultimate foundation on which the class phenomenon rests consists of individual differences in aptitude. What is meant is *not differences in an absolute sense, but differences in aptitude with respect to those functions which the environment makes "socially necessary"* – in our sense – at any given time" (Schumpeter 2007: 160; our italics).

Thus, selection has a first social component because, depending on the times, certain activities are valued highly and allow (or not) individuals to reach higher positions. Skills can fully develop if they are perfectly adapted to the social functions identified as very important. In capitalist societies, the Schumpeterian archetype of social success and ascension remains the figure of the entrepreneur, at the source of the constitution of fortunes and family dynasties. However, entrepreneurial success is more a question of personal qualities than the transmission of a capital or a heritage:

> Actually, among the obstacles in the way of the rise of an industrial family, eventual lack of capital is the least. If it is otherwise in good condition, the family will find that in normal times capital is virtually thrust upon it. Indeed, one may say, with Marshall, that the size of an enterprise – and here that means the position of the family – tends to adapt itself to the ability of the entrepreneur. If he exceeds his personal limitations, resultant failure will trim the size of his enterprise; if he lacks the capital to exploit such personal resources as he does possess, he is likely to find the necessary credit. (Schumpeter 2007: 121)

Capitalism appears as an open system, as those with talent and strong will-power can reach the top of the social ladder by becoming entrepreneurs, regardless of their social origin (Schumpeter 2007: 130–33).

Breaking with the thesis of identical social reproduction, it is social mobility in an "ascending" or "descending" sense that is asserted:

> It is one of the outstanding characteristics of the social structure of capitalism that its 'higher' strata incessantly lose members to, and incessantly recruit themselves from, its 'lower' strata and that this incessant rise and fall in general proceeds relatively quickly: the slogan 'three generations from overalls to overalls' expresses a great deal of truth. (Clemence 1951: 196)

Indeed, the very functioning of capitalism, as it is animated by "creative destruction" (Schumpeter 1976), leads to a downgrading of certain individuals, of certain families, by the competition of novelty and new firms, and those activities that are not able to adapt disappear. Thus, if class structure remains globally identical, the individuals comprising the structure actually change: "For the duration of its collective life, or the time during which its identity may be assumed, each class resembles a hotel or an omnibus, always full, but always of different people" (Schumpeter 2007: 126).

For Schumpeter, the typical way to rise to the top of the social ladder remains entrepreneurship. Nevertheless, not everyone can become an entrepreneur: a certain profile is required. This is where the second type of selection – the biological selection – comes in. Schumpeter also emphasizes, beyond the social determinism of which he recognizes the importance, the "social force of individuality," and the fact that individualities do not all have the same weight in a social system (Schumpeter 2007). However, the aptitudes and character traits that correspond to the entrepreneur-innovator are not acquired through education, but by heredity. He refers to the eugenics of Francis Galton (1822–1911),[2] and takes again the principle of the normal law of distribution of talents: "In an ethnically homogeneous environment, special and general aptitudes, physical and mental, those of will and of intellect, are probably distributed according to the normal curve" (Schumpeter 2007: 164; see also Schumpeter 1949: 81, n.2). To this we must also add the following assumption: the category of entrepreneurs finds its source in a pool of people of the "quarter in a measure above the average" of a population, which forms "a type characterized by super-normal qualities of intellect and will" (Schumpeter 1949: 81–2, n.2).

Talents and skills are therefore unequally distributed within a population and there is a category of individuals with extraordinary intellectual qualities and determination. Then, "the carrying out of new combinations is a special function, and the privilege of a type of people who are much less numerous than all those who have the 'objective' possibility of doing it. Therefore, finally, entrepreneurs are a special type (. . .)." And Schumpeter outlines that this type of conduct "is accessible in very unequal measure and to relatively few people," in the sense that it is peculiar in two ways: (1) "it is directed towards something different and signifies doing something different from other conduct"; (2) "it presupposes aptitudes differing in kind and not only in degree from those of mere rational economic behavior" (Schumpeter 1949: 81, n.2).

So, regarding equality, Schumpeter view essentially is that, "its very meaning is in doubt, and there is hardly any rational warrant for exalting it into a postulate, so long as we move in the sphere of empirical analysis" (Schumpeter 1976: 265).

Even though Schumpeter was greatly impressed by Galton's works (see Gislain 1991),[3] it seems to us exaggerated and reductive to associate one's thought with eugenics. To qualify the point, note first that the work of Galton had a very broad impact. As stressed by Leonard (2003, 2005), in American Progressive Era economics, eugenic approaches to social and economic reform were popular, respectable and widespread, and economists of quite different politics could even be found promoting racist views, in the context of eugenics and elsewhere. Secondly, the fact that Schumpeter finds some elements of truth (hereditary talent) in Galton's work does not lead to adherence to the doctrine, that is to say, eugenics as a set of beliefs and practices aiming at improving society by the selection of the best heritable human characteristics. This supposes a normative and ethical judgment that is absent from the Schumpeterian theoretical construction.

In that regard, we can stress that when Schumpeter refers in his *History of Economic Analysis* to Galton's major scientific contributions, he notably mentions the discovery of "correlation as an effective tool of analysis," and the recognition of the importance of "a new branch of psychology" ("the psychology of individual differences") (Schumpeter 2006: 758). We can also argue that Schumpeter's individualist standpoint of the role of the entrepreneur leads neither to a genius nor a heroic representation of entrepreneurs (Ballandone 2017). In his *Theory of Development*, Schumpeter (1911) emphasizes that his "analysis of the role of the entrepreneur does not involve any 'glorification' of the type . . . We do hold that entrepreneurs have an economic function as distinguished from, say, robbers. But we neither style every entrepreneur a genius or a benefactor to humanity . . ." (Schumpeter 1949: 90, n.1). At the same time Schumpeter's attitude is somehow ambiguous: for instance, dealing with forces that undermine the pillars of capitalist order, Schumpeter stressed as a central argument the growing of an "anti-heroic" civilization (Schumpeter 1976). Regarding intellectual faculty and the theory of the entrepreneur, Schumpeter's writings are more ambiguous (Ballandone 2017). On the one hand, he describes entrepreneurs as having "super-normal qualities of intellect and will" (Schumpeter 1949: 82, n. 2; see also Clemence 1951: 197). On the other hand, in the first edition of his *Theory of Development*, Schumpeter puts forward the new combinations as a process that is, according to him, possible "even without particularly brilliant intelligence" (Becker and Knudsen 2002: 414). And in an earlier article, he had already noted: "Successful innovation is . . . a task sui generis. It is a feat not of intellect, but of will" (Schumpeter 1928: 379).

3. INEQUALITY AS A BASIC ANALYTICAL PREMISE: INTRODUCING DYNAMIC HUMAN TYPE INTO THE PICTURE

As emphasized strongly by De Vecchi (1995: 3), despite the impression that Schumpeter's work may sometimes seem incoherent, in reality it is a comment from constantly varying viewpoints on a single affirmation: "The world is full of life and movement" (Schumpeter 1908). The only central issue Schumpeter always has in mind is that every aspect of social life is continually being transformed under capitalism.

According to Dekker (2018), what makes Schumpeter's theory of capitalism so different from the Austrian School is that it is truly "avant-gardist." Schumpeter's entrepreneur shows the way forward and leads the masses where they neither imagined nor dared to go. Schumpeter fully recognizes that this is a theory of the avant-garde, more generally, and not just of entrepreneurship. So toward the end of his book he develops a distinction between the dynamic and the static type into a general theory of social change:

> We observe these differences in art, in science, in politics. They emerge everywhere with the same clarity. Everywhere these two types are very clearly demarcated, letting those spirits stand out who create new directions of art, new 'schools', new parties. (. . .) On the one hand we find that the behavior of the majority consists in the copying, recognition of, and adaptation to, a given state of affairs of materialistic and idealistic nature, and, on the other hand the behavior of a minority who shape the state of affairs. (Schumpeter 1926: 543)

Some commentators also shed light on the influence, on Schumpeter's vision of dynamics, of Nietzsche's concept of "will of power" (Santarelli and Pesciarelli 1990; Swedberg 1991), and in support of this connection we find as one argument among others, the fact that the ideas popularized in *Also Sprach Zarathustra* had a profound and wide-ranging influence on generations of German-speaking artists and intellectuals (Reinert and Reinert 2006). Behind the fact of an unequal distribution of individual aptitudes, there is above all a methodological claim: one cannot pretend that providing a satisfactory and realist picture of the functioning of economic life (especially of capitalism as a process of qualitative change), starts with the assumption of a hedonistic type of rationality as the sole conduct and motive to be dealt with. This is the main breaking point between the Schumpeterian theory and the dominant economic theory, but also with the Austrian liberals (e.g. Hayek, Mises).

Inequality does not consist only in a socio-biological fact; it is also and mainly a necessity, as it is a motive force for social change: "Looking back into the past, we can hardly fail to perceive the prime importance of the stimulating atmosphere of inequality. The lure of big prizes coupled with the threat of complete destitution no doubt produced a scheme of motivation of perhaps unique effectiveness" (Clemence 1951: 199). But more fundamentally, without "super-normal" individualities, the economic system would be doomed to be reproduced repeatedly, condemned to a stationary state, limited by rational, adaptive behaviors and routines. The importance placed by Schumpeter on different types of human conduct is clearly set out, again, in 1939 in *Business Cycles*:

> (. . .) The assumption that business behavior is ideally rational and prompt, and also that in principle it is the same with all firms, works tolerably well only within the precincts of tried experience and familiar motive. It breaks down as soon as we leave those precincts and allow the business community under study to be faced by new possibilities of business action which are as yet untried and about which the most complete command of routine teaches nothing. (Schumpeter 1989: 72–3)

The "creative response" (Schumpeter 1947) of the ideal-type entrepreneur allows an economic system to break with the static scheme and endogenizes dynamics.

So, as a central Schumpeterian assumption, heterogeneous actors consist mainly in two conflicting opposing forces, creative and innovative actions on one side (actions which also mean destruction, in line with the principle of "creative destruction"[4] (Schumpeter 1976)) and adaptive and routinized conducts on the other side: "While innovation disrupts existing equilibrium, adaptation absorbs the consequences of innovation as a new order, just as Apollo's harmonizing form integrates Dionysos's disruptive forces of life" (Shionoya 1997: 7). For Reinert and Reinert (2006), there is no doubt about that: "The main features of Schumpeter's economics, both the entrepreneur, the instigator of change, and his 'will to power' and creative destruction, are truly Nietzschean creatures." And for Santarelli and Pesciarelli (1990), Schumpeter shared with Nietzsche the same view of the world based on the irreconcilable co-presence on the historical stage of two opposing human types, so that the Schumpeterian idea of leaders emerging from the mass is very close to Nietzsche's "overman" facing the so-called "mass" or "herd."[5] As a matter of fact, as soon as they deal with the key theme of the entrepreneur, Schumpeter's writings are filled with words and expressions that are very close to Nietzsche's core concepts – especially the "will of power."

As a consequence, there is another core divergent idea in Schumpeter's theory, regarding the picture drawn on Walras–Marshallian lines: leadership. Whereas in a "circular flow" the consumer needs to appear to be the central influence of economic life, these needs henceforth become subordinated to the entrepreneur's motives of action: he shapes the individuals' tastes, creates new needs and urges the whole society to follow him in paving new ways. This leads Schumpeter to argue that: "If we define hedonist motive of action as the wish to satisfy one's wants," then "hedonistically (. . .) the conduct which we usually observe in individuals of our type would be irrational" (Schumpeter 1949: 92).

However, diverging from normal ways of doing things necessarily means facing many difficulties. Firstly, as a consequence of the introduction of novel processes, previously established values are cast aside, familiarity of the status quo established through learning and experiment disappears, and radical change in the productive structure results in market disruption. In a nutshell, innovation is a "hazardous enterprise" that plunges the entire life of the economy into radical uncertainty (Schumpeter 1947: 234). Secondly, the one who wants to do something radically new still faces resistance that will inevitably rise in society (Schumpeter 1949: 86–7). For all these reasons, Schumpeter sees in the entrepreneur above all the incarnation of a leader, endowed with a power of command that can compel individuals to dispense with their habitual practices. It is only in the presence of new possibilities that the specific task and the type of the leader appears: "For its success, keenness and vigor are not more essential than a certain narrowness which seizes the immediate chance and *nothing else*. 'Personal weight' is, to be sure, not without importance" (Schumpeter 1949: 89).

The opposition between leaders and the masses in Schumpeter is not only reflected in Nietzsche's philosophy: the influence of Wieser is also evident (Samuels 1983; Gislain 1991; Kolev 2017). The first similarity is methodological: Wieser and Schumpeter did not limit their field of study to pure economics exclusively, but extended their thinking to social sciences more broadly and especially to economic sociology.

One of the fundamental characteristics of Wieser's epistemology is the importance given to the fact of power in analyses (Wieser 1967: 154). Furthermore, in *The Law of Power* (Wieser 1926) then in *Social Economics* (Wieser 1967), he criticizes the neoclassical theory and presents his postulate which he describes as "hyper-individualism": individuals act in an entirely autonomous way and their actions originate only in their will. For Wieser, however, it is necessary to take into account the mutual interrelations and the combined influence of two factors: coercion (the authority that opposes individual desire; forces of compulsion or domination: *Zwangsmächte*) and the need for affirmation of individual desire (the forces of freedom: *Freiheitsmächte*).

But the naive individualism prevailing in the orthodox theory neglects the forces of constraint (linked to the existence of forms of domination and power). In Wieser, the action of the respective weights of the two social forces (*Zwangsmächte* and *Freiheitmächte*), explains the stratification of social structures and the strong differences in individual behaviors. The heterogeneity of individuals is affirmed by the distinction between "leaders" and "masses," which Wieser analyzed more systematically in *The Law of Power* (1926: 35). In any society, the social structure is always such that there is a minority of leaders who impel social action. This structuring into leaders and masses is characteristic of "social economies" which, moreover, are characterized by complexity and thus require a specific coordination process: social power. Wieser considers that the "masses" are incapable of generating spontaneous coordination, so that they must be guided and controlled by "leaders." This coordination is based essentially on a process of imitation, a social action requiring the masses to act according to the success of their leaders (Wieser 1926: 37–8). With the advent of economic power peculiar to the capitalist era, the entrepreneur becomes the typical figure of the leader.

Somehow, leadership acts as a special process of coordination in a dynamic world. To found a new business is not easy – success is not guaranteed. Society resists novelty: consumers, and more generally those who feel threatened by innovation, do not easily embrace change. As supply does not create its own demand spontaneously, firms will employ manipulation, educating recalcitrant people with "elaborate psychological advertising techniques" (Schumpeter 1989: 73). In Schumpeter's theory, opposition between leaders and followers is a keystone not only for an alternative representation of economic life, but also for his analysis of the political system, which leads to a procedural view of democracy as a method.

4.   LEADERSHIP AND DEMOCRACY: SCHUMPETER'S ELITIST VIEW

For Schumpeter, "the democratic method is that institutional arrangement for arriving at political decisions in which individuals acquire the power to decide by means of a competitive struggle for the people's vote" (Schumpeter 1976: 269). In his 1942 book *Capitalism, Socialism and Democracy*, Schumpeter strips the concept of democracy of any ideal and proposes a renewed theory that conceives a political regime as a purely competitive method of selection of leaders. This Schumpeterian redefinition has become canonical in the field of political science of the postwar period.

In the literature, the Schumpeterian conception of democracy is often associated with the tradition of elite theory (Medearis 2001),[6] conveyed at the beginning of the twentieth century by the heirs of the Italian school, Mosca,

Pareto and Michels (Blaug and Schwarzmantel 2001). In the United States, the elitism and influence of Pareto's work has been mobilized in order to provide a more realistic thought and to demystify the classical doctrine of democracy. The reception of elitist theories in the United States is intimately linked to the strategy of certain actors, their resources and the positions they occupied in the intellectual field and the connections between this world and the political sphere in general (Grynszpan 1999).[7] One of these important actors was Arthur Livingston (a specialist of Italian literature), translator of Pareto and publisher of Mosca. After a university career (at Columbia University in New York between 1911 and 1917), he became in 1918 the Italian publisher of the *Foreign Press Bureau*, one of the divisions of the US Committee on Public Information (*Creel Committee*), created in 1917 under the Wilson presidency to turn American public opinion in favor of the country's participation in the First World War, using propaganda techniques. This committee included Walter Lippmann[8] and public relations professionals, including E. Bernays.[9] In the book *Capitalism, Socialism and Democracy*, Schumpeter never quotes the works of Lippmann and Bernays. Nevertheless, the references to Graham Wallas[10] (from whom Lippman took courses at Harvard in 1910) are numerous and positive, as well as recognition of the importance of advertising and propaganda techniques in the manipulation of opinions, which raises questions about the classical doctrine's stance on a citizen's independence and free will.

For Schumpeter, basically, a more "realistic" view of democracy begins with the deconstruction of the "classical doctrine." This doctrine is based on a fatal misconception, which is both an inaccurate representation of human behavior (the one inherited from the utilitarian tradition, especially what we call today instrumental rationality) and, as a logical consequence, an irrelevant theory of political coordination. Firstly, he criticizes the unrealistic assumption that attributes to individual will both independence and rational capacity. The rationality of the citizen is here understood as the ability of individuals to "observe and interpret correctly" the available information (political parties' programs and policies) in order to obtain quickly, according to the "rules of logical inference," a conclusion on political problems. Contrasting with this naive representation, for Schumpeter the individual will is more akin to "an indeterminate bundle of vague impulses loosely playing about given slogans and mistaken impressions" (Schumpeter 1976: 253). In order to capture a more realistic "human nature in politics," Schumpeter makes claims for a broader theory of behavior, which points to the influence of the social framework, as well as "associative" and "affective" factors, on individual decision processes. Thus, in *Capitalism, Socialism and Democracy* we find many borrowings from social psychology, including explicit references to the work of G. Le Bon (crowd psychology), a central reference he shares with Bernays. Later, in his *History of Economic Analysis*, Schumpeter also refers to psychoanalysis as a "general theory of the working of the human mind" and underlines its "vast possibilities of application to sociology – political sociology especially – and economics" (Schumpeter 2006: 798).

Secondly, Schumpeter criticizes the way classical doctrine analyzes political coordination. The underlying utilitarian conception admits the idea of the "common good," which determines the will of the people. This common good, however, means that unanimity exists or is likely to be the aggregate result of individual rational arguments. As a center towards which individual wills should converge spontaneously, it is supposed to be determined perfectly and unambiguously. Adopting a cognitive approach, Schumpeter denies any merit to the concept of common good:

> There is, first, no such thing as a uniquely determined common good that all people could agree on or be made to agree on by the force of rational argument. This is due not primarily to the fact that some people may want things other than the common good but to the much more fundamental fact that to different individuals and groups *the common good is bound to mean different things*. (Schumpeter 1976: 251; our italics)

Along with the rejection of the common good, this "center" also collapses:

> They frankly derived their will of the people from the wills of individuals. And unless there is a centre, the common good, toward which, in the long run at least, *all* individual wills gravitate, we shall not get that particular type of 'natural' '*volonté générale.*' (Schumpeter 1976: 252)

Two questions then arise: facing the diversity of individual representations and beliefs, how can one imagine political and collective action? How can a common will emerge from such complexity? Political aims and coordination must be totally rethought. The political model proposed by Schumpeter is based upon an analogy between economic and political phenomena. In Schumpeter's perspective, a politician, who plays the same role as an entrepreneur-leader in economic life, leads the political struggle. As an entrepreneur, the politician is an innovator, a strategist and an organizer. The analogy with Schumpeter's conception of economic competition is clear here, as this competitive political process includes movements of both innovation and imitation. Political innovation consists of the introduction of new themes and new discussion topics, breaking with traditional discussion. Imitation reflects the tendency of politicians in competition with one another to adopt the themes that have proven successful. The economic analogy can even be extended further: the needs of men and women do not exist as preliminary and independent data. They are created and manipulated by suppliers in competition with one another.

In the same way, in politics, politicians create public opinion:

> The ways in which issues and the popular will on any issue are being manufactured is exactly analogous to the ways of commercial advertising. We find the same attempts to contact the subconscious. We find the same technique of creating favorable and unfavorable associations, which are the more effective the less rational they are. We find the same evasions and reticences and the same trick of producing opinion by reiterated assertion that is successful precisely to the extent to which it avoids rational argument and the danger of awakening the critical faculties of the people. (Schumpeter 1976: 263)

Hence "the shaping of [public opinion] is an essential part of the democratic process" (Schumpeter 1976: 282).

The theory of political command developed by Schumpeter accounts for a coordination of citizens determined by the actions of political entrepreneurs: the politicians. This coordination does not involve a search for convergence of opinion and individual, autonomously determined wishes, but instead operates via the influence exerted by politicians who manage to create or sway public opinion. The analogy between the economic and political spheres enables us to highlight the specificity of politics, which is fundamentally linked to the minor role played by rationality in citizens' judgment. While, in the marketplace, repeated purchases, a direct and visible link to personal interest, and familiarity with economic activities enable a learning curve to counterweight the entrepreneur's will to condition the consumer, no such regulatory behavior exists in the field of politics. The politician has a much freer and broader scope for action than the entrepreneur.

5.   CONCLUSION

For Schumpeter, in a capitalist society, inequality (of incomes) is due to two main facts (Schumpeter 1946). Firstly, unequal incomes are the result of pricing processes and reflect the market values of products and productive services. Secondly, once acquired, wealth may be transmitted by inheritance. To sum up briefly, we can put forward two arguments in Schumpeter's view on social inequalities. The typical way of reaching the top of the social ladder and achieving the highest incomes in a capitalist economy is to become an entrepreneur and to bring innovation. But because talent and will are not evenly distributed among people, not everyone wins during periods of radical change, or at least not in the same way. Moreover, the process of creative destruction always challenges acquired positions in society.

So, creation and dynamics imply individual inequalities and inequality acts as an encouraging factor for change. When considering the long run, if capitalism does not eliminate disparities in the distribution of wealth, it tends to raise the standard of living of the most disadvantaged social classes (Schumpeter 1976: ch. 5). And the main error of reasoning that can be currently found in public opinion regarding inequalities is to think "the majority of people is poor because a minority is rich" (Schumpeter 1946: 204).

At the same time, for Schumpeter, it is clear that a reasoned awareness of the economic performance of capitalism and of the hopes that people are entitled to base on it, would imply on the part of non-possessors and disadvantaged groups an almost inhuman self-sacrifice (Schumpeter 1976). This is why the capitalist system can hardly withstand the various protest movements that will soon rise in the social sphere and, in particular, on the part of those groups that are directly threatened by its modus operandi – especially, this means that radical change and innovations necessarily bring economic cycles, depressions and crises, unemployment and bankruptcies. This loss of legitimacy is all the more accentuated by the fact that the sacrifices imposed by the process of "creative destruction" do not fit well with the principles of an individualistic society swayed by the democratic ideal, which holds the postulate of equality as the rank of supreme value.

So, Schumpeter's thought is fundamentally opposed to utilitarian philosophy and equalitarian ideology.

NOTES

1. Recently, in the USA, a debate was raised about high-tech startups and tech workers being blamed for rising inequality in leading tech hubs such as San Francisco: a masterful illustration of that is the protests over Google Buses shuttling employees from the city to its Silicon Valley campus, while the rest of San Francisco's public transportation system is underfunded.
2. In the prefatory note of his study, Schumpeter identifies (among others) eugenics as a relevant discipline for the analysis. More precisely: "Our subject owes much more to legal and social history; to ethnology (. . .); to the study of the family; and to eugenics" (Schumpeter 2007: 103).
3. Schumpeter considered Galton as "one of the three greatest sociologists, the other two being Vico and Marx" (Schumpeter 2006: 758).
4. According to Reinert and Reinert (2006), the term "creative destruction" was brought into economics not by Schumpeter but by Werner Sombart (1863–1941), the economist who was probably most influenced by Nietzsche.
5. At the same time, this influence should not be over-estimated. Firstly, Schumpeter himself never referred to Nietzsche, especially when introducing the emblematic type of the entrepreneur. Secondly, Nietzsche is mentioned as a source of influence among others in Schumpeter's thought: for instance, Gislain (1991), Streissler (1994) and Kolev (2017) find premises of Schumpeter's theory in Wieser's thought.
6. For Schumpeter it would be better to avoid the term "elite," because it has been often "and without justification" used in the sense of a "positive evaluation" (Schumpeter 1919: 130).

7. The appropriation of Pareto's work was significant at Harvard University, including systematic seminars by biochemist L. J. Henderson, who became interested in the social sciences in the late 1920s. The seminars gained so much notoriety that participating in them or mobilizing references and discussions on Pareto could be a guarantee of access to a position at Harvard. Participants at this seminar included J. A. Schumpeter and T. Parsons.
8. Walter Lippmann (1889–1974) was an American intellectual, writer and journalist. In *Public Opinion* (1922), and *The Phantom Public* (1925), Lippmann analyzes the manipulation of public opinion. Inspired by Graham Wallas' theses on human nature in politics, he seeks to show how the people, endowed with limited rationality, can nevertheless participate effectively in the functioning of democracy. For him, democracy is necessarily linked to the "manufacture of consent."
9. Bernays' book, *Propaganda*, consecrates a collusion of propaganda with advertising. E. Bernays merged what he learned from his experiences as a press agent, advertising agent and war propagandist into a single mass manipulation doctrine, which he sees as the cement of the only possible democracy. Inspired by Gustave Le Bon's work on the psychology of the masses, he advocates "intelligent manipulation" of the masses by the enlightened minority, in order to protect it from the threats of democracy. He exposes his theses in *Propaganda* in 1928: "Propaganda is the executive organ of the invisible government."
10. A footnote is devoted in particular to Graham Wallas' book, *Human Nature in Politics* (1908), of which Schumpeter repeats the title for one of the chapters of *Capitalism, Socialism and Democracy*.

REFERENCES

Aghion, Philippe. 2002. "Schumpeterian Growth Theory and the Dynamics of Income Inequality." *Econometrica* 70, no. 3: 855–82.
Aghion, Philippe, Ufuk Akcigit, Antonin Bergeaud, Richard Blundell and David Hemous. 2015. "Innovation and Top Income Inequality." *CEPR Discussion Paper* 10659.
Ballandonne, Matthieu. 2017. "On Geniuses and Heroes: Gilfillan, Schumpeter, and the Eugenic Approach to Inventors and Innovators." *SSRN*, April 27, available at http://dx.doi.org/10.2139/ssrn.2959651.
Becker, Markus C. and Thornbjørn Knudsen. 2002. "Schumpeter 1911: Farsighted Visions on Economic Development." American Journal of Economics and Sociology 61, no. 2: 387–403.
Blaug, Ricardo and John Schwarzmantel (eds). 2001. Democracy: A Reader. New York: Columbia University Press.
Clemence, Richard V. (ed.) 1951. *Essays of J.A. Schumpeter.* Cambridge, MA: Addison-Wesley Press.
De Vecchi, Nicolo. 1995. *Entrepreneurs, Institutions and Economic Change: The Economic Thoughts of J. A. Schumpeter (1905–1925).* Cheltenham, UK and Northampton, MA, USA: Edward Elgar Publishing.
Dekker, Erwin. 2018. "Schumpeter: Theorist of the Avant-Garde. The Embrace of the New in Schumpeter's Original Theory of Economic Development." Review of Austrian Economics 31, no. 2: 177–94.
Gislain, Jean-Jacques. 1991. "Schumpeter: Inégalitarisme Analytique et Méthode Individualiste." Economies et Sociétés. Série Oeconomia 25, no. 5: 167–224.

Grynszpan, Mario. 1999. "La Théorie des Elites aux Etats-Unis: Conditions Sociales de Réception et d'Appropriation." Genèses. Sciences Sociales et Histoire 37, December: 27–43.

Kolev, Stefan. 2017. "Reincorporating Friedrich von Wieser and the Concept of Power into the Austrian Research Program." Center for the History of Political Economy Working Paper 06, Durham, NC.

Leonard, Thomas C. 2003. "'More Merciful and Not Less Effective': Eugenics and American Economics in the Progressive Era." *History of Political Economy* 35, no. 4: 687–712.

Leonard, Thomas C. 2005. "Eugenics and Economics in the Progressive Era." *Journal of Economic Perspectives* 19, no. 4: 207–24.

Mackie, Gerry. 2009. "Schumpeter's Leadership Democracy." *Political Theory* 37, no. 1: 128–53.

Medearis, John. 2001. *Joseph Schumpeter's Two Theories of Democracy*. Cambridge, MA: Harvard University Press.

Pakulski, Jan. 2012. "The Weberian Foundations of Modern Elite Theory and Democratic Elitism." *Historical Social Research* 37, no. 1: 38–56.

Reinert, Hugo and Erik Reinert. 2006. "Creative Destruction in Economics: Nietzsche, Sombart, Schumpeter." In *Friedrich Nietzsche (1844–1900): Economy and Society*, ed. Jürgen G. Backhaus and Wolfgang Drechsler. Boston, MA: Springer, pp. 55–85.

Samuels, Warren J. 1983. "The Influence of Friedrich von Wieser on Joseph A. Schumpeter." *History of Economics Society Bulletin* 4, no. 2: 5–19.

Santarelli, Enrico and Enzo Pesciarelli. 1990. "The Emergence of a Vision: The Development of Schumpeter's Theory of Entrepreneurship." *History of Political Economy* 22, no. 4: 677–96.

Schumpeter, Joseph Alois. 1908. *Das Wesen und der Hauptinhalt der Theorestichen Nationalökonomie*. Munich and Lepipzig: Duncker & Humblot.

Schumpeter, Joseph Alois. 1911. *Theorie der wirtschaftlichen Entwicklung*. Leipzig: Duncker & Humblot.

Schumpeter, Joseph Alois. 1919. "Classes in an Ethnically Homogeneous Environment." In Joseph Alois Schumpeter (2007). *Imperialism and Social Classes: Two Essays by Joseph Schumpeter*. Cleveland, OH and New York: Meridian Books.

Schumpeter, Joseph Alois. 1926. *Theorie der wirtschaftlichen Entwicklung: Eine Untersuchung Über Unternehmergewinn, Kapital, Kredit, Zins und den Konjunkturzyklus* [2nd edn]. Munich and Lepipzig: Duncker & Humblot.

Schumpeter, Joseph Alois.1927. "Die Socialen Klassen im Ethnisch Homogenen Milieu." *Archiv für Sozialwissenschaft und Sozialpolitik* 57: 1–67. Reprinted in Joseph Alois Schumpeter. 2007. *Imperialism and Social Classes: Two Essays by Joseph Schumpeter*. Cleveland, OH and New York: Meridian Books.

Schumpeter, Joseph Alois. 1928. "The Instability of Capitalism." *Economic Journal* 38, no. 2: 361–86. Reprinted in Richard V. Clemence (ed.). 1951. *Essays of J. A. Schumpeter*. Cambridge, MA: Addison-Wesley Press.

Schumpeter, Joseph Alois. 1946. "Capitalism." In *Encyclopaedia Britannica*. Vol. 4. Chicago, IL, London and Toronto, pp. 801–807. Reprinted in Richard V. Clemence (ed.). 1951. *Essays of J. A. Schumpeter*. Cambridge, MA: Addison-Wesley Press, pp. 184–205.

Schumpeter, Joseph Alois. 1947. "The Creative Response in Economic History." *Journal of Economic History* 7, no. 2: 149–59.

Schumpeter, Joseph Alois. 1949 [1934]. *The Theory of Economic Development: An Inquiry into Profits, Capital, Credit, Interest and the Business Cycle.* Cambridge, MA: Harvard University Press.

Schumpeter, Joseph Alois. 1976 [1942]. *Capitalism, Socialism and Democracy.* New York: Harper & Brothers.

Schumpeter, Joseph Alois. 1989 [1939]. *Business Cycles: A Theoretical, Historical and Statistical Analysis of the Capitalist Process* (2 Vols). Philadelphia, PA: Porcupine Press.

Schumpeter, Joseph Alois. 2006 [1954]. *History of Economic Analysis.* London: Routledge.

Schumpeter, Joseph Alois. (2007). *Imperialism and Social Classes: Two Essays by Joseph Schumpeter.* Cleveland, OH and New York: Meridian Books.

Shionoya, Yuichi. 1997. *Schumpeter and the Idea of Social Science.* Cambridge: Cambridge University Press.

Streissler, Erich W. 1994. "The Influence of German and Austrian Economics on Joseph A. Schumpeter." In *Schumpeter and the History of Ideas*, ed. Yuichi Shionoya and Mark Perlman. Ann Arbor: University of Michigan Press, pp. 13–38.

Swedberg, Richard. 1991. *Joseph A. Schumpeter: The Economics and Sociology of Capitalism.* Princeton, NJ: Princeton University Press.

Wieser, Friedrich von. 1926. *The Law of Power.* Vienna: Verlag von Julius Springer.

Wieser, Friedrich von. 1967 [1927]. *Social Economics.* New York: M. A. Kelley.

16. W. E. B. Du Bois on poverty and racial inequality

Steven Pressman and Thomas Briggs

1.   INTRODUCTION

W. E. B. Du Bois was a philosopher, sociologist, historian, advocate of racial justice and social critic, a sort of twentieth-century Renaissance man. He is best known for several works that studied poverty and the socio-economic condition of African Americans at the turn of the twentieth century, as well as for numerous books and articles advocating racial justice and opposing racial prejudice. Below we focus on Du Bois' work measuring poverty in the United States and analyzing the plight of African Americans at the end of the nineteenth century and beginning of the twentieth century.

But first some background on Du Bois, which Section 2 provides. The following two sections discuss the two main contributions of Du Bois to progressive thought. Section 3 looks at his pioneering work defining and measuring poverty. Section 4 looks at his work on racial discrimination and inequality. We conclude with some remarks on the place of Du Bois in intellectual history.

2.   BIOGRAPHICAL DETAILS

Du Bois was born on February 23, 1868 in Great Barrington, a small town in Western Massachusetts where his ancestors had lived for many generations. In *The Souls of Black Folk*, Du Bois (1903: 2) reports that he had a happy childhood, generally free of racial prejudice. One incident, however, left its mark – a classmate refused to exchange greeting cards with him because he was black. This experience drove Du Bois to combat racial prejudice and promote "personhood" for African Americans. In order to achieve this goal, he realized he would need an excellent education.

Although wanting to go to Harvard, Du Bois lacked the necessary financial resources; instead, he attended Fisk University in Nashville, Tennessee. Fisk was an all-black southern college, where Du Bois was surrounded by other blacks for the first time in his life (Alexander 2015: 8). This was also the first time Du Bois lived in the American South, which gave him his first close look at racial discrimination. The experience reinforced his determination to work for racial equality. Graduating from Fisk in 1884 at the top of his class, Du Bois enrolled as a junior at Harvard, where he studied philosophy and history, earning a BA in 1886.

Next Du Bois went to the University of Berlin to pursue graduate work. There he studied with leaders of the German Historical School, especially Adolf Wagner and Gustav Schmoller, as well as sociologist Max Weber. While in Germany Du Bois traveled to other European nations, where he observed discrimination against various minorities and began to study the impact of discrimination (Alexander 2015: 15).

According to the German Historical School, economic laws must be discovered in data analysis and in historical facts accumulated over long periods of time. Universal economic laws could not be deduced from assumed characteristics of people or markets that had no empirical grounding. Until such facts were known, they argued, it was premature to develop economic theories. The right way to understand an economy was to look at historical data, find regularities, and then make inferences about how the economy worked. For the German Historical School, the world worked differently at different times and in different places. This approach supported the thinking of Du Bois on racial inequality; it affirmed the possibility of changing the world and improving the economic condition of African Americans. The German Historical School also adopted an ethical view of the state; they saw the state as a way to meet the varied needs of its citizens, including public health, transportation and the protection of weaker members of society such as women and workers. This was very different from the standard economic view of the state as an institution to protect property rights (Shionoya 2001; Tribe 2003). It also supported the practical ambitions of Du Bois in promoting racial equality.

Returning to the USA, Du Bois enrolled in the philosophy graduate program at Harvard; in 1895 he became the first African American to receive a doctorate from Harvard University. While studying philosophy, he grew impatient with its inability to connect with real-world problems and its unwillingness to seek to improve the real world. He preferred the empirical and reformist approach that he absorbed in Germany and began to study sociology and economic history. His dissertation, *The Suppression of African Slave-Trade to the United States of America, 1638–1870*, the first book ever published by Harvard University Press (Du Bois 1896), concludes that attempts to abolish the slave trade failed due to apathy and inadequate enforcement of existing laws.

In 1896 Du Bois accepted an offer from the University of Pennsylvania to study the Negro community in Philadelphia, which resulted in his book *The Philadelphia Negro* (Du Bois 1967).[1] It provided a detailed socio-economic analysis of African Americans (a phrase Du Bois disliked because he did not feel comfortable with this linking), and was highly influenced by the methodology of the German Historical School. Its goal was to understand the socio-economic condition of Philadelphia Negros by empirical observation – *before* seeking to analyze the causes of inequality or proposing policy solutions.

As noted above, Du Bois was a lifelong advocate for racial equality and a pioneer in the study of race relations in the USA. He was one of the founders of the National Association for the Advancement of Colored People (NAACP) in 1909 and became its research director. He also edited its magazine, *The Crisis*, between 1910 and 1934. In these roles, Du Bois sought to demonstrate that Negros received an inferior education in the South, which disadvantaged them economically and reinforced prejudices that led to continued discrimination against blacks.

What was the solution? Du Bois (2011) argued that the black and white races had cultural as well as spiritual differences that the world should acknowledge. Long before terms like "cultural pluralism" came into vogue, Du Bois made a case for cultural nationalism in many books and articles. For example, *The Souls of Black Folk* (1903), a collection of 14 essays argued against conciliatory policies that appealed to the white power structure. In many essays Du Bois raged against the rise of the Jim Crow system from 1890 to 1910, and described the deep physical and mental suffering of Negros in America as a result of this system. A great deal of mental suffering took place through "double consciousness," or the idea that the Negro must see himself through the eyes of others and never can see himself for whom he truly is; this meant that the Negro could never truly be free. In effect, Jim Crow laws and double consciousness undermined cultural nationalism through physical and mental segregation.

Du Bois believed that the social sciences could provide the knowledge needed to help solve the problem of race in America by demonstrating that blacks were not inherently (or genetically) inferior or less intelligent than whites. As Katz (2000: 116) notes: "Like other social scientists of the Progressive Era, Du Bois . . . believed that facts gathered impartially with scientific methods would lead – ineluctably – to conclusions that evoked only one legitimate response." However, after seeing lynchings, peonage, Jim Crow segregation laws and race riots, Du Bois came to the conclusion that the solution had to be political rather than intellectual. Protests were needed rather than scholarly monographs. This led to conflicts between Du Bois and Booker T. Washington (probably the most influential black man at the time), who was preaching accommodation and urging blacks to accept discrimination for the time being while gaining the respect of whites through hard work. In response Du Bois helped found the Niagara Movement,[2] which sought to oppose the position of Washington and advance the cause of racial justice. Du Bois (1903) argued that Washington's strategy would only perpetuate the oppression of blacks and that more was needed than accommodation.

After decades struggling to combat racism in the USA, Du Bois gave up on solving America's race problems and moved to Ghana. Shortly thereafter he renounced his US citizenship and became even more radical, using ideas from Marx about exploitation as key elements in his analysis of US race relations. He died in Accra, Ghana on August 27, 1963.

3.   MEASURING POVERTY

Numbers have a way of focusing one's attention. They help organize and order information. They let us measure matters of great concern and see how we are doing over time. This helps us understand how economies work and guides us in developing policies to improve economic performance.

Most of the world today employs a relative notion of poverty, where being poor means having less than others. Poverty is typically defined as living in a household with less than half the median income (after adjusting for household size) in that nation at a particular point in time. The USA is one of very few countries with an official poverty rate measured in absolute terms. Developed by Mollie Orshansky (1965), it calculates the fraction of the population lacking the minimum income needed to survive for an entire year. In 2017, the official US poverty rate stood at 12.3%. For blacks, it was nearly double that, 21.2%. The pioneering work of Du Bois was influential in developing the official US poverty rate according to the historian of this measure, Gordon Fisher (1997a, 1997b). Du Bois' contributions were contained in his pioneering study of the condition of Negros in Philadelphia, where he developed a poverty threshold that provided an objective poverty measure and then went on to measure the poverty rate of Philadelphia Negros.

Once Du Bois agreed to study the Negro community in Philadelphia, he approached his job methodically, putting in regular eight-hour days between August 1896 and December 1897 (Du Bois 1967: 1). He went into the Negro community and interviewed as many people as he could, gathering data about their lives and meticulously keeping track of it. Du Bois also consulted records from city almshouses, reports from the Children's Aid Society and the Charity Organization Society, as well as police records of the arrest of vagrants (Katz 2000: 112). His book documented the condition of Negros living in Philadelphia, and provided statistics on the health, family relations, education, crime, literacy and employment of Negros in the city as well as a detailed description of the social institutions within the Negro community. In total, he interviewed 2,500 households, nearly the entire African American population in the 7th Ward of Philadelphia. While having the largest Negro population in Philadelphia at the time, it was not representative of all Negros in the city.

It was an upper-class area, around one-third Negro, most of whom worked in nearby businesses as domestic servants to wealthy whites. To deal with this lack of representativeness, Du Bois (1967: 2–3) surveyed Negro households in other Philadelphia Wards and used this data to correct for sampling errors.

According to Fisher (1997a: 13), Du Bois was one of the first to select a poverty line and was the first American to estimate poverty rates based upon a poverty threshold. Prior to Du Bois, the Massachusetts Bureau of Labor Statistics (BLS) (1871) drew a poverty line for the state, and Charles Booth (1887, 1888) in England drew a poverty line and sought to measure the percentage of the population that was poor in several communities there. Based on his interviews, which yielded knowledge of the needs of Negro families in Philadelphia, Du Bois called families "poor" whose weekly income was $5 or less per week. This figure applied to a family of five – a husband, wife and three children. No corrections were made for families with fewer or more members; every family faced the same poverty line, or was assumed to have the same needs. To put this into some historical perspective, Du Bois set an annual poverty line at $260 per year. Inflating to today's dollars, the Du Bois threshold is less than half the official Orshansky poverty threshold for a family of four.

Still, Du Bois thought that poverty should be defined in relative terms. He (Du Bois 1967: 1– 2, 170–78) did not think that his poverty line was applicable to the entire country and he even implied that if he were to study whites in Philadelphia, he might set a higher poverty rate for them (Hunter 1904: 48). Although not selecting different poverty lines for families of different sizes, Du Bois did set different poverty thresholds for different occupations and for different racial and ethnic groups. This seems to have been a common view at the time (Hunter 1904: 48), one that has continued until the present. For example, when developing the official US poverty rate, Mollie Orshansky (1965) set a lower poverty threshold for rural areas on the assumption that they would be able to grow their own food. Even today, the USA sets higher poverty thresholds for people living in the states of Alaska and Hawaii, due to the higher cost of living there.

Based on his survey data and poverty threshold, Du Bois estimated that 18.5% of Philadelphia Negros were poor. Another 47.8% had incomes greater than $5 per week but not greater than $10 per week. He called the economic condition of these families "fair" (Du Bois 1967: 171). As many scholars have noted, the poverty rate Du Bois calculated was rather low due to the low poverty thresholds he selected. Something closer to the eventual Orshansky poverty line (the $10 figure) would have yielded a Negro poverty rate of 64%, although it should be noted that this rather high estimate assumes that all families have five members and that smaller families do not have lower income needs.

Going further, Du Bois categorized the causes of poverty — sickness, crime, excessive drinking, lack of employment, bad luck, and so on. And he realized these causes were inter-related, presaging the idea of cumulative causation (usually attributed to Wicksell: see Pressman 2013) and Gunnar Myrdal's (1944) study of the condition of blacks in the USA (see Outlaw 2000). Du Bois (1967: 18, 269–75) realized that lack of employment causes crime; crime causes sickness and misfortune; sickness causes lack of work; and that all these things reinforce prejudices against blacks. Nonetheless the main cause of these related problems, the one cause that needed to be opposed, was discrimination.

Du Bois (1967: 29f.) calculated that Negros made up 8% of the poor population in Philadelphia, even though they comprised only 4% of the entire population. From this he concluded that Negros were discriminated against, and kept out of positions with higher pay and possible advancement. A few years later, Du Bois (1901) estimated that 78% of Negros in Philadelphia's 7th Ward were employed, compared to only 55% of the entire population in the city, which provided evidence that Negros were not lazy, since they were more likely to work than the overall population.

Following the lead of Du Bois, others began selecting poverty thresholds in early twentieth-century America, including the sociologist Albion Small, Robert Hunter (a settlement house worker who published an important book on poverty), the New York BLS and John Mitchell, president of the United Mine Workers (Fisher 1997a: 14). Small set the highest poverty line, $1,000 per year; most figures were in the $500–$600 range. A few years later, the US BLS set poverty thresholds between $408 (in southern towns) and $700 for urban areas (Fisher 1997a: 21ff.). After the Second World War, a consensus formed that single individuals making less than $1,000 a year and families with an income under $2,000 were poor. These figures translate into $13,105 and $26,210 in 2019 dollars (a bit larger than the actual 2019 poverty thresholds for single individuals and a family of four).

In the early 1960s, Mollie Orshansky began developing the official poverty lines for the USA in an empirically grounded manner, as Du Bois had done in his Philadelphia study. She began with US Agriculture Department data on the minimum food requirements for families of different sizes as compiled by the Agriculture Department. This step was an advance on Du Bois' assumption that all families, regardless of size, had the same needs. Orshansky then obtained data on the cost of purchasing this food in the early 1960s. Next, she examined extensive government surveys of household expenditures undertaken during the 1940s and the 1950s. This data indicated that families, on average, spent around one-third of their income on food. So Orshansky multiplied the cost of a minimum food budget for each family type by three to arrive at its poverty threshold. These thresholds represented the minimum income needed by families (of different sizes) to survive during the year.

Each year poverty thresholds are increased by the inflation rate over the past year. US poverty thresholds thus represent a fixed and constant real living standard, taken to be the minimum income necessary to survive for an entire year. The poverty rate measures the fraction of households falling below its poverty threshold.

The Office of Economic Opportunity adopted Orshansky's poverty definition in 1965. Federal agencies then began using it to determine whether someone qualifies for federal programs. Eligibility for housing vouchers, Medicaid, school lunches, Supplemental Nutrition Assistance Program (SNAP, formerly called Food Stamps) and other government programs depend on household income levels that are some percentage of their Orshansky poverty threshold. The work of Du Bois, therefore, had an important policy impact. And since, as noted above, black poverty rates far exceed white poverty rates, Du Bois' pioneering work has been instrumental in improving the economic condition of black Americans.

4.   THE NEGRO PROBLEM

From its inception as a nation, race relations have been a problem in the USA. The first Negros came to America as slaves. A war was fought to end the institution of slavery; and while it succeeded in outlawing physical bondage, it didn't solve the problem of institutional racism or the problem that freed slaves had income and wealth levels far below those of whites. This limited their ability to escape poverty. Fast forwarding to today, Thomas Piketty (2014) argued that wealth and income inequality are mutually reinforcing, and this is the main cause of inequality. Something similar was true of newly freed slaves following the Civil War – even if they could increase their standard of living in absolute terms, due to their lack of wealth, they continued to fall behind whites in relative terms. While in theory freed blacks were supposed to receive 40 acres and a mule, thereby mitigating the wealth inequality problem, in practice they became sharecroppers for their former white masters rather than slaves of their masters (Oubre 1978).

Du Bois spent a good part of his life analyzing the inequalities facing African Americans. Much of his work focused on how to solve America's "Negro problem," which he felt to be at the heart of the nation's inequality problem. Initially, Du Bois saw the problem as due to slavery and the impact of emancipation; then it became political enfranchisement followed by civil rights. Eventually Du Bois came to see the Negro problem in another light, or a perspective that was misunderstood even by Negros. He viewed the problem as one of belonging or inclusiveness, stemming from the lower relative incomes of Negros. Negros wanted the civil liberty to participate in conspicuous consumption, just like white Americans, according to Du Bois;[3]

but they had difficulty accomplishing this because of their history as slaves, and because their economic and social status was so far below that of whites.

There was yet another complicating factor. As early as 1861, the dawn of the Civil War, America faced a challenge – what should be done about the Negro? This conundrum persisted throughout the US Civil War and grew increasingly troublesome as Negros living in southern states were liberated. The problem began with a mass of refugees coming to northern army encampments searching for salvation in a country where they had only known enslavement. No effort was made to sustain the newly freed men; this problem was thought to require a larger solution when the war effort was complete, and the South surrendered. Du Bois describes this as a labor problem where a swath of idle people who, even if they were given tasks sporadically, had no real concept of pay or what to do with it. As a solution, he supported efforts to cloth, feed and educate these refugees; but he saw these as temporary experiments rather than policy solutions that would solve the problem permanently. Integrating freed slaves and soon-to-be-freed slaves into the US labor market challenged a system that did not fully respect these individuals as deserving the rights afforded to others by its Constitution.

The Negro problem following emancipation of the slaves had two sides, according to Du Bois. For whites, the problem was – what does America do with the people who lack the training and skills that their newly granted freedom and citizenship requires? For the Negro, the problem was – what can the freed slave do? Negros had learned just enough to realize their poverty, ignorance and second-class status in America (Du Bois 2011). With this came self-realization, self-consciousness and self-respect; but these were still people who were handicapped, yet expected to keep up with whites.

One possible solution was political. Du Bois (1903: 23) described the right to vote as one sign of true freedom. The 15th Amendment to the US Constitution gave freed slaves the potential to vote for the liberty that the Civil War only partially granted them; it allowed for the possibility of ending the oppressive behavior of the labor industry, the courts and the education system. Negro voters could elect champions of freedom and supporters of racial equality. But although guaranteed the right to vote, the same system was used to disenfranchise Negros. Poll taxes, property requirements, and citizenship and literacy tests were set up in effort to suppress the vote of freed slaves. This led to the next stage of the Negro problem – for Negroes it extinguished their hope of true freedom after being oppressed and enslaved; for whites it created a facade of inclusion, while in reality creating laws guaranteeing its defeat.

Another possible solution to the Negro problem was self-awareness, which created a desire to be treated as equals with whites. This led to a demand for civil rights. According to Du Bois, civil rights was a problem for whites as well as Negros, due to how the world viewed "whiteness." People throughout the world were trained to believe that whatever the white man does, it is done for the betterment of society and all the people that live in it. But this belief would not improve the economic condition of minorities; rather, past experience has shown that it has led to their continued oppression. Du Bois (1920: 31) characterizes the white moral mentality this way:

> To make children believe that every great soul the world ever saw was a white man's soul; that every great thought the world ever knew was a white man's thought; that every great deed the world ever did was a white man's deed; that every great dream the world ever sang was a white man's dream. In fine, that if from the world were dropped everything that could not fairly be attributed to White Folk, the world would, if anything, be even greater, truer, better than now.

Each race came to believe that the white way was the right way; no other race could be equal to the white race. For Negros, countering this belief set became the basis of the fight for civil rights. Given this constraint, Du Bois believed that respect, honor and recognition could be gained only through education and the leadership demonstrated by those most exceptional within the race. This view put Du Bois at odds with the views of other African American leaders, such as Booker T. Washington and Marcus Garvey, who spoke of subservience and separation rather than fighting for equal rights.

Du Bois (1903) identified four ways that newly emancipated Negros sought to achieve economic autonomy using the skills they obtained while enslaved. First, they could gain employment as servants. This was closest to their former duties as slaves but gave them exposure to the master's culture, city life and a small amount of education. Second, they could migrate to cities and towns, seeking to enter the industrial labor pool. A third solution was land ownership; this effort, however, was largely thwarted by the system of share cropping. Finally, there was "The Group Economy." By forming a separate economy, Negros would become self-sufficient and act as an inclusive group, comprised of Negro laborers, managers, owners and consumers. All these efforts would have to prevail under the shadow of racial prejudice and, therefore, could never succeed at providing economic emancipation for American Negros. Du Bois eventually gravitated toward two solutions – migration and education.

While editing *The Crisis*, Du Bois wrote frequently about the migration of blacks from the South to the North. He attributed this mass migration to three things – the cropping conditions in the South (the floods of Alabama and Mississippi and the devastation caused by the Boll Weevil), an increased demand for common labor due to a decrease in immigration from Europe (as a result of the First World War) and increasing violence against Negros in the South (Du Bois 1917: 270). Du Bois saw migration as a means to a better life. He also noted that a delicate balance of Negro migration was required. Most Negros migrating from the South were less intelligent and less efficient than established northerners, and if the white majority felt threatened by the mass of newcomers, racial conflict, hatred and segregation would ensue, turning the North into something resembling the South. Still, Du Bois advocated that Negroes migrate north in search of a better economic life and greater respect because of their greater chances of success in the North.

Furthermore, Du Bois (1916: 63) declared that any Negro wanting his children to have a good education, wanting to be part of a civilized society, and wanting brighter future prospects should move to the North. He did not think that these ends were possible in the South, and that Negros should leave the South as quickly as possible. He also thought that the North would be able to adjust to a massive flow of Negros from the South. While Du Bois was likely right about the first proposition, and while he did raise concerns about the balance of migration, he didn't foresee the reaction in the North to the mass migration of southern Negros. This first migration wave began during the First World War due to the great demand for labor in northern factories in support of the war effort. But even by 1940, nearly 80% of Negros lived in the South. Mass migration did not begin in earnest until after the Second World War and then continued until the 1960s. Rather than leading to integration, it led to racial separation in the North, and rather than assimilation it led to increased racial animosity (Lemann 1991).

A second solution was education. As we saw in Section 2, for Du Bois this was a personal solution for gaining respect and achieving some degree of freedom and equality. This is one reason he likely thought that education was a path to harmonious living between the races and greater equality between them. Du Bois also saw education as a means to help Negros make progress in both absolute terms and relative to whites.

Taking the lead in this endeavor were the most educated, thrifty, and economically secure Negros – "The Talented Tenth" as Du Bois (2015) called them. They were the leadership class of the Negro community. Du Bois posited that every race has a most exceptional 10%, and improvement of the entire race depended on the efforts of these people. For the black race, the talented tenth were those whom after emancipation, began political organizations, and engaged in writing and moral regeneration. The talented tenth also consisted of members of the servile class that managed to gain some economic and social capital in larger cities via education and thrift.

Similar to Du Bois, Myrdal (1944) advocated better education and fair employment institutions that would allow the most talented African Americans to succeed and be recognized for their accomplishments. Recognition would then begin to change perceptions of African Americans in the white community. As more whites saw a larger number of educated, successful and prominent blacks, the less likely they would discount them as people making few contributions to the nation. But there was another reason Du Bois supported greater education for Negros – the danger of the untrained mind, which he thought would lead to prejudice against Negros and an inability to earn money. He (Du Bois 2015) emphasized that education disciplined the intellect/mind and enhanced one's understanding of life, both of which made life worth living. He also thought that education would lead to "the ideal of sacrifice" and noted that the more people were willing to sacrifice, the less each person would have to sacrifice. Du Bois (1903: ch. 6) believed that relegating an entire race to ignorance and poverty, despite their natural aspirations, would be detrimental to the entire nation. Improving the lives of Negros required they receive a good education, especially higher education.

Du Bois did recognize one potential problem with this solution – whether this group of exceptional men could increase economic mobility for other American Negros. One issue was that the talented tenth would include a large number of partially educated rural Negros that sought the income advantages of northern industrial cities. This meant that northern whites would be less likely to change their perceptions of blacks. Du Bois thus implicitly recognized the race problem that faced the USA in the latter part of the twentieth century.

5.   CONCLUSION

This chapter has identified two areas where Du Bois made significant contributions to intellectual thought in the early twentieth century – the measurement of poverty and his analysis of "the Negro Problem" in the United States. But there are other areas where Du Bois made important contributions to progressive thought that should be mentioned.

First, Du Bois should be regarded as a founder of the discipline of sociology, especially the Chicago School (Cavan 1983). *The Philadelphia Negro* (Du Bois 1967) employed empirical methods in sociology that are now the hallmark of the Chicago School, particularly its emphasis on qualitative research – careful observation and face-to-face interviews in order to understand the economic and social lives of people. Also in accord with the Chicago School, Du Bois employed data to draw conclusions about blacks in America and the attitudes of whites toward blacks in lieu of the history of slavery. This empirical orientation sets his work apart from much work in sociology, as well as economics, at the time Du Bois was writing. Both disciplines focused on theory, and making theoretical pronouncements about how the world worked, rather than gathering data about the world. Du Bois contributed by bringing the empirical approach he learned in Germany to the USA and using it to analyze problems surrounding poverty and racial injustice.

Second, Hattery and Smith (2005) contend that Du Bois should be seen as a founder of the social stratification approach in sociology, which makes the occupation, wealth, income and social status of an individual an important determinant of individual success and how people are treated. Du Bois documented these facts of life for Philadelphia Negros at the end of the nineteenth century. His work also stressed that, due to their history, Negros comprised a lower class in America and that it was difficult to move from one social class to another. As such, he employed the stratification approach to understand racial discrimination in the USA and the lack of economic mobility. This work predates such work at the University of Chicago and that is now referred to as the Chicago School of Sociology.

Finally, as mentioned throughout this chapter, we can view the work of Du Bois as a precursor to the pioneering Myrdal (1944) study on race relations in the United States. Myrdal held up the ethical standards of the USA as a reason that discrimination could be ended and that the economic condition of black Americans could be improved. Viewing economic, social, ethical, cultural and other factors as related, he advocated policies that would address one or two problems, knowing that this would improve things in other areas for blacks (see Pressman 1994). At least for most of his life, this approach seemed foremost in Du Bois' mind, especially his emphasis on migration and education (including the development of a talented tenth) to improve the economic and social status of African Americans.

NOTES

1. The *Oxford English Dictionary* notes that the term "Negro" has fallen out of favour in recent years, and is considered out of date or offensive by some. We retain its usage in this chapter as a reflection of the period under discussion and as it was used by Du Bois.
2. Named for Niagara Falls, where the original meeting that led to the NAACP took place.
3. See https://www.youtube.com/watch?v=Ilc92N5vWEo, speech at Mt. Zion Congregational Church in Atlanta, March 15, 1953.

REFERENCES

Alexander, Shawn L. 2015. *W. E. B. Du Bois: An American Intellectual and Activist.* Lanham, MD: Rowman & Littlefield.

Booth, Charles. 1887. "The Inhabitants of Tower Hamlets (School Board Division), Their Condition and Occupations." *Journal of the Royal Statistical Society* 50, no. 2: 326–401.

Booth, Charles. 1888. "Conditions and Occupations of the People of East London and Hackney." *Journal of the Royal Statistical Society* 51, no. 2: 276–339.

Cavan, Ruth S. 1983. "The Chicago School of Sociology, 1918–1933." *Urban Life* 11, no. 4: 407–20.

Du Bois, William Edward Burghardt. 1896. *The Suppression of African Slave-Trade to the United States of America, 1638–1870.* Cambridge, MA: Harvard University Press.

Du Bois, William Edward Burghardt. 1901. "The Black North, a Social Study." *New York Times*, November 17.

Du Bois, William Edward Burghardt. 1903. *The Souls of Black Folk*. Chicago, IL: A. C. McClurg.

Du Bois, William Edward Burghardt. 1916. "The Migration of Negroes." *The Crisis* 12, no. 4: 63–70.

Du Bois, William Edward Burghardt. 1917. "Editorial." *The Crisis* 14, no. 2: 267–71.

Du Bois, William Edward Burghardt. 1920. *Darkwater: Voices from Within the Veil*. New York: Schocken Books.

Du Bois, William Edward Burghardt. 1967 [1899]. *The Philadelphia Negro: A Social Study*. New York: Schocken Books.

Du Bois, William Edward Burghardt. 2011 [1897]. "The Conservation of the Races." In *The Sociological Souls of Black Folks: Essays by W. E. B. Du Bois*, ed. Robert A. Wortham. Lanham, MD: Lexington Books, pp. 111–19.

Du Bois, William Edward Burghardt. 2015 [1903]. "The Talented Tenth." In *The Problem of the Color Line at the Turn of the Twentieth Century: The Essential Early Essays*, ed. Nahum Dimitri Chandler. New York: Fordham University Press, pp. 209–42.

Fisher, Gordon. 1997a. "From Hunter to Orshansky: An Overview of the (Unofficial) Poverty Lines in the United States from 1904 to 1965." Unpublished manuscript.

Fisher, Gordon. 1997b. "The Development of the Orshansky Poverty Thresholds and their Subsequent History as the Official U.S. Poverty Measure." Unpublished manuscript.

Hattery, Angela and Earl Smith. 2005. "William Edward Burghardt Du Bois and the Concepts of Race, Class and Gender." *Sociation Today*, 3, no. 1: available at http://www.ncsociology.org/sociationtoday/v31/smith.htm.

Hunter, Robert. 1904. *Poverty*. New York: Macmillan.

Katz, Michael. B. 2000. "Race, Poverty, and Welfare: Du Bois's Legacy for Policy." *The Annals of the American Academy of Political and Social Science* 558, no. 1: 111–27.

Lemann, Nicholas. 1991. *The Promised Land: The Great Black Migration and How it Changed America*. New York: Random House.

Massachusetts Bureau of Statistics of Labor. 1871. *Report of the Bureau of Statistics of Labor, Embracing the Account of Its Operations and Inquiries from March 1, 1870 to March 1, 1871*. Boston, MA: Wright & Potter, State Printers.

Myrdal, Gunnar. 1944. *An American Dilemma: The Negro Problem and Modern Democracy*. New York: Harper & Row.

Orshansky, Mollie. 1965. "Counting the Poor: Another Look at the Poverty Profile." *Social Security Bulletin* 25, no. 1: 3–29.

Oubre, Claude F. 1978. *Forty Acres and a Mule: The Freedmen's Bureau and Black Land Ownership*. Bâton-Rouge: Louisiana State University Press.

Outlaw, Lucius T. 2000. "W. E. B. Du Bois on the Study of Social Problems." *The Annals of the American Academy of Political and Social Science* 568, no. 1: 281–97.

Piketty, Thomas. 2014. *Capital in the Twenty-First Century*. Cambridge, MA: Harvard University Press.

Pressman, Steven. 1994. "An American Dilemma: Fifty Years Later." *Journal of Economic Issues* 28, no. 2: 577–85.

Pressman, Steven. 2013. *Fifty Major Economists*, 3rd edn. New York and London: Routledge.

Shionoya, Yuichi. 2001. "Rational Reconstruction of the German Historical School". In *The German Historical School*, ed. Yuichi Shionoya. London: Routledge, pp. 7–18.
Tribe, Keith. 2003. "Historical Schools of Economics: German and English." In *A Companion to the History of Economic Thought*, ed. Warren J. Samuels, Jeff E. Biddle and John B. Davis. Oxford: Blackwell, pp. 215–30.

17. A reconsideration of James Africanus Beale Horton of Sierra Leone (1835–1883) and his legacy

Odile Goerg

1.   INTRODUCTION

A renowned scientist and an eminent figure of his time, James Africanus Beale Horton (1835–1883), and his main work *West African Countries and Peoples* (1868), remained neglected by commentators for a long time before his role as a pioneer in the emerging tradition of political thought on the African continent (Martin 2012: 48), and as a trailblazer of pan-Africanism (Shepperson 1969: xvi), was later acknowledged.

His biography goes some way toward explaining this historiographic trajectory: his death in 1883 at the age of 48 occurred precisely when a radical turning point in history was underway, and one in which he was not able, or did not want, to anticipate. His rhetoric, which extolled the virtues of British civilization and the benefits to be derived from spreading its cutting-edge political and economic principles in Africa, was no longer in vogue at the onset of the twentieth century, as the continent was convulsed by colonial domination. Not only does Horton typify a particular period in time (1865–70), but he also represents the very specific society of Sierra Leone, which symbolized the abolition of the Atlantic slave trade. Both time and place heralded hope for the possibility of social change.

If we investigate Horton more deeply – his writings as well as the man himself – we can indirectly sense the spirit of a whole generation of intellectuals. Horton ranks as one of the most influential thinkers of the age, alongside his contemporaries A. B. C Sibthorpe (1840–1916)[1] and especially Edward Blyden (1832–1912), who originated from the Dutch island of St Thomas but became a citizen of Sierra Leone (Lynch 1970). His treatises outlined the road that Africa was to take. They all belonged to the educated elite, having gone through a British-style education, and stood on an equal footing with British colonizers, whether they were missionaries, merchants or magistrates.

Besides, although Horton's optimism died out soon after his passing, his ideas were resurrected under a different guise, when the struggle for decolonization erupted. The turbulent fortunes of his ideas, which were derided as bearing the hallmarks of (colonial) alienation even while essentialist or idealist analyses[2] were gaining traction, should not dissuade us from revisiting James Africanus Beale Horton: by turns a "rare creature, a literate, black Victorian, moving between the two worlds of the old, agrarian Africa and the new, brassy Britain of triumphant industrialism" (Shepperson 1969), a "Prophet of Modernization" or one of many "hybridized, transmogrified, and passionate borrowers of Western values" (Ayandele 1971: 691), one of the best thinkers of the self-conscious African "Mid-Victorian Optimism" (Boele van Hensbroek 1998, 2004).

A doctor and a scientist by trade, Horton published several works which all feature palpable political undertones. My purpose here, however, is to focus on his most explicitly political and global treatise, *West African Countries and Peoples*, which I argue constitutes a landmark as an African intellectual taking a stand against the spread of pseudo-scientific racism and taking an active role in the debates of his time (Section 2 of this chapter). It is also my view that this work clearly sets out a political manifesto for Africa at a decisive moment when everything yet seemed possible (Section 3). It is no surprise, therefore, that *West African Countries and Peoples* sometimes appears in various political science anthologies these days.

Before the advent of triumphant imperialist expansion, premised on a racial hierarchy, Horton expounded a dynamic reflection on the future of Africa. Although his life preceded the Progressive Era, his thoughts are firmly consistent with its spirit, as shown by his insistence on equal dignity for all human beings, as well as his more practical considerations on the appropriate methods for achieving both political organization and the foundations for sustainable economic development on the continent. Race and self-government were therefore intrinsically interlinked.

2. *WEST AFRICAN COUNTRIES AND PEOPLES*: AN AFRICAN MILESTONE

The full title of *West African Countries and Peoples*, as well as the name of its author, illuminate the true scope of this work, a decisive landmark in the genealogy of African political and philosophical thought.[3]

2.1 An Extraordinary Name for an Extraordinary Career

James Horton was a man of his time and of his society, that of the recaptives,[4] or the freed African slaves of Sierra Leone, whose enclave around Freetown was designed to help develop a new post-slavery world.[5] The variations in his family name reflect his political career as well as his ties to the history of this British settlement – a chartered company at first (1787), later a Crown company (1808).

Born into a recaptive Ibo (southeast Nigeria) family, he was christened James Horton, in honor of a British missionary stationed in Sierra Leone from 1816 to 1821.

Horton's decision to add "Beale" followed the same spirit, this time paying tribute to the Reverend James Beale who had taken him under his wing from his primary school days in Gloucester – his native town – and had funded his studies in Freetown, first at the Church Missionary Society (CMS) Grammar School in 1845, and then at the CMS Fourah Bay Institution (known later as the Fourah Bay College) in 1853, with the intention that Horton would become a parson. In 1855, Horton earned a scholarship to study medicine, first at King's College London for three years, and afterward in Edinburgh, where he matriculated as "James Africanus Beale Horton" in 1858 (Fyfe 1972: 33). The new second name affirmed his African roots, a move which was strongly encouraged by Edward Blyden and which was common among his contemporaries, as they would relinquish the names given to them by missionaries. He signed his work "Africanus Horton, MD, Staff Assist-Surgeon, Native of Sierra Leone," ranking his names in decreasing order of importance.[6] He became the first African medical student to graduate with honors from the University of Edinburgh in 1859. The shadow of *The White Man's Grave*, the title of a book dealing with Sierra Leone published in 1836 (Rankin 1836), loomed over Africa, as the War Office expected to train black African doctors, in keeping with the view that whites would be unable to survive in the tropical climes.

Upon his return to Africa, he was appointed surgeon in the British Army at the Gold Coast. He would mingle among the British and Creole elite, both within and without his professional duties, but was also the victim of the most blatant racism, as experienced during the first post he took up in Anamboe in 1860. Nevertheless, Horton was highly respected on the grounds of his sheer abilities. For over twenty years, he would roam the coasts of West Africa, flitting from one British settlement to the next, before finally retiring in Freetown in 1880. Afterward, he put into action several of his economic projects, such as opening a new bank or investing in the pit mining industry. At the same time, he was instrumental in wider society and particularly championed educational causes: for example, he called for the creation of a university in Freetown which would be open to all Africans (Nwauwa 1999). In 1882, he chaired a debate on higher education for women (*Is High Class Education for Women of any Advantage in Africa?*) organized by the Wesleyan Female Educational Institution, of which his daughter was an active member.[7]

As his multiple names suggest, Horton kept one foot in Victorian Britain through his educational background, his beliefs and his profession, while planting the other one firmly on his beloved Africa. Few sources explicitly mention his time in Britain,[8] but we may surmise that it was during this period that his African consciousness – what we would usually think of as a more recent notion – became fully crystallized, due to the separation from his motherland. That was when he added "Africanus" and tellingly declared in the final page of his MD thesis "that this Publication may be the means of exciting some interest . . . on behalf of Africa" (Ayandele 1970: 14). He believed that his community, the people of Sierra Leone – otherwise known as Creoles or Krio – was a hybrid of two distinct influences, like a new whole coming into existence in a given territory merging into a single entity, a nation, an identity with a plurality of roots (Goerg 1995; Wyse 1989). As he himself put it, "but the inhabitants of the Colony have been gradually blending into one race, and a national spirit is being developed" (Horton 1868: 83).

With historical perspective, we could consider today that he spoke in the name of his vision for Africa, mainly Western Africa. Horton was not fully conscious of the global unity of Africa and of associated pan-Africanism, these concepts appearing later in the history of Africa. Moreover, where his true sympathies lay was not always clear. He would mention various settlements, societies and political ideas of British origin and wanted to apply them to West Africa, which was more familiar to him. Thus he became "the first to face the European confrontation and to produce a public space in which this encounter could be discussed" (Boele van Hensbroek 1998: 11). News of events taking place elsewhere on the continent were slow to spread. Such an inclusive vision of all Africans has earned him the distinction of "pioneer of Pan-Africanism" in the eyes of some commentators (Ayandele 1971: 706). Yet others have rejected this epithet on the grounds that it is anachronistic, since the concept of an "African identity" would not surface until 1893 (Boele van Hensbroek 1998: 21). His writings reveal a defense of "the African race," of the Negro. His African identity went unquestioned in the mid nineteenth century, and was not seen as incompatible with his espousal of British civilization; on the contrary, it corresponds to what Boele van Hensbroek has referred to as "the recaptive exemplar," which is perhaps a more relevant approach to Horton's writings than an appeal to anachronistic ideas (1998: 21, 46seq.).

Paradoxically, as early as the 1880s–1890s, the racist values that Horton opposed came to blight his community, which was cast aside as hybrid and held in contempt by the colonizers as non-African, as opposed to the "pure," unvarnished Africans of the Protectorate.[9] Blyden was an active contributor to this discursive construction in the 1880s, as he grew increasingly hostile toward the Creoles, whom he accused of having gone British – a situation which he derided – and instead advocated uniting Africa around Islam. These

"Black Englishmen" or "trousered niggers" had been blinded by foreign values which they could only imitate at best, rather than assimilate wholeheartedly.[10] In the same vein, the traveler Mary Kingsley described Krio manners as "a second-hand rubbishy white culture" (1982: 20).

The Krio were then fighting to be recognized as Africans:

> They are the flesh of our flesh, the bones of our bones, as pure Negroes as us. Since we reap the benefits of Christianity and of certain privileges bestowed on a civilized government, it is only right that we should strive to bring them under our control. (*West African Reporter* 1883)

Likewise,

> We are one and the same people, under the authority of one and the same government. The difference between us and them resides in the fact that we reap the advantages of education and civilization, while they do not. (*Sierra Leone Weekly News*, 1898)

2.2   Traveling the West African Coasts: the Compilation of *West African Countries and Peoples*

West African Countries and Peoples remained forgotten until it was first rediscovered in the late 1960s, at a time when research in African history was flourishing, with publishers making a point of drawing attention to works by African intellectuals.[11] More recently, Horton's work again resurfaced in the aftermath of the development of political science, insofar as it transcended the paradigms of socialism and economic development which were prevalent in the 1960s and 1970s and provided an alternative to Eurocentric views of knowledge. When it was reissued for the third time, in 1969, awareness of it did not extend beyond a small coterie of experts in African studies. It has now reached a far wider readership, especially in the English-speaking world.

I do not intend to provide a comprehensive critique of Horton's work, but instead to shed light on his approach and methodology. Stationed in various posts and constantly immersed in his employment, Horton remained an open mind, avidly reading anything he would stumble upon and gathering information in his encounters with people from all walks of life. Having received a classical education which asserted the supreme importance of the notion of responsibility, he did not limit himself to the role of healer but rather embarked on a self-styled mission to enlighten his compatriots. Beside his scientific publications, such as his medicine dissertation *The Medical Topography of the West Coast of Africa* (1859) and a work on climate and geology (1867), he took a close interest in current affairs and participated in political debates, notably through some publications in the *African Times*, the African Aid

Society journal, founded in 1860 in London. *West African Countries and Peoples* was an elaborate response to the Select Committee of 1865, which marked a turning point in political expansion following the defeat of the British–Fanti alliance against the Ashanti in 1863.

The Select Committee voted for the gradual withdrawal of British forces and favored the transfer of power to the local elites:

> The object of our policy should be to encourage in the natives the exercise of those qualities which may render it possible for us more and more to transfer to them the administration of all Governments, with a view to our ultimate withdrawal from all, except, probably, Sierra Leone.[12]

Horton entertained no illusion as to the practical motives of British policy (e.g. the high death rates for white men in tropical regions and the prohibitive cost of direct rule). Nonetheless he approved of this measure and saw in it the potential for a positive outcome for Africans who would become masters of their own destiny.

As soon as the 1865 report came out, Horton wrote a pamphlet entitled *Political Economy of British Western Africa; with the requirements of the several colonies and settlements (the African view of the Negro's place in nature[13]). Being an address to the African Aid Society* (London, 1865). This would lay the foundations for his later book, embellishing certain passages, notably those which touched on the growing influence of racist ideological currents. He incorporated new quotations, particularly extracts from the work of the abolitionist writer Wilson Armistead, *A Tribute for the Negro* (1848), of which he had no prior knowledge (Shepperson 1969: xi).[14] He arrived in London just before the date of publication to supplement the manuscript, without completely revising it, which accounts for certain contradictions or inconsistencies (Fyfe 1972). Horton meticulously cites his sources, in an effort to legitimize his discourse – when quoting allies – and condemns aberrations when referring to the exponents of racist ideas. The book was printed by the publishing department of the *African Times* at Horton's own expense, since he noted that books on the subject of Africa did not captivate readers "unless written to attract the fancy or to excite wonder, by recording acts of heroic enterprise, like the gorilla hunting . . ." (Horton's personal correspondence, quoted by Fyfe 1972: 68).

Throughout his volume, Horton consistently relies on the classics – Greek and Latin – which he had encountered as a student, as well as on travelogues and scientific writings of his time. It is not certain what he knew of inland African societies living at that time, nor can we ascertain whether they aroused his curiosity. In this work, he did not seek to make any discovery in anthropology or local history, as he generally repeated the prejudices in vogue in his milieu of origin – the coast – without reflection.[15] As is suggested by the original layout of the subtitle of his work, his purpose lay elsewhere:

WEST AFRICAN
COUNTRIES AND PEOPLES

BRITISH AND NATIVE

WITH THE

REQUIREMENTS NECESSARY FOR ESTABLISHING THAT SELF
GOVERNMENT RECOMMENDED BY THE COMMITTEE
OF THE HOUSE OF COMMONS, 1865

AND A

VINDICATION OF THE AFRICAN RACE

Two objectives can be clearly distinguished: (1) putting forward practical measures to facilitate a transition toward self-determination, in the knowledge that the territory in question numbered as many Britons as it did native Africans, (2) countering the rise of pseudo-scientific racism. Incidentally, the book is dedicated to the Reverend Henry Venn from the CMS, "as a Slight Memento of appreciation for his untiring zeal towards the development of the moral, social, and Christian advancement of the African Race . . ."

West African Countries and Peoples can be considered the symbol of a turning point, both in terms of Horton's writing career and wider historical circumstances. Indeed, it is a polemical work and a volume of ideas. However, he could only manage a faint glimpse of this turning point, and he did so with fear, and struggled against this change, yet remained optimistic and full of faith into the future.

2.3   *On the Negro's Place in Nature*: a Rebuttal against Growing Racism

As Horton published his study, several other works arrived on the scene, which would have a lasting impact on people's perceptions of the African continent: T. J. Hutchinson's *Ten Years' Wanderings among the Ethiopians* (1861), Winwood Reade's *Savage Africa* (1863) and above all James Hunt's *On the Negro's Place in Nature* (1864) and Richard F. Burton's *Wanderings in West Africa* (1863). They all objected to egalitarian and monogenist currents with regard to humankind, and portrayed Africans in a negative light, which they premised on a hierarchy of races and intrinsic, immutable differences in each race's respective abilities. Thus Hunt and Burton widened their audience by using arguments that appealed to morality as well as (apparent) physiology.

They had barely turned their campaign into a political lobby through the Anthropological Society of London, with Dr. Hunt as its founder and Burton as vice president.[16] Horton vehemently attacked their theories, but condemned above all their willingness to spread their ideas outside the limited circles of scientists, given that Negrophobic tendencies were becoming rampant in the political sphere:

> It would have been sufficient to treat them with the contempt it deserves, were not that the leading statesmen of the present day have shown themselves easily carried away by the malicious views of these negrophobists, to the great prejudice of that race. (Horton 1868: v)

And "but the Committee of the House of Commons (. . .) seemed to throw some disparaging remarks on the good effects of missionary operations on the Native African" (Horton 1868: 25). This issue lay at the heart of mid nineteenth-century debates, and was a reminder that politicians had yet to come around to the view that all human beings were equal: "They again revive the old and vexed question of race which the able researches of Blumenbach, Prichard, Pallas, Hunter, Lacepède, Quatrefages, Geoffroy St Hilaire, and many others, had years ago (as it was thought) settled" (Horton 1868: 32).

It was therefore necessary to continue the struggle:

> It is without doubt an uphill work for those who have always combated that vile crusade of prejudice, especially when considering themselves at the point of putting a crowning stroke to the superstructure which had taken them years to erect, to find the foundation undermined by rats of somewhat formidable size, and therefore requiring a renowned and a more unassailable structure. (Horton 1868: v)

It is therefore not enough to pour scorn on these aberrations, with which Horton himself engages uncritically, pointing to these authors' unfamiliarity with Africa,[17] denouncing Burton's mindless generalizations[18] – a positive case for racial equality was needed. As Ayandele writes: "Few educated Africans had the courage to refute this propaganda in nineteenth-century West Africa" (1971: 702). Horton shot back. Vindication – a term previously used by Blyden – unambiguously states the goal at hand: *A Vindication of the Negro Race: Being a Brief Examination of the Arguments in Favour of African Inferiority* (Blyden 1857). There were two sides to these debates in Europe. Those who advocated racial inequality[19] were pitted against those who emphasized the fundamental equality of human beings and appealed to environmental factors, physical or social, to account for differences between the races – which their opponents rejected: "A witty writer, the late Dr Knox, of Edinburgh, believes that the races of men, particularly the negro, as they were several centuries ago, still continue to be now" (Horton 1868: 31).

Horton took on the challenge of rebutting racist rhetoric and in doing so summoned the full range of his scientific, empirical and historical capabilities.

2.4   Vindicating the "Black Race"

Horton's ideas echoed those of a well-represented school of thought which asserted the equality of cognitive abilities between racial groups.[20] Alongside them, he upheld "the principle of racial equality" among men, instead asserting that different levels of development were actually caused by contingent historical and ecological factors. Despite his high regard for British civilization, he noted that Britain had not been insulated from darker times throughout her history: "Nations rise and fall."

He viewed the shortcomings of Africans as being caused by the combined effects of the environment and slavery. Although some of his claims may now seem bizarre in retrospect – such as the supposition that white people exposed to tropical climes might grow a browner skin within a few generations – the foundations remained solid: like many of his contemporaries, Horton had an unshakeable faith in progress, which came in the form of science, technology and education. Once these tools were within reach, Africa would prosper, albeit at first under the benevolent guidance of the British Empire. Harbingers of better times to come were the recaptives, who had sprung up to serve as a local elite within less than half a century. Horton made numerous mentions of them in his work:

> Fancy a lot of slaves – unlettered, rude, naked, possessing no knowledge of the useful arts – thrown into a wild country (. . .); fancy these ragged, wild natives under British, and consequently, civilised influences, after a lapse of a few years, becoming large landowner, possessing large mercantile establishments and money, claiming a voice in the legislative government, and giving their offspring proper English and foreign education; and dare you tell me that the African is not susceptible of improvement of the highest order, that he does not possess in himself a principle of progression and a desire of perfection . . . (Horton 1868: 25)

Such a "Krio success story" – a phrase we owe to Boele van Hensbroek – was at the root of his thinking. Alongside compatriots Reverend James Johnson, Reverend Samuel Crowther, the lawyer Samuel Lewis, and many others, he was living proof of the benefits of accelerated development. While Dr. Hunt pointed to the influence of white blood in Sierra Leoneans, Robert Clarke shared Hunt's enthusiasm for the future of this native African elite:

> No one who has lived – as I have done so many years – among the negro races can entertain the slightest doubt of their mental capabilities. At Sierra Leone nearly all appointments from to the highest to the lowest are held by black or coloured men, the duties being in every respect well performed. (1863, quoted by Rainger 1978: 55)

Horton even extended his case to the whole continent: "But I say that the African race, as exemplified by the results of enterprises in Western Africa, if put in comparison with any race on the face of the globe (. . .) will never be found a whit behind" (Horton 1868: vi).

Horton made a point of using his own empirical research to challenge the generalizations derived from the anatomical and cranial data in vogue among physical anthropologists of the time. He derided the view expounded by Dr. Hunt that the development of Africans stopped upon reaching puberty. According to Ayandele, "the value of Horton's refutation of the biological inequality theory should not be minimized" (1971: 702). However, Africans neglected this aspect as they gave precedence to political issues, also of great concern to Horton.

3.   *WEST AFRICAN COUNTRIES AND PEOPLES*: A MANUAL FOR SELF-GOVERNMENT

As its title suggests, *West African Countries and Peoples* offers a dynamic response to the proposals put forward by the 1865 Parliamentary Committee. Following an articulate and impassioned refutation of the inability of Africans to achieve progress – a necessary condition for achieving self-government – it asserts the political need for each settlement to develop internal practical modes of organization to achieve the goals at hand:

> It will be my province to prove the capability of the African for possessing a real political Government and national independence; and that a more stable and effi-cient Government might yet be formed in Western Africa under the supervision of a civilized nation, in conformity with the present Resolution of the Committee of the House of Commons. (Horton 1868: 3)

Horton was firmly in line with the geopolitics of the age both in his vocabulary (nation, nationality, tribe) and in his political projects, borrowing on the notion of "dominion."

3.1   Ideological Undercurrents

Horton's thought was completely wedded to Britain, construed as the benev-olent nation he had encountered in Freetown and as a nation which depended on the effectiveness of its industrious and liberal Christian model, a beacon of progress, and the dominant country in Europe in the mid nineteenth century. His observations on socio-political systems in place in Africa were usually negative. This led him to forcefully condemn slavery, polygamy and all local religions – which he viewed as sources of ignorance and submission. He did not share Blyden's belief in Islam as an alternative. British education, necessary at first, was bound to give way to full and complete independence of all African nations as soon as was realistically feasible. This account, with its failure to detect an undercurrent of imperialism, was severely criticized at the end of the nineteenth century. The Scramble for Africa shattered Horton's hopes and expectations and saw him derided as the flagbearer of an alienated elite.

These two factors explain why his thought, so revered in the 1870–80 period, gradually fell into desuetude. His project, however, was not only coherent in the 1860–70 context, but also far-sighted in nature. He was the first person to militate for a genuine form of self-government, made up of all the various political entities united by their African nationality. This would entail a supra-national governing body and a legislative chamber for West African countries. In addition, he connected political transformations to economic projects, aware of Africa's rich mining and agricultural resources. He provided a detailed plan of the reforms to implement, covering subjects as diverse as access to water, the banking system, the army, town planning and the introduction of new plants.[21] Only through education, the use of techniques of industrialization, and also a strong work ethic and a sense of collective responsibility would societies fully attain their objectives of growth and independence.

3.2   What Kind of Political Community: Monarchy or Republic? United or Scattered? Federal or Centralized?

In an effort to facilitate the British plan of withdrawal from the colonies, Horton sketched out a string of constitutional settlements, paying close attention to the specificities of each society (Horton 1868, part II, "African Nationality": 65–179; Fyfe 1972: 74–83; see also Fyfe 1988). He emphasized the role of a paternalistic educated elite leading the people in its footsteps, which alone would be capable of enforcing radical reforms "to civilize the natives under its rule." This elite, which was meant to expand in numbers as a result of education, would not be excessively self-serving:

> The rising generation especially should bear in mind that they have a special mission to fulfil on earth; that they are not exclusively their own property, but that by indus-try and perseverance they might so better their circumstances and position as to give material aid to those less favoured than themselves . . . (Horton 1868, personal correspondence, cited in Nicol 1969: 14)

He alternately voiced support for authoritarian and benevolent monarchy – with a preference for the latter overall – and even sketched out the outline of a Republic, with or without assemblies, federal (Fanti territory being politically separate from Ga territory) or centralized (a single Ibo territory). As for his own native country, Sierra Leone, he called for the election of a king on the basis of male suffrage, and the creation of two legislative chambers, one whose constituent members would be elected by landowners, and another whose members would be directly appointed by the king. Despite his instance on the need to educate women, he did not entertain the thought of bringing women into the political arena. Some of his constitutional insights proved irrelevant to his twentieth-century readers, and were not viewed as indisputable truths, but they were nevertheless extolled as a "veritable inspiration to the first- and second-generation African educated elite in West Africa" (Ayandele 1970: 5). As the struggles for independence erupted, Horton's political thoughts, which were predicated on the need for Africans to take matters into their own hands, unsurprisingly gained renewed traction.

Horton was directly involved in the events of the Gold Coast and published *Letters on the Political Condition of the Gold Coast* (1870), a collection of letters sent to the Colonial Office in which he had propounded his support for the creation of a Fanti confederation, a political structure to which the British were sympathetic.[22] Following this publication, the governor demanded – in vain – his estrangement. Yet, having bravely stood his ground as an advocate of independence for these local provinces, Horton refrained from expressing his stances on the subject in his writings. Around that time, he would focus on his medical work and finished his life as Surgeon Major in 1879 whilst in charge of the entire army medical department on the Gold Coast. Since he was deeply imbued with ideas of progress – as much for the individual as for nations – he failed to acknowledge the warning signs of the changes in British politics, which he criticized as a retrograde step caused by circumstances, rather than a break from the status quo. In 1881 he once again wrote: "I feel deeply the gratitude I owe to the most civilized and generous Government in the world."[23]

4.   CONCLUSION

Africanus Horton died in Freetown on October 15, 1883, just over a year before the start of the Berlin Conference of November 1884, which would herald momentous change. The world, or at least Horton's perception of it, collapsed, not only in his own country but across the continent and everywhere beyond. The Sierra Leonese elite were barred from the corridors of power and shunned by polite society, against a backdrop of all-powerful imperialism. Social gatherings "at home," with the British governor or at Horton Hall and other upper-class residences where Africans and Britons intermingled, could no longer be held, as the latter moved from Freetown to Hill Station, built in 1902 (Goerg 1998). The legal exclusion of Africans from Hill Station went in tandem with their exclusion from the administration of the Protectorate (annexed in 1896), from the West African Medical Service instituted in 1902, and from the highest civil service positions.[24]

In this context, Horton's optimistic discourse, which was proven wrong by the rest of nineteenth-century history, may be seen as out of step with its time. Although his demand for change was groundbreaking, it regained relevance a century later, after 1945. Colonial authorities lately recognized the importance of education and the need for drastic economic reform and thus acknowledged African activists as the driver of socio-political change. Besides, the notion of independence itself soon returned to the forefront of the agenda. This serves as an invitation to reflect not only on the institutional frameworks but also the ideological underpinnings of progress, whether one opts for Western modernity – as in Horton's case – or a return to the lost pre-colonial paradise, in the name of a fantasy vision of Africa. Having been ostracized and satirized as a representative of an elite that championed the colonial and Western cause, Africanus Horton is finally regaining his rightful place in the history of African political thought. Rereading his works is therefore still imperative today.

NOTES

1. "Sibthorpe's *The History of Sierra Leone* (1868) was also published in London. This author, who missed the chance to study in Great-Britain, has been largely forgotten (see Fyfe 1992; Goerg 2014, 2018).
2. See how intellectuals writing in the language of the "colonizer" were dismissed in the 1950s–1960s.
3. Barely mentioned in Langley (1979), his works are now cited and discussed in various works and anthologies, such as *African Political Thought* (Martin 2012) or *African Philosophy* (Wiredu 2004). He also appears in most encyclopedias and academic "biographies" of Africa.
4. The most recent estimate is 99,466 (da Silva et al. 2014: 369). The recaptives succeeded the first wave of colonists (the Black Poor, Loyalist, Nova Scotians, Maroons from Jamaica).
5. On the history of Freetown, see, inter alia, Fyfe (1962), Peterson (1969) and Wyse (1989).
6. For a biography of Horton, see Nicol (1969), Shepperson (1969), Ayandele (1970, 1971) and Fyfe (1972).
7. For a more detailed account, see *The Methodist Herald and West African Educational Times* (1882).
8. Shepperson (1969: xii) and Fyfe (1972) provide an account of his studies in Britain (one of Horton's sources estimates he studied as much as 14 hours a day); not a hint of evidence pointing to his agitation for the abolitionist cause exists, however.
9. A concept bandied around by colonizers during the Scramble for Africa for the sole purpose of marginalizing educated local elites along racial lines.
10. See Wyse (1989). These often vicious attacks were known as Krio baiting, as Krio was – along with Creole – the local name for the inhabitants of the colony of Sierra

Leone, as opposed to the Aborigines of the Protectorate, which was established in 1896.

11. Facsimile editions were published both by Frank Cass (London, Africana Modern Library) and by Edinburgh University Press (the first one being Edward Blyden, *Christianity, Islam and the Negro Race*, in 1967, the second by Horton in 1969).

12. *Select Committee of the House of Commons on Africa (Western Coast)*, 1865.

13. This not only refers to the debate on races but also to Dr. Hunt's 1864 work.

14. The subtitle of this work may perhaps have inspired his own subtitle: *Being a Vindication of the Moral, Intellectual, and Religious Capabilities of the Coloured Portion of Mankind; with Particular Reference to the African Race*.

15. Horton thus wrote: "Not being acquainted with letters, they have no history" (1868: 5). Ayandele rather harshly deplored "the serious limitation of his book as source material for West African history" (1971: 701). Similarly, "his contempt for Islam, his ignorance of its remarkable achievements in the Sudanic belt, and his ignorance of the history of West African kingdoms limited Horton's horizon" (1971: 703).

16. See Rainger (1978) for more information on the role played by Dr. Hunt in mid nineteenth-century debates on race.

17. "On Dr Hunt we must truly state that he knows nothing of the negro race" (Horton 1868: 33).

18. "I must say a few words on some grave errors in generalization which men of science with restricted observation have arrived at respecting the capacity of progression in the African race" (Horton 1868: 31). He quoted from Carl Vogt (*Lectures on Man*, 1864) and Pruner-Bey (*Mémoires sur les Nègres*, 1861).

19. Gobineau, *Essay on the Inequality of Races* (1853–55, translated into) and Darwin, *On the Origin of Species* (1859), are two authors surprisingly not quoted by Horton.

20. On these debates, see Curtin on "The Africans' 'Place in Nature'" (1965: ch. 2).

21. Part III, "Requirements of the Various Colonies and Settlements": 181–245.

22. Re-edited by Frank Cass, London, in 1970 with an introduction by E. A. Ayandele (dated 1968).

23. *West African Reporter*, March 26, 1881 (quoted by Fyfe 1972: 155).

24. Out of a total of 40 high-level civil service positions, 18 were Krio in 1892; by 1912 there were 92 posts, 15 of which were occupied by Krio, including five which were later cut.

REFERENCES

Armistead, Wilson. 1848. *A Tribute for the Negro*. Manchester and London: W. Irwin.

Ayandele, Emmanuel Ayankanmi. 1970. *Introduction: Letters on the Political Condition of the Gold Coast*. London: Frank Cass.

Ayandele, Emmanuel Ayankanmi. 1971. "James Africanus Beale Horton 1835–1883: Prophet of Modernization in West Africa." *African Historical Studies*, 4, no. 3: 691–707.

Blyden, Edward W. 1857. *A Vindication of the Negro Race: Being a brief Examination of the Arguments in Favour of African Inferiority*. Monrovia: G. Killian.

Blyden, Edward W. 1967 [1887]. *Christianity, Islam and the Negro Race*. Edinburgh: Edinburgh University Press.

Boele van Hensbroek, Pieter. 1998. "African Philosophy, 1860–1995: An Inquiry into Three Families of Discourses." Centre for Development Studies, University of Groningen, PhD Dissertation.

Boele van Hensbroek, Pieter. 2004. "Some Nineteenth-Century African Thinkers." In *A Companion to African Philosophy*, ed. Kwasi Wiredu. Hoboken, NJ: Blackwell, pp. 78–89.

Burton, Richard F. 1863. *Wanderings in West Africa*. London: Tinsley Brothers.

Clarke, Robert. 1863. "Sketches of the Colony of Sierra Leone and Its Inhabitants." *Transactions of the Ethnological Society of London*, 2: 329–35.

Curtin, Philipp. 1965. *The Image of Africa: British Ideas and Action, 1780–1850*. London: Macmillan.

da Silva, Domingues, David Eltis, Philip Misevich and Ojo Olatunji. 2014. "The Diaspora of Africans Liberated from Slave Ships in the Nineteenth Century." *Journal of African History*, 55, no. 3: 347–69.

Darwin, Charles. 1859. *On the Origin of Species*. London: John Murray.

Fyfe, Christopher. 1962. *A History of Sierra Leone*. Oxford: Oxford University Press.

Fyfe, Christopher. 1972. *Africanus Horton. 1835–1883: West African Scientist and Patriot*. New York: Oxford University Press.

Fyfe, Christopher. 1988. "Africanus Horton as a Constitution-Maker." *The Journal of Commonwealth & Comparative Politics*, 26, no. 2: 173–84.

Fyfe, Christopher. 1992. "A. B. C. Sibthorpe: A Tribute." *History in Africa*, 19: 327–52.

Gobineau, Arthur. 1853–1855. *Essai sur l'Inégalité des Races Humaines*. Paris: Librairie de Firmin Didot Frères, trans. by Adrian Collins. 1915. London: William Heinemann, and trans. by Hotze. 1856 as *The Moral and Intellectual Diversity of Races,* Philadelphia, J.B: Lippincott & Co.

Goerg, Odile. 1995. "Sierra Leonais, Créoles, Krio: La Dialectique de l'Identité." *Africa*, 65, no. 1: 114–32.

Goerg, Odile. 1998. "From Hill Station (Freetown) to Downtown Conakry: Comparing French and British Approaches to Segregation in Colonial Cities." *Canadian Journal of African Studies/Revue Canadienne des Etudes Africaines*, 32, no. 1: 1–30.

Goerg, Odile. 2014. "A.B.C. Sibthorpe: Un Historien Précurseur en Sierra Leone". In *Historiographies d'Ailleurs. Comment Ecrit-On l'Histoire en Dehors du Monde Occidental?*, edited by Nathalie Kouamé. Paris: Karthala, pp. 105–17.

Goerg, Odile. 2018. "A.B.C. Sibthorpe (v. 1840–1916), Historien Sierra-Léonais: Au Centre ou à la Marge?" In *Histoire en Marges. Les Périphéries de l'Histoire Globale*, edited by Hélène Le Dantec-Lowry, Marie-Jeanne Rossignol, Matthieu Renault and Pauline Vermeren. Tours: Presses Universitaires François Rabelais, pp. 259–87.

Horton, James Africanus Beale. 1859. *The Medical Topography of the West Coast of Africa*. London: John Churchill.

Horton, James Africanus Beale. 1867. *Physical and Medical Climate and Meteorology of the West Coast of Africa: With Valuable Hints to Europeans for the Preservation of Health in the Tropics*. London: John Churchill.

Horton, James Africanus Beale. 1868. *West African Countries and Peoples, British and Natives*. London: W. J. Johnson.

Horton, James Africanus Beale. 1870. *Letters on the Political Condition of the Gold Coast.* London: William John Johnson.

Hunt, James. 1864 [1863]. "On the Negro's Place in Nature." *Journal of the Anthropological Society of London*, 2: xv–lvi.

Hutchinson, Thomas J. 1861. *Ten Years' Wanderings Among the Ethiopians; With Sketches of the Manners and Customs of the Civilized and Uncivilized Tribes, from Senegal to Gaboon*. London: Hurst and Blackett.

Kingsley, Mary. 1982 [1897]. *Travels in West Africa: Congo Français, Corisco and Cameroons*. London: Virago.

Langley, Ayo J. 1979. *Ideologies of Liberation in Black Africa 1856–1970: Documents on Modern African Political Thought from Colonial Times to the Present*. London: Rex Collings.

Lynch, Hollis R. 1970. *Edward Wilmot Blyden 1832–1912: Pan-Negro Patriot*. Oxford: Oxford University Press.

Martin, Guy. 2012. *African Political Thought*. New York: Palgrave Macmillan.

Nicol, Davidson. 1969. *Africanus Horton: The Dawn of Nationalism in Modern Africa: Extracts from the Political, Educational, Scientific and Medical Writings of J. A. B. Horton M.D., 1835–1883*. London & Harlow: Longmans, Green and Co Ltd.

Nwauwa, Appollos O. 1999. "Far Ahead of his Time: James Africanus Horton's Initiatives for a West African University and his Frustrations, 1862–1871." *Cahiers d'Etudes Africaines*, 39, no. 153: 107–21.

Peterson, John. 1969. *Province of Freedom: A History of Sierra Leone 1787–1870*. London: Faber & Faber.

Pruner-Bey, Franz. 1861. *Mémoires sur les Nègres. Mémoires de la Société d'Anthropologie*. Paris: 293–339.

Rainger, Ronald. 1978. "Race, Politics, and Science: The Anthropological Society of London in the 1860s." *Victorian Studies*, 22, no. 1: 51–70.

Rankin, Harrison. 1836. *The White Man's Grave: A Visit to Sierra Leone, in 1834*. London: Richard Bentley.

Reade, William Winwood. 1863. *Savage Africa*. London: Rarebooksclub.com.

Shepperson, Georges. 1969. *Introduction to West African Countries and Peoples*. Edinburgh: Edinburgh University Press.

Sierra Leone Weekly News. 1898. "The Aborigines." 23, 5 February.

Vogt, Carl. 1864. *Lectures on Man: Place in Creation, and in the History of the Earth*. London: Pearson Longman.

West African Reporter. 1883. "Our Aboriginal Brethen." 291, 29 September.

Wiredu, Kwasi (ed.). 2004. *A Companion to African Philosophy*. Hoboken, NJ: Blackwell.

Wyse, Akintola J. G. 1989. *The Krio of Sierra Leone: An Interpretive History*. Freetown: W. D. Okrafo-Smart & Cy.

18. Sol Plaatje: an intellectual giant in the twentieth-century history of black South Africa

Tidiane N'Diaye and Guillaume Vallet

1. INTRODUCTION

Today, few historians dare to recall the role played by the British, during the colonial era, who laid the foundations for a system of racial segregation. In the aftermath of two prolonged imperial wars, waged against the Zulus and the Boers respectively, Britain set out to establish the Union of South Africa, which covers the same borders as the state of modern-day South Africa (1961). The 1910 Constitution tightened Britain's grip, while delegating some degree of autonomy to the Boers, all at the expense of black populations, which had gained little in return from these developments. At no stage were they requested to participate in the issues affecting the country, whether it be land ownership, mining resources or political institutions. Not even any provisions concerning their political representation were in sight. A string of segregationist laws had been adopted to exclude them from the outset. In particular, the Intercolonial Native Affairs Commission – ironically made up exclusively of Britons – intended to create indigenous reserves all across South Africa in order to resettle Africans.

To a considerable extent, it may be surmised that British indigenous policy paved the way for apartheid, which in turn brought about the struggle for liberty and equality in South Africa. Indeed, as soon as the British withdrew from South Africa in 1948, Nazi Afrikaners affiliated to the National Party embraced apartheid, in effect perpetuating the status quo of British indigenous policy. There again, their purpose was to deny blacks any involvement in political life, and assign them to Bantustans, which were expected to turn into independent, separate nations over time. Faced with the callous deafness of a racist regime, oppressed black populations therefore mounted a resistance under the aegis of eminent figures such as Oliver Tambo and Walter Zizulu, along with a certain man gifted with exceptional charisma, Nelson Mandela.

Yet, it may be averred that the struggle for liberty and equality in South Africa had already been ongoing as early as the start of the twentieth century. Before the aforementioned figures came to prominence, a man of no lesser charisma had shown the way for the resistance: his name was Solomon Tshekisho "Sol" Plaatje (1876–1932). A Zulu who had studied both in the United States and in England, Sol Plaatje founded the South African Native Nation Congress (SANNC) on January 8, 1912, which later morphed into the African National Congress (ANC). He had drawn inspiration from an Indian political party, the Natal Indian Congress, founded in 1894 by a young barrister named Gandhi.

A talented intellectual and an erudite, Sol Plaatje employed his literary skills to write essays, pamphlets and academic literature, which align his thought with a certain form of militancy (Plaatje 1970). The aim of this chapter is to explore the foundational role Sol Plaatje played in bolstering the campaign on behalf of the black populations of South Africa, and elsewhere as well. Not only was he shaped by politics, but his life was also culturally well-informed. All his life, he sought to promote Tswana language and culture in numerous works. To that extent, it would be little exaggeration to regard him as the founder of the "black press."

The chapter is organized as follows: the second section surveys a range of historical events in South Africa which exerted a lasting influence on Sol Plaatje's thought. The third section reveals the emancipatory influence of Sol Plaatje's thought, through his involvement in the struggle against inequalities faced by blacks. Section 4 offers concluding remarks.

2.   A HISTORICAL CONTEXTUALIZATION OF SOL PLAATJE'S SOUTH AFRICA

The peopling of South Africa – Sol Plaatje's home country – through successive waves of immigration was the consequence of an accident of history. Following the sack of Constantinople by the Turks in 1453, the Turks gained complete control of the key trade routes and were a major obstacle to the eastward road. New routes were explored. In 1487, the Portuguese seafarer Bartolomeu Dias thus discovered an alternative passage leading to India via South Africa. The place became known as Boa Esperança in Portuguese, later known as the Cape of Good Hope. The Dutch were the first nation to show an interest, as they needed a port of call halfway between Amsterdam and their colony of Batavia (present-day Jakarta, Indonesia). Upon reaching the cape, mariners would replenish their supplies of drinkable water, food, vegetables and fresh meat. They noticed that Table Bay – the natural bay on the Atlantic Ocean overlooked by Cape Town, South Africa – was open and sheltered from high winds.

Table 18.1   *South African Population by Race in 1911 (by percentage of total)*

African	67.3
White	21.4
Colored	8.8
Indian	2.5
Total	100.0

Source: www.sahistory.org.za, 2019

The native inhabitants of these coasts also happened to raise sheep and cattle. All the conditions were therefore in place to establish a factory: a task which the East India Company entrusted to one Jan Van Riebeeck, explorer and sea-farer, who had already acquired some experience in the region. Among the first European settlers to set foot there were, naturally, Dutch mariners. They were soon followed by a huge influx of immigrants from Switzerland, Scandinavian countries and German-speaking countries. They were also joined by French Huguenots, who had initially found refuge in the Netherlands to avoid reli-gious persecution from France's Louis XIV. Such was the story of white settlement in South Africa, a historical process Sol Plaatje was well aware of.

By the time of Sol Plaatje, the various ethnic groups of South Africa were divided as shown in Table 18.1.

This factor had not been neglected by Sol Plaatje when he campaigned for equality between ethnic groups. An outstanding thinker, he devoted a large part of his life to the political and cultural liberation of South Africa in the context described above. Two national monuments in the province of North Cape bear architectural witness to his legacy and a museum in Mafeking carries his name. Sol Plaatje was not formally well educated – apart from his studies abroad – yet his acute sense and dynamism made him a literary and political icon in South Africa. The Sol Plaatje library in Kimberly – the "diamond city" where he lived for many years and was eventually buried – contains a wealth of evidence pointing to his fame. The town and the university were also named after him (the latter since 2014). He was born on a farmstead at Doornfontein, in the then Free Orange State, into the Barolong tribe, a subdivision of the Tswanas. Of royal lineage, his father traced his descent from Modiboa, the disgraced Barolong king of the sixteenth and seventeenth centuries. His mother was none other than the granddaughter of Tau, king of the Barolong in the eighteenth century. Yet, both of her parents were of Christian heritage.

As a child, he reveled in stories and legends of the Barolong, which were told to him by the women of his family. He belonged to a group of black South Africans who had been educated by missionaries. Plaatje, who declined to take the reins of the SANNC in 1917, spent much of his time traveling to London and to the United States, carried there by his desire to raise awareness of the racial injustices in his native land. Among other things, he was the first black to be published in a newspaper in wartime, as he reported on the siege of Mafeking during the Boer War. He also translated Shakespeare's works as well as some novels into his mother tongue, Tswana. Plaatje's works consist of several publications. Chief among his literary contributions is his first book *Mhudi, An Epic of South African Native Life a Hundred Years Ago*, first written in 1919 and first published in 1930 (Plaatje 1970), no less than the first publication authored by a black man in South Africa.

But he also held the post of chief editor at vernacular newspapers – to whom he contributed himself – and was a fluent speaker of English, Afrikaans, Dutch, German, French, Sotho, Setwana, Sesotho, Zulu and Xhosa. Both his tomb in Kimberly and his residence on Angel Street were declared national treasures as a tribute to a man whose resilience, self-esteem and intellect propelled him to the heart of South African life, despite the potentially destructive and humiliating effects of racial injustice.

On October 11, 1899, the Second Boer War broke out. Three days later, the Boer general Cronje was already besieging the city of Mafeking – today's Mmabatho district, capital of South Africa's North West province. It was also the city where Nelson Mandela uttered one of his last campaign speeches, in the heart of what had been – prior to April 1994 that is – the capital of the former bantustan of Bophuthatswana. Mafeking, meaning "rocks" in Setswana, had been the site of a large village peopled by the Tshidi Barolong, a Tswana tribe, before a train station opened on the railway line connecting the diamond city of Kimberly to another El Dorado, Rhodesia. Going westward, the Tswana steppe gives way to the Kalahari Desert, while in the north the main track cuts between the Limpopo River, which flows eastwards, and the Okavango delta, which feeds the Zambezi River. During the rainy season the delta streams run to the Victoria Falls.

In 1885, Mafeking became the capital of the colony of Bechuanaland and of its protectorate (today's state of Botswana). Troops had been stationed there, at the junction between the railway and the route connecting the southwest of Africa, under German control, to Pretoria. More than 5,000 blacks and 1,700 whites inhabited this area by the end of the nineteenth century. Seventy years after the siege, in 1969, an exciting discovery was made: the private diary of the court's official interpreter, Sol Plaatje himself, which casts a singular light on relations between black and white communities. In the words of the anthropologist John Comaroff, the book revealed "a black man's outlook on a white man's war" (Comaroff 1973).

Indeed, the Barolong were conscious that they had a stake in the matter: they themselves had fought the Boers some twenty years earlier, when the latter had invaded their pastures and demanded taxes. A young Sol Plaatje – aged only 23 at the time – shrewdly presented the problem in his journal. The indigenous issue had always been the most thorny question of the day since the abolition of slavery. Plaatje's journal on December 8, 1899, mentions a conversation between two white men: Lord Baden Powell, a British military officer and founder of the Scout movement, in conversation with General Snyman. Baden Powell warns General Snyman, whose soldiers have stolen indigenous peoples' cattle – among other things – that the indigenous population is now ready to rebel and to fight (Comaroff and Plaatje 1989: 50).

Before hostilities began, the High Commissioner commanded the native tribes to stay calm and not take up arms unless their territory was invaded – in which case they would only be within their rights to defend themselves. In his reply to Baden Powell, Snyman, the Boer general who had succeeded Cronje, admitted that Africans were entitled to self-defense, a notion of which he took a rather loose definition. After the conflict ended, Snyman suggested that the Barolong chief was worthy of the Victoria Cross – a military decoration – but Her Majesty's Government replied that a lesser award would be enough to placate the natives.

Because of such indecision among the colonizers, which suggested that they might be willing to engage with the Barolong, Sol Plaatje was optimistic about the prospects for a peaceful resolution. He had no doubt that he would retain his position as an administrator, especially in the civil tribunal, where he had proved his mettle. From a lowly interpreter, he rose to become a sharp-minded and indefatigable advocate of the black cause, at a time when blacks were being forcibly evicted due to the law of 1913, which allocated 87% of all land to whites and only leaving the remainder to blacks. "We have become pariahs on our own soil," wrote Plaatje in the introduction to his book *Native Life in South Africa*, which was first published in 1916 (Plaatje 1987). What he had seen with respect to the Barolong had made a great impression on him.

Overall, Plaatje should mostly be viewed as an activist, which is why his writings may be viewed as falling into two categories: essays and pamphlets on the one hand, and works that aimed to safeguard the language and culture of his people (such as anthologies of tales, proverbs and dictionaries) on the other. Moreover, Plaatje also authored a work of fiction in English (so as to attract a worldwide readership): *Mhudi, An Epic of South African Native Life a Hundred Years Ago*. This was the first work in English written by a black man in South Africa. *Mhudi* tells the story of two Barolongs, Mhudi and Ra-Thaga. The narrative opens with the king of Ndebeles, Mzilikazi, about to lead a bloody attack against the Barolong. Driven out of their homes by the bloodshed, the protagonists wander the country before finally encountering some of their kin who had survived the slaughter. Their people then enter an alliance with the Boers to exact revenge on Mzilikazi.

In his pan-Africanist novel *Mhudi*, Plaatje strives to rewrite his fellow black peers into the narrative of South African history, which had hitherto been exclusively dominated by whites and the Great Trek. He condemns Boer aggression, but makes no attempt to conceal the horrors perpetrated by blacks during the Mfecane. The story ends with the black characters finally united by a common yearning for peace, and yielding to their tragic or violent fate.

However, some criticized the content of the book. For instance, Snyman attacked the book for a supposed lack of imagination from Plaatje:

> In *Mhudi* (1930), Plaatje deals with the times of Mzilikazi, and especially with the war between the Matabele and Barolong. He has examined the causes of this war and finds that its origin lay in the murder of Mzilikazi's tax-collectors by the Barolong. He shows also that the Matabele had justification for some of their deeds. Plaatje takes pride in his people, and attempts here to interpret to the reading public 'one phase of the back of the native mind', as well as to gain sufficient money to arrest the lack of interest of his people in their own beliefs and literature, by collecting and printing Sechuana folk-tales which are in danger of being forgotten through the spread of European ideas. Although *Mhudi* would seem to be authentic, it lacks the spontaneity of Mitford's Untuswa series. The reader is aware that the writer is recounting events which occurred a hundred years ago, and it seems as if Plaatje is unable to span the gap and live in the period about which he is writing. Little fault can be found, however, with his account of life at Mzilikazi's kraal in the Matabele capital. (Snyman 1952: 141)

In spite of that kind of criticism, the relevance of both Plaatje's thought and creative prolificacy is worth a reminder. Indeed, he wrote *Native Life in South Africa* in the same year (1916) as the collection of Tswana poems he had completed before his departure. In 1916, his collaboration with the British phonetician Daniel Jones led to the publication of *A Sechuana Reader in International Phonetic Orthography* (Jones and Plaatje 2010).[1]

On his return to South Africa, he translated a number of plays by Shakespeare into Tswana and wrote a series of pamphlets on the South African government. He made several trips to England, the United States and Canada, where he gave public lectures on the plight of blacks in South Africa. Until the very end of his life, Sol Plaatje kept faith in his advocacy of black people's rights and did his utmost to protect Tswana language and culture, through the publication of tales and dictionaries. The alliance with Britain, in which he had had faith, and which had materialized in the united front at Mafeking, was not to survive the harsh realities of imperialism.

The civil rights granted to blacks in Cape Province, in 1910, had almost turned Plaatje into a normal citizen, or at the very least a subject worthy of white politicians' notice when they canvassed for local elections. Yet, these "civil rights," as the Boers called them, seemed to be the remnants of a bygone era, a time during which Livingstone and Moffat evangelized the Batswana under the kindly yoke of Queen Victoria. Some might venture to say that these were the early signs of black empowerment under a constitutional settlement which granted every man a vote. Indeed, Plaatje wanted to believe that it was so.

Unfortunately, the combined effects of racial segregation and property rights legislation resulted in dire poverty and violence. What Plaatje could not have foreseen, however, was the military prowess of the South African Defence Force – the successor to the Boer army – in liberating Mafeking. Meanwhile, they crushed an attempted uprising by far-right white separatists, at a putsch in Bophuthatswana. Thus, at least officially, the Bantusta regime, which had been a by-product of the iniquitous land grab of 1913, ended. For the first time in its history, the country became one: the struggles of Plaatje and his successors had been long drawn out, yet not in vain. These exceptional individuals were the object of two outstanding biographies (see Willan 1984; Jeal 1989). Sol Plaatje will be remembered as one of the leading black intellectuals of the twentieth century and his works have gradually been rescued from oblivion throughout the past twenty years.

3.   THE EMANCIPATORY INFLUENCE OF SOL PLAATJE'S THOUGHT

For Sol Plaatje, the struggle for equal access to land ownership was a crucial aspect of the global struggle for equal rights between whites and blacks. He had awoken to this reality as he had witnessed first-hand the horror of South African farmers being evicted from their lands, especially in the period follow-ing the Native Land Acts of 1913[2] passed by the South African government (Plaatje 1987). This piece of legislation, which regulated land ownership, legitimized white supremacy in the aftermath of the political unification of the South African territory (1910). Indeed, only as little as 7% of the territory was allocated to black communities. Worse, these populations were denied the right to acquire or rent out land outside of "scheduled native areas" – rebranded as "bantustans" under the apartheid regime.

Although it is generally crucial for each worker to own "tool capital," whereby one constructs one's identity through work, in the words of the soci-ologist Albion W. Small (Vallet 2016; see also Chapter 3 in this volume), this issue became all the more sensitive in view of South Africa's huge resource wealth. Indeed, he invariably railed against the injustice of the inequality which blacks were made to suffer as a result of exploitation. Drawing inspira-tion from his first-hand experiences in Kimberley, he made a point of arguing that the diamond mines which served the interests of white industrialists did not "grow by themselves," by which he meant that the wealth derived from them was built on the backs of blacks. This was a form of "management capital," to return to another concept developed by the aforementioned Small.

Seen from this perspective, the question of how land should be redistributed emerged as the prerequisite for black people's emancipation and their journey toward civil and material equality. The right to make a decent living off one's labor, Plaatje argued, was of the utmost importance to all people, and he tirelessly asserted the urgency of ensuring that black workers could reap the full and just benefits of their work.

In doing so, Plaatje was addressing the issue of incipient South African nationalism, and of the ways in which to help bring it to fruition (Willan 1984). At stake was the internal division of the state into regions, ethnic populations and cultures at a time of lingering political divisions. Failing to manage and allocate resources fairly would inevitably cause a large-scale socio-political breakdown, and might jeopardize the country's institutional and economic stability for generations to come (Plaatje 1916).

At the same time, Plaatje wished to preserve the cultural identity of South African peoples, in particular by making each constituent of these peoples reflect on their own cultures. His fear was that political and economic unity might swiftly bring down regional and ethnic barriers, thereby strengthening British, and more generally, white, domination. Consequently the legal reassertion of some laws – as of property rights and language rights – was key to preserving local cultures. Independence, achieved by land ownership, he argued, was closely enmeshed with the question of identity. The relationship between the two depended on the ability of local peoples to take an active part in managing resources. In modernist terms, it might be said that Plaatje had pioneering insights as to the best way to administer common goods.

For these reasons, he excoriated black workers' living conditions, in particular those of women. He frequently did not shy away from deploring the misery of African workers – a true "race-class" in his eyes (Limb 2003: 41). To that extent, Plaatje can be viewed as having emphasized the identity-based and liberalizing facets of the emancipation of African workers (Limb 2003). For example, during the Rand strike of 1913, his stance was met with some controversy. In his dedication to improving workers' conditions, he urged his peers not to sacrifice racial justice on the altar of worker solidarity. If a black representative of striking workers behaved unlawfully, justice required that he be dealt with according to the rule of law, that is, in the same way as a white person would. This was a bold stance at a time of rampant racism within the labor movement.

Plaatje in fact yearned for equal rights between blacks and whites, desiring that both groups be properly recognized as British subjects. For Plaatje, the necessary conditions for black emancipation lay not in radical conflict but in institutional change. Under a thin veneer of moderate critique was a vehement condemnation

of black exploitation and a willingness to bring a kind of Black Power movement into being (Limb 2003). This exploitation, he argued, came in the form of
stereotypes and the refusal to register black victims of work-related accidents,
as well as racial segregation in the workplace.

Even so, Plaatje disapproved of the violent remedies advocated by the
radical proletariat (Limb 2003) and repeatedly worried about the rise of
equally radical socialist ideas. His activism was unusual insofar as he wanted
to maintain the institutions of the British Empire whilst simultaneously
encouraging African solidarity and condemning the racism and exploitation
which characterized British colonial power, and that of whites more generally.
Plaatje frequently resorted to irony and sarcasm to lay bare the contradictions
and hypocrisy inherent in British cultural and economic dominance (Limb
2002).

4.   CONCLUSION

This chapter has sought to delineate Sol Plaatje's progressive thoughts in
early twentieth-century South Africa. His thought, which was expounded in
various outlets – such as poems, stories, articles and so on – aimed to bring
about a radical transformation in the ethnic makeup of South Africa. Plaatje
put a clear emphasis on the urgency of reforms in property rights, which were
a necessary step to give everyone a chance for self-emancipation, within the
broader framework of achieving equality of opportunity for all humankind.

This explains why this militant thinker, albeit little known outside of South
Africa, was nonetheless instrumental in initiating a series of pioneering reflections on the subject of blacks in this country, before Mandela's time. Plaatje
was undeniably a progressive at heart, which puts him on a par with other
figures discussed in this book.

While he was occasionally accused of a lenient attitude toward the imperial structures in place in his days, or deemed insufficiently radical, his real
purpose was to lay the foundations for a sense of equality and justice in
South African society, and make it possible for blacks and whites to coexist
in harmony. Certainly, it may be argued that his "pacifist" and compromised
vision prevented him from taking a fully active and influential role in the
political transformations of the 1920s. This attitude ceded more ground to
his critics. Regardless, his intellectual contributions have undeniably shaped
the prospects for social change in South Africa, as well as in similar contexts
elsewhere.

Plaatje lived through a crucial moment in South Africa's history. Although
racism, discrimination and the exploitation of blacks by whites were on
the rise – culminating in the introduction of apartheid in 1948 – his ideas
ushered in new modes of anti-colonial resistance. In that sense, Plaatje may

be considered, alongside Franz Fanon or Aimé Césaire, as one of the intellectual standard-bearers for black identity. Likewise, Plaatje's thought echoes the works of Horton presented in Chapter 17 of this book by Odile Goerg. Even though they have been sometimes underestimated, these two great thinkers definitely brought paramount progressive ideas for Africa during the Progressive Era.

NOTES

1.   With English translations.
2.   Later referred to as the Bantu Land Act and the Black Land Act.

REFERENCES

Comaroff, John (ed.). 1973. *The Boer War Diary of Sol T. Plaatje.* Johannesburg: Macmillan South Africa.

Comaroff, John (ed.) and Sol Plaatje. 1989. *Mafeking Diary: A Black Man's View of a White Man's War.* Johannesburg: Southern Book Publishers.

Jeal, Tim. 1989. *Baden-Powell.* London: Pimlico.

Jones, Daniel and Sol Plaatje. 2010 [1916]. *A Sechuana Reader in International Phonetic Orthography.* New York: Sagwan Press.

Limb, Peter. 2002. "Early ANC Leaders and the British World: Ambiguities and Identities." *Historia* 47, no. 1: 56–82.

Limb, Peter. 2003. "Sol Plaatje Reconsidered: Rethinking Plaatje's Attitudes to Class, Nation, Gender, and Empire." *African Studies* 62, no. 1: 33–52.

Plaatje, Sol. 1970 [1930]. *Mhudi: An Epic of South African Native Life a Hundred Years Ago.* Greenwood, NY: Negro Universities Press.

Plaatje, Sol. 1987 [1916]. *Native Life in South Africa.* London: Longman.

Snyman, Lannice. 1952. *The South African Novel in English 1880–1930.* Potchefstroom: University of Potchefstroom.

Vallet, Guillaume. 2016. "Cooperation rather than Competition in Industrial Organisations: Albion W. Small's Underestimated View." *Business History* 59, no. 3: 453–70.

Willan, Brian. 1984. *Sol Plaatje: South African Nationalist, 1876–1932.* Johannesburg: Ravan Press.

19. Stephen Leacock on political economy and the unsolved riddle of social justice

Robert W. Dimand

> To avoid all error as to the point of view, let me say in commencing that I am a Liberal Conservative, or, if you will, a Conservative Liberal with a strong dash of sympathy with the Socialist idea, a friend of Labour, and a believer in Progressive Radicalism.
>
> Stephen Leacock (1919: 232)

1. INTRODUCTION

Stephen Leacock, "Canada's Mark Twain,"[1] the best-selling humorist in the English language between 1910 and 1925 (Leacock 1973: ix) and head of McGill University's Department of Economics and Political Science from 1908 to 1936, was an incisive satirist and social critic like his teacher Thorstein Veblen (see Legate 1970; Moritz and Moritz 1985; Macmillan 2009; Dimand 2017). Unlike Veblen, Leacock varied the sharp, even bitter, satire of *Arcadian Adventures with the Idle Rich* (1914) with the warmer humor of *Sunshine Sketches of a Little Town* (1912), depicting the rural values abandoned by the urban plutocrats in the Mausoleum Club and the tame academics of Plutoria University. Although no Progressive in the Canadian sense (see Morton 1950 on Canada's Progressive Party as an agrarian protest movement) and only debatably one in the US sense, Leacock was Canada's best-known social scientist in the "Progressive Era," an outspoken reformer and British Imperialist, a founder of the Canadian tradition of "red Tories" chronicled, in the last days of that tradition, in Charles Taylor's *Radical Tories* (1982, especially pages 9–16 on Leacock).[2] He was a distinguished political scientist who was misunderstood by contemporaries in several ways: "When I stand up before an audience to deliver my serious thoughts, they begin laughing. I have been advertised to them as funny, and they refuse to accept me as anything else" (quoted by Erika Ritter in Staines 1986: 11). In 1933, Leacock refused US$1,000 plus expenses to entertain the American Bankers Association in New York City, but offered instead to speak at his own expense "on the restoration of the gold standard or some equally important subject" (quoted by Frankman 1986: 52). Largely because Canadian economists, political scientists and sociologists shared the same academic departments, professional association and (from 1935) journal in his time, Leacock was also often mistaken by the general public and by himself for an authority on economics (e.g. Leacock 1910–11, 1930, 1932, 1933). His disdain for the technical side of economics as incomprehensible, subversive mathematical mumbo-jumbo, forcefully expressed in such works as *Hellements of Hickonomics in Hiccoughs of Verse Done in Our Social Planning Mill* (1936a), produced a reaction against the contemporary acceptance of Leacock as an economist (or, in the case of *Hellements*, as a poet), reinforcing the view of him as just a humorist.

But Leacock, while certainly no master of Marshallian or later economics, had serious contributions to make to political economy as a social critic and political scientist – and as a satirist whose satire was meant no less seriously for being made jestingly. His main work of political economy and social criticism was *The Unsolved Riddle of Social Justice* (1920a), based on six articles he had published in the *New York Times* the previous year, from "Social Unrest After the War" on August 31 to "Socialism in Operation: A Prison" on October 5. This was an intensely felt, serious work of political and social reflection, responding to post-First World War unrest that included, in addition to the Russian Revolution and in the United States the Seattle general strike, the Boston police strike and "Red scare", in Canada the labor unrest exemplified by the Winnipeg general strike and the agrarian protest that brought the United Farmers of Ontario (the provincial wing of the Progressive Party) to office in 1919. Strongly opposed to socialism (but also critical of materialism, unrestrained individualism and inequality), Leacock (1920a) nevertheless saw a need for government to maintain full employment, support the aged and infirm, regulate minimum wages and working conditions, and have high levels of progressive taxation to fund social security. Yet publishing *The Unsolved Riddle of Social Justice* (1920a) and *Winsome Winnie, and Other New Nonsense Novels* (1920b) with the same three British, US and Canadian publishers in the same year contributed to readers' tendency to treat all Leacock's writings as humor – especially since the previous year he had presented his political views in the heavy-handed jests of *The Hohenzollerns in America; With the Bolsheviks in Berlin and Other Impossibilities* (1919)[3] and since, of Leacock's two 1920 books, it was *Winsome Winnie* that over time appeared in eight editions. In a similar juxtaposition, the December 10, 1910, issue of *Saturday Night* had two contributions from Leacock: "Gertrude the Governess" (reprinted the following year in his *Nonsense Novels*) and an article on bimetallism, the fifth of twenty-five weekly articles by Leacock on "Practical Political Economy" (1910–11).[4]

2.   POLITICAL ECONOMIST: A POLITICAL
SCIENTIST TURNS TO TEACHING ECONOMICS

Born in England in December 1869, Leacock was 6 years old when his family moved to Canada. Educated in languages ("living, dead and half-dead" according to Leacock (1998: 3)) at Upper Canada College and the University of Toronto, he taught school for a decade ("the most dreary, the most thankless, and the worst paid profession in the world") before going to the University of Chicago in 1899 for a PhD in political economy, writing a dissertation on "The Doctrine of *Laissez-Faire*" (accepted in 1903 but first published in Leacock 1998): "The meaning of this degree is that the recipient of instruction is examined for the last time in his life and is pronounced completely full. After this, no new ideas can be imparted to him" (Leacock 1912: viii). One of Leacock's colleagues at Upper Canada College, Edward (later Sir Edward) Peacock, although teaching English, had recently graduated in economics from Queen's University, Kingston, Ontario, and later chaired the British merchant bank Baring Brothers from 1924 to 1955 and became the first non-British-born director of the Bank of England. Peacock tutored Leacock in Alfred Marshall's *Principles of Economics* (1890) while Leacock gave Peacock lessons in French so that, chairing a lecture by Leacock in England circa 1921, Peacock claimed "to have been a better teacher than Doctor Leacock because he is now the head of the Economics Department of McGill while I still speak no French" (Leacock 1998: xiii). Despite Peacock's claim to have taught Marshall to Leacock, Leacock did not cite Marshall in his thesis and, like his Chicago teacher J. Laurence Laughlin,[5] taught "Elements of Political Economy" at McGill from John Stuart Mill's *Principles of Political Economy* (first published in 1848, with the last edition in 1871, two years before Mill's death) for decades, as if the neoclassical economics of Jevons and Marshall had not transformed classical political economy. Leacock was not impervious only to then fairly recent neoclassical innovations in economics: his protectionist views were unshaken by an even older, classical contribution to economic theory, David Ricardo's 1817 numerical example of comparative advantage, half a century older than Leacock himself.

At Chicago, Leacock

> took many lectures from Thorstein Veblen and was deeply impressed by him. He had no manner, no voice, no art. He lectured into his lap with his eyes on his waistcoat. But he would every now and then drop a phrase with a literary value to it beyond the common reach. In the first lecture I heard, he happened to say, "Hume, of course, aspired to be an intellectual tough." That got me, and kept me; the art of words is almost better than truth, isn't [it]. Veblen's only failing was weakness for lecturing on the Navajo Indians . . . The lectures, I suppose, were the beginning of what has grown into behavior economics, and institutional economy, which, I thank God, I am too old to learn. (Leacock 1998: 6, written in 1942 or 1943)

Leacock did not discuss his admiration for Veblen's "beautiful and thoughtful mind, free from anger and dispute, and heedless of all money motive" in print until *My Discovery of the West* (1937: 137–8), but his affinity with Veblen's *Theory of the Leisure Class* (1899), including use of the phrase "leisure class," was noted by Clarence Ayres (1920), who found Leacock's *Unsolved Riddle of Social Justice* "in the spirit of the younger group of 'institutional' economists (who are not mentioned, however); a trained psychic might even sense the presence of the spirit of Mr. Veblen" (quoted by Frankman 1986: 53) – and the president of Plutoria University[6] in Leacock's *Arcadian Adventures with the Idle Rich* (1914) is satirized for tedious lectures on the Navajo. In contrast to his response to Veblen, Leacock

> saw very little of Dr. Laurence Laughlin, the head of the department. This was largely my own fault as I was very slow in selecting and starting a thesis and Dr. Laughlin was too busy a man to waste time in mere colloquy with students. We, the students, did not at the time think much of Laughlin's work on money [opposed to the quantity theory]. But later on I have come to think that his books of succeeding years, especially his *Credit of the Nations*, among the best works on economics of peace and war. (Leacock 1998: 5)

Laughlin, who was a formidable and combative public intellectual (see André-Aigret and Dimand 2018), long remained in correspondence with Leacock, who returned to speak at the University of Chicago in 1917, 1920, 1923 and 1925 (on literature, not political economy; Spadoni in Leacock 1998: xxxviii–xxxix).

Leacock's first book, a textbook expounding the *Elements of Political Science* (1921 [1906]), established his credentials in that field. Adopted by three dozen US universities, widely used in the British Empire, translated into eighteen other languages, the textbook sold better and earned Leacock more royalties than any of his humorous works. Beyond the standard topics, Leacock included a chapter on "Imperial Federation," although in the 1921 revision he conceded that this was no longer a practical hope. He wrote a scholarly monograph in the "Makers of Canada" series on the men who achieved responsible government (legislative control of the executive) in Canada (Leacock 1907a), contributed to the inaugural volume of the *American Political Science Review* on responsible government in the British dominions (1907b), and in December 1906 was elected to the Executive Council of the American Political Science Association (Staines 2006: 21) so he was an established political scientist by 1908 when he succeeded A. W. Flux as head of McGill's Department of Economics and Political Science. Jacob Viner, by far the most famous economist to study with Leacock (graduating from McGill in 1914), wrote to Leacock's biographer David Legate that Leacock's "teaching of what he thought advanced economics was a farce, and I'm afraid some of us gave him a rough time, until the girls in the class, out of pity for him, asked us to lay off"[7] but was "much more respectful of Leacock as a teacher of political science" (quoted by Legate 1970: 53). Yet Caroline Clotfelter (1996: 38) offered, as a reason to accept Leacock as a serious economist, that "Jacob Viner was his student."

Craufurd Goodwin (1961: 193), the leading historian of Canadian economic thought and a proud McGill graduate, judged that "It was unfortunate both for Leacock and for Canadian economics that he was forced to earn a living from a subject which he disliked, was unable to comprehend, and took time away from areas where he made best use of his talents" (see also Innis 1944; Kushner and MacDonald 1977; Frankman 1986; Spotton 1995; and Kushner 2006 on Leacock as an economist). But Leacock was not forced to teach or write economics: he fought for the opportunity to teach economics in addition to political science. He joined McGill's newly founded Department of Economics and Political Science in 1901 as a lecturer in political science (promoted to associate professor of political science and history in 1906 upon publication of his first book), after a semester as a sessional instructor in history and political science. He was a successful lecturer in political science: Leacock wrote to the *McGill News* in 1936, at the time of his forced retirement, that he "never knew that my students went to Dr. Peterson in 1902 to speak for my permanent appointment" (Staines 2006: 292). The founding head of the department, A. W. (later Sir Alfred) Flux, had studied economics with Alfred Marshall at Cambridge and then become Stanley Jevons Professor of Political Economy at Manchester before bringing neoclassical Marshallian economics to Canada (Dimand and Neill 2010). Flux was not pleased when, without his permission, Leacock strayed from political science and began teaching courses in economics. Flux wrote to Veblen demanding to know whether Leacock was competent to teach economics but, characteristically, an amused Veblen replied in "curiously vague terms" so "for the sake of peace" Flux let Leacock continue teaching economics (Flux to Principal Peterson, quoted by Legate 1970: 42; see also Leacock to Peterson, January 31, 1906, in Staines 2006: 18–19). In 1908 Flux left Canada for the British Board of Trade and, because of his standing as a political scientist, Leacock succeeded as Head of the Department of Economics and Political Science, at first temporarily (permanently appointed by McGill's Board of Governors only in 1933 when someone noticed that this had never been done).

Succession to Flux as the William Dow Professor of Economics and Political Science did not imply that Leacock embraced mainstream economics. Already in February 1909 he wrote in the *University Magazine* that "economics is being buried alive in statistics and is degenerating into the science of the census" and in April 1910 in the same journal that "Political Economy is that which proves that we can know nothing of the laws of wealth . . . When

I sit and warm my hands, as best I may, at the little heap of embers that is now Political Economy, I cannot but contrast its dying glow with the generous blaze of the vainglorious and triumphant science that once it was," sentiments befitting a student of Veblen (both articles reprinted in Leacock's *Essays and Literary Studies* in 1916 and quoted in Spadoni's introduction to Leacock 1998: xxviii).

3.   FROM ACADEMIC TO PUBLIC INTELLECTUAL

Two happenstances transformed Stephen Leacock from a successful Canadian teacher and textbook writer in political science and a shakier teacher of economics to an internationally known public intellectual who would be commissioned by the *New York Times* to write the series of articles that became *The Unsolved Riddle of Social Justice* (1920a); to receive, by 1920, honorary doctorates from Queen's and the University of Toronto in Canada, Brown University and Dartmouth College south of the border; and by 1923 to be the subject of a volume in the "Makers of Canadian Literature" series (see Legate 1970, following page 162, for a photograph of Leacock and Herbert Hoover taking doctorates at Brown in 1917).

In 1905, Earl Grey, the Governor General of Canada (and donor of the Canadian Football League's Grey Cup), asked Principal Peterson for a lecturer to "wake up Ottawa + keep it awake." Every second Friday from January to April 1906, Leacock gave a series of six lectures on the British Empire to students, Cabinet ministers, members of Parliament, civil servants and, at the last two lectures, Lord Grey and his entourage (see Leacock's summary of the lectures in a Toronto speech, "Greater Canada: An Appeal," in Leacock 1973). Leacock called for Great Britain and the Dominions such as Australia, New Zealand, South Africa and Canada (but not India or African colonies[8]) to join as partners in an imperial federation. His denial that the Monroe Doctrine protected Canada and his urging that Canada build a navy[9] as a contribution to the Empire provoked a rebuttal from the audience by the Minister of Militia. Although Grey found Leacock's otherwise-impressive Ottawa lectures too anti-American ("treading on one's neighbor's corns"), he resolved on "turning Dr. Leacock loose . . . as an Imperial missionary." McGill University granted Leacock a year's leave (the original request to the board of governors, made directly by Lord Grey rather than by Leacock, was for two years) to lecture from April 1907 to March 1908 in Montreal, London, Oxford, Australia, New Zealand, South Africa and Vancouver. The Rhodes Trust sponsored the tour, while Lord Grey promised to pay personally for any cost overrun. "When I state that these lectures were followed almost immediately by the Union of South Africa, the Banana Riots in Trinidad, and the Turco-Italian War, I think the reader can form some idea of their importance" (Leacock 1912: ix). In England,

Leacock presented his views on the proper increased role of the Dominions in Imperial decision-making in a colloquial parable about "John Bull, Farmer" that Rudyard Kipling hailed as just what was needed but that Winston Churchill, then a Liberal and Parliamentary Undersecretary at the Colonial Office, dismissed as "offensive twaddle" (Legate 1970: 44–6; Moritz and Moritz 1985: 109–16; and Bowker's introduction to Leacock 1973: xii–xiv). In 1908, when Leacock returned from his triumphal tour of the British Empire and Flux vacated the professorial chair, Leacock was the obvious choice as William Dow Professor of Political Economy and Head of the Department.

Lord Grey made Leacock a public intellectual. In 1910 the British publisher John Lane,[10] on a visit to Montreal, happened to pick up a copy of Leacock's *Literary Lapses*, a collection of humorous sketches that Leacock had published at his own expense after they were rejected by Houghton Mifflin, the publisher of his politics textbook. Lane, who had prospered from British rights to Robert Service's Klondike poems, recognized a potential best-seller in the book that he had casually bought at a newsstand to read on the ship back to England and so Leacock's other, lucrative career as a humorist began and flourished (Staines 2006: 58–87). With assistance from Lord Grey and John Lane, from his own wit and charm, and from economics and political science sharing the same department at McGill (as at other Canadian universities such as Toronto, Queen's and Saskatchewan), Leacock acquired extraordinary prominence as a Canadian political economist, public intellectual, and popular and scholarly writer by the time that Jacob Viner found Leacock's teaching of advanced economics farcical (which, in turn, was Leacock's opinion of economics). Leacock went on to publish sixty or so books and hundreds of articles ranging from scholarly articles (Leacock 1928, 1935, 1943 on the economics of aviation, "What is Left of Adam Smith?" and the need for geographical science, respectively) to newspaper serializations of his humorous books (e.g. Leacock 1912, the oft-reprinted *Sunshine Sketches of a Little Town*, was originally commissioned as twelve articles in the *Montreal Star*) and of his more serious books (e.g. Leacock 1937, winner of the Governor General's Award for Nonfiction, serialized as twenty-seven articles in the *Globe and Mail* and twelve in the *Montreal Star*). Even the four-act stage version of *Sunshine Sketches* appeared in *Maclean's Magazine* from May to July 1917 (with articles by Leacock in seven of the other monthly issues that year).

Few if any other economics professors had either such a wide audience or Leacock's problem that his audience expected his work to be funny. As another admirer of Veblen remarked, in the best-known evocation of bygone small-town Ontario since Leacock's *Sunshine Sketches*, "Humor is richly rewarding to the person who employs it. It has some value in gaining and holding attention. But it has no persuasive value at all" (Galbraith 1964: 76).

4.   THE UNSOLVED RIDDLE OF SOCIAL JUSTICE

Stephen Leacock wrote *The Unsolved Riddle of Social Justice* in the shadow of the Winnipeg general strike (see Bercuson 1990; Kramer 2010; and, for the history of the strike compiled by the strikers themselves, Penner 1973), the Canadian counterpart of the upheavals shaking the world from Petrograd to Seattle at the close of the Great War. A more local provocation was the acerbic young English socialist Harold Laski, who had lectured in political science at McGill from 1914 to 1916. Although a Tory and anti-socialist, monarchist and Imperialist, Leacock was no partisan of *laissez-faire* or free trade and shared Veblen's jaundiced view of the idle rich, including (or especially) Leacock's relatives by marriage: "the obvious and glaring fact of the money power, the shameless luxury of the rich, the crude, uncultivated and boorish mob of vulgar men and over-dressed women that masquerades as high society . . . The plutocrat, unfettered by responsibility, seems as rapacious and remorseless as the machinery that has made him" (written in 1917, quoted by Bowker in Leacock 1973: xxiii, xxix). Plutoria, the setting of *Arcadian Adventures with the Idle Rich* (1914), was no gentle satire but a dire warning of the cultural disaster of modern, urban money-getting (American, in Leacock's mind) threatening the bucolic Mariposa of *Sunshine Sketches of a Little Town* (1912), where Leacock's satire had been gentle (even if not always appreciated as such by the residents of Orillia, the model for Mariposa). Leacock had before his eyes the example of his wife's uncle, Sir Henry Pellatt, the extravagant builder of a never-completed castle, Casa Loma, a vast folly that is today a tourist attraction in Toronto (see Staines 2006: 199, for a February 1929 letter from Leacock trying to dissuade his mother-in-law from lending her grandson's inheritance to Sir Henry to use in his failing projects).

"With all our wealth, we are still poor," wrote Leacock (1920a, 1973: 79–80). "After a century and a half of labour-saving machinery, we work about as hard as ever ... There are many senses in which the machine age seems to leave the great bulk of civilized humanity, the working part of it, worse off instead of better. The nature of our work has changed. No man now makes anything. He makes only a part of something." But "only a false medievalism can paint the past in colours superior to the present" because of "the universal spread of elementary education, the universal access to the printed page, and the universal hope of better things, if not for oneself, at least for one's children."

Like John Stuart Mill, Leacock distinguished immutable laws of production from mutable arrangements for distribution: "The real truth," according to Leacock (1920a, 1973: 114), "is that prices and wages and all the various payments from hand to hand in industrial society, are the outcome of a complex of competing forces that are not based upon justice but upon 'economic strength'" – an opinion more typical for a social reformer than for an economics professor in Canada, or elsewhere, in 1920. Leacock recognized the injustice of the existing inequality and deplored unrestrained individualism, yet he considered socialist utopias such as Edward Bellamy's *Looking Backwards* quixotic: elected managers would be self-interested and no better or different from current short-sighted, squabbling, corruptible politicians. "Socialism is a mere beautiful dream, possible only for the angels. The attempt to establish it would hurl us over the abyss. Our present lot is sad, but the frying pan is at least better than the fire" (1920a, 1973: 83). He stood firm against inflationary creation of paper money to try to expand output and employment.

If capitalist society is unjust but socialism is unpracticable, what is to be done? Leacock (1920a) called for public support of the aged and infirm, for sanitation, housing, education and children's nutrition, funded by maintaining the high wartime levels of taxation on high incomes and for production to be privately organized and operated but publicly regulated. Minimum wages and working conditions were to be regulated. Recognizing the incentive problems of government provision of employment, he nevertheless held that, providing the wages in make-work projects were low enough to make them a last resort, government should guarantee jobs for all. Written by a Tory, but in the context of general strikes and fear of revolution, it is an approach that sounds more Progressive (in the American use of the term) than Tory, let alone Imperialist. Once the crisis of general strike and potential world revolution abated, Leacock turned from remaking the world to amusing it, carrying on from *Winsome Winnie* (1920b) more than from *The Unsolved Riddle of Social Justice* (1920a), and he also attended to his teaching career, revising *The Elements of Political Science* (1921). But *The Unsolved Riddle of Social Justice* was the fullest revelation of the serious social analyst and reformer who was to be so often overlooked in the public's preoccupation with the humor of "Canada's Mark Twain." When Canada was gripped by another convulsive crisis, the Great Depression, such ideas from Leacock (1920a) as minimum wages, regulated working conditions, government regulation of business, and government responsibility for the unemployed reappeared in the "Bennett New Deal," proposed in radio talks by Prime Minister R. B. Bennett that were published with a preface by Stephen Leacock.

5.   THE LATER LEACOCK

Upholding the British connection against closer American ties, Leacock had campaigned for the Conservatives in the 1911 election against Liberal Prime Minister Laurier's reciprocity treaty for tariff reduction with the United States.[11] In *Economic Prosperity in the British Empire* (1930) and *Back to*

Prosperity: The Great Opportunity of the Empire Conference (1932), Leacock responded to the Great Depression by embracing what was then being promoted in Britain by the Canadian-born newspaper publisher Lord Beaverbrook as Empire Free Trade, the British Empire as a trading block with internal free trade but an external tariff wall (although Leacock's booklets did not mention Beaverbrook's Empire Crusade).[12] Even though the USA had begun tariff hikes with the Smoot–Hawley Tariff Act of 1930, most economists doubted that a trade war between the British Empire and the United States would have benefited Canada, or that the world depression could be ended by taxing trade. According to Margaret Macmillan (2009: 90), "when Keynes was asked by an English publisher for his opinion on Leacock's . . . *Economic Prosperity in the British Empire*, on how to deal with the Depression, he dismissed it as 'extraordinarily commonplace' and recommended against publication." The Macmillan Company of Canada published Leacock (1930) in Toronto, but the parent company did not publish it in Britain.

More helpfully (but unoriginally), Leacock (1933), an eighteen-page pamphlet, proposed public works, lowering tariff walls, and reducing the gold content of the Canadian dollar, but insisted that reducing the metallic value of money be done without any price inflation. Myron Frankman (1986: 56) claimed that "some of the central elements of analysis and policy in Leacock's 1933 *Plan to Relieve the Depression* are at the heart of Keynes's *General Theory*" merely because Leacock (1933: 1) remarked that a worker thrown out of work spends less, causing further contraction. Such secondary rounds of spending and employment were well known to Walter Bagehot and to Alfred and Mary Marshall, and even appeared in a funeral oration by Pericles as reported by Plutarch. As Frankman conceded, Leacock lacked Keynes's explanation of how an initial change in spending and employment would lead to a finite change in equilibrium income and employment rather than unbounded contraction or expansion. Faced with an impending election after years of ineffectual response to the Great Depression, R. B. Bennett, Conservative prime minister since 1930, gave five radio addresses in January 1935 belatedly proposing an activist "New Deal" for Canada (Bennett 1935; see also Wilbur 1968), following on the previous year's creation of the Bank of Canada.[13] Leacock, who had campaigned with Bennett against free trade in 1911, was consulted by Bennett about monetary policy and wrote the introduction to the published version of the radio talks, but wisely declined Bennett's invitation to stand as a Conservative in the 1935 election in Orillia, site of Leacock's summer home (see Legate (1970: 197) for Bennett's flattering letter offering nomination). Acts for minimum wages, unemployment insurance and other reforms were passed by Parliament but rejected by the Supreme Court of Canada and the Judicial Committee of the Privy Council as intruding on the powers of Canada's provinces.

In the *Atlantic Monthly*, Leacock (1936b) rebuked Keynes for using mathematical formulas, imagined well-known poems such as "The Charge of the Light Brigade" translated into mathematics, and pronounced that "Mathematical economics is what in criminal circles is termed 'a racket'" (Macmillan 2009: 91; Clotfelter 1996: 60). Although Leacock insisted in the preface to *Hellements of Hickonomics in Hiccoughs of Verse Done in Our Social Planning Mill* (1936a: vi, x)[14] that readers "will find no ill-nature in it," he declared that

> Forty years of hard work on economics has pretty well removed all the ideas I ever had about it. I think the whole science is a wreck and has got to be built up again. For our social problems there is about as much light to be found in the older economics as from a glow-worm.[15] Only one or two things seem to me clear. Cast-iron communism is nothing but a penitentiary.

Among the few economic truths that did seem clear to him (1936a: ix), "I do not mean . . . to deny the need and the expediency of tariff protection. We are not yet ready for the Kingdom of Heaven of Universal Free Trade. In our present world it would tend to force down the wages of all nations to the wages of the lowest" although he did think that the post-First World War world had "gone tariff-mad." Monetary heretics, such as the Social Credit regime that won office in Alberta in 1935 (see Leacock 1937), were no more insightful than mainstream economists: "my old friend and one-time colleague,[16] Professor Frederick Soddy . . . and others hold that the banker in 'coining credit' defrauds the public of what belongs to society at large. Personally I don't see it: as witness below" (Leacock 1936a: 55).

Leacock did not feel obliged to read deeply in contemporary economics before judging it. Carl Goldenberg recalled that Leacock

> had his prejudices, particularly against mathematical economists. I always suspected that this was in part due to the fact that Irving Fisher of Yale was one of this breed. He was a teetotaler [and Prohibitionist] and so Leacock had no use for him or his approach to economics. I remember buying Keynes's *General Theory of Employment, Interest and Money* when it appeared in 1936 and proudly showing it to Leacock. He opened the book but, unfortunately, at one of the few pages with algebraic equations. He thereupon threw it down and, in disgust, as he walked away, said: 'Goldenberg, this is the end of John Maynard Keynes.' (Collard 1975: 49)[17]

Ridiculing the formula for Keynes's investment multiplier (which he garbled in attempted quotation), Leacock declared, "now I do not know what all that Delta and Y stuff just quoted means, but I am certain that if I did I could write it out . . . plainly and simply" (quoted in Clotfelter 1996: 60).

In 1936, to Leacock's widely publicized outrage,[18] he was one of thirteen professors retired by McGill University upon reaching the age of 65. As Lewis

Douglas (McGill principal from 1937 to 1939) recalled regarding another case, retirement was mandatory at 65 but "There were, however, escape clauses" (Collard 1975: 246). Such "escape clauses" would no doubt have been invoked for Leacock's benefit by General Sir Arthur Currie, commander of the Canadian Corps in the First World War and then from 1920 Principal and Vice-Chancellor of McGill. But Currie, Leacock's student at Upper Canada College in the 1890s (see "Generals I Have Trained" in Leacock 1945a), had died in 1933. Leacock's outrage against being retired had a weakness: in January 1935 Leacock had written and printed a four-page "confidential and not for circulation" pamphlet of *Suggestions for Economy at McGill*, expanded as *The Restoration of the Finances of McGill University, Suggestions Submitted to the Consideration of My Fellow Members of the University*, proposing to save money by pensioning off senior professors nearing retirement age (Legate 1970: 196; Staines 1986: 151), with the unspoken, and in the event unfounded, assumption that of course he would be exempted.

6.   CONCLUSION

First as a lecturer upholding Canada's place in the British Empire and then as a best-selling humorist, Stephen Leacock attracted an audience exceptional for a professor of economics and political science while his success as a political scientist combined with the appointment to head a two-discipline department gave him a more debatable public standing as an economist. Although the success of his popular writings also gave him a vast audience for books and newspaper and magazine articles on serious political and economic subjects, it also led to his being pigeonholed as a humorist. But though he was indeed a humorist and a "character" (and a Tory and Imperialist), and though he disdained, and lacked training in, technical economics (unlike political science), Leacock was a social scientist and political economist in the tradition of Mill who thought seriously about social justice and the alleviation of inequality and poverty, as well as a fierce critic and satirist of plutocracy, the idle rich and mainstream economics in the tradition of his teacher Veblen, while also upholding the gold standard and stridently warning against inflation in the tradition of his teacher Laughlin (see Leacock 1945a, 1945b). Leacock occupied an extraordinary position in political economy in Canada and to an extent in other English-speaking countries in the "Progressive Era."

NOTES

1. However, when the International Mark Twain Society awarded Leacock the Mark Twain Medal in 1935, they cited him as "The Modern Aristophanes" (Moritz and Moritz 1985: 266).
2. The Conservative Party took the name Progressive Conservative in 1942, when it chose John Bracken, the Progressive Premier of Manitoba, as national leader in the hope of attracting Progressive votes against the Liberals in the 1945 election, and governed Canada under that name from 1957 to 1963, 1979 to 1980, and 1984 to 1993. The Progressive Conservatives were eventually absorbed at the federal level by the Canadian Alliance (originally, as the Reform Party, a right-wing breakaway from the Progressive Conservatives) into what is again the Conservative Party, although most provincial counterparts (e.g. in Ontario) retain the name Progressive Conservative (exceptions include the United Conservative Party in Alberta and the Saskatchewan Party in Saskatchewan, while the provincial conservative party in British Columbia is called the Liberal Party, not affiliated with the Liberal Party of Canada). Non-Canadian readers are exempt from the quiz at the start of the next class.
3. Although David Legate (1970: 100) wrote of the title piece that "From the standpoint of popular satire, this was one of his best pieces," Margaret Macmillan (2009: 61) characterizes Leacock (1919) as "nasty and not at all funny. At its end, the former Kaiser, now a ragged street peddler in the Bowery, dies of his injuries after a traffic accident." However, the book does include an account of a club raising funds for Belgian war relief (Leacock's first humorous lecture tour was for the Belgian Relief Fund): when the treasurer announces the campaign has a deficit of $200, there is a motion to donate the entire deficit to the Belgian refugees.
4. "Gertrude the Governess" became famous when, in a political speech, Theodore Roosevelt quoted the sentence in which the lovelorn Lord Ronald "flung himself from the room, flung himself upon his horse and rode madly off in all directions" (Legate 1970: 55). Leacock's article on bimetallism attracted no such attention.
5. Laughlin edited an abridged edition of Mill's *Principles*, adding American examples and omitting the chapters on applications to social philosophy that enabled Mill, in his later years, to consider himself as in some sense a socialist. As Frankman (1986: 52) noted, Leacock exempted Mill from his aspersions on mainstream economics because Mill was "a human being first and an economist afterwards" (Leacock 1930: 165), "one of the makers of the modern world . . . as noble-minded as he was clear-headed."
6. In *Arcadian Adventures*, Leacock shared Veblen's disdain for the conduct of universities by businessmen yet he later became close to Sir Edward Beatty, president of the Canadian Pacific Railway and chancellor of McGill University from 1920 until his death in 1943. Like Beatty, Leacock opposed the (Conservative) federal government turning two bankrupt transcontinental lines (whose bonds had government guarantees) into Canadian National Railways.
7. Leacock opposed higher education of women as distracting to male students but at least once wrote to Laughlin recommending a female student for graduate study in economics at Chicago (and helped pay for the medical education of his sister, Dr. Rosamond Leacock, who became a pathologist at Toronto's Hospital for Sick Children). His gibes at women's supposed incapacity for practical business are ironic given his most famous essay, "My Financial Career" (in Leacock 1910),

about his hapless attempt to open a bank account. Leacock's defense of women's traditional place in the home reflected personal trauma as well as conservative commonplace: clutching a buggy whip, the 17-year-old Leacock drove his drunken, wife-beating father from the family home, threatening to kill him if he ever returned. Leacock never again saw his father, who lived until 1940 (Legate 1970: 22; Moritz and Moritz 1985: 58–9, 309–10; Taylor 1982: 105; Staines 2006: 441 – but see Alex Lucas in Staines 1986: 124–5 for skepticism about the story). However, Leacock's opposition to women's suffrage (Leacock 1911 and his 1915 essay on "The Woman Question" reprinted in Leacock 1973) rested largely on suffragist support for prohibition of alcohol.

8.   Margaret Macmillan (2009: 114–16) documents that Leacock's views about non-white colonized peoples and non-British immigration were fully as problematic in modern eyes as those of the Progressives discussed in Thomas Leonard's *Illiberal Reformers* (2016), with the qualification that Leacock sharply revised those views in his writings during the Second World War, when he denounced "race hatred," and with the exception, surprising for his class and background and the McGill University of his day, that "One of the few prejudices of his time he seems not to have shared is against Jews."

9.   The Royal Canadian Navy, which barely existed at the start of the Great War, was the world's fifth-largest navy at the end of the Second World War.

10. John Lane was the father of Allen Lane, who founded Penguin as a paperback imprint for the family firm.

11. Reciprocity was rejected at the Canadian election of 1911, but at the time of writing, ratification of the successor to the North American Free Trade Agreement is before the US Congress.

12. But see Beaverbrook's letter praising Leacock (1930), quoted by Moritz and Moritz (1985: 237–38). At the time of writing, as Britain is about to leave the European Union, advocates of "Brexit" again dream of Britain leading a Commonwealth trading bloc based on the former British Empire.

13. To Leacock's "heartiest approval," his former student Graham Towers became the first Governor of the Bank of Canada, serving for two decades: "Graham Towers has distinguished himself as that happy combination of a practical banker and theoretical economist for which the world usually looks in vain" (Leacock, "Graham Towers," *McGill Daily*, December 5, 1934, quoted by Fullerton 1986: 18, 21). In 1943 Keynes, supported by Peacock, proposed Towers to head the Bank of England (Fullerton 1986: 192–4). Nearly three quarters of a century later a governor of the Bank of Canada was translated to the Bank of England but in 1943 the Court of Directors was appalled at the suggestion of electing a colonial and "a dollar man" as governor.

14. Leacock considered *Hellements* his favorite among his entire lighter output (Legate 1970: 208) and it is excerpted in Clotfelter (1996: 125–6) but "I had a hard knock when I got my New York publishers returns. – My poor Hickonomics didn't sell at all!" (Staines 2006: 294). Nonetheless his economic views remained in demand from the press, with his series on "The Gathering Financial Crisis of Canada" appearing in Britain's *Morning Post* starting July 6, 1936, the day after the arrival of Canada's Finance Minister (Moritz and Moritz 1985: 278–9; the articles were published in Canada as a book, by Macmillan of Canada). In the last months of his life, Leacock published a series of ten articles on "What's Ahead for Canada?" in the *Financial Post* from December 4, 1943, to February 5, 1944, expanding an article in *Maclean's* magazine. In January 1936 he had declined to

commit to a twice-weekly column in the *Financial Post*, but often contributed serious economic and political articles there. On August 20, 1939, again mixing humor with critique of economics, he published "Lost in the Jungle of Economics" in the *New York Times Magazine*. While primarily directing his economic views to the general public (Leacock 1930, 1932, 1933) and ridiculing academic economics (Leacock 1936a, 1936b, 1939), he also on occasion tried to persuade the discipline (Leacock 1934).

15. In a chapter "Has Economics Gone to Seed?" (in Leacock 1939: 144), he elaborated on this image: "When the world is in danger of collapse from the dilemma of wealth and want, the college economists can shed no light – or only a multitude of crosslights that will not focus to a single beam – in place of a lighthouse, wreckers' signals, or at best, fireworks, elaborate and meaningless."

16. Soddy wrote his monetary books while holding the chair of chemistry at Oxford but had been teaching chemistry at McGill when participating in the research on radioactivity that won Soddy the 1921 Nobel Prize in Chemistry and his McGill colleague Ernest Rutherford the 1908 Nobel Prize in Chemistry. Leacock reported that, like mathematical economics, "the whole mass of the Einstein geometry" was dismissed by "the real modern physicists, such as Rutherford and Soddy" as "neither here nor there" (quoted in Clotfelter 1996: 60).

17. Margaret Macmillan (2009: 89–90) suggests that the only book by Keynes that Leacock seems to have read thoroughly was *The Economic Consequences of the Peace* (1919), not likely to appeal to the fervent Imperialist who published *The Hohenzollerns in America* the same year. Myron Frankman (1986: 53) reported that Leacock's handwritten chapter outline in 1926 for a never-completed anthology of political economy since Adam Smith included Keynes along with Frank Taussig, Gustav Cassell and Norman Angell (but not Veblen) for the twentieth century, but that Keynes's name was crossed out.

18. His statement in the *Montreal Star* was "I have plenty to say about the governors putting me out of the university, but I have all eternity to say it in. I shall shout it *down* to them" (Legate 1970: 200). Legate (1970: 210–11) reported that "In an editorial the *New York Times* saw benefits for any American university which might employ Leacock 'to smoke at its post-graduate students,' or create a post of resident wit or satirist" and that the University of British Columbia offered him a professorship in economics.

REFERENCES

André-Aigret, Constance and Robert W. Dimand. 2018. "Populism versus Economic Expertise: J. Laurence Laughlin Debates William (Coin) Harvey." *Forum for Social Economics* 47, no. 2: 164–72.

Ayres, Clarence E. 1920. "Review of *The Unsolved Riddle of Social Justice* by Stephen Leacock." *Journal of Political Economy* 28, no. 5: 439–40.

Bennett, Richard Bedford. 1935. *The Premier Speaks to the People*. Ottawa: Dominion Conservative Headquarters.

Bercuson, Donald Jay. 1990 [1974]. *Confrontation at Winnipeg: Labour, Industrial Relations and the General Strike*. Montreal and Kingston, ON: McGill-Queen's University Press.

Clotfelter, Caroline Postelle (ed.). 1996. *On the Third Hand: Humor in the Dismal Science, an Anthology*. Ann Arbor: University of Michigan Press.

Collard, Edgar Andrew (ed.). 1975. *The McGill You Knew: An Anthology of Memories 1920–1960*. Don Mills, ON: Longman Canada.

Dimand, Robert W. 2017. "Canada 150: Canadian Social Scientists and the Making of Public Policy since Confederation." *Canadian Public Policy* 43, no. 4: 376–90.

Dimand, Robert W. and Robin F. Neill. 2010. "Marshall in Canada." In *The Impact of Alfred Marshall's Ideas*, ed. Tiziano Raffaelli, Giacomo Becattini, Katia Caldari and Marco Dardi. Cheltenham, UK, and Northampton, MA: Edward Elgar, pp. 53–8.

Frankman, Myron J. 1986. "Stephen Leacock, Economist: Owl Among the Parrots." In *Stephen Leacock: A Reappraisal*, ed. David Staines. Ottawa: University of Ottawa Press, pp. 51–8.

Fullerton, Douglas. 1986. *Graham Towers and his Times*. Toronto: McClelland & Stewart.

Galbraith, John Kenneth. 1964. *The Scotch*. Toronto: Macmillan of Canada.

Goodwin, Craufurd D. W. 1961. *Canadian Economic Thought: The Political Economy of a Developing Nation 1815–1914*. Durham, NC: Duke University Press.

Innis, Harold A. 1944. "Stephen Butler Leacock, 1869–1944." *Canadian Journal of Economics and Political Science* 10, May: 216–26.

Keynes, John Maynard. 1919. *The Economic Consequences of the Peace*. London: Macmillan.

Keynes, John Maynard. 1936. *The General Theory of Employment, Interest and Money*. London: Macmillan.

Kramer, Reinhold. 2010. *When the State Trembled: How A. J. Andrews and the Citizens Committee Broke the Winnipeg General Strike*. Toronto: University of Toronto Press.

Kushner, Joseph. 2006. "Leacock, Stephen (1896–1944)." In *Biographical Dictionary of American Economists*, ed. Ross B. Emmett. London and New York: Thoemmes Continuum, pp. 548–52.

Kushner, Joseph and R. Douglas MacDonald. 1977. "Leacock: Economist/Satirist." *Dalhousie Review* 56, Autumn: 493–509.

Leacock, Stephen B. 1907a. *Baldwin, Lafontaine, Hincks: Responsible Government*. Toronto: Morang.

Leacock, Stephen B. 1907b. "Responsible Government in the British Colonial System." *American Political Science Review* 1, May: 355–92.

Leacock, Stephen B. 1910. *Literary Lapses*. London and New York: John Lane.

Leacock, Stephen B. 1910–11. "Practical Political Economy." Parts I to XXV *Saturday Night*, November 12, 1910 to April 29, 1911.

Leacock, Stephen B. 1911. "The Political Rights of Women – The Case Against Suffrage." *Toronto Star Weekly*, May 13.

Leacock, Stephen B. 1912. *Sunshine Sketches of a Little Town*. Toronto: Bell and Cockburn; London and New York: John Lane; illustrated edn Toronto: McClelland & Stewart, 1996; also, as a series of 12 articles in the *Montreal Star*, February 17 to June 22, 1912.

Leacock, Stephen B. 1914. *Arcadian Adventures with the Idle Rich*. London and New York: John Lane.

Leacock, Stephen B. 1919. *The Hohenzollerns in America; With the Bolsheviks in Berlin and Other Impossibilities*. London: John Lane, The Bodley Head, and New York: John Lane.

Leacock, Stephen B. 1920a. *The Unsolved Riddle of Social Justice*. New York: John Lane, London: John Lane, The Bodley Head, and Toronto: S. B. Gundy; as reprinted in Leacock (1973), pp. 61–145.

Leacock, Stephen B. 1920b. *Winsome Winnie, and Other New Nonsense Novels*. New York: John Lane, London: John Lane, The Bodley Head, and Toronto: S. B. Gundy.

Leacock, Stephen B. 1921 [1906]. *Elements of Political Science*. [2nd edn]. Boston and New York: Houghton Mifflin, and London: Constable.

Leacock, Stephen B. 1928. "The Economic Aspects of Aviation." *Proceedings and Transactions of the Royal Society of Canada*, 3rd series, 22: 213–32.

Leacock, Stephen B. 1930. *Economic Prosperity in the British Empire*. Toronto: Macmillan of Canada, London: Constable.

Leacock, Stephen B. 1932. *Back to Prosperity: The Great Opportunity of the Empire Conference*. Toronto: Macmillan of Canada, London: Constable.

Leacock, Stephen B. 1933. *Stephen Leacock's Plan to Relieve the Depression in 6 Days, To Remove It in 6 Months, To Eradicate It in 6 Years*. Toronto: Macmillan of Canada.

Leacock, Stephen B. 1934. "The Economic Analysis of Industrial Depression." *Papers and Proceedings of the Canadian Political Science Association* 5: 5–24.

Leacock, Stephen B. 1935. "What is Left of Adam Smith?." *Canadian Journal of Economics and Political Science* 1, no. 1: 41–51.

Leacock, Stephen B. 1936a. *Hellements of Hickonomics in Hiccoughs of Verse Done in Our Social Planning Mill*. New York: Dodd, Mead.

Leacock, Stephen B. 1936b. "Through a Glass Darkly." *Atlantic Monthly* 158, July: 94–8; reprinted in Clotfelter 1996, 53–60.

Leacock, Stephen B. 1937. *My Discovery of the West: A Discussion of East and West in Canada*. Toronto: Thomas Allen; also, as a series of 27 articles in *The Globe and Mail*, March 6 to May 24, 1937, and as 12 articles in the *Montreal Star*.

Leacock, Stephen B. 1939. *Too Much College; or, Education Eating Up Life*. New York: Dodd, Mead.

Leacock, Stephen B. 1943. "Plea for Geographical Science." *Queen's Quarterly* 50, February: 1–13.

Leacock, Stephen B. 1945a. *Last Leaves*. New York: Dodd, Mead.

Leacock, Stephen B. 1945b. *While There is Still Time: The Case against Social Catastrophe*. Toronto: McClelland & Stewart.

Leacock, Stephen B. 1973. *The Social Criticism of Stephen Leacock: The Unsolved Riddle of Social Justice and Other Essays*, ed. Alan Bowker. Toronto: University of Toronto Press.

Leacock, Stephen B. 1998. *My Recollections of Chicago and the Doctrine of Laissez Faire*, ed. Carlo Spadoni. Toronto: University of Toronto Press.

Legate, David M. 1970. *Stephen Leacock: A Biography*. Toronto and Garden City, NY: Doubleday.

Leonard, Thomas C. 2016. *Illiberal Reformers: Race, Eugenics and American Economics in the Progressive Era*. Princeton, NJ: Princeton University Press.

Macmillan, Margaret. 2009. *Stephen Leacock*. Toronto: Penguin.

Marshall, Alfred. 1890. *Principles of Economics*. London: Macmillan.

Mill, John Stuart. 1848. *The Principles of Political Economy, with Some of their Applications to Social Philosophy*. London: John W. Parker.

Moritz, Albert and Theresa Moritz. 1985. *Leacock: A Biography*. Toronto: Stoddart.

Morton, William Lewis. 1950. *The Progressive Party in Canada*. Toronto: University of Toronto Press.

Penner, Norman (ed.). 1973. *Winnipeg 1919: The Strikers' Own History of the Winnipeg General Strike*. Toronto: James Lewis & Samuel.

Ricardo, David. 1817. *On the Principles of Political Economy and Taxation.* London: John Murray.
Spotton, Brenda L. 1995. "Stephen Leacock, Economist." *Canadian Forum*, May: 12–13.
Staines, David (ed.). 1986. *Stephen Leacock: A Reappraisal.* Ottawa: University of Ottawa Press.
Staines, David (ed.). 2006. *The Letters of Stephen Leacock.* Toronto: Oxford University Press Canada.
Taylor, Charles. 1982. *Radical Tories: The Conservative Tradition in Canada.* Toronto: Anansi.
Veblen, Thorstein B. 1899. *The Theory of the Leisure Class.* New York: Viking.
Wilbur, Richard H. (ed.). 1968. *The Bennett New Deal: Fraud or Portent?.* Toronto: Copp Clark.

20. Trailblazing feminists at the turn of the twentieth century: a focus on Marianne Weber and Lou Andreas-Salomé

Christine Castelain-Meunier

1.   INTRODUCTION

At the turn of the twentieth century, politicians and scholars worldwide were busy wrestling with the issue of how society should be organized. In countries like France, the United States or Germany, social issues were discussed with much fervor throughout these troubled times, punctuated by great trade union gatherings and World's Fairs. The question of women's rights gained momentum, owing to women from a wide range of backgrounds. In what follows, I have chosen to focus on two such women (Marianne Weber and Lou Andreas-Salomé), who, despite having very little in common, are nevertheless emblematic of the trends just emerging at the time and which hold sway to this day. It should be borne in mind that, as early as antiquity, democratic systems have pitted the impoverished against the wealthy. This perennial theme runs from Aristotle's *Politics* to Machiavelli's *Florentine History*, in which the *popolo minuto* are distinct from the *popolo grasso*, a precursor to Marx's theory of class warfare (Vallet 2011).

In the past two decades, the impecunious have not only vied with the opulent, but they have also grappled with an even more destitute group, namely migrants. Today, the gulf between rich and poor has continued to widen, while xenophobia remains a constant threat on the horizon. The problem has been compounded by a combination of stalling social mobility and people's heightened fears of losing their position in society. At the same time, one of the most prominent forces shaping society may be described as *the flexibility of identity* (Castelain-Meunier 2002, 2005, 2013).

The *malleability of identity* would have been inconceivable, if it had not been for the blurring of boundaries between "masculine" and "feminine" identities. The liberalization of moral attitudes, to which women greatly contributed in the 1970s in the wake of previous feminist struggles, was characterized by the abolition of the patriarchy, first in the agrarian sector and then in the industrial domain. In the following sections, my focus will be on the works produced by Marianne Weber and Lou Andreas-Salomé, a key element of these struggles which were a hallmark of the turn of the twentieth century.

2.   THE AFTERMATH OF AGRARIAN AND INDUSTRIAL PATRIARCHY

The emergence of the woman question closely followed the advent of the industrial patriarchy, as the economy soon demanded that women contribute to the nation's output. This took place against the backdrop of a society ever more insistent on capital accumulation, which called on every man to be economically productive while maintaining the illusion of social improvement. On the one hand, women were denied all civic and social rights, and confined to the domestic sphere, while on the other hand, men assumed control of – and consequently restricted women's access to – the public sphere.

With the industrialization of the economy came the gradual separation of the public sphere from its private counterpart, a distinction which had previously been blurred in agrarian society, as described by Peter Laslett (1969) in *The World We Have Lost*. Capitalist society sought to replace a traditional agrarian way of life, which believed in monarchy, religion and a sacred/profane distinction which mapped onto the gender binary. Men were seen as the holy guardians of knowledge, while women could only thrive on base animal instinct.

Indeed, in the twelfth century the French term "homme" related to the impersonal pronoun "on," which echoed ideas of the collective, or of responsibility, whereas "femme" only referred to what was literally female. In France, this transition from traditional agrarian society to an industrial one was complete by the time of the French Revolution of 1789, which in the words of the historian Jean Delumeau (2005) could be thought of as "the end of patriarchy's golden age," with fathers losing their power over their adult sons and their rights to exclude women from inheriting property. This was a milestone for gender equality. Further advances were made a century later, when in 1883 primary school education was made compulsory for both boys and girls. Formal education, and the associated opportunity to earn a qualification, would enable women to stand out in their families.

In her book, Katherine Blunden (1982) highlighted an undercurrent of deep injustice and frustration which was increasingly prevalent among the women of her time. As growing numbers of women entered formal employment and had their first taste of independence, they became all the more conscious of the yawning discrepancy between their genuine contribution to society and their lack of civil rights, as well as their continued subjection at the hands of men. It was expected of women to play their part in the apparent social progress which came in the wake of capitalist modernization, while tolerating the continued denial of their just political rewards.

3.   WOMEN'S POSITION IN THE WEST, 1900–1950

When the First World War erupted, British and French women were recruited into arms factories as substitutes for their male counterparts who were now on the Western Front. The usual gender divisions were temporarily suspended to further the war effort. As early as 1920, the French feminist Nelly Roussel campaigned to separate sexuality from procreation and called for a sex strike on the Day for Celebrating Mothers of Extended Families (Michel 1979). But that did not prevent the French Parliament from passing legislation criminalizing birth control and increasing the fines for abortions. Simultaneously, a burgeoning school of thought called "personalism," which emphasized the dignity of human beings, laid the foundations for the feminist struggle for women's rights (Michel 1979). In the case of women, "personalism" rejected their conventional role as spouses or mothers, which in effect reduced them to little more than baby factories, which in turn justified the suppression of their political and economic rights. Not only did "personalism" reject all forms of gender discrimination, but in fact it also vehemently opposed any other kind of discrimination that pitted social classes or racial and ethnic groups against one another.

Taking a leaf out of Kantianism, one branch of "personalism" placed the subject at the center of human experience in general, and of moral experience in particular. Its purpose was to exalt the individual self, capable of being its own end. Communitarian "personalism," by contrast, was more of a spiritual school of thought, founded by Emmanuel Mounier, whose main medium was the journal *Esprit*. It sought a humanist third way, somewhere between *laissez-faire* capitalism, Marxism and anarchism. Mounier viewed liberty and creativity as the backbone of personhood and as essential for a healthy spiritual life.

And yet, in countries such as Germany, Italy or Spain, the conception of women as inferior beings proved unshakeable. Women were still regarded as not much else than a housewife expected to cater for her husband and the national-socialist state through child-bearing. Nazi Germany revolved around the three Ks: *Kinder, Küche, Kirche* (children, kitchen, church) and became the first country to decree that all women in the public sector be systematically laid off.

The Italian journalist, writer and former Communist politician Maria Antonietta Macciocchi (1922–2007) provided a telling account of the Nazi perception of women: "A woman is an animal of some sort. Her only natural bond is with the family; a woman who claims sexual liberty becomes just as impure as a Jew, a black man or a homosexual. Feminism is a *bourgeois* perversion, a violation of the natural order of things" (Macciocchi quoted in Michel 1979: 79).[1] In Spain, all the progressive breakthroughs made under the Republican regime (voting rights in 1931, abortion rights in Catalonia) were soon overturned by the Francoist regime.

After the First World War, women earned the right to vote in 21 countries, including England, Germany, the United States and the Netherlands. In 1936, the French socialist Leon Blum refused to grant voting rights to women. But four years earlier, women who were married to foreigners became allowed to retain their French citizenship. In 1938, women gained the right to hold their own ID cards without the explicit consent of their husbands. On April 21, 1944, women were officially able to vote as well as stand for election, just as men were. One year later, they would cast their first votes. These developments were made possible, in part, by feminist figures like Marianne Weber and Lou Andreas-Salomé, who, each in their own ways, exposed women's lack of civil rights as iniquitous, absurd and archaic, to the extent that the status quo was no longer tenable.

4.   MARIANNE WEBER, A CUTTING-EDGE SOCIOLOGIST AT THE HEART OF FEMINIST STRUGGLES

Considered one of the founding fathers of sociology, the German thinker Max Weber (1864–1920) made seminal contributions to our understanding of society's entrance into modernity, the advent of industrial capitalism, bureaucracy, industrial rationalism, Protestant ethics, and the relationship between meaning and action. His wife, Marianne Weber (1870–1954) was also a leading figure of German feminism (Dupré et al. 2016). Her work did not attract the attention it deserved at the time and has only recently begun to attract serious academic interest.

In Germany, some feminists had added their voices to the Revolution of 1848. Among their ranks were a number of societies and newspapers run by women. Radical new ideas started to permeate trade unions, political parties and professional circles. The International Women's Congress, which gathered in Paris in 1888, put their movement front and center on the world stage. Among their most pressing demands were reforms to the Napoleonic Code's provisions concerning the status of married women, voting rights, maternity rights and the professionalization of social work.

A politically committed activist, Marianne Weber became a Member of Parliament under the banner of the German Democratic Party. She served as chairman of the Federation of German Women's Associations from 1919 to

1923, and became an honorary Doctor of Laws in 1924. Two years after that, she published a biography of her husband entitled *Max Weber: Ein Lebensbild* (Weber 1926).

As an academic, she was interested in domestic labor and the extent of women's access to university. Weber was also a pioneer in investigating the lives of those who were socially, legally and politically disenfranchised. She denied the existence of value-neutral ways of thinking and inquired into the pace of change in a world of both new ideas and prejudices. Her treatise *The New Woman* (Weber 1919) (first published in 1914[2]) attacked the view which held that universal human rights were separate from women's rights. On her view, the rise of feminist figures, the issue of women's position in the workplace and female prototypes such as those of the prostitute and the *bourgeois* woman were all part of the emergent social realities of industrial society, as the rigid separation of public and private became increasingly challenged. New rights to education, autonomy and decision-making overturned the established order. Additionally, Marianne Weber produced innovative reflections on universalism and female exceptionalism. She did so by leading the way for change, denying women's inferior status and pushing for equal rights and opportunities. All in all, she advocated that women should have their ability "to unleash their full feminine potential."

Unlike the sociologist Georg Simmel (2013), Marianne Weber did not perceive the masculine and the feminine as two complementary poles. For Weber, women and men are both generic and gendered beings all at once. Both writers ran salons – providing areas of stimulating intellectual discussions on a variety of fields – which numbered several educated women among their attendees, at a time when women were beginning to gain access to universities.

Marianne Weber's *Wife and Mother in the Development of Law*, a multidisciplinary work blending sociology, law and history, was published in 1907. She also wrote a biography that flattered her husband tremendously, and his sociological articles were compiled into *Frauenfragen und Frauengedanken* (Weber 1919). In these papers, we find accounts of the political problems of the day – the future of Germany, the rise of the labor and feminist movements, the consequences of the defeat of 1918 and the impending revolution which followed, as well as the birth of the Weimar Republic – which are helpful for contextualizing women's militancy in the period (Hadot 1977).

Among Marianne Weber's preferred research themes were the role of women as producers of knowledge, evolutions in marriage legislation, women's position in romantic or sexual relationships, the value of domestic work, sexual differences from both objective and subjective viewpoints, Parliamentary work and the new woman (Dupré 2016). These variables were key to transforming the feminine condition and remained the order of the day as the next generation of civil rights advocates took over. The goal was invariably the same: enabling women to embrace their full potential, breaking away from the confines of the reductive dichotomy of housewife or mother.

Marianne Weber should be credited with exposing the political ideologies that legitimized the division between private and public sphere for the benefit of male domination. She revealed the politics underpinning this hierarchy, even whilst insisting on a concern for equality. By contrast, Weber's feminist ally Lou Andreas-Salomé concentrated her efforts on another facet of female struggle, namely the question of identity.

5.   LOU ANDREAS-SALOMÉ: THE WILL TO REUNIFY MIND AND SPIRIT

A German novelist and psychoanalyst of Russian extraction, Lou Andreas-Salomé (1861–1937) was another distinguished figure of female emancipation. Her works were burnt by the Nazis along with those of her fellow psychoanalyst Sigmund Freud. In this section I seek to echo her willingness to reunite mind and spirit at a time when institutions reflected an appetite for production, rationality, materialism and economic expansion which invariably marginalized women. A woman who cared for liberty, tolerance and love, Andreas-Salomé sought to identify the conditions which might generate "acquiescence to life," "love of the living" and "wholeness" (Andreas-Salomé 1984). In Europe, she stood at the forefront of the creative process which would end with the First World War. She explored the idea of the inner life and "being fully oneself." Yet, despite having authored about twenty books, articles and various literary texts and autobiographies, she is usually cited in relation to other luminaries of her time whom she knew. This does not do justice to the variety of her intellectual writings, whose topics ranged from God to narcissism, not to mention her commentaries on Nietzsche's works.

Andreas-Salomé's conception of the "self" is a direct allusion to the disappearance of God that goes hand in hand with the pursuit of individuality. According to Dorian Astor (2017), the delineation of the individual clarifies the boundary between self and world. This is to be contrasted with Andreas-Salomé's idea "whole," of a "return to wholeness," which in her view is aligned with maternity and creation (Astor 2008). The self, initially lonely, morphs into a creature that has the power to create. Also at stake is the problem of narcissism, which should be construed as the indifference of the self toward the world. Andreas-Salomé's acute grasp of femininity must not be forgotten. It permeated her writings as well as her sentimental life: the consequence of any psyche committed to a life of creation.

The friendship and mutual admiration between her and Freud is seen in their correspondence between 1912 and 1926, as well as in Freud's decision to entrust Lou Andreas-Salomé with the task of helping his own daughter find her own feminine self. That was in spite of their personal disagreements on the hypothesis of the fundamental unity and oneness of humanity. Freud was indebted to her for his own insights into both feminine sexuality and the myriad instincts that drive religious sentiment. He also owed her a significant part of his conception of life and the spirit, as expounded in his last work *Moses and Monotheism* (1939).

In Marianne Weber and Lou Andreas-Salomé, we find exponents of two complementary shades of feminist activism. One is concerned with the exclusion of women from public life and their desire to break free from the chains of the household, while the other is more interested in women's inner lives, their liberty and their creativity (Hirt 2017; Michaud 2017).

Regrettably, their output has been severely neglected in comparison with more illustrious men. As a result, we have been unable to fully appreciate their own specific thoughts, influences or contributions to life, whether at the intellectual, social or cultural level. Fortunately, a wave of publications has emerged in recent years, which has shed light on their innovations; consequently we have been able to uncover both their personal insights and their connections with the more well-known figures around them.

Of equal interest is the startling prescience of their cause, which is in keeping with the forces that have shaped modern times. Indeed, these two women were not only responsible for considerable change in their time, but they also unleashed a tide of feminist agitation which has endured to this day. They raised awareness of the major obstacles to women's liberation – that is to say, institutions, norms, rules and stereotypes. Wary of the pitfalls of pejorative labels and narrow forms of sisterhood, they championed reflective thinking and a return to one's feminine self. They were successful in opening up a conversation within a framework of gender dialectic and otherness, gaining ground in the fight against gender discrimination, either through a career in politics – Marianne Weber – or in a more introspective and lyrical fashion – Lou Andreas-Salomé. To be precise, Marianne Weber's efforts were directed toward civil equality between men and women, which necessitates/requires a realignment of gender relations in both the public and private spheres. Lou Andreas-Salomé, for her part, was involved in the fight for the sake of women's identity, free from religious interference and the images of femininity and stereotypes which were manufactured by men.

Marianne Weber and Lou Andreas-Salomé epitomized two complementary approaches to what was then groundbreaking research on gender. In this regard, their cumulative efforts aptly reflect the two aspects identified by Guillaume Vallet (2018), the one comprising "the socially constructed dimension of sex" and the other being "the gender binary and masculine domination." The feminist struggles of the second half of the twentieth century would essentially be organized along these two lines. Between 1900 and 1950, however, any campaigns in favor of equal living standards between all individuals made scant reference to the plight of women. For many women, the First World War had awoken a sense of profound mistrust toward masculine culture, which frequently returned to the tropes of conquest, victory and trench warfare. Such unprecedented suffering as was experienced during the Great War led to new challenges to masculine ideals (Cabbanes 2018).

6.   CONCLUSION

The 1920s saw a greater focus on the struggle for equality, fueled by Enlightenment philosophy and a desire to put culture at the center of education. As rural patriarchy was on the wane, the French political scientist Alexis de Tocqueville promoted the notion of social mobility in the industrialized world in his work *Democracy in America* (1961), as he saw it necessary to look at social dynamics through the prism of equality. This also applied to the condition of women, including the likes of Marianne Weber, who made noticeable inroads in the field of gender inequality, paying attention to its manifestations in culture, work and politics as well as its symbolic forms. She did so not only as an intellectual, but also as a political activist and a standard-bearer for feminine identity, the latter applying equally to Lou Andreas-Salomé.

Yet, although women celebrated the decline of aristocracy which had resulted in individuals being able to aspire to social mobility, the thought of pushing for the extension of social equality to encompass gender equality was still a leap too far. Women did not yet show much concern for civil liberties, focusing their efforts instead on economic equality, and only began to undergo the most subtle of awakenings as they started to realize the power of asserting their own subjective feminine selves. Equality was gradually blending with identity.

Feminists successfully dismantled the previously dominant political ideologies, which turned on the distinction between public and private spheres in order to sanction the confinement of women to private spaces and granted men free rein throughout public space. They decried the political underpinnings on which this distinction was predicated, as well as its role in entrenching the structural oppression of women. Shackled to family life, women provided the labor force required by society and were expected to receive nothing in return, on the grounds that they were acting in accordance with their biological role, and not as economic actors. As neofeminists in the 1970s emphasized the sexual and reproductive rights of women, progressive inroads in this respect helped succeeding generations of feminists to gain greater awareness of other forms of sexism which hindered women's emancipation.

Lastly, history's first unanimous condemnation of violence against women originated in the notion of female dignity and the attendant respect rightfully accorded to them. This implied a rejection of all forms of violence inflicted on women: rape, incest and sexual harassment, whether in the form of prostitution, pornography, female circumcision, polygamy or others. In a similar spirit of global resistance against misogynist violence, the 1993 United Nations World Conference on Human Rights culminated in the establishment of the Vienna Declaration and Programme of Action (Part I, paragraph 18), which was ratified by states and non-governmental organizations. It states that

> the human rights of women and of the girl-child are an inalienable, integral and indivisible part of universal human rights. The full and equal participation of women in political, civil, economic, social and cultural life, at the national, regional and international levels, and the eradication of all forms of discrimination on grounds of sex are priority objectives of the international community.

Contemporary research leads us to acknowledge the *flexibility of identities* as a new force in the social dynamics of postindustrial societies. Individuals have broken free from the customs, norms, values and representations spawned by their socio-cultural surrounding institutions and have been empowered to assert themselves through personal choices relating to areas of their identities which may be social, cultural or sexual. This advance came about due to a combination of factors: that is, a shift from an economy of capitalist accumulation to a redistributive welfare state, women's campaigns in favor of gender equality in the 1970s, birth control, the rise of new family structures, the decline of gendered roles, the attack on stereotypes, an increasingly interconnected world and, lastly of course, the period of transition that our society has been witnessing at the turn of the twenty-first century.

NOTES

1. Maria Antonietta Macciocchi held a seminar at the University of Vincennes on the theme of "Insights on fascism, from its origins to the present day" (published by the same university as "*Eléments pour une Analyse du Fascisme,*" Vol. 1, Paris VII-Vincennes, 1974–75).
2. In *Centralblatt*: see https://journals.openedition.org/socio/2473.

REFERENCES

Andreas-Salomé, Lou. 1984. *Eros*. Paris: Editions de Minuit.
Astor, Dorian. 2008. *Lou Andreas-Salomé*. Paris: Gallimard.
Astor, Dorian. 2017. Conference on the theme "Lou Andreas-Salomé: The Challenge of Love," Collège des Bernardins, December 2, Paris.
Blunden, Katherine. 1982. *Le Travail et la Vertu*. Paris: Payot.
Cabanes, Bruno. 2018. *Histoire de la guerre. Du XIXe à nos jours*. Paris: Seuil.
Castelain-Meunier, Christine. 2002. *La Place des Hommes et les Métamorphoses de la Famille*. Paris: Presses Universitaires de France.

Castelain-Meunier, Christine. 2005. *Les Métamorphoses du Masculin*. Paris: Presses Universitaires de France.

Castelain-Meunier, Christine. 2013. *Le Ménage: la Fée, la Sorcière et l'Homme Nouveau*. Paris: Stock.

Delumeau, Jean. 2005. *Une Histoire du Monde aux Temps Modernes*. Paris: Larousse.

Dupré, Michèle, Gwenaëlle Perrier, Isabelle Berrebi-Hoffmann and Michel Lallement. 2016. "Marianne Weber et la Femme Nouvelle." *Socio* 7: 119–29.

Freud, Sigmund. 1939. *Der Mann Moses und die Monotheistische Religion*. Amsterdam: A. de Lange.

Hadot, Jean. 1977. "Weber (Marianne) Max Weber: A Biography." *Archives des Sciences Sociales des Religions* 43, no. 2: 314–15.

Hirt, Jean-Michel. 2017. Conference on the theme "Lou Andreas-Salomé: The Challenge of Love," Collège des Bernardins, December 2, Paris.

Laslett, Peter. 1969. *Un Monde Que Nous Avons Perdu*. Paris: Flammarion.

Michaud, Stéphane. 2017. *Lou Andreas-Salomé: L'Alliée de la Vie*. Paris: Points Essais.

Michel, Andrée. 1979. *Le Féminisme*. Paris: Que Sais-Je, Presses Universitaires de France.

Simmel, Georg. 2013 [1890]. *Psychologie des Femmes*. Paris: Payot.

Tocqueville, Alexis de. 1961 [1840]. *De la Démocratie en Amérique* (Vol. 2). Paris: Gallimard.

Vallet, Guillaume. 2011. *Petit Manuel de Sociologie à l'Usage des Economistes*. Grenoble: Presses Universitaires de Grenoble.

Vallet, Guillaume. 2018. *Sociologie du Genre*. Paris: Bréal.

Weber, Marianne. 1907. *Ehefrau und Mutter in der Rechtsentwicklung*. Tubingen: J. C. B. Mohr.

Weber, Marianne. 1919. *Frauenfragen und Frauengedanken*. Tubingen: J. C. B. Mohr (including Die Neue Frau).

Weber, Marianne. 1926. *Max Weber: Ein Lebensbild*. Tubingen: J. C. B. Mohr.

21. Silvio Gesell's vision on monetary reform: how to reduce social inequalities

Florencia Sember

1.   INTRODUCTION

Silvio Gesell was born in St. Vith in 1862, in the region of Malmedy, situated on the border between Germany and Belgium. His family struggled to pay for his education, as he was the seventh of nine brothers. He worked first as a post-office employee, later with his brother, and afterward in different commercial activities in Germany and Spain. In 1887, he emigrated to Argentina, where he stayed for twelve years. It was in Argentina that he opened a commercial activity selling dental and medical supplies. The Baring crisis of 1890 inspired him to reflect on monetary problems, specifically referring to Argentine monetary problems (Gesell 1893, 1898a, 1898b). His first work, though, was not about Argentina, but about the reform of money in general (Gesell 1891). His most complete work was *The Natural Economic Order*, written between 1906 and 1911 and published as a single volume in 1916.

Gesell became widely known because of Keynes's extensive reference to him in his famous *General Theory* (Keynes 1978) where he devotes to him what may seem "disproportionate space," praising his work for containing "flashes of deep insight and who only just failed to reach down to the essence of the matter" (Keynes 1978: 7–353). The essence of the matter was, to Keynes, the fact that Gesell built only half a theory of the rate of interest because "the notion of liquidity-preference had escaped him."[1] Irving Fisher also recognized the significance of Gesell's work in his *Stamp Scrip* (1933), where he devotes a section to Gesell's proposal.

The aim of this chapter is to assess Silvio Gesell's contribution on money reform and its relationship to the matter of social inequalities, in a time when this was a subject addressed by many authors of the "Progressive Era."

The remainder of the chapter proceeds as follows. The second section deals with Gesell's views on eugenics and inequalities of his time. The third section presents Gesell's concepts of "free land" and "free money," while the fourth section explains Gesell's theory of interest. The fifth section offers some concluding remarks.

2. GESELL AND HIS TIME: EUGENICS, INEQUALITIES AND THE PROGRESSIVE ERA

Gesell's economic reforms were directed to the establishment of what he called a "natural economic order." It was not natural in the sense that it "arises spontaneously as a natural product. Such an order does not, indeed, exist, for the order which we impose upon ourselves is always an act, an act consciously willed" (1958: 9). The most natural economic order was one in which men thrive. Gesell associated closely the prosperity of mankind with the evolution of the division of labor: "Only through competition, chiefly competition in the economic sphere, is right evolution, eugenesis, possible" (1958: 9).

Eugenic ideas were widespread at the time, not only among racist and conservative thinkers, but also among many authors considered progressive.[2] In Gesell's vision, and differently from other eugenic advocates, superiority was not given by race, religion or culture, but exclusively by the capacity of succeeding in the economic sphere. The most natural order was one in which success was determined exclusively by innate characteristics, these successful traits being transmitted genetically to offspring and eventually "added to the common characteristics of mankind" (1958: 9).

Free competition would favor the efficient, who would succeed because of their personal achievement through work, and experience easier conditions in which to form a family and bring up children, while the losers in the competition would meet greater obstacles and therefore have a smaller number of descendants. Efficient men would become the prevailing type, and society would be free of the "burden of inferior individuals" (1958: 9).[3] Contrary to most authors of the Progressive Era, Gesell was not an advocate of a strong role for the state in eugenics, except guaranteeing that competition among individuals took place under equal conditions. Rather, Gesell thought that nature should determine which individuals could found a family.[4] In systems where the state controls economic life, the type of individual that is privileged is the one that conforms with authority, in a way that the "cleverest intriguers would leave the largest number of descendants – endowed of course with the qualities of their parents" (1958: 17).

The aim of Gesell's monetary and land reform was to achieve an economic order which would allow "the best of mankind" (1958: 10), to develop, as eugenic selection required. This new order had to be founded upon justified egoism, in which everyone must be assured of the full proceeds of their own labor, and dispose of them as they think fit. Justified egoism was self-interest, which drove men to competition among themselves and was different from selfishness, which Gesell called "the vice of the short-sighted" (1958: 11).

To Gesell, the natural economic order had to remedy the defects of present society, led by people who obtained their advantages from money or inherited privileges, that is, through a system of unnatural selection. In the natural economic order, competition between individuals had to take place on equal grounds, that is, eliminating the privileges originating in money or other kind of prerogatives not related to inborn characteristics of individuals. Gesell justified as follows the final aim of his reforms: "We are confronted with the problem, to whom is the further evolution of the human race to be entrusted? Shall nature, with iron logic, carry out the process by natural selection, or shall the feeble reason of man – of present-day, degenerate man – take over this function from nature? That is what we have to decide" (1958: 15–16).

Under the "natural economic order," leadership would fall to the fittest, and every individual would have the possibility to fully develop their potential and at the same time take personal responsibility for their life. Gesell called his ideal of the fully developed individual the "a-crat," an individual who rejects the control of others. He rejected cooperation, gilded socialism and nationalization because they would lead to rule by officialdom and eliminate personal freedom and independence. To Gesell, the choice was between private control and state control of economic life.

Gesell associated his proposal to the Manchester School, in the sense that both proposed a system governed by the free play of economic forces. The problem with the Manchester economists was that they did not see that traditional forms of money and the private ownership of land were the obstacles that prevented competition to take place on a level playing field. To Gesell, it was not enough that the state did not interfere with economic life, to reduce interest rates to zero or reduce rents on land: money and land reform were necessary.

By addressing inequality Gesell meant providing everyone in society with the same opportunity to develop themselves and abolishing all inherited privileges. Once free competition according to the laws of nature was guaranteed, the most efficient members of society would succeed. To achieve this kind of free competition, the workers as a collective had to be guaranteed the full proceeds of their labor, which could be achieved only by the elimination of interest and rent. The distribution among workers, then, would not be equal, but subject to competition.

Gesell advocated a non-Marxist socialism: "The abolition of unearned income, of so-called surplus-value also termed interest and rent, is the immediate economic aim of every socialist movement" (1958: 27). He insisted on the fact that the proposal of socialising the means of production was based on an erroneous interpretation of the nature of capital. According to Gesell, only

Proudhon saw that capitalist advantage did not derive from ownership of the means of production, but from the prevalent form of money: "Marx succumbs to a popular fallacy and holds that capital consists of material goods. For Proudhon, on the contrary, interest is not the product of material goods, but of an economic situation, a condition of the market" (1958: 28–9).

However, Proudhon's solution was faulted because he wanted to combat the privilege of money by raising goods to the level of money; the solution was instead to lower money to the level of goods. Accordingly, Gesell's monetary reform proposal, described in the next section, consisted of the introduction of paper money that deteriorated over time at the same level of goods.

As Dillard (1942: 3) affirms, "Gesell's position is both anti-classical and anti-Marxian. Although he avowed himself a socialist and professed to be attacking capitalism as a whole, his anti-capitalistic position must be interpreted in terms of his definition of capitalism as the 'interest exploiting system'."[5]

3.   FREE LAND AND FREE MONEY

The aim of Gesell's reform was to abolish unearned income – rent and interest – as a means to guarantee that competition among individuals developed on a level playing field and so assure the success of the fittest, in the sense described in the previous section. Free land and free money were the reforms proposed to defend the wage-fund from "parasites," by granting that the whole product of labor was distributed among its creators (Gesell 1958: 85). The proceeds of labor should go entirely to workers, with no part of it surrendered to capitalists as interest or rent.[6]

We will not go deeply into Gesell's explanation of the determinants of rent, as we consider the core of Gesell's theory is his theory of interest. Briefly, Gesell stated that landowners had no incentive to let others use land (for agriculture, building or mining) without compensation. This was because land supply was limited. However, landowners could not demand an arbitrarily high rent. If the whole surface of the earth were needed to support mankind, the owners of land would be able to claim the whole produce of land except the part necessary for the maintenance and propagation of workers. Since in other continents there is still free available land, the landowner could only claim as rent the difference between the proceeds of labor on his field and the proceeds of labor on unclaimed land in other continents.[7]

Gesell's proposal of free land consisted in land nationalization. The state would purchase land from its present owners, paying with government securities bearing the same interest as rent on land would have yielded. Then, land should be leased for cultivation without distinction of race, religion or culture: "The idea of Free-Land admits no qualification. It is absolute" (Gesell 1958: 89).

Any inhabitant of the world would be allowed to compete in the auctions in any place of the world he pleased, and borders would be only administrative.[8] This idea had been stated already in Gesell's book about the Argentine–Chilean conflict on borders: "The civilised man hates borders. The modern man is individualist and cosmopolitan" (Gesell 1898c: 5).

After the implementation of free land, the rent on land would flow to the Treasury, and would be distributed among mothers, proportionally to the quantity of children under the age of 15. In that way, women would be independent from the financial support of a man: "A woman would then be free to consider the mental, physical and race-improvement qualities, and not merely the money-bags of her mate. Women would thus recover the right to choose their mates, the great right of natural selection, which is something vastly more important for them than the illusory right of choosing their political represent-atives" (Gesell 1958: 115). This reform would not only suppress rent, but by the distribution of rent revenues would also in other ways contribute to his conception of the evolution of mankind.

Gesell emphasized that, contrary to what most land reformers asserted, the problem of rent did not solve the problem of interest. Rent was a problem of distribution, as it was the part of the harvest the tenant had to surrender to the landowner. There was not any exchange because the owner simply pocketed rent offering nothing in return. Interest, unemployment and economic crises, instead, were problems of the sphere of exchange: land reform could not abolish interest.

Gesell inquired into the nature of money to show that it was the traditional form of money that originated interest, which was at the core of his explanation of the faults of the capitalistic economic system. The starting point of his rea-soning was that he considered that the base of civilization, to which we owed our wealth, was the division of labor, the fact that we produce more than we consume. Once the division of labor is in place, producers manufacture wares only to exchange them for other goods: in this way, they are compelled to sell. When the division of labor has reached a certain degree, barter becomes impracticable, and money as a medium of exchange becomes indispensable.[9] And the more advantageous the division of labor, the more indispensable is money (Gesell 1958: 147). The material of which money is composed is indif-ferent, for anyone who wants to engage in the usufruct of the division of labor instead of producing only for his own consumption (primitive production) must accept money, which is always controlled by the state.[10]

Everyone who has given up primitive production and participates in the division of labor is compelled to sell, and in this way creates with his products a demand for money. "All wares without exception are the embodied demand for money" (Gesell 1958: 172). This happens because wares deteriorate; there-fore, it is not possible to stock them without incurring great losses.

Gesell emphasized that the "Demand for money is not merely proportional to the stock of wares, it is the stock of wares" (1958: 215). The stock of wares increased because of improvements in the division of labor and the means of production, and by the introduction into the market of new and better-quality goods. There were factors that instead decreased the demand for money, such as improvements in commercial organization and the existence of credit: the demand for money is reduced by the exact amount of the wares exchanged by way of credit.

There is a strong asymmetry between the supply of and the demand for goods, which are subject to different laws. The supply of money is the demand for commodities: only those persons offering money for commodities create a demand for them. Thus, supply of money is not equal to the stock of money (as in the case of the supply of wares) because money can be withdrawn from the market at no cost. The stock of money is only the upper limit to the demand of wares.

A trivial fact, according to Gesell, that had been overlooked, was that because of the nature of the present form of money, demand for goods could be delayed at no cost, while their supply could not be postponed without creating losses to their possessors, since goods deteriorate and become antiquated. The only way the possessors of wares have to protect themselves against loss is to sell them, even if they must be sold at a loss.

Gold, on the contrary, "may be regarded almost as foreign matter intruded upon the earth and successfully withstanding all the destructive forces of nature" (Gesell 1958: 227). The possessor of gold must eventually offer it for sale because it is useless to him in itself, but he can choose the time at which he does so. The principle of usury, says Gesell, is the principle of commerce in general: everyone who brings something to the market tries to obtain the highest price possible. In this way, the possessors of money will not surrender it for nothing; they will ask as much as market conditions allow them to ask.

The asymmetry between supply and demand, stemming from the superiority of money to goods, gave origin to money interest. In Gesell's words: "On the one hand compulsion, on the other hand freedom; and the two together, compulsion and freedom, determine price" (1958: 228). The possessor of money can demand a tribute to act as intermediary for the exchange of wares, because by withholding his money he can paralyze exchange. Moreover, the tribute is contained in the difference between the buying and the selling price, so it can be paid only if between the time of buying and the time of selling prices do not fall. As a consequence, "commerce is mathematically impossible with falling prices" (1958: 230).[11] In the present system "money is the thing people want to own. [. . .]. Let the 'others' have the goods. But who, economically speaking, are these others? We ourselves are these others; all of us who produce goods.

So if, as buyers, we reject the products of others, we really all reject our own products" (1958: 268–9).

The traditional form of money is at the origin of recurring crises and unemployment. When prices fall, money withdraws from the market, as its tribute is not assured. Producers, instead, are compelled to sell their products. Production continues, but prices fall because the supply of money is insufficient. "Demand becomes smaller because it is already too small, and supply becomes larger because it is already too large" (1958: 232). Moreover, if prices fall, credit retires, so more wares must be exchanged by means of money, which depresses prices further. In deflationary crises, "the fear that what is offered cheap to-day will be offered still cheaper to-morrow closes all purses" (1958: 234). There are no equilibrating forces: "This is, therefore, the law of demand, that it disappears when it becomes insufficient" (1958: 235).[12]

Gesell's proposal of free money is an attempt to eliminate the asymmetry between demand for and supply of goods, that is, the superiority of money over goods that gives rise to interest. Free money would be composed of paper money that lost 5.2% of its value annually. To each 100 dollar banknote, a ten cent stamp must be attached each week so the banknote keeps its face value. In this way, free money loses value as wares do. Possessors of money are under compulsion to buy goods, or lend it, whatever the conditions of the loan. Now possessors of money act under compulsion, exactly as possessors of goods. The loan takers, for the same reason, will rapidly invest money and so immediately create demand. In this way, demand would no longer depend on the will of the possessors of money. Gesell calls this a "proposal of compulsory demand" (1958: 273).

Free money is a medium of exchange that prevents prices from falling. According to Gesell, prices can fall for three reasons: because the production of gold is not enough for the supply of money to be adapted to the supply of goods; because when the production of wares, and therefore the production of real capital, is increasing, interest on real capital falls; and because in times of prosperity money is melted.[13] Free money, can prevent all these possible causes as it will be paper money separated from gold; it will be produced by the state according to the needs of the market, and will be offered even if interest on money or real capital falls or disappears.[14]

4.　　THE THEORY OF INTEREST

As shown in the previous section, money interest, which Gesell called basic interest, had its origin in the traditional form of money. The capitalistic quality of money originated from the facts that money was indispensable for a highly developed division of labor, and the physical properties of the traditional form of money allowed it to be withdrawn from the market at no cost. The merchant could force the possessor of goods to pay a tribute, which is interest on commercial capital, amounting to 4–5% a year.[15]

Basic interest cannot be arbitrarily high, as it is limited by its competitors: primitive production, barter and bills of exchange. If the interest rate is higher than the difference of efficiency between the division of labor and primitive production, producers might return to the latter.[16] The same happens with barter: if the interest claimed by money is greater than the advantages of using money over barter, the owners of goods will return to barter, organizing markets to exchange their products. The third competitor of money is bills of exchange. They are not as safe and convenient as money but, particularly in wholesale commerce, they are close substitutes: the higher the rate of interest, the higher the stimulus to use bills of exchange. As in the other cases, the goods that circulate by means of bills of exchange are lost to money, so prices rise in proportion to the circulation of bills of exchange.

When basic interest rises above a certain limit, competitors enter the scene, fewer goods are traded by means of money, and prices rise. The rise of prices forces money into the market, as it means that the possessor of money will lose in proportion to inflation. "We can therefore say that to raise the tribute claimed by money above a certain level automatically liberates the forces which again reduce the tribute" (Gesell 1958: 381). The converse happens when money interest falls below this limit. So interest on money must return to the point where it represents the advantages of money over primitive production, barter and bills of exchange.[17]

Because of the superiority of traditional money over goods, basic interest is the "payment for the activity of the capitalist – and this activity consists of putting obstacles in the way of commerce" (Gesell 1958, 385). Commodities must be able to pay their cost price, plus basic interest, from the selling price. This is to Gesell the true meaning of Marx's formula Money – Wares – Surplus Money.

If someone parts with his money to build a house, a ship or a factory, then he will put an end to the flow of interest coming from that money. Therefore, he will do so only on condition that the house can exact at least the same amount of interest from its tenants, or the ship from its freight, or the factory from wages. All real capital needs at least to yield interest equal to basic interest. In this way, basic interest is transferred to real capital:

> Money takes jealous care that its creatures shall not degenerate; it is given only for the construction of as many houses as can be built without causing the yield of interest to fall below basic interest. [. . .]. So-called real capital is therefore anything rather than 'real'. Money alone is true real capital, basic capital. All other capital objects are completely dependent upon the characteristics of this existing form of money. (Gesell 1958: 391)

Real capital can exact interest because of its scarcity, because it can be created only by spending a sum of money and this money is capital. If the supply of real capital increased to the point where demand was no longer greater than supply, these goods would lose the characteristics of capital. They are capital only because money is capital: "Real capital, just as the wares, merely makes use of a state of the market forcibly established for its own ends by money, namely an artificial limitation of the production of real capital with the aim of keeping the supply of it constantly below the demand" (Gesell 1958: 392).

Gesell shows that interest on real capital must oscillate around basic interest. If it falls below basic interest, no new real capital will be produced. This, plus the natural rate of destruction of real capital, will move the rate of interest on real capital back to the level of basic interest. If the rate on real capital is larger than basic interest, the increased production of houses, factories and ships will bring the rate back to its equilibrium level. This happens because an interest rate rise increases the earnings of capitalists, who are the members of society that save. They will take the opportunity to create new capital.

With the traditional form of money, saving was impossible for most workers. After the money reform, interest and rent would fall to zero and so the proceeds of labor would rise, increasing the capability to save, assisted by falling prices due to a reduction in commercial costs. Moreover, with traditional money, the scarce amount of money saved by workers had to be used up in periods of unemployment, due to recurrent crises. After the introduction of free money, crises would be eliminated, and so savings could accumulate. Even if there were no interest rate on savings, the combination of the factors just described would have a stronger effect than the loss due to absence of interest. Workers would open savings accounts in banks that would lend those funds at zero interest to build real capital.

After the introduction of free money and the consequent disappearance of basic interest, houses, factories and ships would prove the best means of storing savings. They would pay no interest but instead resolve themselves into sums set aside for depreciation. If a person saves and lends his surplus under the condition of receiving the same amount (without interest and without loss), he has an advantage because he would avoid the expenses of upkeep of his savings: "Private ownership of the means of production will then present no advantage beyond that which the owner of a savings-box derives from its possession: the savings-box does not yield him surplus-value or interest, but he can gradually use up its contents" (Gesell 1958: 35).

The form of real capital built by the possessor of savings will change according to the rate of depreciation he wishes to receive. If he wishes to receive 2% annually, he will build a house for letting. If he wishes to receive 10%, he will build a ship. The sums annually written off for depreciation will cover the whole cost of capital. The saver will be able to carry his surplus to the period when he wants to use it at no cost. As soon as free money is introduced, basic interest will disappear. But interest on loans will not. This is because at the beginning there will still be a demand of real capital larger than supply (and so a demand for loans larger than supply). The scarcity of houses, ships and factories will continue for some time, and therefore as long a real capital yields interest, loans will pay interest:

> Up to the introduction of Free-Money interest on real capital depends on basic interest, after the introduction of Free-Money basic interest will disappear, and interest on loans will be exactly determined by interest on real capital. Borrowers of money will no longer pay interest because money can exact a tribute from the wares, but because the demand for loans, for the time being, exceeds the supply. (Gesell 1958: 416)

Basic interest and loan interest are determined by different causes. Basic interest corresponds to the difference of efficiency between money and the substitutes for money. No loan could eliminate this difference. With the interest on real capital we don't have an exchange but a loan. Interest on real capital is determined by demand and supply: "Basic interest has up to the present escaped observation because it was concealed behind its offspring, ordinary interest upon loan-money" (Gesell 1958: 419).

In the end, the process set in motion by the implementation of free land and free money reform would in time result in the fall of loan and real capital interest rates to zero, and the suppression of unearned income. As Dillard (1942: 351) affirms, "Gesell's ideas on long-run social reform are closely analogous to Keynes's 'euthanasia of the *rentier*'". Both agree that in time, the accumulation of real capital would make it so abundant that it would cease to yield interest, that is "pure interest can be made disappear without socialising the instruments of production" (1942: 351).

5.   CONCLUSION

Silvio Gesell was a man of his time. The reforms proposed were functional to his conception of the evolution of society. As many progressives, he believed in the explanatory power of scientific social inquiry to get at the root of economic and social problems and expert management of public administration.[18] However, contrary to most progressives, he was not fond of the legitimacy of social control. His ideal was a society formed by individual members responsible for themselves and free from the control of others or the state. He thought that the problem of interest had remained unsolved because "capital-interest (interest on loans as well as interest on real capital) is the child or by-product of our traditional form of money and can therefore be scientifically explained only with the help of a theory of money" (Gesell 1958: 139). The ends of his reforms were to achieve a system in which the ones who succeed are also the most capable men, those who possess inborn characteristics that are worth adding to the genetic heritage of mankind. After the implementation of the reforms and the suppression of unearned income, "free money will clear away the present ignoble motley of princes, rentiers and proletarians, leaving space for the growth of a proud, free, self-reliant race of men" (Gesell 1958: 285).

It is worth mentioning that, to Gesell, the reforms he proposed had to be implemented worldwide. If the system were to be implemented in just one country, the Banks of Issue would have to choose between keeping prices stable or keeping the exchange rate stable. Moreover, "capital interest is an international quantity" (Gesell 1958: 394), so if interest on real capital falls to zero in one country but is positive in another, real capital will not be built anymore in the former and will be built in the latter. In this way, with time, supply of real capital in the first country will be lower than demand, and interest will become positive again. To attain stable rates of exchange between countries, it would be necessary to adopt a uniform currency policy. Between two countries with paper currency, there was no limit to the fluctuations of the rate of exchange. Under the gold standard, instead, fluctuations in the rate of exchange could not exceed the cost of shipping gold: "At a low level of civilisation, in which no intelligent State control is possible, such automatic compensation of currencies has certain advantages. But at the present day, the retention of the gold standard for this reason is an insult to the national administrations" (Gesell 1958: 355).

Gesell proposed the creation of an International Valuta Association, which would regulate the currency standard and the exchanges, by issuing an international paper money called the "Iva." The currency systems would remain national but had to be based on uniform principles, valid for all countries forming part of the association, no matter the circumstances or their stage of development.[19] The necessity of a worldwide reach of the reforms is normally overlooked, but it turns Gesell's proposals into an impracticable solution.[20] Gesell did not give enough importance to the political feasibility of his proposals; he just thought that the reforms would be carried on by those who "recognise that war and interest are inseparable [. . .]. Such persons have the right inner preparation for understanding The Natural Economic Order; it is for them that the book has been written, and it is they also who, undeterred by opposition, will carry through the reform it proposes" (Gesell 1958: 442).

NOTES

1.　Keynes (1978: 7–356). In this chapter we won't focus on the Keynes–Gesell relationship. For more on this issue, see Darity (1995) and Dillard (1942).
2.　On eugenics and economics in the Progressive Era, see Cot (2005); Diane (1984); Fiorito and Foresti (2018); Fiorito and Orsi (2017); Leonard (2003, 2016); and Peart and Levy (2003).
3.　Gesell affirms that medical science favored the propagation of "defective individuals," and this made even more pressing the need of natural selection. "Medical art can then delay, but it cannot arrest eugenesis" (Gesell 1958: 17).
4.　Leonard (2005: 210) shows that most of the authors of the Progressive Era advocated for "the substitution of State selection for natural selection of the fittest."
5.　Capitalism is "an economic condition in which the demand for loan-money and real capital exceeds the supply and therefore gives rise to interest" (Gesell 1958: 244, fn.).
6.　This is valid for the collective proceeds of labor. Distribution among individual workers will be subject to competition.
7.　Rent of land was thus limited by the existence of what Gesell called free land. There were different classes of free land: uncultivated land in other continents, large areas not cultivated whose owners lived far off, and free land near cities that could become available or increase productivity as a result of technical progress. For more details, see Part 1 and Part 2 of Gesell (1958).
8.　Gesell thought that to be really successful his reform had to be adopted worldwide.
9.　It would be possible to exchange wares by barter, but it is so complex that producers may prefer to cease to work rather than to have recourse to it. Later, Gesell would say that barter becomes a possibility only if the rate of interest is higher than the advantage of using money over barter.
10.　Be it paper money or gold.
11.　Gesell had already noted this previously, talking about the economic situation in Argentina: "The interruption of exchange is the necessary consequence, fatally necessary, of the laws that favor the valorization of money, the general fall in prices, since while those laws are in force, interest loses all its driving force" (Gesell 1898c: 28, my translation).
12.　The converse happens when demand is too large.
13.　In times of prosperity, the demand for gold for industrial use increases, because the demand for jewelry and other gold ornaments is higher. In this way, gold is melted just when its demand is higher because of the increased production of goods. "Money is the condition for the division of labour, the division of labour leads to prosperity, and prosperity destroys money" (Gesell 1958: 239).
14.　Gesell thought prices had to be measured with an index price built from a basket of goods. Prices had to be kept constant by the Bank of Issue, which should put money into circulation when prices fell and withdraw money from circulation when prices increased. The stability of prices was also a matter of justice between creditors and debtors. What mattered was the stability of the price index, not to keep constant the relative prices, which depended on the conditions of production.
15.　This figure is, according to Gesell, given by historical experience.
16.　In this case the quantity of goods traded in the market diminishes and prices rise.

17. In developed societies, the most important competitors that limit money interest are the bills of exchange, while in underdeveloped societies they are barter and primitive production.
18. Leonard (2005: 217) mentions the most important characteristics of Progressive thought.
19. Some of Gesell's ideas in this respect can be found in Keynes's proposal for an International Clearing Union and the Bancor.
20. Blanc (1998) shows that Gesell's experiment was tried, and could be only tried, on a small scale. Onken (2000) also provides examples of organizations promoting Gesell's free economy. With this we are not saying that the need to apply the reforms at an international level is the only obstacle to their implementation.

REFERENCES

Blanc, Jérôme. 1998. "Free Money for Social Progress: Theory and Practice of Gesell's Accelerated Money." *The American Journal of Economics and Sociology* 57, no. 4: 469–83.

Cot, Annie L. 2005. "'Breed out the Unfit and Breed in the Fit': Irving Fisher, Economics, and the Science of Heredity." *The American Journal of Economics and Sociology* 64, no. 3: 793–826.

Darity, William. 1995. "Keynes' Political Philosophy: The Gesell Connection." *Eastern Economic Journal* 21, no. 1: 27–41.

Diane, Paul. 1984. "Eugenics and the Left." *Journal of the History of Ideas* 45, no. 4: 56–90.

Dillard, Dudley. 1942. "Silvio Gesell's Monetary Theory of Social Reform." *The American Economic Review* 32, no. 2: 348–52.

Fiorito, Luca and Tiziana Foresti. 2018. "Eugenics and Socialist Thought in The Progressive Era: The Case of James Medbery Mackaye." *Journal of the History of Economic Thought* 40, no. 3: 377–88.

Fiorito, Luca and Cosma Orsi. 2017. "Survival Value and a Robust, Practical, Joyless Individualism: Thomas Nixon Carver, Social Justice, and Eugenics." *History of Political Economy* 49, no. 3: 469–95.

Fisher, Irving. 1933. *Stamp Scrip*. New York: Adelphi.

Gesell, Silvio. 1891. *Die Reformation des Münzwesens als Brücke zum sozialen Staat*. Buenos Aires: Selbstverlag.

Gesell, Silvio. 1893. *El Sistema Monetario Argentino. Sus Ventajas y su Perfeccionamento*. Buenos Aires: Selbstverlag.

Gesell, Silvio. 1898a. *La Cuestión Monetaria Argentina*. Buenos Aires: La Buenos Aires.

Gesell, Silvio. 1898b. *La Plétora Monetaria de 1909 y la Anemia Monetaria de 1898*. Buenos Aires: n.p.

Gesell, Silvio. 1898c. *La Razon Económica del Desacuerdo Chileno–Argentino*. Buenos Aires: Imprenta y encuadernación "La Buenos Aires."

Gesell, Silvio. 1958. *The Natural Economic Order*. London: Peter Owen Limited.

Keynes, John Maynard. 1978. *The Collected Writings of John Maynard Keynes: Volume 7: The General Theory*, ed. Elizabeth Johnson and Donald Moggridge. London: Royal Economic Society.

Leonard, Thomas C. 2003. "'More Merciful and Not Less Effective': Eugenics and American Economics in the Progressive Era." *History of Political Economy* 35, no. 4: 687–712.

Leonard, Thomas C. 2005. "Retrospectives: Eugenics and Economics in the Progressive Era." *The Journal of Economic Perspectives* 19, no. 4: 207–24.

Leonard, Thomas C. 2016. *Illiberal Reformers: Race, Eugenics, and American Economics in the Progressive Era*. Princeton, NJ: Princeton University Press.

Onken, Werner. 2000. "The Political Economy of Silvio Gesell: A Century of Activism." *The American Journal of Economics and Sociology* 59, no. 4: 609–22.

Peart, Sandra J. and David M. Levy. 2003. "Denying Human Homogeneity: Eugenics and the Making of Post-Classical Economics." *Journal of the History of Economic Thought* 25, no. 3: 261–88.

22. Football culture and sports history in Latin America: from the Progressive Era to contemporary times

Bernardo Buarque de Hollanda

1.   INTRODUCTION

This chapter examines the intellectual discussion around the idea of Latin America, shaped during the "Progressive Era" and under the historical influence of the United States. The main goal is to show the direct or indirect repercussions of this debate on the framework of professional football in the region. The argument is that, although the continents have undergone identity processes that mark differences and similarities among neighboring nations, the concept of a Latin America unity has experienced special difficulties in identity construction throughout its history, more precisely between the late nineteenth century and the end of the twentieth century.

Geographical territories often go through continuous historical periods of frontier exchange, of unity and fragmentation, of approximation and distancing, exemplified in the Latin American case by particular characteristics of its colonial heritage – the multiple influences of colonial metropolises, particularly Spain, Portugal, England and France. Although these represent a past dimension, they became more complex throughout the twentieth century with the emergence of the United States as a hegemonic power that began to have decisive effects on Latin American economy, politics and culture. Our purpose here is to suggest that, although the USA's hegemony is uncontested in all spheres of collective life in Latin America, its presence was not so directly felt regarding modern sports, especially in the world of professional football through intercontinental tournaments between clubs and national teams. In this respect, the otherness remained focused on the other side of the Atlantic: either on the United Kingdom, responsible for inventing the rules of sports, or to Latin European countries – France, Italy, Spain and Portugal – that influenced the styles and playing techniques in South America in cultural and institutional terms.

Firstly, we will highlight the nature of intellectual debates around the idea of Latin America. Then, we will describe a history of creation of sports tournaments between clubs and countries selected in Latin America in order to show the slow institutional process of identity construction through sports and a dialogue with temporality and the European football calendar. Finally, we conclude with a summary about the limits and the potential of the establishment of a Latin American sports unity in the beginning of the twenty-first century.

2. THE LATIN AMERICAN IDENTITY CONSTRUCTION: CONTINUITIES AND INTERMITTENCES

At the end of the nineteenth century, the intellectual self-awareness of being Latin American was sought by writers such as José Martí (1999), in Cuba, and José Enrique Rodó (1985), in Uruguay. In Brazil, the physician Manoel Bomfim (1993) is representative; in 1903 he formulated a critique of the parasitic conditions experienced in the region, because of the legacy of a colonial mindset and practices by European metropolises.

In a Latin American intellectual ambience, it can be said that, on the one hand, "arielism" has preponderated, an expression inspired by a supernatural character in William Shakespeare's *The Tempest* (1611), one of his last works. This current of thought opposed a modernizing and scientistic view, proclaiming a return to an Iberian past. On the other hand, in Argentina the strand represented by Domingos Sarmiento (2010) excelled, who rejected the provincial reality of caudillismo and was in favor of the old Hispanic American colonies' alignment with the North American model.

An expression coined in nineteenth-century France (when the country was ruled by Napoleon III), "Latin America" was standardized in the United States in the second half of the nineteenth century in order to identify a geographic area south of the North American Rio Grande on the Mexican border, which was explored by a French scientific-military expedition to Mexico – its coinage in a book dates back to 1862. The United States stopped being only the opposite to Europe and started to aim the contiguous territory, situated South of Ecuador.

In 1856, the Colombian poet and diplomat José María Torres Caicedo had already contrasted "Latin America" to "Anglo-Saxon" America in his poem *Las Dos Américas*. Caicedo founded intellectual societies with a view to bringing Latin American countries together, which was clearly a political project. In its turn, this was settled in an old idea about the "Latin race," coined by Michel Chevalier, a Frenchman, in 1839, in order to bring French, Spanish, Portuguese and Italian speakers together. The approach pleased Spanish American *criollo* elites, as they appreciated the francophone culture (Burke 2009: 159).

In view of this, Latin America was soon placed in contrast to the emerging pan-Americanist policy in the United States. Pan-Americanism intensified in the late nineteenth and early twentieth centuries with the emergence of a North American hegemony, which aimed to amplify its expansionist policy and international influence zone. The period was marked by wars perpetrated by the United States, like the one against Spain in 1898 in a dispute over the Caribbean Antillean islands, such as Cuba and Puerto Rico. Also at this time, expansionist mottos become well known following the disclosure of the Monroe Doctrine, drawn up in 1823 and resumed in the early twentieth century by Theodore Roosevelt – "America for Americans" – in the wake of "big stick" diplomacy, sponsored by the North American Secretary of State James Blaine.

There were not a few difficulties in achieving the pan-Americanist project. One of the obstacles was due to the Iberian culture specificities transplanted to the US territory. Iberianism and Americanism constituted antithetical poles, triggered by authors of social thought, in contrasting comparison to the models of development in each region. The counterpoint was also used by politicians interested in using North America's colonization case to legitimize the North American supremacy; colonization was considered successful due to the concept of "settlement colonies," a term devised by the French economist Pierre Paul Leroy-Beaulieu. As for the endemic Latin America backwardness, it was explained by the Iberian heritage, materialized on the basis of its "exploitation colonies" experience, to refer to Leroy-Beaulieu's antithetical pair.

North American researcher Richard Morse (1988) was one of those who dared to think of that equation in a less predictable way, without immediately contrasting one to the other and without using a one-way principle. The Brazilianist would enhance the ideological and institutional heritage contained in concepts of Ibero-America and Anglo-America. Since then, he has dealt with Latin American specific values, and the region's allegedly racial, linguistic and cultural unity, proposing a different valuation principle for each one of them. The explanatory tradition stressed Iberian backwardness, with a predominance of holism, annihilator of individual differences. As for the Anglo-Americans, the supremacy of Protestant individualism was acclaimed as a cultivator of democratic, Republican and constitutional ideals. This has shaped American history with the ideals of civic virtues, free will, political decentralization and economic liberalism. It was a country typified by a cosmopolitan intelligentsia since *Democracy in America* (1835), a book by French author Alexis de Tocqueville (1985), which derived from the rationalist, materialist and liberal aegis of the United States and encouraged belief in the autonomy of the individual over the whole. As for the Hispanic and Lusitanic heritage countries, based on the historical legacy of Catholicism, they were formed under the principle of a more centralized and incorporating state, based on the experience of a hierarchical community.

According to Morse, this trait, far from being an obstacle, conferred an advantage to the Ibero-American experience. Its more open and more fraternal sociability allowed it to reverse traditional devaluation in the face of North American alterity. To his mind, the idea of the superiority of the USA over the inferiority of Latin America should not be conceived. Yet in ideological terms, it is known that in the period between the world wars (1919–39), intermediated by the Great Depression and the damaging effects of the New York stock market crash, the USA used physical force, employing warlike military power. However, the bellicose prominence in foreign policy coexisted with other forms of coercion. North America started to engage with the southern hemisphere of the continent using a blend of diplomacy and violence. Development of mass media on a global scale enabled a more sophisticated domination exercise, in a form well-established by the Frankfurt School, employing the concept of cultural industry.

Alongside the debate on cultural industry, the continent lived with frequent tensions in the political sphere. In constant ambiguity with the governments of the U.S.A., In the 1930s, 1940s and 1950s, successive administrations in the USA watched the emergence of various presidents and dictators in Latin America, who could be called populists by certain strands of sociological interpretation. In Brazil, in the midst of historical vicissitudes, the concept of populism was drafted by university graduates from Escola de Sociologia Paulista (Miceli 2012). These sociologists underlined the frailties of the kind of capitalist transformation in Latin America in the mid twentieth century, far from the ideal type erected by Marxism on the basis of the Industrial Revolution. They did not deny the advent of the "masses," but argued the undue consideration of social contradictions that underlay political clashes. They sought to draw the attention to the fact that the aliancista rhetoric of nationalism had the effect of covering up the fundamental question of capitalism. This focused on the conflicts of class, in the fierce disputes between capital and labor, in the historical role of the working class and in ruptures more drastic than reforms initiated by populist leaders.

Despite these criticisms, inspired in the context of academic Marxist debates of the time, whose assumptions have also been the object of revision and more accurate analysis in recent decades, the projects of Lázaro Cárdenas in Mexico, Getúlio Vargas in Brazil and Juan Domingo Perón in Argentina would become important nationalist and labor references in their respective countries. Their centrality can be measured in the historical developments and balanced lineages of their successors. In place of the primary agricultural exporting system, industrialization would be the touchstone of government speeches. It was believed that the industrial process would be the driving force of the region's emancipation and, in view of this, it was channeled by personalist leaders and by a national feeling of anticolonial aspect, as an elementary contrast to external influences and interferences.

At an institutional level, after the Second World War, it is worth mentioning the local search on Latin America would be propelled by the creation of the Economic Commission for Latin America and the Caribbean (ECLAC) in 1948. As noted by the economist Celso Furtado, the organization, linked to the United Nations, experienced strong opposition from Washington in its early years. Headquartered in Santiago in Chile, ECLAC was composed of a generation of Latin American intellectuals with technical training in economics and, at the same time, with a developmental concern that intended to overcome structural backwardness and conquer the region's autonomy. Foremost in the ECLAC environment were men like Raúl Prebisch from Argentina (see Dosman 2011) and Celso Furtado from Brazil (see Furtado 2007). They were responsible for outlining public policies based on economic studies and social interpretations aligned to the continent's historical evolution.

Latin America comprises a very extensive territorial region of more than 20 million square kilometers. The regional framework encompasses South America, Central America and the Caribbean Islands. There are at least three subsets – Northern Mexico, the American isthmus and the South American continent – and three languages of colonial origin – Spanish, Portuguese and French. These, throughout the history of colonization, undermined pre-Columbian cultures and African ethno-cultural traditions.

According to the observation of Celso Furtado:

> Latin America has ceased to be a geographical expression in order to become a historical reality as a result of the disruption of the traditional framework of international division of labor, of the problems generated by a late industrialization and of the evolution of its relations with the United States; when the U.S.A. became a hegemonic global power they conceived for the region a status of its own, involving a more direct and ostentatious control, and at the same time, requiring increased cooperation among the countries of that area. (Furtado 2007: 32)

In continuity with the dialogue of developmentalism in the 1940s and 1950s, but also with criticism of the dualistic reading then in force (which substantiated industrialization by import substitution), in the late 1960s the generation responsible for laying the foundations of Dependency theory emerged, under the political impact of a series of events: among the most important ones it is worth citing the Cuban Revolution, the Alliance for Progress, President Kennedy's Peace Corps and the military coups supported by the USA.

The intellectual debate of that scenario would be enriched in 1970, when the Brazilian sociologist Fernando Henrique Cardoso and the Chilean historian Enzo Faletto published *Dependency and Development in Latin America*

(2004). The authors seek to undo the illusion of the possibility of actually breaking the dichotomic center–periphery model. Against the grain, the authors propose integrated regional development between the various Latin American countries, so as to constitute a concrete alternative to the greed of international division of labor and to the compelling domain of big business on national markets.

Radicalization was a constant at the time, with extremism in both US political parties amid the deployment of dictatorial and discretionary regimes that would prolong their hold on power. Discourses and practices revolved around revolutionary processes in the Caribbean island of Cuba with insurrectional movements in Central America (Nicaragua and Guatemala) and reformist and coup projects in South America (Argentina, Brazil, Chile, Peru and Uruguay). This was a period when it was hard to distinguish between politico-ideological militancy and production of scientific knowledge, especially in the social sciences. Perhaps the most emblematic book of this generation was written by Uruguayan writer Eduardo Galeano, *Open Veins of Latin America* (1980) (first published in 1971) – it has been both censured and praised, embodying factual data and a description of the systematic despoilment the region underwent over centuries of colonization and independence.

In a panoramic view, the contribution of literature in the constitution of the Latin American imaginary of the period should also be highlighted. The literary influence manifested from at least the nineteenth century, when its function was both fictional and foundational, constitutive of history and identity conformation of each country in the region (see Sommer 2004). In the contemporary phase, during the second half of the twentieth century, the so-called "Latin American boom" occurred, with an affirmation of literature through writers such as the Colombian Gabriel Garcia Marques, the Peruvian Manuel Scorza, the Mexican Juan Rulfo, the Cuban Alejo Carpentier, the Guatemalan Miguel Ángel Asturias and the Uruguayan Cristina Peri Rossi, among others. International critics endorsed the work of these writers and gave it the cognomen of "magical realism."

This literary movement was responsible for the projection of Latin America in the framework of the most cosmopolitan literate culture and obtained positive receptions in both Europe and the United States. Originally published in 1967, *One Hundred Years of Solitude* by García Márquez was one work that achieved the highest editorial impact. Alongside the projection of Latin American literature, the novel won the author a Nobel Prize in 1982, which inspired his speech "The Solitude of Latin America."

3. SPORTS IMAGINARY AND CONSTRUCTION OF FOOTBALL IDENTITY IN LATIN AMERICA

The historical framework drafted so far has stressed the great power of North American influence on the heterogeneous set of Latin American countries. Nevertheless, it is worth pointing out the existence of singularities of the relationship between the United States and Latin America regarding sports culture, in general, and football culture, in particular. It is known that the introduction and implementation of modern sports in Latin America during the second half of the nineteenth century and early twentieth century originated in the economic and cultural activities of imperial Great Britain in the region. The clearest expression of this phenomenon was the codification and diffusion of a number of sports practices that conformed to ideals of modernity and civilization.

The influence of England in the Victorian period has been directly and indirectly noted. In many cases, the modalities of sports arrived in Latin American cities through ports and railways through the action of other European contingents. While English engineers introduced sports' practice in the American continent, the nations of Continental Europe, for their part, also practiced modern sports such as football, for example. By assimilating the habits and tastes of British countries they introduced those habits and tastes in other regions of the globe. The Platine region countries of Argentina and Uruguay stood out in this process, both in the absorption of physical activities invented and coded in Britain, and in the filtering of their moral values – race, fiber, elegance – as the Argentinean anthropologist Eduardo Archetti (2003) elaborates in an exemplary manner. One of the explanatory factors for the creation of sports clubs in Latin America was due to the massive exodus of European emigrants from Italy, Spain and Portugal, among others, to take root on the American continent. English historian Bill Murray synthesizes this phenomenon with propriety:

> At the end of the 19th century, the economy and the football expanded in the southern coastal regions of South America, especially in large cities located in the estuary of Río de la Plata: Buenos Aires and Montevideo. In this region, sailors and British workers, especially of railways, played football in the 1860s. Twenty years later, several clubs appeared, some of them still very well known. Early in the 20th century, the British influence was replaced by the one of southern European immigrants, mostly Italians. However, teams with British names refused to change them when Italians took control. (Murray 2000: 55)

Therefore, the introduction of football in South America has made the zone of influence of the United States limited in terms of sports culture. A multi-sports country in which activities such as baseball (created in 1839), American football (different from soccer and adapted from rugby in 1869), basketball (created on North American soil in 1891), and hockey, stand out, as the USA influenced the Caribbean and Antilles regions (Echevarría 2004) but only affected the Southern Cone countries in a transitory manner. According to British historian Peter Burke in "Football vs. Cricket in the New World" (2009), the US Army introduced baseball to Cuba and the Dominican Republic in the late nineteenth century.

Thus, the "criollization" of sports, that is, the hybridization of which Eduardo Archetti spoke to address polo and football in Argentina (Archetti 2003; Toledo 2009) manifested a hegemony in the reverse direction with the process of assimilation by native elites of a British sports-cultural phenomenon. In regard to the American territory, this favored to some extent a backward pan-Americanism, as advocated by the Brazilianist Richard Morse.

This point is developed by Uruguayan historian Andrés Morales:

> The Pan Americanism on the one hand and the Hispanic Americanism on the other hand, sometimes opposed, sometimes together, were two distinct forms of constructing national identity. In football speeches, both postures were present at the time of narrating victorious Cups and championships. The football is appropriated as a tradition but in this period and in the triumph speeches, the idea that the Uruguayan were the inhabitants of the Republic started to take shape. It is in *Ariel*, by José Enrique Rodó, that we have found the biggest influence of the speeches that revolve around victories.
>
> In 1924's victory, the idea of a team formed by hispanic-latins – fundamentally conformed by players of Italian and Spanish origin – had proved to be superior and won national representations of Anglo-Saxon countries as Holland, the United States or Switzerland. It was proudly said that the team that had conquered the gold medal spoke Spanish. In 1928, the identity construction was held in concentric circles. With the triumphs against Holland and Germany, once more there is the idea of the hispanic-latins' superiority over the anglo-saxons in the football. But after defeating Italy (in which the confrontation is taken as a shock between two Latin football powers), the basic otherness comes to be America against Europe. (Morales 2013: 202)

The USA's men's national soccer team actually participated in some World Cup competitions in the first half of the twentieth century, as in 1930 in Uruguay and in 1950 in Brazil. However, it was only in the course of the 1970s, due to the world popularization of football, that the North American sports universe recognizes the value of *soccer* and starts to financially invest in this modality by means of internationalized clubs, such as the New York Cosmos. In the 1990s, the USA (increasingly home to Latin athletes), accepted the institutional incorporation of soccer and won the right to organize, for the first time, a World Cup in their territory.

Thus, it is possible to propose the reversal of the structural center–periphery pair. While international relations between the United States and Latin America polarized, the Latin American peripheral condition had to be relativized in the ambience of football. At least in South America, the fundamental otherness was formed against the institutional control of football by Continental Europe. With the advent of the francophone FIFA in 1904, the relationship of South American sports bodies had to go through the mediation policy of countries such as France and Italy, among others. Firstly, until the 1920s football matches were arranged by tours of teams and selected players, who crossed the Atlantic, from one coast to the other. Again, as stated by Murray (2000: 63): "The first foreign team to tour South America was Southampton, in 1905. They won all five matches played in Argentina, conceding just three goals. Nottingham Forest, in the same year, won all seven matches, conceding only one goal." Then, the process expanded with the creation of competitions of international importance, such as the FIFA World Cup, since 1930. As we know, this organization became a vehicle for professional soccer and created its own international tournament, although it does monitor amateur soccer in the Olympic Games. The early World Cup, a quadrennial event, showcased the technical supremacy of European over South American "schools," using the journalistic jargon of the time. Following on from this, Uruguay, Argentina, Brazil and Chile professionalized their soccer between 1931 and 1933.

Football imagery, both of clubs and of national teams, was built in a dialogic sense and ascending scale order: from local to national to continental; and then to the international sphere. In 1910s South America, mutual knowledge of national selected teams intensified with the organization of tournaments contested between neighboring countries. There are examples of smaller competitions, such as Taça Bernardo O'Higgins (Brazil–Chile), Taça Rio Branco (Brazil–Uruguay), Copa Júlio Roca (Brazil–Argentina) and Taça Osvaldo Cruz (Brazil–Paraguay).

In the post-First World War era, South American participation in the football competitions of the Olympic Games would be both positively and negatively highlighted. In positive terms, the focus was Uruguay winning the championship twice, in 1924 and 1928, against Switzerland and Argentina, respectively. As for the 1936 Olympics, an incident in extra time during the quarter-final match between Peru (sole representative of South America) against Austria, sparked a brawl. Austrian players clashed with Peruvian supporters who invaded the pitch at Hertha Berlin stadium (Dietschy 2010: 248). Eliminated from the tournament by the Organizing Committee, the Peruvian players and every Peruvian athlete withdrew from the competition by order of general officer Benavides, the then president of the Republic. The case unleashed a series of diplomatic disputes between the leadership of the Peruvian Football Federation and the International Olympic Committee members, with threats to German and Austrian consulates in Lima. Aside from this incident, we must recognize that the Olympics would not be enough to arouse great interest on the part of the South American teams. This can be inferred if we observe that the Brazilian national team, for example, debuted at Olympic football only in 1952, at the Helsinki Olympics, and until the 2016 Rio Olympics it had never won a gold medal in the sport (Giglio 2013).

In the second half of the twentieth century, another major competition occurred in the pan-American Games, whose first meeting took place in Buenos Aires in 1951. In addition, from 1956 on, the Atlantic Cup based in Rio arranged matches among all these national teams. Such matches have allowed a certain traffic of players and coaches, in addition to playing styles. One of the negative effects of the increase in soccer tournaments was the growth of rivalries within sports, potentiated by neighboring relations. Government provocation, polemics between journalists, players fighting with fans, and the burning of flags and racist insults set the tone of a few matches in South American tournaments. After consecutive disagreements, Argentina and Brazil, through their representative entities, spent ten years not watching matches between their teams (1946–56).

In a positive way, we can consider that the championship circuit also brought benefits. The largest stadiums were built, though under the mantle of the delicate relationship between football and politics (Rein 2015). In Argentina, General Agustín Justo contributed to the construction of *El Monumental* stadium, in 1938, which had the support of the municipality of Buenos Aires. At government expense, already under the aegis of Peronism, in the following decade, the Racing Stadium was inaugurated in Avellaneda to 60,000 fans, named after the president of the Republic, Juan Perón (Gaffney 2008; Hémeury 2013).

On the field, the counterpoint with European football, for example, gave rise to the "diagonal," a Latin American variant of the WM,[1] a system developed in Europe and seen as rational in the strategy of players' distribution on the field. The change defined the Latin American style for at least 30 years, since the Uruguayan Olympic title in 1924. The internal circulation of coaches and players, at least in South America, was a contributing factor to this change. As an example, the players strike in Argentina in 1948 should be remembered (Frydenberg and Sazbon 2015), followed by the Argentinean exodus to Colombian football in its golden phase, including Alfredo Di Stéfano, recruited by Millonarios of Colombia; the Paraguayan coach Fleitas Solich should also be mentioned, who served in Brazil during the same period; and it is worth noting athletes like the strikers Leônidas da Silva, Domingos da Guia and Heleno de Freitas, who passed by Platine football clubs at different times.

Before the intensification of movement of footballers, coaches and leagues, the previously mentioned binational confrontations were the embryo of the South American Championship. Played from 1916 onward, it was renamed Copa América in 1975, as the counterpart of the UEFA European

Championship. Whereas in South America the national teams' competition took place during the First World War, its continental European equivalent would only be created in 1960. The event organizer was the South American Football Confederation, which brought together the football federations of each of those Southern Cone countries. In addition to Bolivia, Colombia, Peru, Paraguay and Venezuela, there are a total of ten countries, whose governing body is known as CONMEBOL. To extend the range of action, two more countries from other regions have been invited since the early 1990s, Mexico being the most frequent of them. Mexico, a country under the North American influence zone, has been integrated (with the three Guyanas) in The Confederation of North, Central American and Caribbean Association Football (CONCACAF) since 1982.

Regarding spectators, travels of football fans have been multiplied by continental and world tournaments of national teams. The 1930 FIFA World Cup's final, contested between Uruguay and Argentina in Montevideo, was watched by more than 90,000 spectators. Of this total, about 20,000 were Argentineans. Using ships, thousands of Porteños crossed Río de la Plata to watch the match. However, despite the civilizing pedagogy embodied in modern sports, matches of national teams and clubs have been marked by endemic hostilities, virulent clashes and serious tensions, both inside and outside stadiums. For example:

> In South America in 1920 the police officers had to dig ditches and make a barbed-wire fence to keep fans off the field. Stadiums were overcrowded and fans loved invading the field to celebrate with the player who scored the goal, that is the reason for precaution. But there were also cases of violence against referees and players. (Murray 2000: 88)

Besides some occasional championships and friendly matches, fans of South American clubs had to wait until the 1960s to witness the emergence of a continental championship among clubs, the CONMEBOL Libertadores (Castro 1988). In competitions like this, not only did South American clubs and their supporters begin to circulate on the continent with greater regularity, but the event also allowed confrontations between South American champions and victorious European clubs of the UEFA Euro Cup. The structural relationship – South America versus Europe – was thus fed back in the second half of the twentieth century, passing from the level of national teams to that concerning national club associations.

During its 55 years in existence, Copa Libertadores has enabled the publicizing of clubs such as Peñarol and Nacional (Uruguay); Olimpia and Cerro Porteño (Paraguay); Colo-Colo, Universidad Católica, Universidad de Chile and Cobreloa (Chile); Once Caldas, América de Cali, Atletico Nacional and Deportivo Cali (Colombia); LDU and Emelec (Ecuador); Universitário and

Sporting Cristal (Peru); Bolívar (Bolivia), among many others, out of a total of 168 teams that have already contested this cup competition.

The list can be expanded if Argentine and Brazilian teams are also included. As for Argentinean clubs, the most renowned on the continent were Independiente, Racing, Boca Juniors, River Plate, Estudiantes de la Plata, the Argentinos Juniors, Vélez Sársfield, Newell's Old Boys and San Lorenzo, concentrated in the cities of Buenos Aires and La Plata. With respect to Brazil, we should mention clubs such as Santos, Cruzeiro, Flamengo, Grêmio, São Paulo, Vasco da Gama, Internacional, Palmeiras and Corinthians, coming from the south and southeast of the country, which arrived at decisive phases and won titles. Recently incorporated into the competition, the Mexicans have stood out because of clubs such as América, Tigres and Cruz Azul. In addition to these three, from the capital, it is worth mentioning Chivas, from Guadalajara (Vital 2014).

4. CONCLUSION

This chapter has provided us with enough elements to conclude with a few more general reflections on the potentialities and limitations concerning the existence of a Latin American football imaginary. Firstly, we must consider the historical limits of the scope of the idea of Latin America as a cultural, intellectual and territorial unity. Such limitations relate to the fragmented relationship of its countries with the various metropolises that colonized it, sharpening particularities. Perhaps one of the most clamant examples of that is the difference, in the nineteenth century, between the independent republics of the so-called Hispanic America and the case of Brazil, country of continental dimensions, colonized by Portugal and considered "America's exotic plant," for retaining the monarchy after its independence.

The configuration of a unified Latin America acquires a more convincing sense in the course of the twentieth century, less by its similarities and more by the growth of importance of the United States. The contrasting reaction of other countries on the American continent can be observed in the face of North American power in political, economic and cultural terms. However, we suggest that, interestingly, despite all the penetration of Anglo-Saxon values, modern sports codified in Victorian England were partly undertaken during the American Progressive Era, by a country that was not able to shape its own sports with the same force seen in Latin American sports culture. In the particular case of football, the influence was reversed, from Latin America to the United States, with initial resistance. Over time, the gradual incorporation of the world of *soccer* has been achieved in the United States, due to global and, in particular, Latin American football popularization.

Thus, the specular relationship of football in Latin America continued to be built in relation to its European metropolises or the economic influence of Britain, regardless of the various cultural and football exchanges among South American and Latin European countries. It is certain that the World Cups were essential in this process, as they showed the contrast between continental and Latin American playing styles, but it is also right that other competitions involving national teams were important. Similarly, the tour of European clubs by Latin America in the 1910s, and the movement of Latin American clubs across Europe from the 1920s on, are equally important in the formation of such exchanges and identities.

Of all the experiments throughout the twentieth century, it can be concluded that the most important ones to reflect upon transnational identities in football, such as the region or the Latin American continent, are the clashes between national teams, especially for Copa América. This was created in 1975 as an expansion to the South American Championship, invented in 1916. A landmark of this competition in this imaginary occurred in 1993, when CONMEBOL incorporated Mexico into Copa América, a nation that had joined the North American Free Trade Agreement (NAFTA), an economic bloc, led by the United States and of which Canada was also a member. If, from a geographical point of view, Mexico is officially part of North America, it is known that in social, ethnic and cultural terms the Mexican people has historical affinities with Latin America; this places the country to a certain extent in an ambiguous and frontier identity position.

As for the club context, continental teams and organizations watched a decisive step with the creation of the suggestively titled *Copa Libertadores da América* (Liberators of America Cup) in 1960. The reunion of South American clubs in this tournament follows the guidance of what happened in Copa América and, at the end of the 1990s, it began to invite Mexican teams to participate in the competition. Thus, this is an important reason in the scale expansion, from South to Latin America. This helps in the formation of a Latin American identity of football, although the Central American and Caribbean countries and the Antilles continue without participating in the said competition, being more integrated into the North American sphere of political, cultural and sports influence.

Far from being a passive reflection of what happens in society, modern sports constitute thought-provoking observation laboratories of decision-making powers, political directions at stake and vectors of identity collectively formulated by a certain people, by a particular culture or by a particular continent. The example of football in Latin America is one of the perfect expressions of that.

NOTE

1. WM is the name of a tactical football system invented by Herbert Chapman. In 1930, as manager of Arsenal (United Kingdom), he moved from the traditional 2-3-5 system by making three changes of position: he retreated the midfielder, putting him between the two defenders, and created a second midfield line from the retreat of the two inside forwards. Reading this diagram, a 3-4-3 (or 3-2-2-3) formed two letters on the field – W in attack, M in defense. WM was born.

REFERENCES

Archetti, Eduardo P. 2003. *Masculinidades: fútbol, tango y polo en la Argentina*. Buenos Aires: Editorial Antropofagía.

Bomfim, Manoel. 1993. *América Latina: Males de Origem*. Rio de Janeiro: Topbooks.

Burke, Peter. 2009. A ideia de América Latina; Futebol versus Críquete no Novo Mundo. *O historiador como colunista*. Rio de Janeiro: Civilização Brasileira.

Cardoso, Fernando Henrique and Enzo Falleto. 2004. *Dependência e Desenvolvimento Na América Latina: Ensaio de Interpretação Sociológica*. Rio de Janeiro: Civilização Brasileira.

Castro, Moacir Werneck de. 1988. *O Libertador: A Vida de Simon Bolívar*. Rio de Janeiro: Rocco.

de Tocqueville, Alexis. 1985 [1835, 1840]. *Democracy in America* (2 vols). New York: Alfred A. Knopf.

Dietschy, Paul. 2010. *L'Histoire du Football*. Paris: Éditions Perrin.

Dosman, Edgar J. 2011. *Raul Prebisch: a construção da América Latina e do Terceiro Mundo*. Rio de Janeiro: Contraponto.

Echevarría, Roberto Gonzales. 2004. *La Glória de Cuba: História del Béisbol em la Isla*. Madrid: Editorial Colibri.

Frydenberg, Julio and Daniel Sazbon. 2015. *La Huelga de Jugadores de 1948. La Cancha Peronista: Fútbol y Politica (1946–1955)*. Buenos Aires: UNSAM Edita.

Furtado, Celso. 2007. *A Economia Latinoamericana*. São Paulo: Companhia das Letras.

Gaffney, Christopher T. 2008. *Temples of Earthbound Gods: Stadiums in the Cultural Landscapes of Rio de Janeiro and Buenos Aires*. Austin: University of Texas Press.

Galeano, Eduardo. 1980. *As Veias Abertas da América Latina*. Rio de Janeiro: Editora Paz e Terra.

Garcia Marquez, Gabriel. 1967. *One Hundred Years of Solitude*. New York: Harper & Row Publishers.

Giglio, Sérgio Settani. 2013. "COI X FIFA: A História Política do Futebol nos Jogos Olímpicos." PhD dissertation. University of São Paulo.

Hémeury, Lucie. 2013. "Le pouvoir Hors-jeu? Football et Péronisme em Argentine (1946–1955)." *Cahiers des Amériques latines* 74: 55–74 [published online].

Martí, José. 1999. *La edad de oro*. Habana: Editorial Gente Nueva.

Miceli, Sergio. 2012. *Vanguardas em Retrocesso: Ensaios de História Social e Intelectual do Modernismo Latinoamericano*. São Paulo: Companhia das Letras.

Morales, Andrés. 2013. *Fútbol, Identidad y Poder (1916–1930)*. Montevideo: Editorial Fin del Siglo.

Morse, Richard M. 1988. *O Espelho de Próspero: Cultura e Ideias nas Américas*. São Paulo: Companhia das Letras.

Murray, Bill. 2000. *Uma História do Futebol*. São Paulo: Hedra, 2000.

Rein, Raanan (ed.). 2015. *La Cancha Peronista: Fútbol y Politica (1946–1955)*. Buenos Aires: UNSAM Edita.

Rodó, José Enrique. 1985. *Ariel: Motivos de Proteo*. Caracas: Biblioteca Ayacucho.

Sarmiento, Domingo. 2010. *Facundo, ou Civilização e Barbárie*. São Paulo: Cosac Naify.

Sommer, Doris. 2004. *Ficções de Fundação: Os Romances Nacionais da América Latina*. Belo Horizonte: Editora UFMG.

Toledo, Luis Henrique de. 2009. *Estilos de Jogar, Estilos de Pensar. Visão de Jogo: Antropologia das Práticas Esportivas*. São Paulo: Terceiro Nome.

Vital, Nicholas. 2014. *Libertadores: Paixão que Nos Une*. São Paulo: Cultura Editora Sustentável.

Index